LAW AND DEMOCRACY IN NEIL MACCORMICK'S LEGAL AND POLITICAL THEORY

Law and Philosophy Library

VOLUME 93

For further volumes:
http://www.springer.com/series/6210

LAW AND DEMOCRACY IN NEIL MACCORMICK'S LEGAL AND POLITICAL THEORY

The Post-Sovereign Constellation

Edited by

Agustín José Menéndez

Universidad de León, Spain and ARENA, University of Oslo, Norway

John Erik Fossum

ARENA, University of Oslo, Norway

Springer

Editors
Agustín José Menéndez
Facultad de Derecho
Universidad de León
León
Spain
agustin.menendez@unileon.es
altierospinelli@gmail.com

John Erik Fossum
ARENA Center for European Studies
University of Oslo
Oslo
Norway
j.e.fossum@arena.uio.no

ISSN 1572-4395
ISBN 978-90-481-8941-0 e-ISBN 978-90-481-8942-7
DOI 10.1007/978-90-481-8942-7
Springer Dordrecht Heidelberg London New York

Library of Congress Control Number: 2011922621

Printed on acid-free paper

Springer is part of Springer Science+Business Media (www.springer.com)

Acknowledgments

This book is a tribute to Neil MacCormick. It contains a range of chapters all of which engage critically with his work, and, as such, are cast in his reflexive spirit. We thought that this was the most appropriate way of paying tribute to his wide-ranging scholarship and also the best way for us to help carry forward his legacy. The chapter composition is a mere faint reflection of the breadth of Neil's intellectual interests and scholarly output. The contribution is also hopefully only a first attempt to use Neil's institutional theory of law as a proper invitation to engage in more comprehensive bridge-building across academic disciplines.

The book consists mainly of revised and updated contributions that were delivered at the workshop and doctoral course "The post-sovereign constellation – Law and Democracy in Neil MacCormick's legal and political theory", which we organised at the University of Bergen during 7–9 November 2007. This workshop was, in fact, the second in a series of events aimed at engaging in broader conversations with contemporary legal and political philosophers on transversal themes. The first one was held in Oslo in 2004 and was devoted to Robert Alexy's jurisprudence (and resulted in a volume in this same series), and the third took place in Bergen in 2009, and was dedicated to the discussion of the political implications of the judicialisation of European constitutional law. Further events will, hopefully, follow in the future.

Neil MacCormick's chapter is his introductory statement to the workshop. In addition to the workshop submissions, we are delighted to have two additional chapters, one from Jeremy Waldron and one from Neil Walker, Neil MacCormick's successor as The Regius Chair on the Law of Nature and the Law of Nations at Edinburgh University.

We are grateful for the support from the Norwegian Research Council and the University of Bergen (the Meltzer Foundation and the Department of Administration and Organisation Theory), which contributed to the funding of the Bergen Workshop, as well as the Law Faculty for hosting the event. We would also like to thank the ARENA Centre for European Studies and the cross-faculty programme on Democracy, both at the University of Oslo, for support in helping to complete the book.

We would like to thank Flora MacCormick for her permission to publish Neil MacCormick's chapter and for her endorsement of this book. Many thanks also to Chris Engert for proficient editing.

Introduction

This book considers the work of one of the key contemporary legal and political theorists. The late Neil MacCormick made decisive contributions to the understanding of law, democracy and justice under conditions of social and ethical pluralism. MacCormick was proud of his triple heritage (H.L.A. Hart's path-breaking reformulation of legal positivism, Smith's and Hume's liberal and progressive political theory, and Scottish democratic nationalism). But he was keen on cultivating that heritage not by teaching it and revering it in any mechanical manner, but by making decisive and fundamental contributions to its further development, as he argues with *gusto* in Chapter 2 of this volume. And, indeed, the distinguished holder of the Regius Chair of Public Law and the Law of Nature and Nations in Edinburgh excelled both as a legal theorist and as a political philosopher. Even a brief and incomplete summary of the main lines of MacCormick's research and publications (as the one included in Part I of this book) is enough to realise its breadth, and the great range of issues and important questions that propelled Neil MacCormick's intellectual curiosity. In this brief introduction, we consider, in some more detail, the key contributions that the author whose path-breaking *Legal Reasoning and Legal Theory* and subsequent string of outstanding books and articles has made to legal and political theory (Part I). In the remainder of this chapter, we summarise the main contents of this book (Part II).

But it is proper to add that what rendered both MacCormick's theory and Neil himself especially inspiring, and also so greatly rewarding to interact with, was his intellectual honesty. In particular, we would like to point to his highly reflexive and theoretically constructive "propensity to self-subversion", to borrow the famous term from Albert O. Hirschman.[1] Neil put his own approach in question by seriously considering alternative viewpoints and positions, and based upon that, actively engaged in a reflexive re-consideration of his theory. In so far as practical reason drives the human spirit forward, this is certainly one of the best ways of ensuring it. It also demonstrates beyond any doubt the exceptional human and intellectual stature of Neil MacCormick.

---

[1]See Albert O. Hirschman, *A Propensity to Self-Subversion* (Harvard, MA: Harvard University Press, 1998).

The Legal and Political Theory of Neil MacCormick

A legal philosopher by vocation, MacCormick led the development of the institutional theory of law. His characterisation of *law as an institutional fact* reveals not only the collective and user-oriented character of legal norms (radicalising some of the key intuitions of Hart's legal theory when affirming that the legal phenomenon cannot be fully understood without taking the standpoint internal to legal practice seriously), but also the inextricably twin nature of law as a functional means of social integration and as a vehicle for the reconstruction of the social order in ways conducive to the realisation of normative ideals (in brief, of justice). MacCormick aimed at keeping neatly distinct the realms of the "is" and the "ought" (here pursuing some of the key insights contained in Kelsen's first edition of the *Pure Theory of Law*)[2] while stressing the necessary connection between law and morality, reflected both at the systemic level of law, and in the underlying claim to the correctness necessarily underlying any legal norm (something which has also been emphasised, in different terms and within different traditions, by Robert Alexy and Ronald Dworkin). By highlighting that *law is an institutionalised order*, MacCormick claimed that the systemic character of law derives not so much from the objective nature of legal norms, but rather from the social practice of making use of the law as a means of social integration; or to phrase it differently, it is because we hypothesise that law is a system, and we do so upon the basis of a normative ideal of such a system, that law can discharge the basic social tasks that it is entrusted to perform in modern societies. Some of these key insights lingered behind the hypothetical assumption of a "*grundnorm*" which would establish the validity of the whole legal order (in Kelsen's theory) and even more explicitly, in the distinction between primary and secondary norms advocated by Hart. But MacCormick goes further than both Hart and Kelsen by taking the elucidation of the social functions of the law very seriously, thereby assigning them a key role in shaping both his theoretical and his practical understanding of law (in ways not very different from Habermas). Indeed, the characterisation of law as an institutional normative order explains, in MacCormick's view, the unavoidable tension in modern law, its divided "soul" between its "empowering" side (providing the subjects of law with the moral knowledge necessary to be just, to know what they have to do, and enabling social co-operation in order to achieve complex collective goals on a large scale), and its "coercive" nature (as the necessary doses of certainty and insurance against default can only be provided by the shadow of enforced compliance). MacCormick has indeed made decisive contributions to the exploration of both the ideal element in law and legal practice, while nonetheless remaining far from oblivious of its unavoidable "partially heteronomous" character.

MacCormick's institutional theory of law has improved our understanding of the concept, nature and practice of law, by elucidating at least five key questions: (1) *the*

---

[2]On the extent to which he succeeded, contrast the chapters in this volume by Massimo La Torre and Stefano Bertea.

societal foundations of law, the close connection between the normative and the institutional imagination of human beings and the integration of democratic societies through law; (2) *the normative character of law*, by determining, in a coherent and systematic manner, the implications of such a character (from the texture and the composition of the legal order and the features of legal norms, to the systemic properties of law); (3) *the pluralist nature of modern democratic law*, showing us that law is closely associated not only (even if mainly) to the nation-state, but can also be the means of integration beyond and below the nation-state; (4) *the unavoidable argumentative character of rule-based legal orders*, by integrating into a coherent theoretical vision the key positivist insight concerning the key role of rules in the integration of modern society and the fundamental post-positivistic vindication of the principled nature of democratic legal orders; and (5) *the open character of law*, by emphasising the limits of law as a means of social integration. These five fundamental themes were explored time and time again by Neil MacCormick, starting with his formidable inaugural lecture of 1974 *Law as an Institutional Fact*, to his *Institutions of Law* of 2007, and through the pivotal *An Institutional Theory of Law*, co-authored with Ota Weinberger in the mid eighties.

The core innovative features of his institutional theory of law go a long way to explain why MacCormick was not only a prominent theorist, but also a scholar who enjoyed dealing with concrete legal problems charged with social and political implications.

Thus, his major contributions to legal reasoning and legal rhetoric are to be found in *Legal Reasoning and Legal Theory* of 1978 and in *Rhetoric and the Rule of Law* of 2005. These two major books and a long series of articles and book chapters were decisive in the transformation of our understanding of legal argumentation, along with Alexy's, Raz', Aarnio's and Peczenick's contributions. The relevance that MacCormick assigned to the analysis of social legal practices led him to be very attentive both to the steering of societal conflicts through rules obeyed in "spontaneous" and "quasi-automatic" fashion by the subjects of law (what, indeed, classical positivism assumed was the core of the legal phenomenon), and to the argumentative practices through which discrepancies in the actual normative implications of legal principles are settled. *Legal Theory and Legal Argumentation* was, indeed, one of the leading treatises which brought back to the forefront of legal theory the analysis of how legal cases were actually argued, and the drawing of conclusions regarding the nature of law itself, and, very especially, the role of the said principles in modern legal orders. Indeed, *Legal Reasoning and Legal Theory* is properly characterised as an attempt to integrate some of the key insights of Dworkin's criticism of Hartian classical legal positivism with a view to rescuing the brand of positivism defended by Hart. But the more that MacCormick explored his original contributions, the more that he came to distance himself from the author of the *Concept of Law*, although this does not necessarily imply that he came to converge with Dworkin's position. As Massimo La Torre claims in his chapter in this volume, it may, perhaps, be fairer to say that MacCormick pursued some of the key insights of Hart's theory to their logical and normative conclusion(s), and, in doing so, integrated theoretical findings coming from other angles and traditions;

his keen interest in "positive" legal topics and his very fruitful collaboration with Ota Weinberger may have rendered a genuine and promising third way possible. Through these works, MacCormick made a decisive contribution to the coming of age of "post-positivism", a form of legal positivism which is conscious not only of the morality necessarily underpinning law, but also of the structural shift implied in the constitutionalisation of national legal orders, making the law bind through principles to be detailed and derived into rules, not through rules which would then be generalised into principles.

And thus also his outstanding contributions to constitutional theory beyond and below the nation-state, reflected both in his theoretical re-construction of European constitutional practice from *Beyond the Sovereign State* to *Revisiting Legal Pluralism*, and to the decisive *Questioning Sovereignty* of 1999. His lifelong preoccupation with legal pluralism, concurrently fuelled by his understanding of the nature of law and his sympathies towards the cause of Scottish nationalism led Neil MacCormick to develop what may be fairly said to be the first theory of European constitutional law which takes the specific features of the European Union as a process of legal, economic and political integration seriously. In particular, the Scottish philosopher aimed at showing that European law is grounded in an overlapping set of legal social practices which pre-suppose different understandings of the validity basis of Community law. In lieu of obsessively focusing upon which of the two alternatives is right (the national constitutional practice which claims that the European legal order rests upon the twenty-seven national constitutions, or the supranational constitutional practice which affirms that integration has led to a mutation in national legal orders, now absorbed into a single European constitutional order framed by the constitutional law of the Union), legal theory should occupy itself also - if not principally - with determining why and how the European legal order does, indeed, keep on discharging its basic social tasks, despite the co-existence of such practices. Or to express it differently, the really intriguing question is not which of the two standpoints is right (both of them *are* from their own perspective) but why a legal order can be pluralistic without descending into chaotic diversity.

MacCormick was also a major political philosopher. He played a major role in vindicating and renovating the political philosophy of the Scottish Enlightenment by means of putting forward a distinctive theory of distributive justice and a theory of liberal nationalism aimed not only at rendering nationalism attractive, but also at rooting his cosmopolitan and liberal political project. This was reflected in his fundamental (and, perhaps, unfairly neglected) *Legal Right and Social Democracy* of 1982, but was already at work in the volume which he edited in 1970 under the title of *The Scottish Debate* (which includes a fundamental exposition of the philosophical roots of his liberal nationalism), would be articulated in *Questioning Sovereignty,* and exposed in its final form in his *Practical Reason in Law and Morality*. This keen interest in the theoretical aspects of constitutional theory reflects a thorough consideration of the theory of the state, and, very especially, of the normative dimensions of the *Rechtsstaat*, closely intertwined with the basic assumptions of his institutional theory of law. Although it is beyond doubt that his interest in nationalism was not only academic, but also reflected a deep existential commitment, MacCormick made a major contribution to the re-thinking and re-positioning, so to say, of nationalism as part of a liberal and cosmopolitan political project. In particular, his reflections cast light on the role that "liberal" nationalism could play in rooting and grounding what, in most cases, remains the abstract and detached political philosophy of cosmopolitanism. In his writings, nationalism becomes the emotional side of democratic federalism. A side which a child of the Scottish Enlightenment could not but struggle to make sense of.

The Contents of the Book

This book engages in a critical reconstruction of MacCormick's work, aimed at the three-fold objective of offering a critical introduction to his work, furthering his insights into each specific field, and revealing the connections between the different sides (legal, political, and philosophical) of his work.

In the chapter which forms Part I, **Neil Walker**, successor to Neil in the Regius Chair of Public Law and the Law of Nature and Nations in Edinburgh, highlights the joyous creative tension between the two sides of the *oeuvre* of MacCormick the intellectual and the person (of temperament and disposition): the local and the cosmopolitan. Indeed, the fact that Neil's biography and convictions attracted him to the "in-between", contributed, to a large extent, to shape and to mould his legal and political theory, by rendering him sensitive to questions which tended to be ignored or sidelined in mainstream theories. This is, indeed, the background against which MacCormick developed his many contributions to legal theory (his post-positivistic institutional theory of law, which Ota Weinberger also contributed to the development of), and political theory (his views on democratic nationalism and supranationalism), which prompted him to analyse the pluralistic structures of the democratic constitutional state, (both at supranational and at infranational levels). The chapter ends by coming to terms with the actual implications and significance of MacCormick's constitutional pluralism. In MacCormickian fashion, Walker reconsiders the tensions in MacCormick's shift from radical to moderate pluralism, and ponders on the extent to which the different strands of the pluralistic literature may be characterised as renderings of the ideas with which MacCormick was struggling.

The second part contains a chapter by **Neil MacCormick** himself, in which he reflects on the seven big themes of his legal and political theory: the normative character of the legal order, the institutional character of the legal order, the central but far from exclusive role played by state law in social integration, the relationship between law and morality, the synthetic and systemic aspects of law, and the relationship between reasons and emotions in practical reasoning. In reviewing these themes, MacCormick both paints an overarching broad-brush picture of his theory, and also reveals the intricate connections and links between the different parts, thus providing a very appealing introduction to the broad range of readers that will be inspired by his work.

The third part deals with MacCormick's concept and conception of law. **Lars Christian Blichner** claims that MacCormick's theory is of special interest to social scientists, because he is one of the rare contemporary legal scholars who was keenly interested in exploring the limits of law as a means of social integration, and law's relationship to other normative orders. Neil's historical sensibility makes of his work a reminder both of the fundamental relevance of the delimitation of the province of law and of the fact that the difference between law and other normative orders is one of degree, rather than absolutes. Blichner's contribution to the theory of juridification and de-juridification (and their multi-faceted character and interaction) is an apt means to highlight, reconstruct and even complete some of MacCormick's basic insights on what concerns the relationship between normative orders, institutional normative orders, and legal orders. Blichner's key message is that processes of juridification and de-juridification should no longer be regarded as "borderline", "marginal" questions which legal theory can blissfully ignore; they should be analysed as determining factors of the social tasks that law can perform effectively. **Massimo La Torre** considers the unfolding of Neil MacCormick's legal theory by reference to the concept of law, which underlies his work. La Torre claims that the legal theory of the Scottish philosopher is the true heir to the normative project underlying Hart's legal theory, in the precise sense that it has pushed to its logical and normative conclusion the quest for a non-decisionistic understanding of law, which stresses the key role played by social legal practices, the centrality of the standpoint *internal* to law as a normative order to understand legal phenomena, and consequently, calls for a theory which focuses on the addressees of the law and not exclusively on institutional actors. **Stefano Bertea** focuses on MacCormick's contributions to legal theory on what concerns the identity and validity of legal systems, and, in particular, MacCormick's master rule. While the Scottish professor started by building upon Hart's characterisation of the distinction between primary and secondary norms as the key to jurisprudence, thus affirming that the identity and validity of the legal system are tied up with the rule of recognition as a conventional rule supported by a social practice, he was to engage in a long-term critical reconsideration of the problem. Moved by the inadequacy of the rule of recognition to serve as the basis of a plausible recognition of the legal order of constitutional states, especially of the open, co-operative and pluralistic European *Rechtsstaat* (of the post World War II period), and influenced by his reading of Kelsen's views on the matter (and very especially by the "fundamental norm" of a legal system as a hypothetical norm that plays a rather similar structural role as the one proper of the rule of recognition), MacCormick came to affirm that the identity and validity of the legal system is based upon a master rule, which is defined by reference to a more inclusive (more democratic) social practice, wherein citizens are considered relevant as norm-users, and not only judges as norm-givers. Bertea finds that, while the institutional theory of law in general, and the master rule in particular, have made major contributions to our understanding of law, the master rule fails to provide a complete and sufficient account of the normativity of law. As long as the master rule is *conventional*, as Hart's rule of recognition is (and thus not hypothetical as Kelsen's fundamental norm is), its capacity to account for the normativity of law is conditioned on the finding of a proper explanation of how such a convention can become normative, how the *is* becomes an *ought*, without indulging in the naturalistic fallacy. Bertea considers the three main characterisations of legal conventionalism in the literature (legal conventions as indicators of acceptance, as co-ordination conventions, and as constitutive conventions) and finds that all three are inadequate. This casts a long shadow over MacCormick's master rule, which nonetheless, does not impair the standing of the institutional theory of law as one of the most powerful contemporary legal theories.

The fourth part considers three aspects of MacCormick's post-positivistic jurisprudence and its relation to a liberal political theory. **Marina Lalatta** explores the systemic nature of MacCormick's legal theory by focusing on the underlying tension between his claim to uphold a "moderate" relativism in moral questions, and his late acceptance of the existence of a systemic connection between law and morality, which comes close to the "claim to correctness" theory of Robert Alexy. While she acknowledges that MacCormick's reluctance to abandon a moderate relativistic position is not without good reasons (recently highlighted by the enthusiastic endorsement of non-relativistic theorists and political actors of blatant violations of fundamental rights in the so-called war on terror), Lalatta claims that MacCormick should endorse a non-relativistic position without having to endorse the less attractive aspects of cognitivism. **Jeremy Waldron** takes issue with a core premise of MacCormick's post-positivistic characterisation of the relationship between law and morality, his "reservation principle", which reconciles the autonomy of law from morality with the claim that the case for integration through law as an autonomous social medium does not require individuals to abandon their own morality. Building on some of Hart's intuitions on the "thin" intrinsic morality of law and on his opening towards an inclusive legal positivism, MacCormick came to defend the "reservation principle" as a core principle of his political theory in *Practical Reason in Law and Morality*. Waldron challenges the scope of the reservation principle by considering whether it is justified in all cases, or whether, in some circumstances, it undermines law as an effective means of social integration. He does so by contrasting the implications of MacCormick's reservation principle and Hobbes' non-reservation principle in several circumstances. By doing so, Waldron not only problematises one key aspect of the post-positivistic turn of MacCormick (and of *discursive* theories of law in general, which have shifted the centre of gravity of legal systems from rules to principles), but also reveals the underpinning relationships between law and legal culture which, in themselves, may go a long way to account for MacCormick's persistent defence of the central role of rules in democratic legal systems, as in the mass of circumstances in which law integrates society, it is rules that undertake the job. As, indeed, Waldron claims, law is needed as a routine internalised in the lives of its addressees. **Tanja Hitzel-Cassagnes** considers the extent to which MacCormick succeeds in constructing a synthetic theory of law and politics capable of accounting for the various transformations of law as a means of social integration in a "pluralistic" context without renouncing any of the key normative categories of political philosophy inherited from the Enlightenment. MacCormick claims that there has always been a pluralistic potential cloaked behind, so to speak, the apparently monistic political and legal language of modernity; and what had served to conceal this potential was the historical, political and legal pre-eminence of state law, its characterisation as the unique form of institutional normative order. But while we cannot but share MacCormick's "pragmatic" concern, and while there is much to be learnt from his actual theory, Hitzel-Cassagnes rightly points out that it is simply not the case that the universalistic drive of law is a side-effect of the pre-dominance of the "nation-state" paradigm, but that it is actually the constitutive character of law as a means of social integration; this implies not only a "structural" universalistic proclivity of law, but also a "normative" universalistic proclivity. As a consequence, norms governing the relationships between legal orders should also be legal norms underpinned by a universalistic drive. The powerful insights behind MacCormick's democratic celebration of social pluralism are, according to Hitzel-Cassagnes, more fittingly brought to fruition through Kant's vision of law as a reflexive and provisional structure. This reconciles the move away from considerations of the primacy and competence of the law in an ontologising fashion, and towards a reflexive process in which the promise of autonomy and self-determination stand a chance of being realised.

In the fifth part, **Flavia Carbonell** engages with MacCormick's theory of legal argumentation. Carbonell reconstructs, in a critical fashion, MacCormick's concept of coherence in legal reasoning, and places it in the context of his theory of legal pluralism. The salience of the theory is determined by analysing the extent to which MacCormick's theory underlines the jurisprudence of the Court of Justice of the European Union; and the extent to which coherent argumentation may ground the claim of MacCormick to it being the best possible theory of European Community law. Carbonell finds that the resort to coherence by ECJ as a means of increasing the breadth and scope of Community law does not foster a legally pluralistic reconstruction of Community law, but is, indeed, an instrument of its monistic reconstruction. Indeed, it turns the Court into the final decision-maker in charge of solving conflicting interpretations or collisions of norms. This casts some doubts not only as to the *affinity* between legal pluralism and coherence, but also as to the extent to which the European legal order is a pluralistic one.

The sixth part focuses on MacCormick's theory of legal pluralism, and, very especially, on its application to the constitutional theory of the European Union. **Martin Borowski** finds that MacCormick's theory of post-sovereignty represents the most sophisticated attempt to date to explain the "pluralistic" nature of Community law, overcoming the simple confrontation of the "European view" and the "national view" of the European Union, which has characterised legal and political scholarship for decades. However, he finds that legal pluralism is not convincing, either as a general theory or as the basis of the reconstruction of Community law. This is basically so because it fails to reconstruct the derivative nature of Community law, and cannot provide an adequate framework for deciding conflicts between EC law and national constitutional law. However, MacCormick's contribution to tackle the difficult and complex problem of the reconstruction of Community law is taken, by Borowski, as the point of departure for what amounts to a sophisticated and revised version of the national theory of constitutional law, namely, Borowski's derived and nearly unconditional supremacy of Community law. This entails that the actual breadth and scope of the supremacy of Community law is subject to potential exceptions, to be determined by means of weighing and balancing the normative reasons underpinning the claim to supremacy (in concrete, the very weight of European integration) with weighty countervailing reasons which may justify the opposite result in a handful of cases. **Agustín José Menéndez** aims at situating MacCormick's European constitutional pluralism in the *problématique* of European constitutional law. What Borowski labelled as the "European enigma" is de-coupled into two riddles, concerning the *genesis* of the European legal order (how what formally were international treaties could result in the establishment of a constitutional polity), and the *relationship between legal orders* (how Community law is granted almost unconditional primacy in European constitutional practice). The standard constitutional theories that have portended to solve these problems have failed to provide plausible answers to these two riddles. MacCormick's constitutional pluralism broke new ground and offered a coherent reconstruction of European constitutional practice from a sociological perspective. But it remains unsettled as a constitutional theory. Departing from MacCormick's shift from a radical to a moderate pluralistic position, Menéndez tries to reconsider the key implications of European constitutional pluralism, and to apply the manifold insights left to us by MacCormick to the fashioning of a constitutional theory capable of accounting for the pluralistic traits of Community law, but without reneging on the regulatory ideal of law as a single legal system. That alternative theory is the theory of constitutional synthesis, which assigns a central role, in the legal and political process of European integration, to the *collective* of national constitutions, which were seconded from the entry into force of the Treaty of Paris onwards to the role of the common constitution of the Union.

The seventh part considers the political theory of liberal nationalism put forward by Neil MacCormick. **Joxerramon Bengoetxea** focuses on MacCormick's contribution to the understanding of nation, law and state in contemporary Europe, and, in particular, on his concept of "internal enlargement", or, to express it differently, the possibility that Member States divide or split into new Member States so as to realise the aspirations to self-government of region-states. He reflects on the correlation between MacCormick's institutional theory of law, with his emphasis on non-state institutional normative orders, and his defence of "liberal nationalism", as a legally differentiated and distinct form of liberal political philosophy. Bengoetxea considers in detail the key role that such a form of nationalism could play in rooting and providing support for the cosmopolitan *telos* which characterises the European integration project. **John Erik Fossum** also focuses on MacCormick's liberal nationalism. The first issue with which he grapples is how well the post-sovereign constellation can reconfigure nationalism through disposing of the exclusivist and suppressive (of regional forms of nationalism) propensities built into the sovereign state. Second, is the question of the status of liberal nationalism in MacCormick's broader theoretical conception of the post-sovereign constellation. This also raises the issue as to whether there might be other, alternative, modes of allegiance that might be compatible with MacCormick's general approach to law and politics in the post-sovereign constellation. In the concluding section, it is argued that a cosmopolitan constitutional patriotism might be a more suitable mode of allegiance for the post-sovereign constellation. The potential for harnessing this to a democratic end, the chapter argues, is best ensured by building upon the deep insights in MacCormick's approach, and subsuming them under the theory of constitutional synthesis.

Contents

Contributors

Joxerramon Bengoetxea Universidad del País Vasco/Euskal Herriko Unibertsitatea, Vitoria, Spain, joxerramon.bengoetxea@ehu.es

Stefano Bertea Law School, University of Leicester, Leicester, UK, stefano.bertea@leicester.ac.uk

Lars Christian Blichner University of Bergen, Bergen, Norway, lars.blichner@aorg.uib.no

Martin Borowski Birmingham Law School, College of Arts and Law, University of Birmingham, Birmingham, UK, m.borowski@bham.ac.uk

Flavia Carbonell Universidad Alberto Hurtado de Santiago de Chile, Santiago, Chile, flocarbonell@yahoo.es

John Erik Fossum ARENA, University of Oslo, Oslo, Norway, j.e.fossum@arena.uio.no

Tanja Hitzel-Cassagnes Leibniz University, Hannover, Germany, t.hitzel-cassagnes@ipw.uni-hannover.de

Marina Lalatta Costerbosa Department of Philosophy, Università di Bologna, Bologna, Italy, marina.lalatta@unibo.it

Massimo La Torre Hull Law School, Università "Magna Graecia" di Catanzaro, Catanzaro, Italy, mlatorre@unicz.it

Neil MacCormick University of Edinburgh, Edinburgh, UK

Agustín José Menéndez Facultad de Derecho, Universidad de León, León, Spain; ARENA, University of Oslo, Oslo, Norway, agustin.menendez@unileon.es; altierospinelli@gmail.com

Jeremy Waldron New York University, New York, NY, USA; All Souls College, Oxford University, Oxford, UK, jeremy.waldron@nyu.edu

Neil Walker University of Edinburgh, Edinburgh, UK, neil.walker@ed.ac.uk

About the Authors

Joxerramón Bengoetxea is Professor of Legal Theory in the University of the Basque Country, Vitoria. He was legal secretary at the cabinet of Judge Edwards at the European Court of Justice, Deputy Minister for Employment at the Basque Government, and scientific director of the International Institute for the Sociology of Law at Oñati. He is the author *The Legal Reasoning of the European Court of Justice* and *La Europa de Peter Pan*.

Stefano Bertea is Reader in Law at the Leicester Law School. He previously held teaching and research positions at the University of Bologna, University of Modena, the Law School of the University of Edinburgh, the Christian-Albrechts Universität zu Kiel and the University of Antwerpen. He is the author of *The Normative Claim of Law* (Oxford: Hart Publishers) and has published extensively on legal and political theory in the *Oxford Journal of Legal Studies, the European Law Journal and Law and Philosophy,* among other journals.

Lars Christian Blichner is Associate Professor at the Department of Administration and Organisation Theory, University of Bergen. He has published seminal articles on subsidiarity in the European Union, interparliamentary deliberation and more recently, on juridification.

Martin Borowski is Senior Lecturer at the Birmingham Law School. He completed his *Habilitation* at the University of Kiel and was appointed as 'Privatdozent' in 2004. He is the author of *Grundrechte als Prinzipien* and of *Die Glaubens- und Gewissensfreiheit des Grundgesetzes*.

Flavia Carbonell is Lecturer at the Universidad Alberto Hurtado of Santiago de Chile. She holds LLMs from the Centre of Political and Constitutional Studies and the Universidad Carlos III, was member of the RECON research group at the Universidad de León, and has recently completed her PhD dissertation on the argument from coherence.

John Erik Fossum is Professor at ARENA Centre for European Studies at the University of Oslo, Norway, and substitute coordinator of RECON. He is the author of *Oil, State and Federalism*, co-author of *The Constitution's Gift* and co-editor of *Democracy and the European Union* and *Developing a Constitution for the European Union*, among others.

Tanja Hitzel-Cassagnes is Professor at the Institut für Politische Wissenschaft at the University of Hannover. She is the author of *Geltung und Funktion. Supranationale Gerichtsbarkeit im Spannungsfeld von Praktischer Rationalität, Recht und Demokratie.*

Marina Lalatta Costerbosa is Lecturer at the Faculty of Letters and Philosophy of the University of Bologna and at the Università Magna Grecia of Catanzaro. She is the author of *Ragione e Tradizione. Il pensiero giuridico ed etico-politico de Wilhelm Von Humboldtj* and of *Il Diritto comme Raggionamiento Morale*.

Massimo La Torre is Professor of Legal Philosophy at the University Magna Grecia of Catanzaro and at the Hull Law School. He is the author of *Disavventure del Diritto Soggetivo, La Crisi del Novecento. Giuristi e filosofi del crepuscolo di Weimar* and *Constitutionalism and Legal Reasoning*.

Neil MacCormick was Emeritus Professor of Public Law and the Law of Nature and Nations at the University of Edinburgh, where he was a Regius Professor from 1972 to 2008. He was Member of the European Parliament; during his stint he also served as member of the Convention on the Future of Europe. He was the author of *Legal Reasoning and Legal Theory, Legal Right and Social-Democracy, H.L.A. Hart, Questioning Sovereignty, Rhetoric and the Rule of Law* and *Institutions of Law.* He was also co-author (with Ota Weinberger) of *An Institutional Theory of Law.*

Agustín José Menéndez is Profesor Contratado Doctor Permanente at the Facultad de Derecho, Universidad de León; he is RECON fellow at ARENA, University of Oslo. He is the author of *Justifying Taxes,* co-author of *The Constitution's Gift* and co-editor of *Arguing Fundamental Rights*.

Jeremy Waldron is University Professor of law and philosophy at the New York University School of Law and Chichele Professor in Social and Political Theory at All Souls (Oxford). He has held teaching and research positions at Otago, Lincoln College, Oxford, the University of Edinburgh, Boalt Hall School of Law at Berkeley, Princeton University, Columbia Law School and Cornell University. He is the author of *The Right to Private Property, The Law: Theory and Practice in British Politics, Law's Disagreement, Liberal Papers, The Dignity of Legislation, God, Locke and Equality*, and most recently, *Torture, Terror and Trade Offs*, among others.

Neil Walker holds the Regius Chair of Public Law and the Law of Nature and Nations at the University of Edinburgh. He held teaching and research positions at the University of Edinburgh and was Professor of European Law at the European University Institute in Florence (2000–2008). He is the author of *Policing in a Changing Constitutional Order*, co-author of *Civilizing Security*, editor of *Sovereignty in Transition* and co-editor of *Relocating the Rule of Law*, among others.

Part I
A Life in Law and Politics

Chapter 1
The Cosmopolitan Local

Neil Walker

1.1 Neil MacCormick at Home and Abroad

Any tribute to Neil MacCormick and his work must begin by recognising a striking duality to his character, to his achievements, and, indeed, to his intellectual world-view and considerable body of work. When, in 1948, the sociologist Robert Merton famously coined the terms "local" and "cosmopolitan" to describe two different kinds of cultural orientation amongst members of a community, it was clear that his opposition was a stylised one that admitted of many exceptions.[1] In our own community of legal scholarship, it is difficult to imagine anyone who has so comprehensively and consistently given lie to Merton's opposition than Neil MacCormick. I have never met a more international Scot than Neil MacCormick, just as I have never met a more Scottish internationalist than Neil MacCormick. He truly was the cosmopolitan local.

This duality is manifest both in his professional and in his political life. Professionally, although he received countless attractive offers to relocate elsewhere, he was proud to hold the Regius Chair of Public Law and the Law of Nature and Nations at the University of Edinburgh from the date of his return to Scotland from Balliol College, Oxford in 1972 until his retirement in 2008. This period of 36 years spanned more than half his life, and made him, by a considerable margin, the longest serving member of the Professoriate of the entire University. It should also not be forgotten that his earlier education was predominantly Scottish. As an undergraduate he studied Philosophy and English Literature at Glasgow University, and he cut his teeth as a law lecturer in the city of Dundee. He loved the Scottish university scene and, in particular, Edinburgh University and its Law School – an affair of the heart that was entirely reciprocated. He held many positions of authority

N. Walker (✉)
University of Edinburgh, Edinburgh, UK
e-mail: neil.walker@ed.ac.uk

[1] "Patterns of Influence: A Study of Interpersonal Influence and of Communications behavior in a Local Community", in: P. F. Lazarsfeld and F. N.Stanton (eds), *Communications Research, 1948–1949* (New York: Harper and Brothers, 1949).

A.J. Menéndez, J.E. Fossum (eds.), *Law and Democracy in Neil MacCormick's Legal and Political Theory*, Law and Philosophy Library 93,
DOI 10.1007/978-90-481-8942-7_1,

and responsibility in the university and was a prominent and much respected public intellectual in the city and in the country as a whole.

Yet, for all his academic rootedness, he was also very much an international figure. He was an enthusiastic and tireless traveller, and, in his travels, his *persona* was always that of a member of the global community of scholarship. He was a vital and inspirational figure over many years in the worldwide growth of the International Association for the Philosophy of Law and Social Philosophy (IVR). He had strong and abiding academic relations over five continents, received honorary degrees from a number of leading international universities, and worked tirelessly and selflessly to promote the discipline which he loved worldwide.

Politically, he was, of course, a lifelong Scottish nationalist. Indeed, he was born to it. His father had founded the modern Scottish National Party (SNP) in 1934, his brother had been a Member of Parliament in the 1970s, and Neil himself was active for many years in the party, providing a key bridge between the sometimes sharply opposed gradualist and fundamentalist wings of the movement as well as supplying the party's shining intellectual light. After a lifetime of good political works, and with the constitutional landmark of a new Scottish Parliament at last in the offing, he again demonstrated his cosmopolitan side by departing the Scottish scene and becoming a Member of the European Parliament on behalf of the SNP between 1999 and 2004. He was, by common accord, outstanding in that role and was particularly influential as an alternate member of Giscard d'Estaing's Convention on the Future of Europe, which produced its famous first Draft Constitutional Treaty of the European Union in 2003. His nationalism was of the open and liberal kind, and it was no surprise to those who knew him that it travelled well. There were many, indeed, who wanted him to extend his stay in Brussels, but he had unfinished business at home. After he returned from Europe to Edinburgh – now at last a political, as well as a cultural, capital city – he took great pleasure and pride in acting as a special adviser to Alec Salmond, the First Minister of the first ever SNP government of Scotland. It was a role he carried out assiduously and vigorously even during his final illness.

All of this would be remarkable enough for one life. But, of course, this is without even mentioning the stuff that animates this volume, namely, his extraordinarily deep and diverse contribution to writing and thinking about the place of law in the order of things. Here, again, even in the surface themes of his work, we can see the two sides of MacCormick – the local MacCormick rooted in the particular, and the cosmopolitan MacCormick astride the universal. There was the MacCormick who wrote with poise and passion about nationalism, about sovereign statehood, about subsidiarity, and about the manifold diversity and unique particularity of normative orders. Then, there was the MacCormick who wrote with just as much insight and commitment about European and international law, about post-sovereignty, about the general nature of legal reasoning, about the institutional anatomy of any and all legal systems, and about the deep and universal structure of moral reasoning.

It would take a book-length study to do justice to the inner connections – the inevitable tensions, as well as the notable successes – of such a rich and intricate life, and I know that at least one will be written in due course.[2] My very modest aim here is simply to point to the continuity between the professional, political and intellectual dimensions of Neil MacCormick, cosmopolitan local *extraordinaire,* and to flag up some of the most obvious issues this raises about his life and work.

To begin with, there is the question of causality. To what extent did the professional and political *persona*, and the contrasts thrown up in these aspects of his life, influence his intellectual world-view, and to what extent *vice-versa*? Even to pose the question is to invite the obvious conclusion that the pattern was one of mutual influence. By any standards, and especially by academic standards, Neil MacCormick's was a remarkably integrated life. To read or hear him was to become keenly aware of someone whose thought was deeply informed by personal observation and experience. Equally, to encounter him was to observe someone whose knowledge and belief system was deeply informative of his actions – someone who not only preached, but also acted out the virtues of practical (rather than merely theoretical) reason.[3]

In the second place, there is the question of trajectory. Patently, Neil MacCormick's was a progressive life. His political ambitions and priorities shifted as external circumstances altered and as new opportunity presented itself. His professional life, too, evolved over time, his precocious success in the Regius Chair ensuring the early and relentless accumulation of the responsibilities of office – responsibilities, nevertheless, that he invariably met with great enthusiasm, careful commitment, good humour and skill. And, as we shall see, his intellectual gaze also shifted over the years, especially with regard to his mature interest in questions of post-national legal theory. Again, however, the abiding impression of MacCormick is of a life of integrity – integrity over time as well as between the component parts. Their particular manifestation may have changed, but the deep issues that engaged the mature MacCormick were, by and large, the same deep issues that engaged the young MacCormick. Such was the distinctiveness in both style and substance of Neil's approach, both on the page and on the platform, that the author of this extensive *oeuvre* was, from the beginning to the very end, unmistakably one and the same.

Thirdly, and of most immediate importance for an academic volume, the question of integrity also arises in the narrower intellectual domain. If there is no doubt about MacCormick's remarkable ability to marry theory to practice in his own life, or about the resilience of his commitments over time and often quite profound changes in circumstances, what of the body of thought itself? Neil was drawn to contrasting orientations in his work not because he was intellectually perverse, or footloose, or

---

[2]An intellectual biography of MacCormick by Maksymilian Del Mar has been commissioned by Stanford University Press as part of their *Jurists: Profiles in Legal Theory* series. It is scheduled to appear in 2013. An edited collection on the Scottish dimension of MacCormick's life and work will appear later in 2011; N. Walker (ed) *MacCormick's Scotland* (Edinburgh: Edinburgh University Press, 2011).

[3]This holistic approach is never more apparent than in his final book, written in the last year of his life; *Practical Reason in Law and Morality* (Oxford: Oxford University Press, 2008).

determined to dazzle with his virtuosity, but simply because the hard questions that he was interested in often drew him to the difficult edges and "in-between" zones of theoretical thought. This is true, for example, of his journey from a fairly orthodox positivist position towards something called "post-positivism", which he describes in his contribution to this volume. It is also true, for example, of his increasing interest in his later writings in Luhmannian systems theory or Habermasian discourse ethics, perspectives which he could never wholly endorse, but which helped him get to places that his more familiar intellectual resources could not readily reach.

However, what I want to concentrate on here is a third example, namely, the tension between his long standing endorsement of constitutional pluralism and his belief in the unity of law. This example is an especially apt one, I believe, and not only because it speaks clearly and directly to the present volume's specific concerns with that "post-sovereign constellation" which MacCormick's work did so much to illuminate. It is also particularly appropriate in offering a vivid case-study of just the kind of practical preoccupations that led to his internal theoretical tensions and conflicts; of the seriousness, clarity and candour with which he typically approached these conflicts; and, finally, of the ways in which a body of work as rich as his can allow us to imagine *MacCormickesque* solutions to problems he himself ran out of time to try to fix.

1.2 Constitutional Pluralism and the Unity of Law

Neil MacCormick was always very good at developing new questions out of old ones. He was also extremely adept at persuading his audience, including many who were still in thrall to the old questions, that these new questions were both the right and the most important questions to ask and to answer. This aptitude had a lot to do with native intelligence, but it also had something to do with what he calls, in his contribution to the present volume, his preference for a constructive/collaborative, rather than a critical/dialectical, approach to legal study. MacCormick sincerely believed that he always had more to learn from a room full of people than they had to learn from him. He was the most alert of listeners to other people's arguments and the most sympathetic of readers of other people's work. He conducted himself this way out of genuine humility, unfailing courtesy and unremitting intellectual curiosity, but also because he knew that this was the best way to get others to take his arguments seriously.

This quality was, if anything, intensified in his work on European law and polity. It was an area to which, as already noted, he came comparatively late in a multi-faceted intellectual life, and one in which he had, from the outset of his involvement, a direct political interest in developing a voice that would be broadly persuasive. These factors re-inforced his already well-honed instinct to go about his business by seeking to absorb what everyone else had to say and by endeavouring to present his own contribution, however fresh and however challenging, as somehow continuous with that received thought. In a nutshell, in European matters even more than elsewhere, MacCormick's way was to start from the point of view of others, and only gradually work back to his own, and to do so in a manner that focused on opening up new possibilities and lines of inquiry, rather than closing issues down. MacCormick's development of a specifically pluralist understanding of the relationship between national law and supranational law in the EU can be understood in the light of this overall academic sensibility and imperative of political engagement, as well as reflecting his efforts as a "cosmopolitan local" to integrate the universal and particular strands in his work.

Both in its explicitly trans-systemic ambition and in its exclusive concentration on systems displaying an institutional formality akin to that found in the state legal system, MacCormick's pluralist analysis differs in type from the classic tradition of legal pluralism within legal anthropology. This tradition tends, instead, to focus on the relationship between the official legal system of a single law-state and the various other self-styled legal or normative orders operating within the territory of that law-state. MacCormick's starting-point was his observation that there were not one but two main – and fundamentally incompatible – perspectives in play in the understanding of the European legal configuration. On the one hand, there were those for whom the last word in legal authority as to the nature of the European legal configuration rested with the national constitutional authorities, and, according to whom, the whole of European law could be understood as a massive, but reversible and so conditional pooled delegation of national sovereign rights. On the other hand, there were those for whom the last word rested with the supranational institutions themselves, self-conceived and self-constituted as an independent or autonomous authority, within the domain of the national competences and capacities transferred to them in the basic Treaties of the Union.[4]

MacCormick's response to this perceived state of affairs was neither to dismiss either opposing perspective as irrelevant, nor to agree with either position in full. On the one hand, he did not pursue the route of those – more influential in the academy than in the popular or political discourse – whose response was to reject both the state-centred and the EU-centred approach as trapped in an outmoded pedigree-centred attitude to legal authority, and who, instead, looked at the configuration of the EU in combination-with-the-states either as a new kind of complex unity,[5] or as something to which the very idea of bounded order and coherence was not appropriate.[6] On the other hand, he wanted to reject what he saw as the one-sided

[4]See, in particular, N. MacCormick, *Questioning Sovereignty* (Oxford: Oxford University Press, 1999), Chapter 7.

[5]See, for example, D. Curtin and I. Dekker, "The EU as a 'Layered' International Organization: Institutional Unity in Disguise", in: P. Craig & G. de Búrca (eds), *The Evolution of EU Law* (Oxford: Oxford University Press, 1999); A. von Bogdandy, "The European Union as a Supranational Federation: A Conceptual Attempt in the Light of the Treaty of Amsterdam" (2000) 6 *Columbia Journal of International Law*, pp. 27–54.

[6]See, for example, O. Gerstenberg and C. Sabel, "Directly-Deliberative Polyarchy: An Institutional Ideal for Europe", in: Ch. Joerges and R. Dehousse (eds), *Good Governance in the European Union* (Oxford: Oxford University Press, 2002).

sovereigntist bias involved in accepting entirely and exclusively either the state-centred, or the EU-centred, approach.

MacCormick's theory of law as institutional normative order was the device through which he distinguished himself from either set of positions. The idea of law as institutional normative order is one in which an arrangement of norms is grounded in a set of law-making and law-applying institutions and associated practices and attitudes, which, in a mutually reinforcing way, ensure the *systemic* quality of that normative order; that is to say, features such as its settled authority, its internal coherence, its reflexive adaptability.[7] Against those who would move too quickly to embrace the complex unity of European law, the idea of law as institutional normative order as invoked by MacCormick reminds us that quite different systems make up – configure – the whole that is European law, and since a key systemic feature is the recursiveness and resilience of the relevant complex of attitudes, institutions and practices, these different systems of institutional normative order will not easily lose their separate identity. Against those who would not think it interesting or fruitful to think of law in terms of bounded systems *at all*, and so would see nothing of particular interest or critical concern for law at that place of the confluence of different streams of national law, MacCormick would play the system card to the opposite effect. He would insist that, however difficult it was to identify the basic legal warrant for each and every unit in the complex mix of legal norms in the overall European configuration, the nature of that warrant was nevertheless best thought of in system-specific terms; that, as he put it, even in the most crowded normative space, the "settled, positive character" of any particular unit of law remained stubbornly "jurisdiction-relative".[8]

Yet, against those who would plump exclusively for the settled orders of national law or the settled order of supranational law, MacCormick would hold that this takes too narrow a view of the terms of co-existence of different normative orders or jurisdictions. Just as these orders are not fated to merge into a complex unity, so, too, it is unnecessary to the survival of any that one is entirely subordinated to and subsumed under the other. The idea of institutional normative order allows each relevant discrete complex of institutions and practices, and the overall regulative ideal or orientation which recursively feeds into and emerges from it, to be sustained notwithstanding the fact that, from a spectator's standpoint, none has comprehensive or unrivalled normative authority in its own domain, as was paradigmatically the case in the world of mutually exclusive and mutually corroborating sovereign states under the modern Westphalian system.

It is this break from the idea of absolute and unrivalled authority, indeed, which both lies behind and accounts for MacCormick's claim to be a "post-sovereigntist", and also a post-statist.[9] Certainly, an institutional normative order must at least

---

[7] See, for example, MacCormick, note 4 *supra*, Chapter 1; and, at greater length, N. MacCormick, *Institutions of Law: An Essay in Legal Theory* (Oxford: Oxford University Press, 2007).

[8] MacCormick, note 4 *supra*, p. 14.

[9] Ibid., Chapter 8. See, also, N. MacCormick, "Sovereignty and After", in: H. Kalmo and Q Skinner (eds), *Sovereignty in Fragments* (Cambridge: Cambridge University Press, 2010).

make a plausible claim to the plenitude of normative authority in its own terms – its regulative ideal must be corroborated by significant and sustained real-world success – but this is not incompatible with the resilient co-existence of two or more candidate orders and associated regulative ideals in areas where their claimed jurisdictional domains overlap. What is more – and this is where the political MacCormick rejoins the academic MacCormick – it would be a stark refusal to acknowledge the salient political facts of European integration as well as a failure of the theoretical imagination not to recognise the continuing force and plausibility of claims from national and supranational perspectives *alike*.

But to demonstrate the *plurality* of normative orders within the European legal space is not yet to demonstrate their *pluralism*. It is one thing to claim that the EU legal configuration is made up of one or more legal systems. It is quite another to show how these systems interact and cohere in a sustainable fashion. Here, then, we approach the horns of MacCormick's dilemma. On the one hand, if it is mere plurality that he is portraying, then it is not clear that he is adding anything, theoretically, to our understanding of how, if at all, law sounds and connects beyond the boundaries of a particular legal order. Nor is it clear that he is adding anything, practically, to our understanding of how the particular multi-order configuration known as the EU works and sustains itself over time. On the other hand, to the extent that he is able to show us how law functions *qua* law beyond the boundaries of the legal order, how, if at all, can he do so without turning plurality back into a new kind of systemic *unity* that necessarily denies the distinctiveness and independence of the parts? The fear is that we are here faced with a truly Procrustean dilemma. Either we have too little to say about the relationship between the parts, and so there is no additional properly legal step through which to turn legal plurality into an arrangement in which the connection of the legal parts is itself regulated by law, or, in so providing this extra step of legal regulation, we end up saying too much about the relationship between the parts and so destroy the distinctive integrity of the parts.

MacCormick's early instincts led him towards *understating* the relations between the parts.[10] In this view, which he subsequently labelled "radical pluralism",[11] he accepted that there was no legal relationship between the different constituent legal systems of the European legal configuration other than those which could be reduced to the terms of either or both systems. Instead, the only connections between the legal orders were (a) relationally contingent in their content, and (b) system-specific in their basis of authority and interpretation. That is to say, (a) they were the product of particular bridging mechanisms negotiated between each order, such as the preliminary reference procedure between national courts and the ECJ, the transposition of European directives into national law, the direct national effect of European regulations, the duty of national courts to implement EU law, *etc.*, and (b) the meaning and implications of the exchanges conducted across these bridges was ultimately decided by each system on its own terms. In addition, there were, of course, strong

[10]See, in particular, his "Beyond the Sovereign State" (1993) 56 *Modern Law Review*, pp. 1–18.
[11]MacCormick, note 4 *supra*, p. 117.

political and cultural relations between the systems. The political institutions of the EU, each in their own way, recognised and represented the constituent Member States in their deliberations and decision-making – the Commission, the Council and the European Council doing so at the level of the states themselves, and the Parliament doing so at the level of the populations of the states. Culturally, the relative convergence of the states of Western Europe, itself re-inforced by legal and political ties, found many expressions – including, reciprocally, indirect legal expression in ideas such as the judge-made and later Treaty-endorsed invocation of the "common constitutional traditions" of the Member States as a source of the human rights jurisprudence of the EU itself.

As already intimated, such an approach was open to both practical and theoretical objections. Practically, it could offer no proof against inter-system conflict. The dense network of bridging mechanisms was clearly very effective in anticipating, resolving, or deferring conflict, but the "contractual" contingency of these mechanisms, and, even more so, the diverse system-specificity of their authoritative interpretation meant that such avoidance of conflict could not be guaranteed all the way down. Political and cultural ties also helped, but, again, could not guarantee against conflict, especially as the EU became larger, more politically and culturally diverse, and more economically unequal. The large set-piece engagements of constitutional courts with European law over questions of the fundamental limits of encroachment on national sovereignty (as in the German *Maastricht* and *Lisbon* cases), over the protection of fundamental rights (as in the *Solange* cases), over the transfer of security functions from the national to the supranational sphere (as in the *European Arrest Warrant* cases), and – particularly telling from the perspective of growing political and cultural heterogeneity – over the power-transferring implication of joining the EU from the perspective of the only recently independent CEE Enlargement states, all speak of the precariousness of the inter-systemic proof against conflict.[12]

Theoretically, too, this approach offered nothing about the nature of law beyond a positivist investment in sources and pedigree. Whatever the general limitations of such a conclusion (to which I turn below), moreover, this could not have but been a cause of unease, and even embarrassment, to Neil MacCormick, who, as already noted, in his later work was wont to describe himself as a "post-positivist". It is also an embarrassment that grows and becomes more acute as we go beyond the EU itself. For, as I have argued elsewhere,[13] it is no accident that the idea of pluralism between constitutional orders first flourished in the European domain. The intensity and sophistication of the EU's contingent bridging mechanisms, together with the strength of the political and cultural ties, provided something of a "regional comfort zone" for this new brand of "constitutional" legal pluralism. As we have seen, on the

[12]For a good recent overview, see J. Baquero Cruz, "The Legacy of the Maastricht-Urteil and the Pluralist Movement" (2008) 14 *European Law Journal*, p. 389.

[13]N. Walker, "Constitutional Pluralism in Global Context", RECON Online Working Paper, 2010/3.

thin positivist understanding of the radical pluralist perspective, the pluralist bond remains a precarious accomplishment even within this comfort zone. Beyond this, however, in the increasingly dispersed networks of transnational legal relations and institutions outside of the EU, in relations between national orders and other regional trading blocks, functional regimes (trade, environment, criminal law), global general institutions (United Nations), private or hybrid forms of sectoral organisations (from ICANN to the International Olympic Committee), the limitations of radical legal pluralism are exposed even more vividly.[14] Here, there are neither the dense, mutually reinforcing bridging mechanisms, nor the solid cultural and political supports that sustain the EU theatre. Here, even more so than in the EU, the question of the necessary glue of legal pluralism is starkly posed.

MacCormick himself was, of course, aware of this wider environment, but tended to restrict his response to the problem of the thinness of radical pluralism to Europe, as his domain of particular interest. His revised proposal, in the light of the thinness objection, was to conceive of Europe's supranational pluralism as "pluralism under international law".[15] This was in recognition that European supranational law had originally emerged as a species of the genus international law – and, here, we see the resilience of MacCormick's positivist, pedigree-based conception of law – but it also arose out of a broader sense that, in the name of moving beyond mere plurality, there had to be some kind of normative *tertium quid* which would stand above the competing particularities of national and European law.

For some, MacCormick's later solution firmly impales him on the second horn of the procrustean dilemma. For is the invocation of a supervening international law not simply the way to a new form of normative unity and therefore a transcendence and so a denial of the very pluralism that MacCormick seeks to embrace? The answer to this is somewhat unclear from looking at MacCormick himself. He does not actually have much to say about the content or the mode of articulation or vindication of this aspect of international law (and to that extent, his new approach is also open to the opposite objection that it is no more than a rhetorical gesture, a mere re-labelling of his radical pluralism which does not begin to address the latter's problems), save that it is the supposed thin solvent that turns plurality into pluralism while avoiding "flat unity".[16] So, let us conclude by briefly posing some new questions, and providing some fresh indications as to what he *might have* meant by this. In so doing, we should bear in mind not only the substantial work that has subsequently been done in this area, much of it inspired by MacCormick's pioneering example, but also some of the "post-positivist" thoughts that may be mined from elsewhere in his body of work.

To the extent that MacCormick was searching for some notion of a unity of law standing beyond particular legal systems, but a unity which was not conceivable in

[14] See, for example, N. Walker, "Beyond boundary disputes and basic grids; Mapping the global disorder of normative orders" (2008) 6 *International Journal of Constitutional Law*, pp. 373–396.

[15] MacCormick, note 4 *supra*, p. 117.

[16] Ibid., p. 121.

terms of a new system to which the original legal systems would inevitably become subordinate, three possibilities, or at least three distinctive areas on a spectrum of possibilities, seem to present themselves. The first is what we might call, following Michael Walzer, a "covering-law universalism".[17] What this entails is a version of legal unity so strong, so insistent on subordinating the particular to the epistemic and moral authority of the universal, that it does not allow internal differentiation and division at all, and so does not recognise the subordination that would flow from that differentiation. Covering-law universalism would require either the global recognition of a powerful strain of natural law or a robust framework of positive law. Patently, such a unitarian solution is neither feasible, nor remotely in keeping with the recognition of the integrity of the local and particular in any new global framework of law – an abiding concern of MacCormick, but also of the vast majority of thinkers on the ethics of global law. Crudely, the covering-law approach only "solves" the problem of pluralism by denying the very baseline plurality out of which the question of pluralism flows.

A second possibility, again borrowing our label from Michael Walzer, is one of "reiterative universalism".[18] Here, again, there is a general or universal quality to the norms that integrate the pluralist configuration. Yet, the articulation of these common norms is not seen as a matter of simply "reading off" the local version from some inert universal covering-law, but as a continuous and progressive process of re-contextualisation in which the universal is not merely realised, but re-shaped by the particular. Some examples of this can be found in the new global legal literature. According to one prominent scholar of Global Administrative Law, for example, the relevant universals can form around notions as general as the principles of legality, rationality and proportionality, together with respect for the Rule of Law and the basic protection of human rights.[19] Over time, these normative ideas, all of which are engaged in key tasks of "channelling, managing, shaping and constraining political power"[20] tend to circulate more widely and more readily. Gradually, "as the layers of common normative practice thicken, they come to be argued for and adopted through a mixture of comparative study and a sense that they are (or are becoming) obligatory".[21] Meanwhile, a similarly cosmopolitan story is being told today about the development of global constitutional law across state and post-state sites, centred upon the nurturing of universal constitutional commitments to principles of legality, subsidiarity, adequate participation and accountability, public reason and rights-protection.[22]

---

[17]M. Walzer, "Nations and Universe", in: David Miller (ed), *Thinking Politically: Essays in Political Theory* (New Haven CT: Yale University Press, 2007), pp. 183–218, at 187.

[18]Ibid., p. 184.

[19]See B. Kingsbury, "The Concept of 'Law' in Global Administrative Law" (2009) 20 *European Journal of International Law*, pp. 23–57, at 31–34.

[20]Ibid., p. 32.

[21]Ibid., p. 30.

[22]See M. Kumm, "The Cosmopolitan Turn in Constitutionalism: On the Relationship between Constitutionalism in and beyond the State", in: J. L. Dunoff and J. P. Trachtman (eds), *Ruling the World?* (Cambridge: Cambridge University Press, 2009), pp. 258–325.

Would MacCormick be attracted to this kind of narrative of authorisation as a way of fleshing out what he meant by pluralism under international law? Possibly so. Certainly, it finds a much better balance and blend between the universal and the particular – the cosmopolitan and the local – than the covering-law version of universalism. And if his idea of the normative primacy of international law is intended as one of the primacy of a body of legal doctrine (however dynamically and dialogically conceived), then reiterative universalism would seem to fit his needs. Given his earlier commitment to radical pluralism and to the integrity of local legal and political self-determination, however, and, just as significantly, given the manner in which he discusses the concept of the universal elsewhere in his work, I suspect that reiterative universalism would, in the end, for MacCormick, continue to err, too much on the universalist side of the argument.

In particular, MacCormick's more general work on practical reasoning and on the relationship between law and morality – work which he concentrated on very closely in his last years – suggest a more modest, but still important, role for the universal domain, and one whose relevance to the present discussion is apparent.[23] In his discussion of the overlapping qualities of legal and moral reasoning, MacCormick, guided by Kant, but, even more so, by Adam Smith, has much to say about universalisability and the process of universalisation. Crucially, his main concern is with the *methodological*, rather than the *substantive*, significance of the idea of the universal in our legal and ethical lives. Just as any positive system of law requires us to act upon its *heteronomous* norms as if they applied to all like situations, i.e., universally, so, too, we should approach our *autonomous* moral choices in a similar law-like manner. We should make *all* these choices and *only* those choices that we would be prepared to defend universally. In this way, we would both, introspectively, avoid treating ourselves as somehow exceptional, as above the moral law, as well as, extrospectively, commit ourselves to accept the broader consequences if all were to act like us.[24]

Arguably, this kind of thinking has relevance at the inter-systemic level as much as at the inter-personal level. Where the positive law of any system runs out, and the terms of trade have to be worked out between the overlapping systems, then perhaps the relevant "law" here is simply the autonomous requirement on all parties to think of their actions and decisions in law-like terms. This involves no requirement that they defer to the same substantive universals, nor even an expectation that they will necessarily generate the same substantive universals in the process of universalisation. However, it does provide some kind of mutually reinforced self-discipline, and some attendant idea of comity which is in keeping with the *ethos,* if not the letter, of international law – something less than positive law, but more than purely strategic interaction.

---

[23] See, in particular, MacCormick, note 3 *supra*; see, also, N. MacCormick, *Rhetoric and the Rule of Law: A Theory of Legal Reasoning* (Oxford: Oxford University Press, 2005).

[24] See, in particular, MacCormick, note 3 *supra*, Chapters 1–5. For an incisive analysis of the Kantian and Smithian influences in his work, see M. Del Mar, "The Smithian Categorical Imperative: How MacCormick Smithified Kant", SSRN (2010).

Some of the ideas that have gradually gained currency in global legal-thinking in recent years, including Miguel Poiares Maduro's contrapunctual law[25] and Nico Krisch's model of pluralist public autonomy,[26] both notably influenced by MacCormick, may, at least on one reading,[27] be understood in terms of the kind of inter-systemic law of universalisability proposed here. Whether MacCormick himself would have approved is another question. But the mixture of dual-sourced and pluralistically-reconciled idealism and deep pragmatism that made him the most cosmopolitan of locals and the most local of cosmopolitans would certainly have drawn him in this direction.

[25] M. Maduro, "Contrapunctual Law: Europe's Constitutional Pluralism in Action", in: N. Walker (ed), *Sovereignty in Transition* (Oxford: Hart Publishing, 2003), pp. 501–538.

[26] N. Krisch "The Case for Pluralism in Postnational Law", LSE Legal Studies Working Papers 12/2009, available at: http://papers.ssrn.com/sol3/papers.cfm?abstract_id=1418707. See, also, his *Beyond Constitutionalism: The Pluralist Structure of Postnational Law* (Oxford: Oxford University Press, 2010).

[27] See, for example, some of the doubts expressed by Krisch himself; "The Case for Pluralism in Postnational Law", note 26 *supra*, pp. 14–17.

Part II
The Seven Big Themes in MacCormick's Legal and Political Theory

Chapter 2
MacCormick on MacCormick

Neil MacCormick

Some colleagues, I think, specialise more in the critical-dialectical method than in the constructive-collaborative one. My dear friend and admired senior colleague, Ronald Dworkin, is an interesting example of somebody who always surveys the world from a single position: his own. Dworkin, although giving very interesting valuable *critiques* of other people's work, always does so by restating them in his own terms, and seeing if he can give what he regards as an improved version of it. His recent writings about legal positivism are an example of this style. This is a very strong and powerful way to do business. I think my own style has tended towards the other direction. I enjoy a good argument as much as anybody else. I like the dialectical-critical bit of the work. But I notice, when I review a book, for example, that I always tend to start by trying to see it from the author's point of view. It takes me a long time to discover if I agree with a book, because if you try to understand it, you should read it sympathetically, with willing suspension of disbelief. Once you master the ideas, you think, "hmmm, that is rather persuasive", even if it says what you do not think; or what you did not use to think. The upshot of this is, of course, that people who have this attitude tend to shift their position. If you read something with sympathy and interest ("there *is* something in that", "*better* take that on board"), you will be willing, from time to time, to acknowledge a change, a shift of position, because you have felt that some other argument which you had not thought about, was a strong one, and you needed to acknowledge and adapt or adopt. This must make it difficult, I realise, reading some of the papers of this book, for people reading the things that I wrote 20 or 30 years ago, to figure out the position of MacCormick. The answer is that he is a moving target. This creates the risk of inconsistency and, perhaps, worst of all, of what we could call mere eclecticism.

N. MacCormick
University of Edinburgh, Edinburgh, UK

Note from the editors: This chapter contains the transcription of the paper that Neil presented at the 2007 workshop at the Bergen Faculty of Law where most of the papers included in this book were first discussed. We have made minor editorial changes, to accommodate the speech to the written form, without tampering with the flow of Nei's discourse (or at least that is what we strived for and hope).

A.J. Menéndez, J.E. Fossum (eds.), *Law and Democracy in Neil MacCormick's Legal and Political Theory*, Law and Philosophy Library 93,
DOI 10.1007/978-90-481-8942-7_2, © Springer Science+Business Media B.V. 2011

You take an idea from here and an idea from there, and you make a certain collage of nice ideas, but maybe you do not have something that makes complete sense. I hope that this is not the case. But there are difficulties about both styles. They need to combine somehow; the critical-dialectical and the constructive-collaborative must be taken altogether. These are difficult things to do, but we must all try. I very much appreciate the spirit of this gathering, which is exactly this kind of collaborative, but also mutually critical, exercise.

It seems to me that what I have done over the years is to address several tasks. I really regard *Institutions of Law* as the centre of what I have really tried to do, or the underpinning of everything else. I do believe that there are important epistemological and ontological issues with which the philosophy of law does have to deal. I remember reading an article by Richard Tur, now in Oxford, then in Glasgow, in which he said, many years ago, that, to understand Kelsen, you must realise that what he was doing was writing a theory of knowledge for legal science. In what sense is there knowledge, in what sense can we *know* things if we are studying law? Law is not just a matter of either naked will, or ideology or interest wrapped up in an attempt at objective theories of justice, or something like that. Kelsen's *problématique* was all along – and Tur is right about this – trying to establish in which sense we can obtain genuine knowledge in a genuinely normative realm. I think that it is important, for us in law schools, to take issues of legal theory seriously, because, to some extent, our claims to be genuine members of the academy, genuine scientists or scholars, depends upon having some reasonably thought-through views about these matters.

Institutions of Law tries to tackle the question, is there really law, and what sort of thing is it? The answer, you know, rather trivially, is that law is an institutional normative order. The method which I try to use, I call explanatory definition. The method is, in part, one of analysis, but not in the rather elaborate one of conceptual analysis developed by Oxford philosophers in the aftermath of the Second World War. What I mean is analysis in the older sense. We are dealing here with a large complex object and the best way to understand large complex objects is to understand them in terms of what their elements are, what their parts are. *To understand the whole by understanding the parts*. Clearly, this also requires a moment of synthesis, as well. Because the parts are what they are only as parts of a whole. You have to have a sense of the parts, as parts, and of the whole, as a whole. A kind of hermeneutic circle, I suppose.

The simplest part of a normative order is norms. We have to think about what norms are, and about the various kinds of norms that there are, and of the various kinds of relationships between persons that you can have. And, indeed, also about the constitution of persons, as persons from the point of view of normative order, as well as the relations that they have. All these things have to be clarified, and can be so clarified.

In addition to normative order, one has to think about institutionalisation, institutional normative order. And these are all questions with which I deal, which we will be discussing in some of the chapters in this volume, so I do not want to go into detail in advance, but just to sketch the main elements of the things with which we are dealing.

As already mentioned, one of the things that I find important is to get straight that state law, the law of the state, as in Norway or Germany, is only one kind of law; one of the merits of using the concept of institutional normative order is that one does not automatically, from square one, so to say, privilege the state as the *locus* of law. The state is, in fact, for most of us, the most important *locus* of law, and it is so for two very important reasons. First of all, the state is territorial; and second, the state is a coercive organisation. It can allocate opportunities to occupy space, and it can endorse such allocations, so that its normative order tackles issues which are, for all of us, vital, and affect the interests and concerns of the other normative orders which there may also be.

However, many more of my fellow citizens are aware of the laws of associated football and the proceedings of the *FIFA* than of the proceedings of the European Union or even the law of Scotland. But, of course, when it comes to the bite, if somebody commits a fierce assault during a football game, the courts of the state will have the first shot at dealing with the issue. But *FIFA* law will still have its effect in terms of the removal of points from a team, or the exclusion from competition. But it is not the case that the only *dissuasive* forms of coercion are those operated by the state. However, only the state can legitimately back coercion with physical force. This is true also from the standpoint of great transnational confederations such as the European Union, although we will have discussions in the course of this volume concerning how to conceive of the relationship of the European Union as a legal order and the Member States as legal orders, and the members of the European Economic Area as connected states. We all know well that, in the last resort, if it comes to the question of physical enforcement, European law will be enforced through the organs of one of the states, and not for the time-being by any specifically EU coercive organ.

There are very important reasons why we have to take, and, in fact, do take, state law very seriously. As teaching institutions, law schools are mainly engaged in assisting people to learn the law of their own jurisdiction; there is money to be made practicing this kind of law because of the serious effects that it has upon the organisation of the economy and upon society. When we discuss notions such as legal pluralism, it is helpful to start with a conception of law which allows us to say why state law is so important, but makes it clear that it is not the *only* kind of law that there is. And it is not law in some radically different sense, or some weaker sense. I will not call canon law in any sense weaker law than Norwegian law. To excommunicate is certainly a different thing than to put somebody in jail. But some people fear excommunication more than they fear jail. There are people who think differently. I am one of the latter. Excommunicate me as much as you will, but I do not want to go to jail.

I guess there is the other question of the relationship of legal order, so understood, and moral order, legal norms and moral norms. Just putting it crudely and simply, it looks as though state law, and law more generally, is institutional, and it thus puts the agent in the situation of heteronomousness. When subjected to the law, one is potentially subjected to the will of others. It is not necessarily the case that I agree with the law of my state, even in fundamental and important things. You only have to contemplate issues such as euthanasia and abortion, for which, whatever the solutions which state law may reach in matters of this kind, there will be conscientious citizens who will be outraged by what their state does or fails to do. In contrast, morality in the conception I defend of it, is neither institutional, nor coercive; indeed, it is autonomous, it presupposes the actual exercise of moral choice. It leaves the agent in a position of autonomy. Each of us is his or her own final judge in matters of morality. Whether each of us is his or her own final legislator is another, and interesting, question which I will attend to briefly at the end. This, I think, marks the contrast between the legal sphere, as I understand it, and morality, as I understand it. I remark, from time to time, that a lot of the discussions about law and morality assume that we know perfectly well what morality is. But the problem is, indeed, how to characterise morality and how to characterise law. The relationship between two objects can only be clear when you establish what the two objects are. It seems to me that, if you take this conception of morality and this conception of law, it is obvious that the one is not identical with the other; this is an important fact. In fact, some people will say that makes you a positivist, if you hold to a clearly demarcated line between law and morality. However, I am not sure about this.

The next thing which is worth thinking about, once we get a clear conception of law, of morality and of institutional normative order, is the practicality of law. Law is not just an inert body of norms. Indeed, norms are not inert things; norms are guides to action. This entails that a reflection on the character of legal reasoning is of great importance and interest to us. How is the institutional normative order operationalised? And, in particular, how it is operationalised in judicial decision-making, and in legal practice more generally. I have always been interested, since the very earliest time, in theories of legal reasoning, and in the attempt to construct a theory of legal reasoning which is compatible with what I originally took to be a legal positivistic view, perhaps the same view as that of my teacher H.L.A. Hart.

My point of view is fairly straightforward. When we connect the theoretical study of legal reasoning with the ontological issues studied in *Institutions of Law* (norms, third rules, principles and guidelines), it is useful to work out definitions of the differences between rules, principles, guidelines and so forth. And I think that I have offered some hopeful suggestions about this in the said book.

Thinking in terms of the Rule of Law, the *Rechtsstaat*, clearly one of the tasks of legal reasoning is to show that, where we do have rules, they are being applied accurately and faithfully. And although there has been a great deal of discussion about whether deductive logic has any part to play in the work of legal systems and legal institutions, I have never been able to be persuaded – other than in a very straightforward way – that there is a kind of simple legal syllogism which is involved in the application of rules to cases. Clearly, to call it a simple legal syllogism can be rather deceiving, because, as Joxerramón Bengoetxea once discovered when he was thinking about it in Edinburgh, you may find complex chains of simple syllogistic reasoning. Take complex tax problems: we say these are easy cases, but only in the sense that they do not necessarily give rise to any problems of interpretation. But they are frantically complex. It involves a great deal of patience and intelligence to work them to an end. So do not under-estimate the importance of syllogistic reasoning in law.

But also do not underestimate the fact that, for good reasons, the scope of syllogistic reasoning is restricted, because we get problems of interpretation, problems of qualification, problems of evaluation and issues about relative values, different consequences of pursuing one course over another, what I call a problem of relevancy, and problems of proof. We can look to the styles and kinds of reasoning that can be brought to these tasks. One thing is clear: there have to be reasons *beyond* the rules. And this means that there is a porousness between both the *activity* of law and the *practice* of law and general moral reasoning, because both of them engage in practical reasoning and relate to questions of practical reasonableness. In general terms, the duty of courts is to reach the most reasonable and plausible solution consistent with the rule of law; and this, in itself, is a kind of loaded dice on the issue of how to unpack this. In *Legal Reasoning and Legal Theory*, I thought that, at the end of the day, one simply had to reach a subjective decision. And, in a certain sense, this is true; if you are a judge, and only limited rules apply, you must reach a decision. This can leave us with the thought that there is really no right answer at all, which is where I was to begin. But my colleague, Ronald Dworkin, has, over the years, cumulatively persuaded me that this is a mistake, and so has Robert Alexy. There is no reason to suppose that there is not, in the last resort, a more reasonable answer to any given problem, and a less reasonable one, even if both of them are fairly reasonable, and even if you take full account of the law. I am now an acceptor of a version of the right answer thesis, which has been a topical dispute among lawyers since Ronald Dworkin first posed the question in his book *Taking Rights Seriously* in 1977.

We nonetheless wonder if, on the other hand, we have to try to figure out the kinds of arguments (for example, arguments about coherence, consistency, consequences), and how they fit together, and, in some way, the issue of reasonableness lies there. Another question, which I think is a unifying point between legal and moral reasoning, a unifying aspect of practical reasoning, that I noticed in some of the papers we will discuss, is the issue of universalisability, Kantian universalibility, i.e., the topic of the universalisable, of generalisation when deciding issues. I have worried about this a lot. It is true that one only decides particular cases, and, indeed, one only takes particular decisions. And you always have particular reasons for doing so. Yet, would these reasons be reasons, rationally acceptable reasons, if we did not think that they were, in some way, universalisable? In my view, they would not, but this has been a considerably discussed subject. And, again, I think the reader will have a further iteration of this in the coming chapters.

Then, having said all this about the analytical and the rational aspects of legal theory, we must come to terms with its synthetic aspect. We need to look at how legal orders come together in different bits, and how this connects with other questions of importance to us. Some of my colleagues, particularly my English colleagues, are inclined to say that the differences between, for example, public and private law, or public and criminal law, are rather arbitrary, that there is no clear line of demarcation. And, perhaps, in a certain way, the particular structure of the English court system makes that seem credible. Yet, it is surely not accidental that all legal thinking in modern states tries to separate issues of public law, issues of criminal law, and issues of private law. This seems to be logical. Public law represents the interface between law and the state, the state both centrally and locally, and we see that, in the modern world, public law is engaged in the efforts by the state which are motivated by political argument to inject a degree of distributive justice into an economic system which, in so far as it is a market order, can sometimes have momentary results which seem unsatisfactory from the standpoint of justice. So that, for example, the provision of public education, public health services, the equalisation devices of one kind or another, are done under the *aegis* of public law. The other interesting thing about public law is if you look at it from the standpoint of legal relationships; powers exercised under public law tend to be unilaterally exercisable. If you are taking a decision on behalf of an agency of the state, we may consult the public beforehand, you may have duties to consult and the obligation to state the reasons for your decisions; the decision binds regardless of the consent of the other party. This stands in sharp contrast with most of the powers which are exercisable in private law. However great the economic disparity between the parties, it remains the case that, generally speaking, a private power cannot be exercised except with the consent or the agreement of the person towards whom it is exercised. So private law powers are bilateral, although they often operate in very sharply distinct power relationships, economic power relationships, while public relations are unilateral in the referred sense. However, it may be that the state sometimes finds that its power of a legal kind is, technically speaking, unilateral, but that de facto it is countervailed by the economic influence which a private corporation can exercise in public affairs (as is the case, for example, when the state tries to regulate Microsoft).

If we think of the state and civil society, the civility of civil society depends, above all, on the criminal law. It used not to depend on criminal law, and it is not only criminal law. But when we talk of civil society, what do we mean? If we depart from Adam Ferguson's *Essay on Civil Society,* the question is that all human beings live in societies, but not all societies are civil, some societies are war-like. My Viking ancestors, when they arrived in Scotland and ventured to rape and pillage, were not unsocial beings; Aristotle would have recognised them as perfectly social people; but civil people? And they met pretty fierce guys there. My other ancestors called them off. It ought to be surprising, but it is not surprising that I can walk down Princess Street in Edinburgh thinking that nobody is about to draw a sword and stab me. By and large, we trust total strangers to treat us amiably and with civility. Among the reasons for this is the state and its coercive power: you can create a sufficient body of competence that there is voluntary co-operation in coercive systems, to use Hart's phrase; people are able to deal in an impersonally trusting way. I passed through London a week ago and went onto the tube-station platform at Oxford Circus at a quarter to six. It was heaving with people. I realised again why I never wanted to live in London. But even then, everybody was going about their business. In these days of heightened fears of terrorism, it was so obvious, being there, that this state of affairs is far from obvious. Still, we do not really think that a terrorist act is going to happen. And we are right. It does not happen. People get through these huge crowds with safety and security. This is a remarkable procedure. The civility of civil society is secured by law, and particularly guaranteed by criminal law.

The economic system is, surely, wholly dependent on private law; first of all, you require secure private property. You will never divide what you can take. Economic relationships depend, to a large extent, upon security supplied by private law. When you put it altogether, you can see. Well, you will be able to make sense of Niklas Luhmann. The legal system, the political system, the economic system and civil society, are all aspects of the same thing, or alternatively, they are different moments of the great social whole. And, as he very brilliantly says, each of these is a system of communication which understands the others imperfectly. And this is also true. What we have to realise, however, is that they are not completely opaque to each other; they are interactive and develop structural couplings between them. I think this view of creating some kind of synthetic, as well as analytical, view of the elements of legal order helps us to build up a sense of what we are talking about: the overall coherence of law and society and political order.

The last problem which is still outstanding is the following. This volume deals with a set of books which for the time being is a trilogy but there is another green book[1] coming which I am trying to write at the moment. I think some of you have noticed that there is a perpetual oscillation between the ideas of universalisibility, and the ideas of Adam Smith, which are surely correct. People who have no sense of fellow-feeling for others will be totally incapable of becoming moral agents, the horizon of otherness of other people; yet, the sameness of their capacity for suffering as one's own kind is the beginning of enlightenment in moral questions.

I suppose, to this day, that psychopaths, people with various forms of social and personality disorder, are simply people who cannot see the world as others see it, who cannot imagine themselves in the shoes of somebody else sympathetically. I think this is correct. This insight from David Hume and Adam Smith, the capacity for empathy and fellow-feeling, is foundational for both the existence and the functioning of moral creatures; that has to be acknowledged.

And, yet, it clearly will not do just to say what is right is a matter of what feels good. One of the most famous eighteenth century critics of David Hume asks, "Why do we call judges judges? If Mr Hume is right, we will call them feelers". It is not true. Feelings may matter, but, at the end of the day, moral judgement is judgement, as legal judgment is judgement. We think of moral reasoning and legal reasoning as being somehow mutually parallel. We go back to the problem of trying to reconcile something out of Kant, and the school of natural law thinking of which he is a

[1]Note from the editors: A reference to *Practical Reason in Law and Morality*, the book in the quartet series *Law, State and Practical Reasons* whose cover is emerald green, and which was published one year after this chapter was presented in Bergen.

combination, and the sentimentalism of some parts of the Scottish enlightenment thought.

I am quite satisfied that I do not yet know the answer to this. What I know is the question: How to reconcile the need to procure a sensible rational theory of moral judgement, which nevertheless takes account of the fact that the matters of which moral judgement judge are the most fundamental feelings and emotions of human beings? This is all I can say about this at the moment, but I am still working on it.

Some people have noted that I have effectively changed camps. I started out as a positivist, and I am now called the muse that only natural lawyers can own. But I am entitled to call myself a post-positivist. Why? The answer is given very well in Massimo La Torre's chapter. I certainly started out my legal thinking very much under the spell of H.L.A. Hart, and I do think that one very fundamental insight of Hart stays with me, and ought to stay with all of us, that is, that we are more fundamentally norm-users than norm-givers. To understand law and legal order, you have to understand it from the user's point of view, not from the manufacturer's. And this is partly because part of our most important normative capabilities relate to norms that nobody ever made. I refer to speech. No natural language was ever deliberatively created, all natural languages are normative codes which tell you the right and wrong ways of expressing yourself. We all speak. If we could not speak, we would not think human thoughts, anyway. So, the roots of our capacity for specific human action is a normative order which we all use, but which nobody has made. This, I think, is a significant point. I am not saying that man-made norms are not important. They are very important, and, for the very reason, I started out with: the law of the state dominates much of practical activity. And, of course, states have legislatures, judiciaries and precedents and so on. But, of course, it is true that most of the most important practical norms that we confront are man-made ones, or partially man-made ones; but bear in mind that the capacity to make them depends on a constitutional framework, and the constitutional framework itself depends upon its customary observation by members of the community. You can always find a constitution as you like, but if Mr Musharraf[2] can tear it up and the people acquiesce, then it stops being a constitution. The issue is, what is functioning as a constitution, and that again depends on the perspective of the user, not the perspective of the provider. From this point of view, I remain a faithful disciple of H.L.A. Hart. I think that, on a number of important points, his theory turns out to be wrong or to be still insufficient. I am not entitled to call myself a natural lawyer given all that I inherited from Hart and Kelsen, but I am no longer a positivist, but a post-positivist.

[2]Note from the editors: At the time the chapter was written, Mr Musharraf was the President of Pakistan (having obtained power through a military coup d'êtat), and incurred several clear breaches of the Constitution, to put it very mildly. He subsequently resigned after impeachment pressure from a newly elected government, and has lived in exile since 2008.

Part III
The Limits of Law

Chapter 3
Juridification from Below: The Dynamics of MacCormick's Institutional Theory of Law

Lars Christian Blichner

> Law is institutional normative order.
>
> *Neil MacCormick*[1]

> Human beings are norm-users, whose interactions with each other depend on mutually recognizable patterns that can be articulated in terms of right versus wrong conduct, or what one ought to do in a certain setting. Understanding this use of norms precedes understanding any possibility of deliberately creating relevant norms that are to become patterns of behaviour. Yet, deliberate creation of norms also occurs. Norm usage can acquire a more formal character, indeed, can become 'institutionalized'. To understand this is to understand the transition into institutional normative order, and thus law.
>
> *Neil MacCormick*[2]

> Law as institutional normative order thus comes to be a complex and systematic whole.
>
> *Neil MacCormick*[3]

Any theory of law should, ideally, include some idea about juridification, although not necessarily using that name. In the vocabulary of this chapter, this would, by implication, mean that any theory of law should also include an idea about the limits of juridification; effectively, the limits of law. In what way does Neil MacCormick's institutional theory of law include an idea about juridification and the limits of law? In order to answer this, I will proceed as follows: first, a concept of juridification is needed, second, a basic idea about MacCormick's institutional theory of law, and

L.C. Blichner (✉)
University of Bergen, Bergen, Norway
e-mail: lars.blichner@aorg.uib.no

[1] Neil MacCormick, *Institutions of Law, An Essay on Legal Theory* (Oxford: Oxford University Press, 2007), hereafter *IoL*, p. 1.
[2] Ibid., p. 20.
[3] Ibid., p. 304.

A.J. Menéndez, J.E. Fossum (eds.), *Law and Democracy in Neil MacCormick's Legal and Political Theory*, Law and Philosophy Library 93,
DOI 10.1007/978-90-481-8942-7_3,

third, a more detailed account of juridification relative to MacCormick's theory. I will concentrate on MacCormick's concept of law in order to answer questions like: What makes juridification possible in the first place? (presuppositions, human ontology); What drives processes of juridification? (dynamics); and Why juridification is accepted? (legitimacy, justification). These are big questions, of course, and we cannot expect to do justice to MacCormick's entire lifelong work. I will concentrate on his book, "*Institutions of Law*", which is his latest and most comprehensive version of his institutional theory of law. Even more specifically, I will focus on the transition from normative order to institutional normative order.[4] This will be my main reference in what follows. The strategy will be one of comparing MacCormick's concept of law with an account of juridification developed elsewhere.[5] In the process, I hope to identify mechanisms[6] through which juridification can be understood, and maybe indicate an answer to the most difficult of questions: What are the limits of juridification; What are the limits of law according to Neil MacCormick?

3.1 The Concept of Juridification

The concept of juridification proposed here, originally developed in collaboration with Anders Molander, takes, as its point of departure, what may be considered to be five basic elements of law.[7] First, law involves authoritative institutions. This means identifiable institutions made up of identifiable people with a limited competence to make decisions on behalf of those whom the law concerns. Institutional procedures concerning decision-making and the limitations on what an authoritative institution may do are governed by rules and principles, and the same goes for changes in the authority's competence. Second, law involves norms. These norms should be such that they can guide human conduct. In order to do this, they have to conform to the most basic rule of law criteria, meaning that norms have to be general and relatively clear, promulgated, non-retroactive, relatively stable, possible to follow, and not contradictory.[8] Third, law involves an equal opportunity for all subjects under law, to appeal to law, and law also involves deciding who is right

---

[4] *IoL*, Chapters 1 & 2.

[5] L.C. Blichner and A. Molander, "Mapping Juridification" (2008) 14 *European Law Journal*, pp. 36–54.

[6] See J. Elster, "A Plea for Mechanisms", in: P. Hedstrøm and R. Swedberg (eds), *Social Mechanisms: An Analytical Approach to Social Theory* (Cambridge: Cambridge University Press, 1998), pp. 43–75; and *idem*, *Explaining Social Behavior: More Nuts and Bolts for the Social Sciences* (Cambridge: Cambridge University Press, 2007), especially p. 32.

[7] These again loosely build on four more basic criteria of law: 1. Law should be able to guide human conduct. 2. A claim to correctness in the weak sense that every decision made by the legal system should be backed by reason. 3. The fulfilment of the basic rule of law criteria. 4. Law should be backed by morally acceptable reasons, meaning reasons that people in general may accept as moral even though they may not agree that these reasons should have any bearing on a given actionable conclusion.

[8] See L. L. Fuller, *The Morality of Law* (New Haven CT-London: Yale University Press, 1964).

and who is wrong whenever someone believes that the law has been violated and makes an appeal to law. Fourth, law involves interpretation. Part of the limited competence of the institutionalised authority is competence to interpret the law. This gives the institutionalised authority power. This power is limited, in that interpretation is, itself, governed by rules and principles. Sometimes this involves interpreting or changing, or even inventing new rules and principles governing interpretation.[9] Fifth, law involves a tendency among strangers to understand both their self and others, and the relationship between the self and others, in view of a common legal order.

All these five elements may be seen as preconditions for any legal system. Our contention, in developing a concept of juridification, however, is that we need a way not only to establish the presence or absence of these elements, but also to establish their relative degree of dominance. According to one formulation, the term juridification may be seen as capturing the process "whereby areas of social and economic life become subject to systematic control through legislation, the application of legislation by state agencies and the adjudication of outcomes through the judicial process and the courts".[10] What we have proposed is five dimensions of juridification that may capture this development in more detail: first, constitutive juridification (A) is a process in which norms constitutive of a political order are established or changed to the effect of adding to the competencies of the legal system. Second, juridification (B) is a process through which law comes to regulate an increasing number of different activities or regulate these activities in greater detail. Third, juridification (C) is a process whereby conflicts are increasingly being solved with reference to law. Fourth, juridification (D) is a process by which the legal system and the legal profession obtain more power (as contrasted with formal authority), due to indeterminacy and lack of transparency in law. Finally, juridification as legal framing (E) is the process by which people increasingly tend to think of themselves and others as subjects under law, sometimes at the expense of other identities. Juridification, as we understand it, takes place within a legal order or a legal order in the making, be it at a national, international or supranational level. It is a process, in the sense that something increases over time. If the process is reversed, we speak of de-juridification.

We have made two propositions on the relationship between the different dimensions of juridification: first, the different dimensions of juridification are not necessarily linked, meaning that a link has to be substantiated empirically. We argue

---

[9]Basically, the more radical the interpretation, the stricter the demand that the rule of law situation should be improved, meaning that, after the interpretation, there should be less room for criticism based upon the rule of law than before. Based upon the premises that the rule of law is an essentially contested concept and that it is never fully satisfied, all we can ask is that the interpretation be reasonably defended with reference to the rule of law. Thus, the rule of law serves as a weak critical standard, in the sense that some interpretations are excluded, but more than one may be acceptable.

[10]See S. Wilks, "Markets and law: Competition policy and the juridification of the economic sphere", Paper presented at the Society for the Advancement of Socio-Economics (SASE) Conference, George Washington University, Washington DC, 8 July 2004, on file with the author.

that, although it is almost inconceivable to imagine a society based upon law in which some juridification have not taken place on all five dimensions, they are distinct, in the sense that one type of juridification may gather speed, halt or be turned around without a parallel effect on the others. Second, the relationships between the different dimensions of juridification may be linked in any way, positively or negatively, meaning that any model has to be substantiated empirically. The problem with this, of course, if even only loosely accurate, is that we may come up with hundreds of models that all give different accounts of the process of juridification. In normative terms, the conclusion was that, even if a level of juridification on all five dimensions seems warranted for any system of law, juridification carried too far might move the very same political order towards total legal domination. At a certain level, juridification may, indeed, turn ugly as Gunther Teubner claims. Saying that too little is as bad as too much, is not exactly a ground-breaking statement, but we may at least postulate a breaking-point, or maybe rather a breaking zone, that a society enters at a certain level of juridification. Such a zone may be seen as being delimited by a point beyond which the benefits of further juridification are questionable and a further point where juridification is carried so far that the effects are clearly detrimental from the point of view of the rule of law, democracy or civil society.

At the same time, it is difficult, based upon our conceptualisation, to establish an ideal model of juridification. The closest that we can get at this stage is to argue that the dimensions of juridification defined here will have to balance each other off. We can establish some rules of thumb, some "stop and think" signs of the type: if juridification B without juridification C, something is wrong; or if juridification D without juridification A+B something is completely wrong; or if juridification ABCD without juridification E, of which the EU legal system may be seen as an example, something has to change or something is going to break, to use but a few possible examples.

We argue then that different dimensions of juridification will have to develop hand in hand, but this alone is not sufficient. There is not only a tension between the different dimensions of juridification, but also an inner tension within each. The logical endpoint of juridification A, for example, is a society run by the judiciary. At some point in moving towards such circumstances, the existing self-understanding and legitimacy base of the legal system would be undermined. In the same way, juridification B carried too far would undermine the very freedoms that law is supposed to protect. Juridification C may, in the end, internalise moral, ethical and instrumental concerns to a degree where the responsibility for solving political disputes becomes indistinguishable from the application of law. With juridification D, the legal system is dependent on the continued construction of a relatively coherent working legal order, a coherence that will be increasingly difficult to sustain as the scope of interpretation and the degree of complexity increases, not least with the development of international law. Finally, juridification E may proceed at the expense of, or subsuming, other conceptions of the self and others, conceptions which the status of a legal person pre-supposes and is meant to protect.

A note on this account of juridification is in order. It was originally meant to cover what MacCormick would refer to as the legal order of the constitutional democratic state, and different legal orders developed in co-operation between these states, such as, for example, the EU legal order. This paves the way for questions relating to the status of this concept of juridification relative to the pluralism of normative and institutional-normative orders that MacCormick's legal theory presupposes. So one question that this chapter may help to answer is whether this concept of juridification may find more general use even relating to the most minimal normative and institutional-normative orders. Before exploring this in more detail, I would like to start by giving an all too brief outline of some of what I take to be the relevant building-blocks of MacCormick's institutional theory of law, which is necessary to understand the discussion that follows.

3.2 MacCormick's Legal Theory, Legal Pluralism and the Limits of Law: Some Preliminary Remarks

It may seem unfair, in a way, to evaluate MacCormick's concept of law relative to a concept of juridification that MacCormick has not used himself. My defence is that MacCormick's concept of law is intimately linked to his institutional theory of law, and that an account of juridification should, ideally, be included in any comprehensive theory of law. To examine law in terms of processes of juridification and de-juridification, as understood here, points to questions relating to the limits of law as well as to the dynamic development of law.

MacCormick defines law as institutional normative order. The institutional normative order that he concentrates on throughout his book *Institutions of Law* is the constitutional democratic state. He starts out, however, by explaining (laying out) how this constitutional legal order can exist, and how it is institutionalised. With a fair amount of simplification, the explanatory exercise has three identifiable levels. First, normative order; second, institutional normative order; and third, the modern constitutional state or "law-state",[11] which is the most comprehensive institutional normative order currently existing. One may loosely say that these are three levels of juridification.

Different orders, at each level of juridification, according to MacCormick, may exist and develop in parallel. The first level is made up of pre-legal normative orders, the second, any, even the most minimal, "legal" order, and the third, the specific legal orders of the modern constitutional state, marked, most importantly, relative to the second level, by a fully-realised separation of powers doctrine. The first two levels are the most basic and are the ones upon which I will concentrate. According to MacCormick, it is the institutionalisation of "norm-usage" that is essential to understanding the transition from normative order "into institutional normative order, and

[11] *IoL*, p. 35.

thus law".[12] This transition is exemplified by the practice of queuing.[13] If our concept of juridification is compatible with MacCormick's concept of law, it should be possible to reconstruct at least parts of MacCormick's argument concerning these levels by way of our five dimensions of juridification.

MacCormick's point of departure, then, is a pre-legal social order, a normative order. It may be called pre-legal because of its importance to MacCormick's concept of law. It is something that precedes an institutional normative order. Without pre-legal social order, a legal order would not be possible. I interpret this in two ways:

- First, that MacCormick argues that normative order serves as confirmation that human beings are capable of guiding their conduct by way of norms, and, moreover, that this is an inherent part of being human. This ontological point of departure is essential for the establishment of any legal order and for juridification. "Humans are, by nature, norm-users",[14,15] meaning that they are capable of differentiating between what ought not, and what may, be done. The question is *whether* this human potential may be filled with *whatever* substantial content.
- Thus, second, it may be argued that it is not only this human quality that matters, but also that legal orders in addition build directly on already developed normative orders in a more substantial way, as the queuing example seems to indicate. The legal order, on this reading, is an institutionalised continuation of a normative order (or normative orders) that is, or are, already present in any society. This, in a broad sense, cultural quality (as in everything from queuing cultures to human rights cultures), whether driven by instrumental, ethical or moral concerns, is essential for any legal order and for juridification; "in the final analysis the formal rests on informal, customary foundation."[16]

These two ideas are, of course, compatible; we can hold both views without contradiction.[17] The real question is whether it is possible to build legal order without the

[12] *IoL*, p. 20.

[13] Queuing as normative order is without any institutional guidance except from the norms of queuing past on from one individual to the next, and this is activated whenever a particular individual encounters another individual in a situation which, according to the norms, calls for queuing. Roughly speaking, this normative order becomes institutionalised when someone other than the queuing individuals imposes some form of order on the queue, be that in the form of a manager of the queue, the putting up of a fence or a machine giving out numbers. This institutional normative order can develop into a fairly complex set of rules and the need for interpretation of these rules. I will return to this in more detail.

[14] *IoL*, p. 245.

[15] This is close to Lon Fuller's view that: "To embark on the enterprise of subjecting human conduct to the governance of rules involves of necessity a commitment to the view that man is, or can become, a responsible agent, capable of understanding and following rules, and answerable for his defaults." See Fuller, note 8 *supra*, p. 162.

[16] *IoL*, p. 304.

[17] It is even possible to see it as a *continuum*, where "norm-user" skill may be filled with ever more specified substantial content.

substantial support of an existing normative order. Or, in more relative terms, how much substance is needed for law to fulfil its function properly, be it civility, social peace, justice, or the common good, or all of these?[18]

According to MacCormick, law is institutional-normative order, as opposed to normative order. To say that it is institutional merely refers to one particular type of institutionalisation[19]; one that establishes legal order or refines this legal order. In the limited vocabulary of this chapter, this would mean juridification. At a given time, in a given society, if I have understood MacCormick correctly, there are always different existing normative orders and different institutional normative orders, and these may interact in different ways. MacCormick's concept of law, then, seems, at first sight, to be almost limitless as "legal orders" (institutional normative orders) may emerge anywhere and may exist independent of any state authority. On closer inspection, however, this pluralism certainly has its limits.

First, laws ubiquity points to a particularistic or contextual quality of law. Law may be used to create order in a host of different and possibly unrelated social circumstances. However, it is still but one of many ways to create social order (the alternatives include everything from pure force to uncontroversial everyday social norms). The question, then, is *when* law may, or should, be used, and when it may not or should not be used. The answer points towards some external normative criteria such as effective social integration, democracy, justice, or, quite simply, order as a quality in itself. From the norm-user perspective, this means that the norm-users have to accept these criteria.

Second, if the concept of law may be used in widely-different circumstances and still be called law, it means that there is a universal quality to law. But what are the elements that have to be present in any social circumstance in order to call something law? The answer points towards some particular internal institutional qualities of law, such as, for example, consistency, non-contradiction or clarity. From the norm-users perspective, these are qualities that any norm-user would have to accept while still being a norm-user under law.

Third, there is a dynamic quality to law as legal orders may develop in response to different demands to social integration. Legal orders differ in their sophistication from the most simple local law to the most complex modern state law. Thus, there is a limit to law as any stability is only temporary. Law may always be challenged, and if it cannot be challenged, it is not law. From the norm-user perspective, norms are always up for grabs; an institutional normative order is never perfect.

Fourth, there is an argumentative quality to law linked to reason-giving, what MacCormick calls "the intrinsic arguability of law".[20] Any decision has to be given with reference to reason, even if this reason is not always perfect "even from the

[18] *IoL*, pp. 216, 221 & 304.

[19] This is one particular type of institutionalisation relative to the many different concepts of institutionalisation currently existing in the social science literature.

[20] *IoL*, p. 260.

perspective of the engaged legal reasoner".[21] This relates to Alexy's "claim to correctness" argument. Thus, there is a limit to law as, for example, "extreme injustice is incompatible with law".[22] From the norm-users perspective, law that cannot be reasonably defended in public is not law.

Finally, there is a placid quality to law. If different legal orders exist side by side, and if they sometimes overlap or infringe upon each other, one may ask in what way does, can or should, one legal order limit another legal order? This means that questions linked to the contextual-, the universal-, the dynamic-, and the argumentative-quality of law have to be restated at the level of a plurality of legal orders. There is, however, a lower limit, as only institutional-normative order is legal order, and an upper limit, as the total domination by one legal order effectively undermines any plurality, be it of normative or institutional-normative order. Law is limited, in the sense that, when it meets another institutional normative order, it has to reason to the satisfaction of norm-users.

All in all, MacCormick's legal theory points towards a democratic quality of law through his emphasis on the norm-users. This does not mean that, wherever there is law, there is also democracy. Law is democratic in the minimal sense that, if a legal order is not generally accepted by the norm-users, it cannot properly be called law (but has to be called something else, such as, for example, a coercive order).[23] Law is limited, in the sense that, if norm-users do not freely accept and internalise a particular legal order, law will not prevail. If the majority of norm-users are would-be criminals, there is no law.

3.3 Normative Order and Juridification

Is it at all possible to identify the different dimensions of juridification in MacCormick's work, and can it help us to understand the dynamics involved and, possibly, the limits of juridification? The first test is whether the five dimensions of juridification proposed may also, in some way, capture what MacCormick calls "informal normative practices" or "normative order", the starting-point or background for any form of juridification. If MacCormick is right in claiming that any legal order has its roots in the pre-legal idea of human beings as norm-users, and that the development of a legal order, from normative order to institutional-normative order, may be called juridification, then it might be possible to identify the presence, or the lack thereof, of the five dimensions of juridification even at the pre-legal level.

[21] Ibid.

[22] Ibid., note 22.

[23] In a democracy, most would contend that law is accepted because it is democratically made, but, in this case, the democratic element is not an intrinsic part of law, but only what makes law democratic. This is in contrast to MacCormick's norm-user perspective, which can be seen to give law an intrinsic democratic quality, albeit a limited one.

As indicated, in order to clarify what he means by normative order, MacCormick uses the practice of queuing as an example. What we need, in order to understand something such as queuing as a normative order, is how people come to act in roughly similar ways. At least three "positive" mechanisms seem to be working in combination, plus one "negative". First, an "underlying guiding idea",[24] a kind of constituting principle such as, for example, "first come, first served", as in the case of queuing. People interpret this underlying idea in a roughly similar fashion, albeit with variations, depending on context and other more particular considerations.[25] The interpretations are potentially contestable and no uniquely right answer exists.[26] Second, mimicking behaviour, as when "we all try to pick up local nuances when we move around".[27] When in doubt, people do what others do. Third, a normative belief that acting in this or that way is the right thing to do for various reasons. This is the idea of overlapping consensus,[28] people may have different reasons for acting in the way that they do, but they are all strong reasons, be it justice, fairness, respect for a particular culture, even efficiency in the "what is most efficient for all" sense, and so on. Fourth, an idea of choice, that people may break with the normative order on their own free will, jump the queue, with no justifiable reason,[29] and with no more serious repercussions than the contempt of others. The normative order is a voluntary practice. Is there a parallel between the dimensions of juridification and such a normative order?

First, no doubt, norms are an important part of a normative order. These may be more or less specified, as in juridification B, and one may even draw the parallel that sometimes a particular normative order conquers new terrain, as when the practice of queuing spreads across different sectors of society, or new normative orders emerge. One way of measuring the different cultural queuing codes would be to measure the specification of the queuing rules and how far it has spread throughout society, or, more generally, to what extent a particular society is guided by normative orders. That the norms are specific, however, would not necessarily mean that they are common to all, although MacCormick seems to believe, as indicated, that a common base norm is a necessary focus point for any normative order.[30] How does this interpretation square with one of MacCormick's main points that "there can be normative order without explicitly formulated norms".[31] Still, he also argues that this "does not mean we cannot reflect on how to make explicit an implicit norm of

---

[24] *IoL*, p. 18.

[25] Ibid., pp. 15 & 17.

[26] Ibid., pp. 16 & 18.

[27] Ibid., p. 17.

[28] Ibid., p. 18.

[29] Ibid., p. 14.

[30] This is similar to Dworkin's distinction between concept and conception. People may have a common concept of queuing, for example "first come, first served", but different conceptions of it. Ronald Dworkin, *Law's Empire* (London: Fontana, 1986), p. 71.

[31] *IoL*, p. 18.

conduct".[32] Thus, it seems reasonable to conclude that norms may be made more or less explicit, while still holding onto the idea of a normative order.

Second, nor can there be any doubt that references to the normative order are used in an effort to solve conflicts, as in juridification C. Even this may vary across time and between different cultures. In some circumstances, it is quite normal to complain when someone is jumping the queue, while, in others, it is less so.

Third, human beings may, to a greater or lesser extent, believe in a particular normative order such as queuing. They may identify with, value, and see themselves as subjects under the normative order, as in juridification E, not only as benefiting from something by adapting or risking something by not adapting.

What, then, about the competence to decide what the normative order is in cases of conflict (A), or the interpretive power that follows from ambiguous, confusing or simply too many and too complex norms (D). Following MacCormick, these elements of juridification, which, in a legal order, are formally institutionalised, are, in a normative order, distributed equally among individuals. When MacCormick speaks of a normative order, he seems to speak of this as a flat structure in which every human being has the same right and, presumably, the same power to interpret the normative order and to act on his or her own understanding of it. There is a pressure to adapt by way of social sanctions, but everyone has the same right to interpret what these sanctions are and how to apply them. However, still remaining within MacCormick's frame of reference, one may speculate that, even within a normative order, some would have a greater say on *what* the proper conduct in a particular situation should be, and *when* the relevant norms should be activated. Newcomers would, for example, look to the more experienced for guidance, or there might exist some cultural codes which regulate who to look to for guidance, without this amounting to anything like a formally institutionalised structure. This means that it may be possible to identify some minimum level of juridification A and D in a normative order, in the sense that there may be some general norms which indicate where to look for guidance when in doubt (A), and there may be some people with more clout than others when interpreting what the norms are (D).

So this seems to be MacCormick's main point in focusing on normative order: that human beings are capable of ordering their lives in order to avoid conflicts or to solve them (C) based upon (more or less) implicit norms (B), anchored in the belief that abiding by the normative order is right (E), and without the guidance of any other formal deciding or interpreting authority than their own, but possibly inspired or influenced by some form of informal authority (A, D).

The main emphasis, however, is on juridification C and E. This is what makes a normative order normative, and it does so in a double sense. The normative order guides people to do certain things and to avoid others in practical instrumental terms because it helps to avoid or to solve conflicts (juridification C), and, at the same time,

[32]Ibid., p. 15.

it is *because* it is the right thing to do so that people identify with the normative order (juridification E). Juridification C and E can then be seen as the normative dimension of juridification in terms of MacCormick's concept of law, "law as institutional *normative* order", in the sense that only these two dimensions of juridification may be developed to their fullest potential while still remaining within a normative order. As indicated, this may also amount to what would be considered by some to be excessive juridification C and E. From the point of view of law, one may, for example, consider queuing for the sake of queuing (in the sense that queuing has minimal or no effects on normative standards such as efficiency or justice) to be excessive juridification E. The reason why people queue would then be because it is a cultural practice that people cherish, not because it has any practical significance other than avoiding any conflict that might arise as a result of a perceived disrespect for this cultural code.

Some normative orders work better than others, and a normative order may disappear all together. Thus, we may at least presume that there are processes of "juridification" and "de-juridification" going on even at this level. It is difficult, however, to understand what drives these processes. Normative order seems to have a practical instrumental side (meaning that it serves a function) to it, as well as an ethical or moral side, and both are needed in order for something to be counted as a normative order. The last man standing when a queue dissolves may be ridiculed because his action has no practical effect, but he will be the hero of all those that believe queuing is the right thing to do, maybe even among those that have given up their ideals for pragmatic reasons. However, one man is not a queue. What we have is normative, but not an order. Likewise those that queue, not because it is the right thing to do, but rather to obtain what they want or to avoid embarrassment, do not really form a queue in the sense of a normative order. It is order, but not normative order.

What we have, then, in terms of juridification, are people who try to solve some practical problems with reference to a normative order (C), a normative order to which they attach value and subject themselves (E), because they believe it to be the solution that is equally best for all considered equal. Juridification C and E mutually reinforce each other. The importance of the normative order seems to be this: people act in an orderly fashion based upon an idea of what is the right thing to do, in order to fulfil some function, even in the absence of explicit norms, authority or coercion. Why, then, would a normative order need institutionalisation as indicated in the queuing example, or, alternatively, why can we not solve all problems of social integration by way of normative orders? Why do institutional-normative orders develop? Why further juridification? To begin with, two reasons may be indicated. First, we fail to solve conflicts because there is disagreement over the interpretation of norms. Juridification B has not developed very far. Second, there is disagreement over who should be in charge and who should interpret the norms. Juridification A and D have not developed very far, either.

3.4 Institutional Normative Order and Juridification

When moving from a normative order to an institutional-normative order[33] MacCormick emphasises two institutional traits, the formulation of common and explicit norms, and the establishment of some form of limited institutionalised authority to keep track of and to uphold these norms, and to interpret them in the event of conflict. The first of these is linked to juridification B, the second to juridification A and D. Thus, the elements of juridification which, in a normative order, are weak or left out, in an institutional normative order, play centre stage; it is what makes the institutional-normative order institutional. We now have all the elements that we need in order to build a legal system. But how does this happen? What is it that triggers this process and what keeps it going?

MacCormick provides a straightforward answer to at least the first part of this question:

> The defining characteristic of this kind of normative order is the possibility it opens to avoid exclusive reliance on somewhat vague implicit norms. Problems of a kind apparently endemic in informal orders can be avoided by resorting to issuance of expressly articulated norms, making explicit what is to be done or decided in expressly foreseen circumstances, the very effect of the explicitness being to diminish vagueness.[34]

So the defining characteristic is the issuance of explicit norms, that is, juridification B, the specification of first-tier norms. However, someone has to issue these norms and interpret what they mean in concrete situations. We have seen that, even in a normative order, there is room for some specification of norms. What is principally new in the institutional-normative order is an authority, an authority that is, itself, limited by norms; that is, second-tier norms. The hallmark of an institutional-normative order, then, is an established authority. It is an authority in the sense that it may construct the norms, interpret the norms, administer them and punish disobedience. Moreover, and more importantly, it has a *right* to do all this. Now, what is it that makes it possible to establish this authority? Where do the second-tier norms come from? What is it that drives the process of juridification A. Why do people generally queue when told to queue by someone in charge? Why do people let themselves be ordered around? In order to understand the dynamics involved in the transformation from normative order to institutional-normative order, one place to start may be to

---

[33]MacCormick's concept of institution contains both a normative and a practical element, in that it refers to a practice that is in some way "infused with value", to paraphrase Philip Selznick (the phrase was coined in his *Leadership in Administration* (New York: Harper & Row, 1957), p. 17). A distinction is also made between formal and informal institutions, based upon the presence or not of stable explicit authoritative norms. Normative order is informal institutions and institutional normative orders are formal institutions. Finally, a distinction between institutions as organisations or not, is made. A court is an institution and an organisation governed by explicit norms. A contract, on the other hand, is not an organisation, but it is still an institution because it is governed by explicit and authoritative norms.

[34]*IoL*, p. 24.

ask why the new system is accepted if it is to be based upon something other than coercion.

There does not seem to be any obvious answer to this question if we presume, as I will for the sake of argument, that there is not already a higher or stronger institutional-normative order, so to speak, which provides this authority for the weak institutional normative orders (for example, a managed queue based upon legally-enforced property rights).

3.4.1 The Point of View of Authorities

The first answer would be that authority stems from the quality of the institutional set-up identified as authoritative (juridification A). The basic point about juridification A is that an institution is given a limited amount of competence, and thus there have to be norms which guide where authority begins and where it stops. But how does MacCormick account for this? The authority seems to be taken more or less for granted. It comes into being equipped with at least some second-tier norms to guide its decision-making activity. The authority applies and lay down norms in order to make norms more explicit "for a certain bounded sphere of activity".[35] Even though queuing norms are now "explicitly laid down by those in charge of providing the service on offer",[36] the institutional composition of this authority is not described in much detail. We have to rely on formulations like this:

> The position held by marshal or manager is almost certainly itself an expressly created job, perhaps with a formal job description set up within an organization with a quite elaborate structure of interrelated roles or jobs and with employees appointed to carry them out. In such context there is clearly what we may call 'institutional normative order', not merely informal normative order, with informal institutions.

Thus, the authority does not seem to get its authority from any external source. It presumably has the right to manage a queue whenever this right has been activated. Even though it seems that juridification A is presupposed, or leads to juridification B, it is not easy to figure out where juridification A comes from.

3.4.2 The Norm-Formulator Point of View

A second alternative then is that the authority is based upon juridification B, meaning that the authority in charge gets its authority from the quality of the first-tier norms, a quality that again depends on the second-tier norms. This seems more promising since most of the second chapter of *Institutions of Law* deals with the explicitness of norms. In this interpretation, it is the specification of first-tier norms that first leads to the establishment of an authority and to the further development of

---

[35]Ibid., p. 25.

[36]Ibid., p. 21.

this authority by the development of second-tier norms to limit or expand its competence. This is B→A. The creation of order, in many circumstances, depends on explicit first-tier norms; somebody has to see to it that norms are made explicit; this somebody needs authority, so authority is given to somebody who, by definition follows some basic second-tier norms. If this is so, how can the quality of first- and second-tier norms be assessed?

One test would be to see if the norms set out conform to the norms of the preceding normative order or have a similar source, such as efficiency concerns or concerns of justice. Then, we have to interpret MacCormick to the effect that norm-users relate to the substance of this preceding normative order. Since there are more than one interpretation of the preceding normative order, we have to presume that people would be content with a range of different possible interpretations as long as this range may be understood to belong to the category of, let us say, queuing. The norms will then be acceptable to the degree that they do not break with the informal institution of queuing. The authority would, for example, get in trouble if it moved people in and out of the queue based upon how much money they were willing to pay. However, this does not seem to be MacCormick's position. In commenting on various formalised queuing practices he argues that "attitudes to queuing may be far removed from those of mutual voluntary cooperation", even though he adds, "though perhaps never quite excluding every trace of this".[37] In order to arrive at this position, a more promising start would be to try to understand what is meant by the explicitness of norms. Three candidates will be considered:

1. Explicitness as Specification of Norms. What happens in an institutional-normative order is that an authority is set up or takes charge in order to "render precise what in the informal setting is vague". The authority's task is to make decisions according to norms. When these norms do not give a satisfactory answer, an answer is given either by pure discretion or it is solved by way of a specification of norms, which makes it possible to reach a conclusion in that particular situation, a conclusion that may serve to solve similar problems in the future. The task is then to make the norms more explicit and less vague. If we read MacCormick's example of queuing carefully, however, we see that what he describes as an effort to create explicitness and lack of vagueness[38] may, in fact, be seen as the opposite. Juridification B, as specification of norms (as MacCormick is fully aware of) does not necessarily make the norms more explicit or less vague. The clear and simple "institutionalised" rule that the person to be served first is the one that can present the right piece of paper, with the right number, at the right time, at the right counter, risks becoming more vague with each new specification that is added, as when the rule involves making "two further calls in a clear, loud voice" and checking "if there are any apparently deaf people" around.[39]

---

[37] Ibid., p. 22.
[38] Ibid., p. 24.
[39] Ibid., p. 24.

The specification of rules does not have to lead to more complexity and indeterminacy, but it certainly may and sometimes does, the reason often being that what is at stake and the reason for specification, is not explicitness in itself, but, for example, justice. Thus, here we seem to have a kind of internal dynamic. Vagueness leads to the formulation of more specific norms which again leads to even more vagueness and the need for even more specified norms and so on. Juridification B (as specification) seems to feed on itself. The downside to this is that explicitness as specification does not, in itself, seem to give the institutional normative order authority. If anything, it would be the authority's effort to render precise what was formerly vague. The effort to specify the norms may also lead to an expansion of the authority's competence (juridification A). The question is whether the manager of a queue has the authority to make specifications, for example, regarding how to handle, let us say, mentally-handicapped people. If not, the manager can take on the responsibility to do so or be given this authority by a superior authority. In either case, it is the need for specification that drives juridification (or de-juridification) A, increased or more limited competence. This means that B→A. In sum, then, juridification B pre-supposes juridification A (A→B). As MacCormick writes, "The existence of the second tier of the practice leads to" (A→B) "or is accompanied by" (AB) "an increasingly explicit articulation of the first tier." But it is also the case that the specification of norms (B) leads to more specification of norms (B), and this again may give the authority more competence (A). A→(B←→B)→A.

2. Explicitness as Adherence to Basic Rule of Law Criteria. Explicitness may mean that, in order to function, rules must be "intelligible and within the capacity of most to obey".[40] One way of putting this is that norms have to conform to the most basic rule of law criteria as laid out, for example, by Lon Fuller.[41] MacCormick does not refer explicitly to the rule of law while discussing informal normative order (Chapter 2 of *Institutions*), although there are frequent more or less explicit references to at least some of the basic internal rule of law criteria, such as, for example, the generality of norms, the precision of norms, the promulgation of norms, the relative stability of norms, non-contradictory norms and elements of due process. Even though MacCormick goes a long way to indicate that the aim of juridification B is to get ever closer to this ideal or to try to get closer to this ideal, as when he refers to the explicitness of norms, and various specifications without contradiction, this does not seem to have the status of a comprehensive "basic rule of law test". However, we have found a second internal dynamic element: juridification B is driven by a desire on the part of the authority to make it possible for people to follow the rules, and

[40] H. L. A. Hart, *The Concept of Law* (Oxford: Clarendon Press, 1961), p. 202.

[41] Lon Fuller that argued that in order to call something law it at least have to conform to these criteria, what he called the inner morality of law, because it would be immoral to ask people to follow rules that would in effect be impossible to observe, whether these rules could themselves be considered moral or not. It is interesting to compare with Lon Fuller here since even he saw law as including a whole range of activities that normally is not called law, like the rules of a sports organisation.

this involves an effort to conform to the basic rule of law criteria, whenever earlier implicit or explicit norms breaks with these criteria. More bluntly put, specification is sometimes driven by the desire for basic rule of law improvements.

3. Explicitness as Formal Structure of Norms. Yet another test would be whether the norms adhere to the "whenever OF, then NC" (whenever *operative facts* then *normative consequences*) formula of a norm. For this to be the case, we would have to presume that this structure has to be relatively recognisable, meaning that anyone should be able to recognise it as a proper norm. The rule "Jeans will not always be accepted" posted on the wall outside a bar in Bergen, Norway, would, for example, not count as a norm, even if the bouncer knows exactly what it means in terms of the ideal formula. If it did, it would not be the explicitness of the norm that gave authority to the bouncer, but something else.

But is this really what MacCormick means? I have already argued that, under a normative order, norms may be more or less explicit, so what is new when we move to an institutional-normative order? Possibly that the norms are now explicitly formulated in the sense that they fulfil the criterion "Whenever OF, then NC". But this does not seem to mean that anyone may easily be able to formulate the norm in such terms. On the contrary, MacCormick seems to suggest that it is the authority's task to figure out this whenever it is unclear. So, the formula seems to give structure to the authority's reasoning in interpretation, but not to demand that the norms, in themselves, should be formulated in such a way that anyone may understand them as such. As with the rule of law criteria, then, it seems to be the belief in the authority's ability to interpret the norm in accordance with the formula that gives authority. People, in general, believe in the formula but realise that a perfect and determinate fit for all kinds of situations is difficult to formulate, and thus are comfortable with leaving this task to a specialised authority. Juridification B, in the sense that all norms, when applied, should be specified in order to conform to the general formula, leads to juridification A, in the sense that the authority is given the competence to interpret any norm in order to make it fit with the formula (B→A).

3.4.3 The Point of View of the Norm-User

A third answer would be that the authority rests with the norm-users, most basically whether they use, want to use and are able to use, the norms laid down by the authority or not. The authority's authority is depended on the degree to which people solve conflicts by reference to norms. It is already established that people are norm-users by nature, but that cannot possibly mean that people will use whatever norms that are handed to them. As in the normative order, people still have a choice; law is always up for grabs. Furthermore, if it is difficult or maybe even impossible to use the norms, they will not be used. Is there an increased tendency to solve conflicts with reference to the norms or not, that is, juridification and de-juridification C, and what is the role of this in the process of juridification generally?

Even though people are free to choose whether to abide by the norms or not, that is, to solve conflicts by way of reference to norms or not, in an institutional-normative order, there is, presumably, more at stake than that in the normative order. In the queuing example, people are "required to follow the norms laid down by the service-provider"[42] and the people queueing "have to orient themselves"[43] to norms. But why would this be so? People may just turn around, let us say because the queue is too long, unfairly managed, in total disorder, or for whatever reason, because they need the service provided, one may argue, but even then people may sabotage the queue, protest, start a fight, organise some kind of resistance to the queuing order and so on. Yes, but then the authority always has the possibility of arranging the queue in ways that make it more difficult to sabotage or it can coerce people in more direct ways. Yes, they probably can, but the more such measures are used, the less people orient themselves to the norms and more to the actual or expected coercion (coercion which MacCormick does not recognise as always a necessary and intrinsic part of law). Juridification C apparently plays a more important role in MacCormick's scheme than what appears at first glance. But what is this role?

The authority, according to MacCormick, "has or assumes authority to determine how to settle disputes". It is this need for dispute resolution that apparently triggers a process of specification of norms. It is a matter of making a decision whenever "some doubt arises about the priority in a queue".[44] Conflicts, then, are solved by the authority, but by reference to norms, norms that people in general accept in order to solve conflict. If it is not possible to solve conflicts with reference to these norms as they stand, the norms are specified. The need for juridification C then triggers juridification B, and, as we have seen, juridification B triggers juridification A and *vice versa*. We then have: C→(B←→A).

But MacCormick goes further than this. Not only does the need for dispute resolution trigger juridification (and de-juridification) A and B, the quality of dispute resolution, that is, the quality both of first-tier and second-tier norms, but it also positively affects the tendency which people have for solving conflict by reference to norms. We see this in the example where inconsistency "could be bad for customers relations"[45] or difficulties of interpretation "are (for example) causing annoyance among the customers, who might take their business elsewhere".[46] So juridification C does not only lead to juridification B, but juridification A and B also positively affect juridification C. When norms become more specified, there will

[42] Ibid., p. 21.

[43] Ibid.

[44] Ibid., p. 22.

[45] Ibid.

[46] Ibid., p. 23.

be an increased tendency to settle disputes by reference to norms (B→C). Thus, we have C→(B←→A)→C. This, however, also depends on the degree of juridification or de-juridification A. In the beginning, the authority has the right to settle disputes which are only limited to a specific area of operation and some implicit ideas about what such an authority has the right to do. Through practical dispute resolution, second-tier norms develop, which may give the authority more, or less, competence, that is de-juridification or juridification A. This would again positively affect juridification C and the quality of juridification B.

3.4.4 The Norm-Interpretation Point of View

So far so good, but what about juridification D, the increase in judicial power? "Judicial power" (in our interpretation) has two sources: indeterminacy and lack of transparency in a system of norms. Clearly, in the beginning, there is a fair amount of indeterminacy; the norms are unclear and vague. With juridification A and B, we would expect de-juridification D. As the norms become more specified and the area of application becomes settled, and when the second-tier norms are in place, there should be less room for doubt. But, as we have already seen, this is not necessarily the case.

First, the sheer number of norms and specifications of norms makes it increasingly difficult for the norm-users to have a clear view of what the norms are. It falls to the authority to keep track of this complexity, even in a fairly simple norm system such as that of ordering a queue. The lack of transparency alone would give the authority increased "judicial power" (B→D).

Second, as argued, specification does not necessarily mean less room for interpretation. On the contrary, it may often enough mean that the norms become harder to interpret (B→D). Similarly, second-tier norms, that may limit, as well as increase, the authorities competence, may sometimes make interpretations more difficult (A→D). According to MacCormick, implicit rules in an institutional normative order are norms that may be derived from a previous ruling (covered by the doctrine of precedence). If the authority has the competence to solve cases both by "establishing" new implicit rules and by reference to existing implicit rules, it will almost surely lead to more complexity and thus less transparency, but it may also provide more room for interpretation. The dilemma, from the point of view of an authority that has to make a decision, is easy to see. Too strict limitations on competence (de-juridification A) leaves less room for interpretation (de-juridification D) and may hurt "customer relations" (de-juridification C) since it may not be possible to make a reasoned decision, and, moreover, the factors that the norm-users see as relevant may not be taken into consideration. If the authority is given more competence (juridification A), it gives more room for interpretation (juridification D), but the norm-user may still not be satisfied if the interpretation made is too difficult to understand or is considered incorrect (de-juridification C).

A partial answer to this dilemma is given in the form of second-tier norms that govern the degree of competence that the authority has when applying different rules. It is presumed, then, that, in some issue areas, more discretionary power is warranted in order to reach a conclusion. Other issue areas may be considered too important in some sense to be left to the authority to decide. Juridification D may then vary across issue areas, but if we ask how this variation is decided, we are again left with "customer satisfaction" as the best indicator. The authority will establish second-tier rules which, as far as possible, ensure that people will continue to use reference to norms in order to solve conflict.

In addition, there is, in MacCormick's work, a more comprehensive answer to the question of interpretation. The formula "whenever OF, the NC" gives direction and structure to legal arguments, but cannot, in itself, solve disputes regarding interpretation. This is left to the rhetoric of law, which is the reasoned deliberation over how to arrive at OF and NC and the relationship between the two.

3.4.5 The Norm-Accepting Point of View

All in all, then, in MacCormick's institutional theory of law, the institutional dimension of juridification may be captured by juridification A, B and D. The relationship between these dimensions of juridification is, as we have seen, complex, with different mechanisms working to balance the three dimensions through processes of juridification and de-juridification. The quality of these processes is, however, in the final analysis, decided by the norm-users. It is the need for an institutional system in order to solve conflicts with reference to law that sets off the process and decides its further development. If the institutional normative order is not actually used (de-juridification C) for whatever reason (inefficiency, injustice and so on), the order will slowly dissolve. In addition, the last issue to be dealt with relates to the tendency among norm-users to frame issues in the light of the existing institutional normative order, a tendency that indicates the degree to which people identify with the institutional normative order (juridification E). It is one thing that people actually use norms to solve conflicts, it is another that they believe this to be something they ought to do, that they subject themselves to norms *because* it is right. Where does this sentiment come from? We have already discussed this in relation to a normative order where we concluded that juridification C and E mutually reinforce each other, but does this also relate to juridification A, B and D?

If we presume, like MacCormick, that some values are good, be they linked to efficiency, fairness or reasonableness or some other value, and, furthermore, that the observance of such values positively affects juridification E, we should look for how MacCormick accounts for this. When it comes to juridification or de-juridification A, the answer is clear enough. Some "general principles" are established in order for the authority to evaluate systematically how and to what degree different values should be considered when making a decision, and there can also be direct reference to such values or norms which indicate, when these should be taken into consideration. This, in turn, irrespective of whether juridification or de-juridification A is involved, would, generally speaking, most certainly make interpretation more complex and difficult as different values have to be balanced against each other.

When it comes to juridification B, values, as indicated, may be built into rules, as discussed by MacCormick.[47] One may, for example, specify a rule by including the word "reasonable" in order to indicate that, when making a decision, this standard should be applied according to common sense, in order to avoid that the norm be used in situations where it would be clearly unreasonable. The word "reasonable" is entered because more concrete specifications would be difficult to make, or, as often is the case in a partly unpredictable world, impossible to provide. This, again, is related to juridification D. The authority in question has the right to interpret and this grants it power, but there is a limit to this power as clearly unreasonable interpretations will be rejected by the norm-users through processes of de-juridification E and C.

3.5 The Norm-User Perspective on Juridification

If this interpretation of MacCormick's institutional theory of law relative to processes of juridification and de-juridification is roughly right, it points towards a rather interesting model of juridification. This is what I will call a democratic theory of juridification, or juridification from below. The model, with a fair amount of simplification, has two basic dimensions.

The model has a "normative" dimension linked to juridification and de-juridification C and E. It is normative, in the sense that it is juridification C and E, which, in the final analysis, determine whether an institutional order is to be accepted by norm-users as law. The acceptance has two sides to it; one practical (juridification C), and one linked to identity (juridification E). Law is dependent on norm-users actually using the law, in the sense of using appeal to law in order to solve conflicts (C), meaning that law has to be useful in this practical sense, that it serves a purpose. Law is also dependent on legitimacy, in the sense that norms not only serve a practical purpose, but that it also does so in a way that norm-users may identify with as right (E). Both are needed in order for law to become law; that is institutional *normative* order.

This acceptance, however, is dependent on a second institutional dimension, that is, institutions that make acceptance possible. Thus, the model also has an "institutional" dimension linked to juridification A, B and D. First, the functioning of institutions will have to be guided by some basic rules that norm users find useful and legitimate (A). Second, the first-tier norms have to have both form and content that norm-users find useful and legitimate (B). Third, the interpretation of both basic norms and the first-tier rules has to be conducted according to principles (most basically, according to a logic of argumentative reasoning) that norm-users find useful and legitimate.

[47] Ibid., p. 30.

With these two dimensions, we may tentatively construct five ideal type orders, and at least come close to establishing the boundaries of law. The basic premises are these: first, juridification, in order for an institutional normative order (legal order) to emerge, has to reach a certain level on all the dimensions of juridification. Second, if carried too far, juridification may reach levels at which it is no longer possible to speak of an institutional normative order. Finally, in any institutional normative order, whatever the level of juridification, the different dimensions of juridification are balanced off against each other.

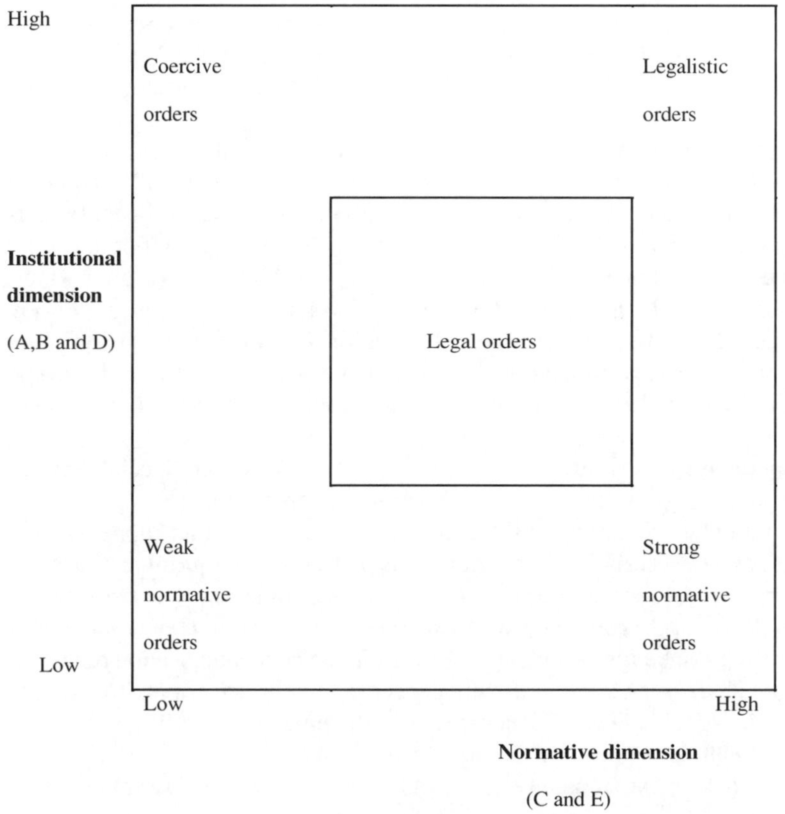

Normative order, as described by MacCormick, is found at the bottom of the figure. There is a certain level of juridification A, B and D as described earlier, but it is too low for an institutional-normative order to develop. The normative orders may, however, have different levels of juridification C and E. Weak normative orders are orders that are not generally accepted by potential norm-users. One example may be special privileges for a particular group of people, let us say, based upon gender or societal position. To the degree that such orders are of any importance to norm-users, they would be unstable without normative acceptance or institutionalisation.

However, one may imagine such orders even in a modern democratic society. As long as these practises are not seen as infringing, in any serious way, upon basic rights, they may be tolerated and even respected, even if most people in general see them as useless to themselves and, in principle, inappropriate. An example of this might be an Internet network restricted to a particular class of people, which gives the people who are members privileged access to particular markets. One may, however, think of situations in which privileges are accepted by everybody as something natural, as is the case when women allegedly accept inferior positions in some societies, or when inherited positions or wealth are sources of both respect and privileges. These would be situations in which privileges are backed by a strong normative order. However, weaker or stronger normative orders are not law, since juridification A, B and D has not developed very far. What happens when these extreme cases of juridification C and E are coupled with institutionalisation, that is, extreme juridification A, B and D?

In the case of the weakest normative orders, in which special privileges are involved, institutionalisation may amount to what one may call a coercive order (upper left corner). Take slavery as an example. It is highly institutionalised, as the slave-owner has the right to establish proper rules and refine these as he or she sees fit (juridification A, B and D). Why is this not an institutional-normative order? Because the normative dimension is missing. Most of potential norm-users would not find it useful, nor accept it as legitimate. Moreover there are no mechanisms to assure de-juridification A, B and D, mechanisms that would possibly bring the order within the realm of an institutional normative order, that is, away from slavery.

In the case of the strongest normative orders, in which special privileges are involved and norm-users accept the situation, it seems more difficult to reject institutionalisation as amounting to institutionalised normative order (upper right corner). The fact that excessive juridification A, B and D without juridification C and E is not law, according to MacCormick, seems compelling, but that excessive juridification A, B and D combined with excessive juridification C and E is not law, but "legalism", something that would follow from the conceptualisation of juridification presented here, seems less self-evident according to MacCormick's theory. In order to explain why I believe this, nevertheless, to be the case, I will go back to the five limiting qualities of law introduced earlier.

First, the contextual quality of law claims that law may be useful in a host of different situations and for a host of different reasons (efficiency, justice, self-interest, the common good, order in itself, *etc*), but not everywhere. There are contextual limits as to the use of law. The usefulness, however, is for the norm-users to decide. If norm-users do not use something as law or accept it as law, then, it is not law. In the case of a legalistic order, however, the norm users accept the order, and this means that we cannot use this contextual limitation to indicate that something is not law. From an external point of view, we can, of course, claim that the norm-users are not autonomous, that they are indoctrinated or pressured in some way, and go on to argue that law is dependent on democracy to some degree or in some form. But this does not seem to be MacCormick's position. An institutional-normative order may exist without democracy as the queuing example indicated. Instead, what I will argue in the following is that MacCormick's concept of law presupposes some democratic elements which, in themselves, do not amount to democracy, but merely point in the direction of democracy.

Second, the universal quality of law, suggests that, wherever you go, law is marked by the same quality; that it is able to guide human conduct. In order to do this, it has to adhere to certain rule of law criteria most famously proposed by Fuller in "*Law and Morality*"; law should be clear enough to be understood, relatively stable, not contradictory, not retroactive, not impossible to follow and so on. This clearly limits law as means to subjection, as juridification A, B and D will have to be limited. However, we may think of laws that fulfil these criteria to an acceptable degree and this still privileges certain groups, as when Saudi-Arabian women are not allowed to drive in their country of origin. If this is accepted by the norm-users, why should we not call it law?

Third, a more promising candidate is linked to the dynamic quality of law. It suggests that law may develop in order to adjust to the norm-user perspective. That juridification A, B and D, for example, are adjusted in order to achieve juridification C and E. But if there is no one left to challenge the system, the dynamic quality is gone. From perceived perfection, there is no escape. An intrinsic part of law is that it can always be challenged. Fourth, then, if law is not challenged, there cannot possibly be any argumentative quality to law and finally, even though other orders may exist be they legal or not, they will have no relevance relative to the "legalistic" order as this order cannot be challenged. A religious sect of fanatics, for example, follow their own rules without regard to state law, international law or whatever other reasonably relevant normative- or institutional-normative order.

So it seems that MacCormick's theory even involves an idea of excessive institutionalisation, be it with, or without, the acceptance of norm-users. One possible way to interpret the Guantanamo Bay detention camp is to look at it as a particular order in its own right. It is heavily institutionalised, in the sense that excessive juridification A and D have taken place, and, whenever a new norm is needed, it is added to the order (juridification B). It is limited to certain activities, but what these activities are may be redefined as being seen fit by the authority, and the authority ostensibly has authority over each and ever living human being on earth. It started out as an order closer to the legalistic end of the *continuum*, accepted by, at least, parts of the American people. Through consecutive challenges brought on by de-juridification C and E, the order has moved towards the coercive end of the *continuum*. At the same time, a process of de-juridification A, B and D has taken place, as the system has been challenged from legal orders proper such as international law and American constitutional law. Perceived as a purely coercive order by norm-users, it will have little chance of surviving if it loses executive backing.

Institutional-normative orders, then, are democratic in the sense that they are dependent on acceptance from the norm-users in order to be called legal orders, and have to be accepted both as useful and right. It is not, however, necessarily democratic in the sense that law-making is necessarily democratic (for example, backed by democratically-accountable law-making institutions). There is still a conceptual difference between law and democracy. Law without democracy is possible. However, if this interpretation of MacCormick has anything to offer, it may help understand why in most models of democracy, democracy is said to presuppose law. In MacCormick's terms, this would mean that modern liberal democracy presupposes an institutional-normative order.

The basic question that we have at least tried to start to answer is this: What drives the process from normative order into the ever more elaborate institutional-normative order? What drives the process of juridification according to MacCormick? Tentatively, we will suggest a combination of three features: first, processes of juridification, second, processes of de-juridification, and third, a commonality between people in general, politicians, law-makers, bureaucrats, lawyers, legal scholars and judges.

3.5.1 Processes of Juridification

There is something intriguingly simple and comprehensible with MacCormick's explication of normative order and institutional normative order, and the relationship between the two. As has been argued, it might not be all that simple after all, as there are more dynamics at work than first anticipated, if we consider the explicitly expressed, as well as the more implicit or implied, dynamics. Is it possible to combine all these (and others that a more comprehensive examination might reveal) in a single model? It probably is, but I will settle for a simplification that I believe can capture the essence of the dynamics of juridification. It begins with norm-users who want to solve conflicts by reference to norms, and it ends with the realisation by norm-users that this ought to be done, something that encourages further juridification. The system, then, is driven by norm-users who try to solve conflicts by reference to norms (juridification C). We do not need to have any other foundation of this point of departure than the premise that people are, by nature, norm-users, that they tend naturally to try to solve conflicts by reference to norms.

What I propose, then, is that juridification C, an increased tendency to use norms to solve conflict, at one point depends on the establishment of some sort of authority with a limited competence to make decisions. This is juridification A. The authority, in turn, specifies and adds to the norms as new and unprecedented cases demand. This is juridification B. Sometimes, this means inventing new principles, doctrines, *etc*, which further expands the authority's competence (juridification A). All this does not, however, lead to less room for interpretation. On the contrary, as the world's complexity presents itself, there is no end to interpretation and this is, in turn, reflected in the complexity of the institutional normative order. This is juridification D. The authority's expertise at interpretation and knowledge of the meandering path to rightfulness, becomes ever more indispensable. In general, most people appreciate this. They will start to see themselves as subjects under the institutional normative order. This is juridification E. But this is not the end of the story. It starts all over again. As people (including those in authority) realise that the institutional normative order works, they start to identify themselves with the established order (juridification E), they become more inclined to make references to institutionalised norms in order to solve conflicts (juridification C), the authority's competence increases (juridification A), and so on. Thus C→((A→←B)→D)→E→C→(A...

3.5.2 Processes of De-juridification

Is there no end to this process of juridification? There certainly is. Such a system, dominated by juridification, will, in the end, collapse under the burden of complexity and incoherence. We will get de-juridification E and C as it becomes ever more difficult to understand what the norms mean. People can no longer orient themselves according to norms, and the rules which both limit and guide decision-makers become incomprehensible. The remedy is de-juridification A, B and D. As the process of juridification moves on, there is a parallel process of de-juridification. The authority takes on new competencies only to give them away (sometimes only partially) if they turn out to be too difficult or too complex to handle. Norms are specified but sometimes the process is turned around and more general principles are established in order to simplify norm-use. Sometimes, principles are established and norms specified in such a way as to make interpretation easier and thereby simplify the system. Sometimes, cases are rejected because the interpretations needed are too far removed from the norms that are to be interpreted, and so on. Overall juridification continues, but is continuously patched up by parallel processes of de-juridification, all in order to achieve a level of coherence, simplicity and thus predictability.

These mutually-adjusting processes of juridification and de-juridification may go relatively unnoticed, but they are sometimes shaken by larger changes, as when an institutionalised authority suddenly loses a big part of its competence by a massive process of de-juridification A, when, for example, the principle of separation of powers is introduced. What would trigger such events, according to the ideas laid out here, is de-juridification E followed by de-juridification C, two processes that cannot be reversed by relatively minor adjustments in the form of de-juridification A, B and D.

The most basic change, when moving from simple institutional-normative orders to more comprehensive ones, such as the modern constitutional state is, first, overall juridification and, second, de-juridification A. De-juridification A happens when the authority is split up into different institutional agencies, "charged with legislative functions, with adjudicative functions, with executive administrative functions and with law-enforcing functions".[48] Since juridification, as defined here, is linked to the adjudicative function, it will lose much of its competence to the other three, but maintains a level of competence in order to control the other institutions. In

[48] Ibid., p. 35.

this new situation, however, we can get juridification or further de-juridification A. The same goes for juridification B, which may be met by revolutionary processes of de-juridification B, the scraping of whole segments of law at the stroke of a pen, as when the freedom of religion is confirmed by law, or laws regulating intimacy are replaced by new laws regulating intimacy. Juridification D also has its limits, and when piecemeal adjustments fail, larger doctrinal change, for example, in order to limit judicial review of administrative action, may be the result. Radical de-juridification D is brought on by de-juridification A.

3.5.3 Towards Commonality?

So, we have an idea of overall juridification, an idea of de-juridification as an adjusting mechanism, and de-juridification as more radical change, punctuated equilibria;[49] big revolutions and smaller revolutions. The different dimensions of juridification counter-balance each other and this gives the overall process, be it dominated by juridification or de-juridification, its direction. Can this, alone, keep the system going, secure continued juridification without total collapse? Clearly, there are some rules which guide the formulation and interpretation of norms, and rules which limit, in one way or another, the authority in question, thereby regulating the decision-making process. In addition, there is a general requirement linked to the deliberative quality of debate. The question is whether we need something more, something more substantial, such as a more comprehensive rule of law, democracy or the integrity of civil society, specific principles necessary for an institutional normative order as complexity increases, standards external to the process of juridification that may direct the process and curb excessive juridification? Not necessarily, if I have understood MacCormick correctly.

The alternative is linked to juridification C and E, the basic elements of a normative order. This is what everyone, supposedly, has in common. We are all norm-users by nature. We tend to solve conflicts, if possible, with reference to norms. This goes for people in general, as well as politicians, bureaucrats, lawyers, legal scholars or judges. They all ask the same question: How is it possible to solve this or that dispute with reference to law? At the same time, everyone tends to frame issues in the light of an institutional normative order, an order to which they voluntarily subject themselves. The institutional part of MacCormick's argument, linked to juridification and de-juridification A, B and D, may be seen as the core elements of a modern constitutional order. Overall juridification of the institutional-normative order, however, is also dependent on juridification C and E. These dimensions of juridification are what keeps the system together as it is what everyone, inside as well as outside the system, is competent to assess. If juridification A, B and D "fail", it will lead to

[49] See S. D. Krasner, "Approaches to the State: Alternative Conceptions and Historical Dynamics" (1984) 16 *Comparative Politics*, pp. 223–246; and *idem*, "Sovereignty. An Institutional Perspective" (1988) 21 *Comparative Political Studies*, pp. 66–94.

de-juridification C and E, and this effect will be picked up by everyone concerned, and lead to adjustments; parallel processes of juridification and de-juridification A, B and D. The system, if left alone, may naturally develop towards something akin to a modern constitutional "rule of law" state, but this process may take many twists and turns, and the end-product of different processes may be quite diverse, as exemplified by the many different, but advanced, institutional-normative orders currently existing.

Chapter 4
Reform and Tradition: Changes and Continuities in Neil MacCormick's Concept of Law

Massimo La Torre

4.1 A Recollection

Speaking about Professor MacCormick's concept of law and its evolution in time means, to me, somehow an exercise of recollection, and it brings about a sort of autobiographical backlash. The academic year 1984–1985, I spent in Graz at the Institute of Philosophy of Law of the local university, whose director, at that time, was Professor Ota Weinberger. As is well-known, the first seminal book presenting a contemporary version of institutional legal theory was *An Institutional Theory of Law* by Neil MacCormick and Ota Weinberger, which was published in 1986. Being in Graz in 1985, I could see – so to speak – the making of this book, which collected a number of papers by the two scholars. I remember very well how much Professor Weinberger was excited about the book and the affinity of his views with those of his Scottish colleague.

During that year, I attended Weinberger's seminars and lectures and had daily discussions with him about the new theory that was slowly taking shape. I found his views and all the process fascinating, and was attracted (and finally seduced) by an approach which, while being solidly anchored in the analytical philosophical tradition, nevertheless had a few subversive traits. I was thus encouraged to read Neil MacCormick's papers and books, and such intense reading, together with the frequent exchange of views with Professor Weinberger, deeply influenced my ideas about law and legal theory.

I had been unhappy with the analytical philosophy of law for a number of reasons. On the one hand, its ontological reductionism, whereby the only relevant dimension of the reality was an empiricist and physicalist one, seemed to me hostile to a serious consideration of law as a domain in which arguments do really matter and are decisive for decisions. I had problems in accepting the view that legal reasoning was just ideology or a variable of a stimulus/response mode of human conduct. I could hardly cope with the neo-positivistic idea that "all propositions

M. La Torre (✉)
Hull Law School, Università "Magna Graecia" di Catanzaro, Catanzaro, Italy
e-mail: mlatorre@unicz.it

A.J. Menéndez, J.E. Fossum (eds.), *Law and Democracy in Neil MacCormick's Legal and Political Theory*, Law and Philosophy Library 93,
DOI 10.1007/978-90-481-8942-7_4,

are of equal value"- to use Wittgenstein's wording (*Tractatus logico-philosophicus*, § 6.4), given that a value – to quote again Wittgenstein's phrasing – "must lie outside the world" (§ 6.41)[1] and hence it could neither be known nor approached in a rational way. On the other hand, I could not see how language might be the central existential category of law, putting aside or downgrading extra-linguistic reality as the mere content for linguistic propositions, thus ending up defining law as just another sort of language function. Finally, I believed to see, lurking behind analytical jurisprudence and legal realism, the old and somewhat terrible figure of law as force and violence. The "fact" celebrated by legal realism was, indeed, the *fait accompli* and the facticity of the hold of the stronger over the weaker. Decisionism – it seemed to me – was, in the end, the final outcome of legal positivism, whatever its philosophical foundation, especially under the crude light of neo-positivism and physicalism.

Now, the mass of all these unhappy features of legal theory under positivistic and analytical conditions seemed to be avoidable through the new legal institutionalism proposed by MacCormick and Weinberger. They raised a number of claims that I found to be sound, especially once one moves to study law from the angle of legal argumentation and constitutionalism. They were, indeed, relatively sound, and deserved being taken on board.

4.2 Hart's Legacy

H.L.A. Hart's impact on the contemporary jurisprudential debate on the concept of law can hardly be over-estimated. Although his work is often seen as a fine re-statement and re-elaboration of the legal positivist *Weltanschauung*, Hart's legal theory is the first, fundamental step away from the revised legal positivism which had been shaped by scholars such as Hans Kelsen and Alf Ross. Hart's criticism, although, in the first place, addressed against John Austin's topical expression of analytical jurisprudence, does not, in fact, spare the "pure doctrine of law". Nor is Hart too condescending towards Scandinavian realists. What actually is attempted by the British jurisprudent is to re-assess and re-organise the core of positivist views by reforming their philosophical and methodological postulates.

In this enterprise, the central, though non-explicitly philosophical, background is Wittgenstein's late programme and its imaginative change of paradigm within analytical philosophy, at least as long as this is explored by Oxford ordinary language philosophy. Hart's views are hardly to be fully understood without such a source. The same holds – I would say – as far as Neil MacCormick's theses are concerned, since their starting-point is a critical re-assessment of Hart's revision of the analytical jurisprudential background. This is why I believe that it is vital for us, today, to examine this foundational moment carefully.

---

[1] L. Wittegenstein, *Tractatus Logico-Philosophicus*, trans. by D. F. Pears and B. F. McGuinness (London: Routledge & Kegan Paul, 1966), p. 145.

Allow me to summarise what I deduce to be the four fundamental tenets of Hart's philosophy of law.

(i) There is a preliminary, general rejection of *per genus et differentiam* definitions.[2] Words, names, concepts to be defined should be referred to the multiple uses that are made of them. Necessary and sufficient conditions for the application of a concept are not to be found predetermined in the concept's semantic content. Likewise, what is law is not just a matter of definition, but is to be found in the very practice of the law itself.

(ii) The second tenet of Hart's legal philosophy, accordingly, is that the law to be defined is to be approached as a practice, and not just as a pure linguistic phenomenon. The point of view to be adopted for this purpose cannot be a purely theoretical perspective. A pragmatist stance should be taken that the relevant point of view is that of the *practice* of law. Said in a slightly different way, the definition of law cannot be performed without taking its practice into account.

(iii) But the law is not just "any" practice; it is a *social* practice. It is not a matter of individual prescriptions or commitments; it presupposes a community in which general conduct is taken by following common rules. The meaning of a (legal) rule is related to its use, and such use is not a private or idiosyncratic habit. There is a community, a tradition – if you like – which backs such use. The law – as Hart points out – is a practice which consists of following different and multiple sorts of rules that are not all imperative or restrictive. Nor are they all to be reduced to one principal format of rule. This is shown through the variety of types of rules that lawyers apply. Rules are something to use, and their purport can only be ascertained and classified from the user's point of view:

> Power conferring rules are thought of, spoken of, and used in social life differently from rules which impose duties, and they are valued for different reasons. What other tests for difference in character could there be?[3]

In the experience that we make of the law, we do, of course, first of all face imperative rules, rules which impose obligations and constraints, and which narrow down our scope of action. But we also face other and, perhaps, even more important kinds of rules: rules that ascribe powers, rules that offer facilities, rules that serve as a sort of signposts, as references in order to recognise further rules and to attribute them legal existence, rules that are canons or criteria of sound judgement and of legal reasoning at large. A primitive legal system might consist only of commands or prescriptions. However, this is not the case with modern developed legal orders that are actually structured along multiple layers of different kinds of rules.

---

[2]See H. L. A. Hart, "Definition and Theory in Jurisprudence", now in *idem*, *Essays in Jurisprudence and Philosophy* (Oxford: Oxford University Press, 1983), Chapter 1.

[3]H. L. A. Hart, *The Concept of Law* (Oxford: Oxford University Press, 1961), p. 41.

(iv) A further consequence of this approach is that the practice of law to be known, to be understood and conceptualised, needs to be considered from a privileged and special perspective, which is not that adopted by an external observer as occurs in a purely descriptive enterprise. This special and privileged perspective here is the one taken from the internal point of view, that is, *from the point of view of those that are taking part in the practice and follow its rules*, in short, from the angle of the main actors of the practice: in the law, advocates and judges. The language *about the law* (which comprises the *concept* of law) is based upon the ordinary language *of the law*. The point of view of a mere observer will not suffice. It will not be sufficient to render the sense and purport of what law consists of. For instance, as we have just seen, the important difference between power-conferring rules and obligation-imposing rules, that is, between what Hart calls secondary and primary rules, could only be perceived from the point of view of the user, that is, from the internal point of view. In a more general sense, it is normativity itself which is "internal", and not just "external", although, according to Hart, this does not imply that normativity is equivalent to feeling obliged. One can be obliged, can have an obligation, without necessarily *feeling* obliged. In brief, "internal" does not mean here "psychological"

Now, if this is Hart's research programme in a nutshell, at least until his posthumous *Postscript* to the *Concept of Law*, the wide range of implications that we can draw from this programme has not yet been fully taken into account or investigated to its furthest borders. For instance, if we have to take Hart's rejection of *per genus et differentiam* definitions and his recommendations of the perspective of the rule-user seriously, it might well be that his philosophy is not affected by the "semantic sting", the positivist and conventionalist view about legal validity, according to which validity's necessary and sufficient conditions are intrinsic to the rule-semantic content.

Of the three prominent scholars whom we may attach both the label and the honour of Hart's disciples, and here I refer to Professors Ronald Dworkin, Neil MacCormick and Joseph Raz, the first (Dworkin) has made his fortune by stressing his distance from, and launching a formidable attack against, the old master's views, while the last (Raz) has, for a while, hoisted the school's flag and has looked after the continuity of Oxford jurisprudence in the wake of the master's teachings. However, Raz has left the law user's perspective out of the scope of legal philosophy and has made it something irrelevant for the concept of law. Whether, by doing so, he has, in fact, been the most faithful of Hart's disciples could, however, be doubted.

Thus, and this is the central contention of mine in this chapter, only the second of the three disciples mentioned above (Professor MacCormick) might, perhaps, be seen as the closest to the original inspiration of Hartian legal philosophy. I contend that it is, indeed, Professor MacCormick who makes all of the four main tenets of Hart's research programme his own and who tries to maintain the promises that the old master could not, or would not, fulfil to the end.

The point of Hart's inheritance is raised by MacCormick himself when he remarks that "the Hartian doctrines in *The Concept of Law* which seemed to me soundest in themselves and yet to require redevelopment in certain ways are the very doctrines Hart himself has either abandoned or restated quite differently in his latest writings".[4] However, the right to disinherit could be denied to the "grand-sire", since "children, even illegitimate ones, nowadays have against their parents legal rights of succession".[5] A child can be a legitimate heir even against the will of his father (at least, under Scots law, says MacCormick not without a pinch of irony); likewise a disciple – we may add – can receive and transmit his teachings even against the master's later retraction.

4.3 An Unfinished Agenda

Two promises or claims are, more or less, explicitly made or raised through the whole of the argument of Hart's *Concept of Law*.

(1) The first claim is that law – as we have already seen – to be understood and conceptualised, should be dealt with from an "internal point of view". Here, we find the promise of a *hermeneutical* theory. Reporting and understanding, explanations by causal laws or by meaning and intention are judged to be distinct cognitive enterprises.
(2) Hart's second claim is that law is much more than a mere matter of commands and imperatives, of decision and sanctions. Here, we have – somehow – the promise of an *anti-authoritarian* conception. Within Hart's theoretical horizon, there is a, more or less, openly declared commitment to a liberal view of law, in which prescriptions and coercion are no longer the fundamental materials of which legal experience is made. Now, these two promises have remained unfulfilled. They are not kept to the end; they seem to be abandoned by the English jurisprudent. Eventually, in his posthumous *Postscript*, we find more than hints of a "change of heart",[6] especially as far as the centrality of the internal point of view is concerned.

As matter of fact, in the inner development of Hart's theory – and much before the *Postscript* – the internal point of view is, on the one hand, moralised, so that it is converted into the perspective of those that approve of the legal order under consideration, and feel, more or less, morally obliged to abide by its rules. In fact, the internal point of view is seen by Hart as sharing the values of the legal system in question. On the other hand, such a perspective is reserved to only a specific class of people within the legal order: legal officers and judges. Ordinary citizens,

---

[4]N. MacCormick, "Commentary", in: *Issues in Contemporary Jurisprudence. The Influence of H.L.A. Hart*, R. Gavison (ed) (Oxford: Clarendon Press, 1987), p. 105.
[5]Ibid.
[6]R. Dworkin, "Hart and the Concepts of Law", (2006) 119 *Harvard Law Review Forum*, pp. 95–104, at 102.

but also, to a certain degree, lawyers in their capacity as advocates, are sent back to the external side of the law – where it is a matter of regularities, expectations of probabilities, predictions, and brute facts.

The second, the anti-authoritarian promise, is also not maintained to the end. It is true that Hart introduces into the system a kind of rules, which is different from that of commands and norms which impose sanctions; it is true that he successfully repeals and confutes Hans Kelsen's idea of the sanction as a defining element of the legal provision. Indeed, a sanction is such if it is so defined through the indication of its being a reaction to a previous violation of a rule. The rule is prior to the sanction and some evil or damage cannot become, or qualify as, a sanction without a previous normative ascription. All this is sharply pointed out by Hart and successively backed and reinforced by MacCormick – who even argues that coercion is not a logical or necessary feature of law.[7]

However, when dealing with judicial deliberation, Hart has to concede that, beyond the semantic core of rules, legal reasoning ends up shifting into a fully discretionary decision. Decisionism is, somehow, Hart's response to the question of both rule-following and rule-application in hard cases. Once we enter – he says – the penumbral area of legal rules, where there is uncertainty about their meaning, and we face always a more or less wide one, we will have very little to reason or to deliberate in a rational or argumentative way. Or rather, we will have very little reason if we move from what positive law as a sum of semantic meaning can offer. Thus, judicial antiformalism will be unavoidable: we will no longer have a semantic point of reference to orient ourselves in our decisions. We will have to decide fully by ourselves, without an intersubjective, more or less, determinate ground for justification. Decisionism seems, then, to be the last word for the practice of law.

Clearly, this conclusion cannot be other than unsatisfactory for a domain in which actors are in search of, and struggle for, "one right answer". Against Hart's decisionism, his three disciples each react in a different way. Dworkin tries to fill the gap of discretion, which Hart kept open, through his "rights thesis" and by recourse to the notion of principles. In the law – he says – rights are claims to be right, and there are not only rules to apply, but also principles. The latter, by their logic, cannot be made precise only through semantic operations (as is the case for rules), but need a justificatory discourse, which is argumentative more than hermeneutic. Now, this exercise in justification leads to moral reasoning, that cannot consequently be kept out of the legal precinct. Moreover, principles are expansive and do not allow for empty spaces; they radiate into the whole of the legal system.

Joseph Raz acknowledges that legal reasoning is driven through principles, and is, therefore, close to a moral practice. But then he insists on defending the legal positivistic view of a strict conceptual separation between law and morality, so that, in the end, he has to expel legal reasoning (which is irremediably morally tinged) from the "nature" of law. His thesis is the following: it is true that legal reasoning

---

[7] See N. MacCormick, *Legal Right and Social Democracy* (Oxford: Oxford University Press, 1982), Chapter 12.

is involved in moral deliberation, but legal reasoning is not relevant as far as the definition of law is concerned. The legal philosopher, in conceptualising law and legal concepts, is not at all bound or referred back to the lawyers' use of these notions. However, by doing so, such a legal philosopher would have to abandon Hart's central assumption, according to which, in order to define the concept of law, one should consider how the law is used and practiced, that is, first of all, *legal reasoning*. It seems that a legal philosopher of the kind suggested by Raz would be, rather than following Hart's research programme, a sort of *pre-Hartian* scholar.

It is only Professor MacCormick – this is my central thesis – who remains faithful to Hart's original methodology. In his first book, *Legal Theory and Legal Reasoning*,[8] the Scottish scholar programmatically declares that "a theory of legal reasoning is required by a theory of law".[9] Here, Hart's idea, that the study of lawyers' use of law and its notion is central to the philosophical enterprise which deals with the very concept of law, is openly vindicated. Accordingly, Professor MacCormick develops a theory of legal reasoning that is compatible with the Hartian research programme. This book, writes MacCormick:

> is something of a companion volume to H.L.A. Hart's classic *The Concept of Law*. The account it gives of legal reasoning is represented as being essentially Hartian, grounded in or at least fully compatible with Hart's legal-positivistic analysis of the concept of law.[10]

In his first monograph, Professor MacCormick, on the one hand, defends the possibility and even the necessity of using deductive reasoning against sceptics and decisionists. "Despite recurrent denials by learned persons that law allows scope for deductive reasoning, or even for logic at all, this book" – so writes MacCormick in a new foreword to his monograph – "stands four-square for the idea that a form of deductive reasoning is central to legal reasoning".[11] The relevance given to the deductive structure of reasoning in MacCormick's reconstruction of legal reasoning corresponds to Hart's focussing on rules when discussing the concept of law. This is explicitly recognised by the Scottish scholar himself:

> The centrality of rule-based reasoning in this book matched the centrality of the 'union of primary and secondary rules' in Hart's jurisprudence.[12]

If there is a non-deductive part of lawyers' reasoning, this, in the end, – it is said – will focus on the deductive part, and will be intelligible by virtue of its relation to this part. On the other hand, he nonetheless tries to integrate Dworkin's criticism of Hart's positivism within a theory of second order justification of judicial reasoning and a conception of external validation of legal reasoning sources.

---

[8]N. MacCormick, *Legal Theory and Legal Reasoning* (Oxford: Oxford University Press, 1978).

[9]N. MacCormick, *Legal Theory and Legal Reasoning* (Oxford: Oxford University Press, 2003) (revised edition), p. 229.

[10]Foreword, in *ibid.*, p. xiv.

[11]Ibid., p. ix.

[12]Ibid., p. xv.

Thus, it is to Neil MacCormick that we owe a serious attempt to maintain Hart's unfulfilled promise of a non-decisionist concept of law, without, however, giving up either the positivist separation between law and morality, or the internal point of view. There is some concession to Dworkin's theses, but only as much as it is necessary to safeguard Hart's concept of law from its own unwished for decisionist slippery slope. In fact, the centrality that MacCormick gives to deductive reasoning allows us to see principles no longer as focal and overarching in the structure of legal reasoning, thereby limiting or controlling the entrance of moral considerations into judicial deliberation. Principles are considered as a matter of external justification without impinging upon the formalist, rational, because deductive, internal justification of the judicial ruling.

In this respect, I would also like to mention MacCormick's thesis of the "imperative fallacy", outlined in an article published in the early 1970s.[13] Here, his contention is that we not only have a descriptive or "naturalistic" fallacy (derivation of an "ought" from an "is"), but that we could also have an *imperative* fallacy, that is the logically unjustified belief that we are able to infer an "ought" ("I ought to shut the door", for instance) whenever we are confronted with "shall" ("you shall shut the door"). A command is a fact and a statement of fact (that is, a statement that there is a command to do such-and-such x) cannot be the major premise for an "ought" or normative statement. I would like to stress that such a thesis might contradict the "source thesis" or – in Dworkin's terminology – the "plain fact view", according to which the existence of a law (or of a legal obligation) could be fully justified in cognitive terms, through the reference to a particular "source" of law (a piece of legislation, for instance, or a concrete, specific judicial decision) without further specification or normative premises. On the other hand, the "plain fact view" which Dworkin ascribes to Hart is hardly consistent with Hart's rejection of the *per genus et differentiam* definitions. By means of stressing the possibility of an "imperative fallacy", MacCormick points out to a justificatory scheme which is, indeed, at variance with the positivistic obsession with "sources". Indeed, sources are thought of as something open to description – which is the argument that the positivistic jurisprudent employs to re-assess the distinction between law and morality as an ontological or logical incommensurability between the two.

Furthermore, Professor MacCormick also picks up and develops Hart's first promise: his legal epistemology centred around the "internal point of view". MacCormick first tries to avoid Hart's moralising move by distinguishing a "volitional" from a "comprehending" internal point of view. "It will be noted", he writes, "that what determines the 'internality' of a statement is the *understanding*, not the *will* of the speaker".[14] Here, we face an ambiguity in Hart's explanation of the

[13]N. MacCormick, "Legal Obligation and the Imperative Fallacy", in: A. W. B. Simpson (ed), *Oxford Essays in Jurisprudence*, Second Series (Oxford: Oxford University Press, 1973), pp. 171–201.

[14]Appendix, in MacCormick, note 9 *supra*, p. 291.

internal point of view. When considering the distinction between "internal" and "external" statements, we cannot avoid the following question:

> Is it a distinction between levels of understanding, or a distinction between degrees of volitional commitment?[15]

Towards a concrete, historical legal system – MacCormick says – we could, indeed, assume an internal point of view and accordingly issue "internal statements" concerning the "internal point of view", without, however, taking a volitional commitment with regard to the considered system of law, that is, without having to identify ourselves morally with that system of law. There is, actually, an internal stance which is *detached*, merely cognitive. Saying that one is *obliged* by the system and *accepting, or willing* to be so are different perspectives. However, the latter – says MacCormick – is the crucial attitude to assume in order to have "internal statements": without a normative internal point of view, we could not have a cognitive internal perspective. The latter is:

> parasitic on – because it presupposes – the 'volitionally internal' point of view: the point of view of an agent, who in some degree and for reasons which seem good to him has a volitional commitment to observance of a given pattern of conduct as a standard for himself or for other people or for both: his attitude includes, but it is not included by, the 'cognitively internal' attitudes.[16]

This implies – I believe – that a sort of moral attitude emerges logically prior to the legally cognitive one: in a sense, by affirming the priority of the "volitional" perspective, MacCormick seems to establish a conceptual bridge between morality and law. His thesis, here, seems to amount to the following: (a) we could not have law without some group ascribing moral force to it; and (b) we could not have a legal (detached) point of view without presupposing a much stronger normative commitment towards those very rules that we are going to understand and report. In short, it would seem that the thesis here is that the law that "is" somehow depends on the law that "ought to be" – which might be considered a violation of the legal positivist neutrality principle. In a sense, what MacCormick is proposing by his distinction of a "volitional" and an "understanding" internal perspective and the additional view that "understanding" is parasitic on "volitional", is something which could be seen as being closer to Dworkin's "rights thesis" – whereby stating that a right implies a claim "to be right".

It might therefore be doubted that, by this distinction, MacCormick was able to overcome Hart's moralising of the internal point of view. A way-out would, perhaps, be to reassess the volitional stance as a normative one (removing its psychological and mentalistic undertones), to root it into a concrete practice (that, for instance, of giving and asking for reasons) switching into a pragmatist mood, and then to try to discriminate between a strong normative point of view (*grosso modo* equivalent to a strong volitional, moral perspective) and a weak normative attitude – which,

[15] Ibid.

[16] Ibid., p. 292.

although it implies a commitment to the relevant rules, would not moralise them, since they were conceived here as a part of an ontological and/or epistemological dimension, well distinguished from the ideality of the moral sphere and of the volitional upholding that such a sphere demands.

MacCormick seems to point in this very direction when he makes a decisive move in his concept of law. He tries to reinterpret Hart's internal point of view in terms of a thesis about *the facts of the law*. He emphasises that the internal point of view is possible within a specific area of experience, that is, when dealing with a special type of *facts*. Thus, we need an ontology of law considered as a special sort of fact which needs to be understood from the appropriate perspective. Law is made of facts which are dealt with by internal statements. These special facts in the world are *institutional facts*.

> If law exists at all, it exists not on the level of brute creation along with shoes and ships and sealing wax or, for that matter, cabbages, but rather along with kings and other paid officers of the state on the plane of institutional facts.[17]

This, actually, is a statement which is not very far from the following statement, recently written down by Dworkin:

> Legal systems are not natural kinds, like bismuth and centipedes, that have essences. They are social kinds.[18]

In MacCormick's words, we find a clear reference to John Searle's theory of "institutional facts", as distinct from "brute" facts, and this is so because of particular rules which constitute or "institute" these facts. This represents a development of views held by J.L. Austin, the Oxford philosopher and a friend of Hart's, who added to language and statements, beyond the usual reality-mirroring function, more creative properties. Language is performative; it not only mirrors, but also principally shapes and produces new states of affairs. Baptising a ship, giving her a name in a ceremony, is not an ostensive operation, or a descriptive enterprise; it entails producing something new: an identity which was not there before. Now, Searle, in a sense, makes performatives impersonal, not fully bound to a pragmatic context between an addresser and an addressee in a concrete specific individualised context. Performatives are thus reinterpreted as *rules*, but rules that do not prescribe something which is independent from the rule, but rules that constitute objects and states of affairs that are not logically independent of the rules themselves. These are "constitutive rules" (as opposed to prescriptive or "regulative" ones). And constitutive rules introduce or produce "institutional facts".

MacCormick prefers to use the notion of "institutive rules". But by doing so – avoiding the idea of "constitutive rules" and introducing a tripartion of "institutive", "consequential", and "terminative" rules – the Scottish scholar seems to narrow down the scope of institutional facts to legal *concepts*, such as contracts, wills, trusts, *etc*. Law is seen as an institution or as an institutional fact – this is step forward from Hart's yet undeveloped ontology of rules and hermeneutics of points of views. However, what an institution amounts to remains a trifle too under-determined.

---

[17]N. MacCormick, *Law as Institutional Fact* (Edinburgh: University of Edinburgh, 1973), p. 2.
[18]Dworkin, note 6 *supra*, p. 98.

4.4 Neo-Institutionalism

MacCormick's first use of institution as a notion for legal theory is to point out a special existential dimension of law that cannot be fully referred to the empirical world. There are more things in human experience and in law than just inert objects or merely empirical states of affairs. (i) In this sense, "institution" is used as an equivalent to institutional fact. But immediately after having introduced this notion, MacCormick refers it mainly to *legal concepts*.

Institutional facts would be an appropriate abstract notion for a concept-like contract, so that, in the end, the former are reshaped in terms of (ii) a device to render the application of rules easier and more efficient: a technique of presentation, a presentational tool of (legal) materials which could, in principle, be manipulated under a different notion, one by one, rule by rule, provision by provision. They are, more or less, what the German doctrine would call *Rechtsinstitute*. But – and I refer here precisely to the argumentative line taken in MacCormick's seminal inaugural lecture *Law as Institutional Fact* – (iii) an institution is also said to be a social collective entity, a social group, a contextual community. Here, MacCormick seems to use "institution" in a sense which is closer to that adopted by traditional legal institutionalism, by scholars such as Maurice Hauriou and Santi Romano.

We are then confronted with a further turn in his use of this notion; (iv) institution is said to be something which has to do with the "institutionalised" or the "organised".[19] "Institutional", here, is opposed to "informal",[20] and it is a dimension in which there are different layers of norms, and people or officials are appointed to enforce the rules and to check their correct application. In this further sense, an "institution", *grosso modo*, is equivalent to the developed normative system singled out by Hart: a system where there are rules and meta-rules; and where meta-rules are not *prima facie* prescribing patterns of conduct, but are meant to ascribe powers about the first order, "primary" provisions. In this sense, we could not have an institution without people charged, or "officers" appointed, to ascertain what the rule to be applied to a certain case and to redress deviant behaviour actually is.[21] Adjudication, in short, would be the "threshold" beyond which we shall find law as a proper "institution".

All these four declinations of the notion of "institution" can be found in the manifesto of MacCormick's institutionalism: his inaugural lecture held in Edinburgh in 1973. What is a little disconcerting for a reflection whose title is *Law as Institutional Fact* is that, in its conclusion, the philosophical declination of "institution" (that is, Searle's proposal of an "institutional fact") is dismissed and only its sociological use is fully admitted. Institutional facts are seen as being too narrowly defined to allow for standards other than rules to be operative within the scope that they would be called to cover in law. MacCormick is sympathetic with Dworkin's vindication of

[19]See, for instance, N. MacCormick, *Questioning Sovereignty* (Oxford: Oxford University Press, 1999), p. 7.

[20]See N. MacCormick, *Rhetoric and the Rule of Law* (Oxford: Oxford University Press, 2005), p. 4.

[21]See N. MacCormick, *Institutions of Law* (Oxford: Oxford University Press, 2007), Chapter 1.

rights and principles as important bricks, or rather, pillars, in the walls of law. The law has a purposive side that rules cannot fully express and implement: principles are inescapable both in legal practice and in the definition of law. MacCormick, in this respect, is much less sceptical than Raz and than Hart himself, at least as the latter's views are expressed in his posthumous *Postscript* to *The Concept of Law*.[22]

Rules do not fully govern their own application. This is stated by Wittgenstein, argued by Hart, and reinterpreted by MacCormick, who does not, however, extract from such a statement a sceptical conclusion in the light of Hart. "We cannot," says the Scottish scholar, "be sure that the conditions of validity which we state as necessary are unquestionably necessary in every case, so we cannot be certain that for every case they are sufficient."[23] To complement the open texture of the semantic content of rules we could, or should, recur to *principles*. If this is so, the conclusion will be that:

> institutive rules of institutions should be taken only as setting the conditions which are ordinarily necessary and presumptively sufficient to the existence or valid creation of a specific instance of the institution.[24]

Such flexibility (or defeasibility) of law and legal concepts depends upon, among other reasons, the elaboration of arguments of principles and policy. The meaning of legal rules is not to be exhausted in their semantic content: they have a "point" – which is to be recognised and traced back in order to make sense of their application. Rights, for instance, rest upon interests (MacCormick is a notorious opponent of the will theory)[25] and these are external to the semantics of rules, but should, nevertheless, be taken into account in order to assess the purport and justification of rights. But if this is so, if the semantics of rules does not offer a full paradigm of their application, then – this is MacCormick's conclusion – "the concept of law cannot be tied down to being simply an institutional concept in the philosophical sense, covering simply the criteria of validity and the rules valid in terms of them".[26]

This is a very important conclusion and one which opens up the possibility of further development for the concept of law. On the one hand, one could try to give to the philosophical notion of institution, Searle's "institutional fact", a clearer pragmatic turn. Institutional facts would then be defined not through their constitutive rules alone, but also, and, indeed, mainly, through the concrete actions made possible through those rules. An institution would thus be a practice, a number of pieces of conduct, not just an ideal object or state of affairs produced by fiat through special semantic contents. Or, following Searle's suggestion, the object would be "just the continuous possibility of the activity".[27] A better definition of an institution might

---

[22]See H. L. A. Hart, *The Concept of Law*, 2nd ed., with a Postscript edited by P. A. Bullock & J. Raz (Oxford: Oxford University Press, 1994), p. 238 *et seq.*

[23]See MacCormick, note 17 *supra*, p. 24.

[24]Ibid., p. 28.

[25]MacCormick, note 7 *supra*, Chapter 8.

[26]Ibid.

[27]J. R. Searle, *The Construction of Social Reality* (Harmondsworth: Penguin, 1996), p. 36.

thus be the following: an institution is a scope of action made possible through constitutive rules, whenever this scope of action is actually "exploited" through actual conduct. In this way, it would also be possible to avoid the usual vicious circle that afflicts many definitions of "institutions", whereby an "institution" is said to be a system of rules *and* the product of these very rules at the same time.

MacCormick's conclusion about the open texture of institutions and "institutional facts" also makes a further move possible. Rules and institutions need a practice to make their range and sense of application precise. But what kind of practice is this? It is clearly a *meaningful* and *judgmental* practice, a number of pieces of conduct not only driven through the contents of rules, but also through their "point" and their underlying "interests" and values. "Norms", Professor MacCormick reminds us, "involve judgments".[28] And "normative judgments and deliberations do not relate to or pre-suppose or derive from single isolated norms. Rather, they depend on some larger conception of normative order".[29]The "institution" is not just a norm, or just a "habit", as in Wittgenstein's *Gepflogenheit*. This being a normative situation, a space where conduct is taken because this is opened up by rules, we cannot but pose the question of justification.

The problem is seen by Wittgenstein, who then refers to the "form of life" within the institution that is valid and "exploited" as a justificatory background. However, this – the "form of life" is not yet the bedrock; a "form of life" is not blind to the game of giving and asking for reasons. True, there are institutional theories which both stop here, and recommend a closed communitarian narrative to us. This may, perhaps, be the case of traditional legal institutionalism. However, this cannot be the case of a legal theory that is open to the question of the "point" of the law. Wittgenstein, too, goes beyond the *Lebensform* and adds to the rule its *Witz*, its "point" (see, for instance, *Philosophische Untersuchungen*, paragraphs 564 and 567), so that there might be room for an underlying principled discourse.

MacCormick does something similar when he stresses that, in order to issue a normative judgement, "some larger conception of normative order" is needed. He then adds that a normative order is first something which "ought to be"- a paradigm "about the way things ought to be and ought to go on" – and only afterwards does it become facticity, as a matter of the world as it is. But here – I would say – we take a path well beyond any "plain fact view" or any "source theory", and we are given a chance to refer (and re-assess) institutional facts (and law) against a justification background.

---

[28]MacCormick, note 19 *supra*, p. 7.

[29]Ibid., p. 3.

Chapter 5
The Master Rule, Normativity, and the Institutional Theory of Law

Stefano Bertea

5.1 Introduction

H.L.A. Hart theorises, in *The Concept of Law*, the existence, in any modern legal order, of a conventional practice which establishes the criteria of legality, a practice that he calls the rule of recognition and regards as both the keystone of every system of laws and the germ of legality.[1] It has since then been accepted by various scholars – especially within the tradition of mature legal positivism, and despite their conceptualising the law in different ways – that any developed legal system will have, at its foundation, a complex master rule, or basic norm, having two main functions.[2]

On the one hand, the master rule operates as an *identifying norm*: it determines which standards are legal and which ones are not. In other words, the master rule sets the criteria and conditions, subject to which something can be said to belong to the legal system: any standard satisfying the criteria set by the master rule will be considered legal, while any standard that fails in this respect will be excluded from membership as non-legal. In this way, not only does the master rule define the boundaries of specific legal systems, but it also establishes what is law and what is not law, thereby having an impact on the very nature of law.

On the other hand, the master rule functions as a *validating standard*, that is, it determines the criteria a provision must comply with in order to be valid.

S. Bertea (✉)
Law School, University of Leicester, Leicester, UK
e-mail: stefano.bertea@leicester.ac.uk

The paper is part of a 5-year project entitled "The Constitution of Globalization" that is funded by an Odysseus research grant of the Research Foundation-Flanders (FWO).

[1]See H. L. A. Hart, *The Concept of Law* (Oxford: Clarendon Press, 1961), 1994 edition with a Postscript, pp. 100–110.

[2]This twofold role clearly expressed by A. Marmor, "How Law is like Chess" (2006) 12 *Legal Theory*, pp. 347–371, at 352, among others, who ascribes two functions to the basic norm: that of "answering the question of how we *identify* the law as such" and that of "answering the question of law's *normativity*".

A.J. Menéndez, J.E. Fossum (eds.), *Law and Democracy in Neil MacCormick's Legal and Political Theory*, Law and Philosophy Library 93,
DOI 10.1007/978-90-481-8942-7_5,

Importantly, what is meant here by *validity* is something different from mere affiliation: to say of something that it is valid does not simply mean that it forms part of a legal system, by virtue of its being a rule or standard established by law; instead, it means that this something has normative force. A legal standard is valid if it is normative, that is, if it partakes of the *ought* of law and can thus affect the normative status of persons under the law, by imposing duties on them or by recognising them as having certain rights and powers. Constructing legal validity as normativity makes it also possible to explain such validity, as the propensity of law to generate not just *any* reason for action, but to generate "reinforced" reasons, or reasons that can actually guide and justify a certain line or mode of conduct or course of action.[3] On an orthodox positivist view, the master rule *qua* validating standard acts as the ultimate determinant of the normativity of law: the standards inhabiting a system of laws become valid, and hence normative, by virtue of their connection with the master rule. And this is relevant to a legal-theoretical explanation of normativity, since it is not the normativity of *every* legal standard that needs to be explained, but only the normativity of that practice which lies at the foundation of law, and this practice is the master rule. From it, flows the normativity of specific legal standards, a normativity accordingly constructed upon this conception as indirect, or systemic: it is a normativity borrowed from that associated with the rule conferring validity on all other legal standards.[4]

The central role that the master rule plays in determining the normativity of law – a normativity that forms an essential part of law itself – justifies an interest in the debate on the validating power of this rule. My aim in this chapter is to contribute to this debate by discussing, in particular, the problems that Neil MacCormick's institutional theory of law comes up against in accounting for the normativity of the master rule. MacCormick takes up Hart's view that the master rule is conventional, and, thus, for MacCormick, to explain the normativity of the master rule is, in the first place, to explain what it is that makes a conventional practice normative – or what turns a complex social *fact* into an *ought*. In discussing MacCormick's account of the normativity of the master rule, then, we will have to enter into the question of the relation between conventions and normativity in law.

The discussion that follows is essentially a critique, and divides into two parts: an introductory part, in which I lay out the background and set up the main problem, and a critical part, in which I argue that the problem remains largely unanswered. I start out, then, in Section 5.2 with an introduction to MacCormick's institutional theory of law: I will do so drawing primarily on his most recent work, since I am

[3] The distinction, then, is between reasons at large offered in support of what is demanded, and reinforced reasons – the ones a valid legal standard can bring into being – which carry extra weight with regard to countervailing reasons and are protected from at least some of the potentially outweighing factors.

[4] As J. Coleman, puts it, "the capacity of almost all legal rules to *govern* conduct depends on their bearing a certain relationship to another rule – the rule of recognition', to the effect that 'a philosophical account of the very possibility of governance by law... rests on the possibility of a philosophical account of how the rule of recognition can be a reason for action".

offering a selective reconstruction of his theory. Because this theory has already been discussed extensively in the literature, I will go straight to the master rule and consider MacCormick's account of its validating properties. We will thus see how the institutional theory conceives the master rule as a conventional practice that lies at the foundation of law, and I will argue that the theory should, accordingly, be understood as a form of legal conventionalism. As mentioned, however, the moment that we endorse a conventionalist approach, we will be faced with the problem of explaining how it is that social facts (which is what conventional legal practices are) can become normative, which means that we will have to explain how normativity finds its way into law to begin with. MacCormick does not work through this problem fully, and so, if we are to see how it might be solved by working from his institutional theory, we will have to look at what other contemporary conventionalists have said in this regard. This ushers in the second part of my discussion, but since there is no single or overall account that contemporary conventionalism offers of the normativity of the master rule – a normativity grounded in such disparate concepts as acceptance, mutual expectations, and constitutive force – the discussion will, accordingly, have to be broken down into separate parts. This is what I will do in Section 5.3, in which I introduce the main conventionalist accounts of the normativity of the master rule, arguing all along the way that none of these accounts is without its problems. If that is, indeed, the case, then, institutional theory has yet to explain adequately the normativity of the master rule and, consequently, the normativity of law in general.

5.2 The Normativity of the Master Rule

MacCormick has been working from the mid-1980s towards an institutional theory that conceives the law as a complex of institutional facts which has a normative content and an orderly arrangement.[5] The law, based upon this conception, "belongs to the genus of 'normative order', and, within that genus, can be further specified as an 'institutional normative order'".[6] This description characterises the concept of law in terms of three main features: institutionalisation, normativity, and orderliness. Thus, the concept of law can be explained, in the first place, by recourse to the idea of *institutional facts*, or facts that – as products of "human will, human convention or human contrivance"[7] – are social, and thus, have an existence which is distinct from,

[5] The institutional theory of law was first set out in its contemporary version in N. MacCormick and O. Weinberger, *An Institutional Theory of Law* (Dordrecht: Kluwer, 1986). Scholars who have contributed to the theory upon the basis of MacCormick & Weinberger's pioneering studies are J. Bengoetxea, *The Legal Reasoning of the European Court of Justice* (Oxford, Oxford University Press, 1993), M. La Torre, *Norme, Istituzioni, Valori* (Rome: Laterza, 1999), and D. Ruiter, *Institutional Legal Facts* (Dordrecht, Kluwer, 1993); and *idem*, *Legal Institutions* (Dordrecht, Kluwer, 2001). The latest statement of MacCormick's own version of the theory can be found in MacCormick, *Institutions of Law* (Oxford: Oxford University Press, 2007).

[6] N. MacCormick, *Institutions of Law*, note 5 *supra*, p. 13.

[7] N. MacCormick & O. Weinberger, *An Institutional Theory of Law*, note 5 *supra*, p. 9.

and not reducible to, natural, or brute, facts. This means that the truth of institutional facts does not follow exclusively from "the condition of the material world and the causal relationship obtaining among its parts",[8] but is, instead, largely dependent on the existence of "a shared framework of understanding and interpretation among persons in some social setting".[9] Second, the law is a *normative practice* addressed to human beings as norm-users. The law and the normative – by which MacCormick means "the idea of our having ways to differentiate right from wrong in what we do, of having common or overlapping conceptions of what one ought to do in various recurring situations" – are conceptually linked up.[10] This means that the law concerns the "ought" of human experience, and, thus, it ultimately incorporates a constraining quality among its distinctive features.[11] And third, we do not mean by *law* just any set of normative institutional facts, but an *arrangement* of such facts, and thus an *orderly* set, as against a set of randomly grouped facts. This means that people under the law relate to one another upon the basis of a shared framework of standards; from which it follows that the idea of orderliness is, for the institutional theory, essential to the concept of law.

We just saw that normativity figures centrally in MacCormick's explanatory description of law: law is described as a *normative* system of institutional facts, and this binds normativity into a conceptual connection with law. For this reason, it becomes fundamental in jurisprudence, given these premises, to offer an explanation of the normativity of law, and MacCormick accordingly discusses the question frontally. He does so by introducing the example of queuing, or standing in line.[12] This is something we are all very familiar with, and it may seem unrelated to law, to be sure, but it aptly serves the purpose because we have here a practice (queuing) that exemplifies the basic features of law: when we queue, we typically enact something having the structure of an orderly and institutionalised practice endowed with normative force. And so, if we look at the fundamental traits of queuing, we can shed light on the nature of law itself, and, if we explain the normative force of queuing, we might just be able to gain some insight into the normativity of law. The normativity of queuing is explained by MacCormick by drawing on such ideas as our habitually behaving in certain ways and according to certain set patterns, our awareness of one another, and our common normative opinion.[13] Our habitual

---

[8]Ibid., p. 10.

[9]N. MacCormick, *Rhetoric and the Rule of Law* (Oxford: Oxford University Press, 2005), p. 6.

[10]MacCormick, note 5 *supra*, p. 20.

[11]On this point, see MacCormick, *Institutions of Law*, note 5 *supra*, pp. 33–34.

[12]See, especially, MacCormick, *Institutions of Law*, note 5 *supra*, pp. 14–24.

[13]By *common normative opinion* is meant the shared sense that the conduct being practiced is obligatory. A common normative opinion obtains whenever "people conduct themselves in relation to others on the basis of an opinion concerning the right thing to do which they suppose to be a mutual opinion" (MacCormick, 2007: 18), and so whenever each member within a social group "acts on the understanding (or the assumption, not necessarily particularly articulate) that each of the others is oriented towards more or less the same opinion concerning what everyone ought to do" (MacCormick, *Institutions of Law*, note 5 *supra*, p. 16).

behaviour is simply, in this case, our lining up whenever the situation calls for it or whenever it is customary for people to do so (at the checkout counter of a supermarket, for example). Now, if enough of us have a sense that it is obligatory for one to conform to other people's habitual modes or patterns of behaviour, then we get a *shared* sense that this must be so, that is, we form mutual beliefs and expectations, generally regarded as legitimate, that each of us *ought to* conform and do what everyone else is doing (in the example in question, queuing). These legitimate beliefs and expectations re-inforce the common sense that the pattern of behaviour (our consistently forming a queue at certain places) is not just a habit, but a model: it is not just something people *do*, but is what people *ought* to do, and this lends force to requests that everyone should behave so, as well as to criticism of deviant forms of behaviour (such as jumping the queue). We can see, then, the basic idea, namely, that the mutual legitimate beliefs and expectations arising around a habitual mode of behaviour turn "what most people do" into "what ought to be done", and so into the "right thing to do".[14]

The mechanism through which a conventional mode of conduct, such as queuing, becomes normative is a general one, and therefore extends to the law, at whose core lies a conventional practice. And while this is a more complex and formal practice than queuing, and, accordingly, requires a more complex theory than that by which to explain the normativity of queuing, the underlying principles of such an explanation remain the same, which is to say that the normativity of law can be explained by virtue of the law being a practice out of which mutual expectations arise: just like the normativity involved in the practice of queuing, so the normativity of law is grounded in a combination of a set mode of habitual behaviour, mutual awareness of what everyone else is doing, shared normative beliefs, and mutual expectations experienced as legitimate.[15] But clearly, as was just noted, the practice of law involves a much greater complexity and formality than the practice of queuing does: the law is structured as queuing is not; the law is a *tiered* practice, since we find here not just primary standards – the ones which govern our modes of behaviour, and to which we refer in forming mutual expectations with regard to such behaviour (the underlying practice) – but also secondary standards, or standards conferring on some people the power to issue primary standards. This means that the normativity of the standards located at the bottom tiers (the primary standards) is dependent on the normativity of the higher standards found in the master rule (the secondary standards). Which, in turn, makes the master rule the ultimate source of the normativity of all other legal standards in a given legal system. And so, the normativity of law as a whole can be explained once the master rule is explained as a practice habitually followed and capable of generating legitimate mutual expectations within the relevant social group.

---

[14]This construction is put forward in MacCormick, *Institutions of Law*, note 5 *supra*, pp. 14–20.

[15]This proposition is presented in MacCormick, *Institutions of Law*, note 5 *supra*, pp. 22–24, among other places.

The idea of a master rule clearly plays an essential role in this construction, considering that the normativity of law is derivative on the normativity of the master rule: the normativity of the entire body of legal standards – namely, of the law as a whole – depends on the existence of a complex conventional practice that holds public officials to a commitment to observe and uphold both the constitution and the laws validly made under it: the legal rules and principles in force within a certain territory owe their constraining and justificatory force to the master rule, that is, to the conventional practice upon which basis the same rules and principles are identified and validated. What ultimately enables the law to be normative, then, is the normative character of the master rule, since any failure of that rule to be normative will cause the normativity of the law as a whole to lapse into inexistence; that is, the normativity of the entire body of standards identified and validated by the master rule will collapse.[16]

It becomes imperative at this point, considering how important a role the master rule plays in MacCormick's account of the normativity of law, to spend a few words laying out the basics of this rule. MacCormick sets up his argument for the master rule by pointing out what he takes to be the shortcomings of the equivalent rule in Hart (the rule of recognition), criticised as being too simplistic an explanation of the systematic and normative force of the law, and thus as failing to give a "satisfactory general account of law in all constitutional states".[17] Many systems, in other words, are so structured that a Hartian rule of recognition cannot make much sense in them: we can appreciate this especially with respect to federal systems and to legal systems that operate under the pressure of globalisation and supranational governance, since, in such systems, we have a situation in which different courts refer to different standards (as against a single, uniformly applied one) in determining the validity of legal norms. MacCormick, then, takes exception to Hart's proposition that there exists a single power-conferring rule that we can point to as the master rule: the complexity of mature legal systems is reflected in the master rule, which must, accordingly, be conceived as a more structured and complex practice than Hart's rule of recognition. This leads MacCormick to recast the idea of a master rule, which he summarises as being the rule requiring that the constitution as a whole be respected. While this restatement incorporates important elements from Hans Kelsen's legal theory, it does not make for a radical departure from Hart's idea of the rule as something whose essential role is to identify and to validate the legal standards in force within a certain territory. Like Hart, MacCormick acknowledges the theoretical utility of a rule that, by operating as an identifying and validating standard, provides the foundations of a legal system. And, like Hart, MacCormick understands the basic rule of law as a conventional practice, that is, as a rule habitually followed by a group, and the reason why those in this group act as the rule prescribes is precisely that everyone

[16]This view is framed most explicitly in MacCormick, *H.L.A. Hart* (Stanford CA: Stanford University Press, 1981), pp. 103–165; see MacCormick, *Institutions of Law*, note 5 *supra*, p. 60.

[17](MacCormick, *Institutions of Law*, note 5 *supra*, p. 57). The full argument is stated in ibid., pp. 56–58.

else in the group does, too, or at least does so consistently enough to make the rule a practice. We can see, then – despite MacCormick's remaking of Hart's rule of recognition in setting out the master rule – that the two rules are conceptually continuous.

The institutional theory can thus be set down as a paradigmatic instance of legal conventionalism, the view that the law has a social convention at its core: it exists and produces normative effects as an institution shaped by a social and conventional practice. If we agree in constructing MacCormick's institutional theory as a species of legal conventionalism, then we should also ask how the theory deals with the question of what makes social conventions normative, in such a way as to make any other standard validated by the conventional master rule likewise normative. This question is theoretically relevant, since conventions are widely conceived of as social facts and so occupy a space – that of factuality – which is altogether different from the normative space of norms, reasons, and justification. Granted the impossibility of deriving an *ought* from an *is* (here, of deriving practical guidance and justification from the conventional practice which substantiates the master rule), the mere fact that people, by and large, act collectively in certain set ways seems neither a necessary nor a sufficient reason for anyone to regard that mode of conduct as a normative standard. Hence, the question: How can the social fact that most people within a community consistently follow a master rule explain the emergence of legitimate mutual expectations, in such a way that that the rule, along with the standards which it validates, ought to be regarded as binding on us and as justifying the corresponding behaviour?

5.3 Legal Conventionalism and Normativity

It is my contention that MacCormick's account of the normativity of law is incomplete, for it fails to clarify how internal states, such as beliefs and expectations, can turn a habit – and thus a normatively inert thing – into a normative practice. MacCormick seems at places to suggest that what makes it possible to transit in this way from the factual to the normative are certain psychological mechanisms.[18] Yet, an appeal to psychology is misplaced here. Indeed, psychology is concerned with "what is" (the factual) as distinct from "what ought to be" (the normative), and so, if we grant that normativity is an autonomous part of human experience, we cannot explain normativity upon the basis of psychological considerations alone, for these are factual or empirical, and thus belong with the *is*, in contrast to normativity, which, instead, belongs with the *ought* and thus is conceptually distinct from factuality and cannot be reduced to it. Relying on an empirical foundation of this sort would amount to effecting a transition from one sphere (the *is*) to another (the *ought*), none of whose properties can be derived from any of the properties of the former. MacCormick's institutional theory, then, fails to give a comprehensive

[18]See, for instance, MacCormick, *Institutions of Law*, note 5 *supra*, pp. 16–18.

account of the normativity of the master rule: it does so by leaving unanswered the central normative question of the transition from the *is* to the *ought* of human experience.

The most obvious place to start in order to bring to completion the theoretical effort left unfinished by MacCormick is from the discussion of the master rule's normativity found in legal conventionalism, the tradition of legal thought to which the institutional theory of law belongs. There are at least three accounts that contemporary legal conventionalism offers of the normativity of the master rule, and it is to these accounts that the remainder of this chapter is devoted, considering each of them in turn and doing so in a critical spirit, to determine whether they have anything to offer that someone working in the institutional theory of law might be willing to take up in pursuing the direction which MacCormick has indicated.

5.3.1 Acceptance as the Source of the Normativity of the Master Rule

On one variant of legal conventionalism, the normativity of the master rule is accounted for by relying upon the idea of acceptance, an idea first theorised (in this sense) by Hart and subsequently refined by Jules Coleman. Hart's focus is on the normative tenor of the language of law, a language made of statements conveying the state of being under an obligation (or being obligated) to do what the law prescribes. The assumption, when we consider statements of this kind, is that the person making them has taken a certain attitude toward the law: Hart calls this attitude the internal point of view and characterises it as the point of view of one who accepts the law as a whole and thus is committed to it. The internal point of view, however, is only meant to explain how the *language of law* becomes normative, not how the law itself does so, for which reason we will not find in Hart's work a comprehensive account of the normativity of law, but only an account confined to its language. And it is in this way that Coleman builds on Hart's conception of the internal point of view and takes it one step further by specifying the conditions subject to which the *law* can impose obligations. Coleman characterises the internal point of view as "a basic and important psychological capacity of human beings", the capacity to "adopt a practice or pattern of behaviour as a norm".[19] The internal point of view thus understood – as a capacity, willingness, and disposition to endorse given standards – can explain how a certain regularity of behaviour can provide practical reasons. The key notion here is that of endorsement: to take an internal point of view with regard to regular patterns of behaviour is to endorse these patterns, and endorsed patterns are more than just social facts, because social facts are, as such, constitutively unable to create reasons for action, whereas endorsed patterns do have an inherent ability to create such reasons, and in this way they ascend or lift off, as it were, from the ground of the *is*. Thus, the moment that we define law as a social practice endorsed

[19]Coleman, note 4 *supra*, p. 88.

by a certain group, we thereby also have an explanation of the normativity of law. And, in Coleman's view (as in MacCormick's), the law does, indeed, have a social practice at its foundation: this practice is the rule of recognition, which, from this view, structures the social convention in effect among the officials who enact and apply the law.

The nature and normativity of the rule of recognition – from which derives the normative force of all other legal provisions – is further specified by Coleman by appealing to Michael Bratman's idea of a shared co-operative activity.[20] A shared co-operative activity is a convention among people who share three basic characteristics: they are mutually responsive, mutually supportive, and are committed to the activity that joins them. It is owing to this inherent commitment that a shared co-operative activity can give rise to obligations to act as prescribed: the participants' mutual commitment supports their reliance on one another and gives rise to legitimate expectations, which, in turn, provide each person with obligations to act in accordance with the legitimate expectations of others. A shared co-operative activity may be said, in this regard, to replicate the normative structure of pacts and promises. Like a pact or a promise, a shared co-operative activity carries a binding force based upon the mutual legitimate expectations brought about by reciprocal commitments. Because conventional practices – when they come in the shape of a shared co-operative activity – can explain how obligations might come about, Coleman concludes that, once we construct the rule of recognition as an endorsed conventional practice consisting in a shared cooperative activity, we have a "plausible and attractive" account of the "practices of officials necessary to create and sustain law".[21] The normativity of law is thus explained by appealing to the existence of a conventional social practice among officials: to the extent that officials adhere to the rule of recognition, this rule imposes on them an obligation to enforce the provisions it validates.[22] Hence, from Coleman's approach, which, in this context, remains faithful to Hart's project, the normativity of law is characterised as a distinctive and specific kind of normativity – call it social normativity – which cannot be reduced without distortion to moral normativity. In contrast to moral normativity, which originates in a critical practice, the (social) normativity of law derives from a conventional practice.[23]

---

[20](Ibid., pp. 92–94). Although Coleman no longer supports this view, it remains the most developed and comprehensive explanation of the normativity of law from within the Hartian tradition of legal positivism, and, for this reason, it will be carefully discussed in this section.

[21]Ibid., p. 97.

[22]Ibid., p. 77.

[23]Although this theory goes beyond Hart's original intent, it essentially remains faithful to Hart's original non-cognitivism and expressivism. For H. L. A. Hart, "as the etymology of 'duty' and, indeed, 'ought' suggests", obligations in law refer to "actions which are due from or owed by the subjects having the duty, in the sense that they may be properly demanded or exacted from them"; *idem*, *Essays on Bentham* (Oxford: Clarendon Press, 1982), p. 160, This is a position that Coleman also subscribes to, and subscribing to it means rejecting any cognitive analysis of obligation, or any analysis under which the existence of an obligation is linked to the existence of objective reasons to act as prescribed.

Granted, this account of the normativity of the master rule does seem, at first sight, to capture something about the law as a practice, but there are two serious problems with the account that need to be pointed out, problems which are significant enough for us not to want to take them up on an institutionalist approach. The first such problem lies in its arbitrarily narrowing the scope of the normativity of law. There is a severe limitation of scope involved in the view that all it takes to explain the normativity of law is an account of how the rule of recognition can be normative for officials. The limitation involved is that the law, from this perspective, generates practical reasons only for a minority of those concerned, the officials, and makes no normative claims at all on the rest of us.[24] In fact, it may well be that ordinary citizens do not see themselves as involved in a shared co-operative activity under the framework of the law, and so they may well not accept the law (at least not in the sense of its enabling a shared co-operative activity) and may, accordingly, have no reason to follow the dictates of either the rule of recognition or of other legal standards. It is unclear, then, how the normative pull of the master rule, and thus the normative force of the laws which this rule validates, can extend to everyone else, so as to also take into account people *not* serving in an official capacity. Any normative claim the law makes on the *citizens* thus remains unexplained.[25]

It is this failure to take the citizens into account that gives us a measure of just how short Coleman's theory falls, with regard to offering a complete account of the normativity of law, and, indeed, of the legal enterprise as a whole. We can appreciate this by way of Sylvie Delacroix' argument that the attitude which ordinary citizens have towards the law ought to be considered an *integral*, rather than an external, part of the law.[26] If law can exercise any normative force on citizens, rather than only on the officials, it is because "law's overall success in giving rise to reasons for action that are deemed 'conclusive' by the non-official part of the population does matter" to legal officials.[27] The shared co-operative activity that officials see themselves as engaged in cannot simply be ascribed to the worship of the rules: officials do not set up the legal machinery and keep it running for its own sake, but, rather, because they see it as a way to attain further objectives which they regard as worthwhile and important, if not as the *raison d'être* of law. The law, then, even on a minimal understanding of it as a co-operative activity shared by policy-makers,

[24]For a full discussion of this limitation, see K. E. Himma, "Conceptual Jurisprudence and the Intelligibility of Law's Claim to Obligate", in: M. O'Rourke, J. Keim-Campbell & D Shier (eds), *Topics in Contemporary Philosophy: Law and Social Justice* (Cambridge MA: The MIT Press, 2005), pp. 311–326.

[25]MacCormick is well aware of this problem: he points out that acceptance cannot explain the obligations that citizens at large have under the law but can only explain the binding force the law has on officeholders, who would incur a pragmatic self-contradiction if they acted contrary to the basic norm requiring observance of the constitution and of the laws enacted under the constitution; *idem, Institutions of Law*, note 5 *supra*, pp. 51–52.

[26]See S. Delacroix, *Legal Norms and Normativity* (Oxford: Hart Publishing, 2006), pp. 174–183, for the argument in support of this view.

[27]Ibid., p. 174.

civil servants, and other officials, is shaped by a family of further objectives and purposes, through which it can be understood why the same officials commit themselves to creating and applying laws. These purposes should thus be acknowledged as elements essential to law itself. If it proves impossible, without these purposes, to explain or otherwise make sense of the officials' commitment to the law and to the entire legal enterprise, the reason is that such a commitment would not even exist but for these purposes, and thus no legal system could emerge, because no one would *set* it up and no officials would *keep* it up. And there is no way the law can serve the purposes for which officials commit themselves to the legal system unless the standards issued by the officials are treated by citizens at large as reasons for action. Because no official would commit himself or herself to a legal system that ordinary citizens did not widely consider to be normative – in fact, such a system would fall apart soon after it had been set up – any legal theory that fails to explain how the law makes normative claims on officials and non-officials alike will show itself to be an inadequate account of law.

In summary, we cannot make sense of the legal enterprise which the officials engage in – and so, ultimately, we cannot explain how the law can even exist – unless we recognise that the scope of the normative claims of law extends to all citizens rather than just to the officials.[28] This shows that any attempt to ground the normativity of law in the notion of acceptance is not only bound to be incomplete but will also prevent us from grasping the role of normativity in law, and, indeed, the very nature of law as a practical enterprise.

This last point introduces the second significant problem with Coleman's theory, a problem that can be illustrated by going back to the central role which the theory envisions for the idea of a shared co-operative activity, for it can be questioned how accurately this kind of activity really describes the way in which people engage with one another under the law. A convincing argument has been put forward in this regard by Matthew Noah Smith, who makes the case that a shared co-operative activity falls under the rubric of hyper-committal activities, by which is meant activities requiring their participants to seek an agreement and to remain committed

[28] An argument in support of this claim is offered as well by Gerald Postema. From the premise that "it is a defining feature of law that it channels social behaviour" – idem, "Co-ordination and Convention at the Foundations of Law" (1982) 11 *Journal of Legal Studies*, pp. 165–203, at p. 187 – and does so in a *special* way, that is, by *guiding* behaviour rather than by manipulating the psychological determinants of action – Postema argues that the law has a public nature which extends beyond the circle of public officials and involves *everyone* subject to the law: "law can direct action to its ends only if its rules are integrated into the practical reasoning of those subject to the rules": Ibid., p. 190. Nor does it suffice to communicate legal standards, because (among other reasons) communication is an interactive process in which each participant's ability to understand depends on the expectations and understanding of the others; so what also needs to happen with regard to these standards is that they must be perceived as binding by people at large. This makes the normativity of law an affair involving public officials and citizens alike, and it means that its normativity cannot be adequately explained without taking the citizens' attitudes into account. If we agree that law is a means to *guide* conduct (and is not just coercive), then we should grant that a legal system is paradigmatically a system whose standards are not just the concern of officials, but also figure in the practical reasoning of all other citizens, too.

to it.[29] The required agreement is both conceptual and epistemic: conceptual because the parties have to agree both intentionally and extensionally to the idea behind the activity in which they are engaged; epistemic because they each need to have accurate beliefs and expectations about the moves that the other participants will make in undertaking this shared activity. These two forms of agreement are matched by two corresponding forms of *commitment*, conceptual and epistemic, on top of which also comes a *practical* commitment, describing the participants' willingness to engage in the activity in mutually supportive forms. Clearly, we cannot lay out Smith's analytic treatment in any detail here, but the point is that shared co-operative activities are grounded in the possibility of close-knit relations among participants, who, in addition to being sensitive to the conduct and aims of the others, must also commit themselves to the social practice at hand and be fully invested in it.

Achieving such a deep participation in a collective enterprise and such a strong commitment to an institution is going to be a tall order even if, following Coleman, we take it that the participants in question are just the legal officials, to the exclusion of everyone else in the population subjected to the legal system. The kind of participation and commitment required by the model of shared co-operative activity may possibly be obtained in legal systems that govern small and homogeneous communities. But it is hard to see how it can be obtained in the legal systems of nation-states and supra-national entities, where the functionaries are not likely to share by default common aims or to be necessarily devoted to a shared cause. The likelihood of disagreement, in legal contexts, at both conceptual level and epistemic level, is reinforced by the consideration that in legal systems officials need not form a homogenous group.[30] The upshot of this manifold composition is that, within the class of legal officials, we will find people with the most diverse education, background, and political commitment to, as well as degree of identification in, the legal system. This diversity makes highly implausible the existence of conceptual agreement over the shared activity of legal officials. In addition, the disparate composition of the class of legal officials makes it most unlikely that fellow bureaucrats will be acquainted with whatever mutual intentions and plans may exist. This stands in the way of epistemic agreement among legal officials. The combination of conceptual disagreement and epistemic disagreement is also bound to jeopardise the possibility of commitment, be it conceptual, epistemic, or practical. This lack of agreement and commitment emerges not only when we consider the workings of remote departments within a legal system, but also the functioning of specific segments of the same department: even functionaries performing similar institutional roles and tasks need not have shared beliefs about, or any commitment to, their mutual agendas. The effect is that, besides being merely possible and not necessary,

---

[29] See N. Smith, "The Law as a Social Practice: Are Shared Activities at the Foundations of Law?" (2006) 12 *Legal Theory*, pp. 265–292, at 278–85.

[30] As Smith notes, in modern legal institutions, legal officials are not just legislators and judges, they also include functionaries working in "many administrative agencies that have the authority to issue regulations that we have no reason not to take to be law"; *idem*, note 29 *supra*, p. 285.

no commonality of objectives extends – of necessity – to all the officials, especially where they occupy different hierarchical levels and have diverse roles within the same institutional body. The degree of agreement and commitment-holding in a legal system is, then, limited, and falls short of what would be needed to have a shared co-operative activity. The conclusion to be drawn from these remarks is that the model of shared co-operative activity can hardly be said to apply to such a large-scale and temporarily extended social practice as the law.

The critique that we have just looked at highlights two problems that we encounter if we follow Coleman in taking acceptance to be the source of the normativity of the master rule: the problem of the limited scope of such normativity (since it only applies to the officials and what they can endorse) and that of the oneness of mind and purpose a shared co-operative activity requires (a commitment the officials themselves cannot be expected to have, let alone all the other people who are subject to the law). These are problems which the institutional theory of law needs to work out before it can completely and fully account in an adequate way for the normativity of the master rule and thus of law itself. But let us turn now to the second of three such accounts that conventionalism offers, as mentioned above.

5.3.2 The Master Rule and Co-ordination Conventions

MacCormick's account of the normativity of the master rule can, alternatively, be made complete, from a conventionalist approach, by recourse to the idea of a co-ordination convention.[31] This is understood as a convention arising in the effort to find a practical solution to pervasive large-scale co-ordination problems, by which are meant situations in which it makes more sense for agents to act in concert than for each to act in the particular way that seems most rational or reasonable to him or her *personally*, regardless of whatever everyone else is doing.[32] For a solution to such co-ordination problems, especially where a spontaneous *ad hoc* agreement is unlikely, we are better off relying on a conventional practice.

There are different accounts in the literature of the normativity of the master rule as based upon a co-ordination convention. Here, I will consider the account offered by Govert den Hartog, who explicitly frames this as a complement to

---

[31] Among those who rely on the idea of a coordination convention as a key tool of legal interpretation are C. Gans, "The Normativity of Law and its Coordinative Function" (1981) 16 *Israel Law Review*, pp. 333–349 (1981), Postema, "Co-ordination and Convention at the Foundations of Law", note 28 *supra*, E. Lagerspetz, *The Opposite Mirrors* (Dordrecht: Kluwer, 1995), and G. den Hartog, *Mutual Expectations* (Dordrecht: Kluwer, 2002).

[32] One such situation (where co-ordination comes into play) is the road, and the problem can be exemplified by way of our choosing to drive on the right side or the left side of the road: as much as we may each have a preference of our own for one or the other of these two choices, we recognise that it makes even more sense (it is more reasonable, rational, or fitting) to have an agreement that will make our overall driving experience smoother and safer than if we each made our choice independently of the other drivers (and of pedestrians).

the institutional theory of law,[33] and who singles out three basic elements of a co-ordination convention: transparent patterns of mutual expectations, cooperative dispositions among people within a social group, and interdependent reasons.[34] Which is to say that a co-ordination convention thus construed emerges when, among agents who have co-operative dispositions, certain patterns of mutual expectations arise, which are supported by interdependent reasons: for agents who are willing to cooperate – namely, who have co-operative dispositions – such patterns of mutual expectations will provide reasons to act accordingly, precisely on the assumption that other agents will do the same, and this facilitates social co-ordination. By virtue of this capacity to foster social co-ordination among agents with a co-operative disposition, patterns of mutual expectations evolve into conventional solutions to co-ordination problems, in the process gaining the status of genuine co-ordination conventions. And in situations in which social co-ordination is regarded by the agents concerned as an essential precondition which makes it possible to pursue certain common goals and interests successfully, a co-ordination convention can give rise to reasons understood not just as hypothetical imperatives but as unconditional or categorical ones; that is, it can give rise to authentic obligations. Once a pattern of mutual expectations of co-operative behaviour has taken root, then, people willing to co-operate will have entrenched reasons to live up to the same expectations.[35]

The major point here is that the master rule can itself be understood as a complex co-ordination convention, and, by so framing the master rule, we can account for its normativity: this normativity is grounded in the legitimate mutual expectations that this rule, by virtue of its function in co-ordinating social interaction, can generate among participants who have a co-operative disposition. It is, in other words, a normativity grounded in the ability of the master rule to serve a co-ordinative function, in that such co-ordination gives rise to the mutual expectation that everyone within a social group will follow the master rule and the standards validated by it. While there needs to be an interest in co-ordination in order for this mutual expectation to arise, once the co-ordination emerges and gives rise to a corresponding layer of mutual expectations, a self-reinforcing process will have been established, in that a sense of mutual trust will spread among the participants in the practice, this being the practice of law. And the normative force of the master rule, once it has taken root, extends to all the standards validated by the same rule: the standards established under the law should be observed (if for no other reason) because they are validated by a rule that says they should be. The standards validated by the master

[33] See den Hartog, *Mutual Expectations*, note 32 *supra*, pp. vii–ix.

[34] By *co-operative disposition*, den Hartog means the attitude of those who are "prepared to honour each other's justified expectations"; ibid., note 32 *supra*, p. 20, and, by *interdependent reasons*, he means reasons that exist whenever "people intend to act in a certain way, only because they believe the others to intend to act in the same way as well"; ibid., note 32 *supra*, p. 6.

[35] As den Hartog puts it, "the underlying form of an obligatory norm… is this: I expect you to cooperate in the production of a common good, because I trust you and it would be untrustworthy or unfair to betray my trust"; *idem*, note 32 *supra*, p. 43 & pp. 32–37.

rule can become normative – and, consequently the law as a whole can, too – by virtue of their connection with an entity (the master rule) which is itself normative, and, indeed, by virtue of their being an issuance of this rule.

The centrality which this account of the normativity of the master rule recognises for mutual expectations suggests on the face of it a good fit with MacCormick's account, which also brings out the central role of mutual expectations in this regard.[36] This coherence might prompt one working from an institutionalist approach to look to contemporary studies of co-ordination conventions in an attempt to complete MacCormick's unfinished effort. Yet, as has forcefully been argued in the literature, an appeal to co-ordination conventions ultimately fails to explain the normativity of the master rule adequately. So let us briefly consider three of the arguments put forward in this regard, and then close this section with a further argument which questions whether an appeal to co-ordination conventions really is coherent with the institutional theory of law.

The first problem involved in modelling the normativity of the master rule on the normativity of co-ordination conventions is simply that the master rule is not a co-ordination convention. True, the master rule may facilitate co-ordination, especially among officials, but this is not its primary purpose, for here we have a practice primarily devoted to *defining* and *delimiting* the legal system, instead; what distinguishes the master rule from all other legal standards is the fact that it contains the criteria of legality. Any role that the master rule may play in sustaining social co-ordination should not obscure the fact that this function is secondary to, and contingent on, its primary and essential function of *constituting* the legal domain. Thus, the master rule's normativity is properly grounded by explaining – in the first place – its constitutive force (the force associated with its primary and essential function), and whether, in this way, we can also account for its co-ordinative force, this can, at best, be considered a beneficial side-effect, but not as the reason why the rule itself has come into being.[37]

This connects to a second problem involved in laying emphasis on the ability of the master rule to co-ordinate social interaction, because it is in this way that we end up obscuring several other functions of the law, the domain both defined and delimited by the master rule: unlike co-ordination, these other functions are *essential* to the law, and they cannot be reduced to co-ordination, either.[38] Although there are occasions when the law can serve a helpful co-ordination function, it is really an impoverished and distorted view of the law that sees it primarily as a device by which a social group can handle the pervasive and persistent co-ordination

---

[36]Thus, for example, MacCormick claims that norms "emerge from practices based on mutual expectations and beliefs"; *idem*, *Institutions of Law*, note 5 *supra*, p. 23, and though he is referring here to *informal* norms, the claim also extends to formal ones – or at least this seems to be the sense of his overall argument; ibid., pp. 22–24; see, also, pp. 39–45.

[37]This critique can be found in A. Marmor, *Positive Law and Objective Values* (Oxford: Oxford University Press, 2001), pp. 1–24, among other places.

[38]This critique is developed in some detail in L. Green, "Positivism and Conventionalism" (1999) 22 *Canadian Journal of Law and Jurisprudence*, pp. 35–52.

problems which it is bound to have. Securing co-ordination is thus a less central function of the law than contemporary students of co-ordination conventions think. This much can be appreciated by considering, for example, that only a sub-set of legal standards arise in response to our need for co-ordination. Some of our most fundamental legal provisions are, instead, rooted in interests and concerns different from co-ordination, and deeper than it, such as a concern with the kind of society in which one would like to live. It thus seems like to be an arbitrary selection to focus on the co-ordinative function of law and ground its normativity in the ability of legal provisions to achieve such co-ordination.[39]

A third problem, as discussed in the literature, is that an account of the sort which we are looking at – in which the master rule's normativity is made to rest on a co-ordination convention – "blurs the distinction between what law is, and what counts as law in a particular order".[40] This is because a co-ordination convention does not determine the nature of a concept but, instead, serves a social function. Construing the master rule as a co-ordination convention would thus amount to denying that this rule has any part in determining the concept of law. The master rule *qua* co-ordination convention can serve certain functions within a legal system – primarily, the function of co-ordinating the activity of officials and other users of law – but it cannot say anything about the nature of the law itself, which consequently is defined independently of the master rule. This conclusion should be of major concern to institutional theorists, for it implies a clear departure from the roots of the theory, which lie in the tradition of legal thought inaugurated by Hart, in which the nature of law is made to depend on the features of the master rule.

This last point introduces a final consideration, which is that if we are working from within an institutional theory and rely on a co-ordination convention to ground the normativity of law, we will fail to achieve consistency with the Hartian component of the same theory: an appeal to co-ordination conventions makes the normativity of the master rule a *moral* normativity; Hart's legal positivism, in contrast, would call for an account which showed the normativity of law to, instead, be social, not moral. This is a point that needs to be expanded on. If we ground the normativity of the master rule in a co-ordination convention, then we will have brought into our account the constituent ideas of mutual expectation and of a co-operative disposition. Yet neither of these ideas is morally neutral: they both rest on values and principles – fidelity, trustworthiness, mutuality, reciprocity, reliance, fairness, justice – the nature of which is distinctively moral, for it takes a moral argument to clarify their content and assess their force.[41] Because moral considerations and

[39]This point is well summarised by Coleman's proposition that in so far as "coordination conventions are solutions to games in which the participants' *ex ante* preferences have a specific structure, or are ordered in certain specific ways", conceiving the rule of recognition as a co-ordination convention "would place an arbitrary and baseless constraint in our concept of law"; *idem*, *The Practice of Principle*, note 4 *supra*, p. 94.

[40]Marmor, "How Law is Like Chess", note 2 *supra*, pp. 347–371, at 357.

[41]This aspect clearly emerges from den Hartog's discussion: see, for example, *idem*, *Mutual Expectations*, note 31 *supra*, pp. 43–46.

arguments figure centrally into the idea of a co-ordination convention, using this idea as a basis upon which to account for the normativity of the master rule is tantamount to making morality a necessary component of the normativity of law itself, a normativity that, in this way, ultimately winds up being constructed as moral. This makes it difficult to show how co-ordination conventions might make something normative without appealing to moral considerations, which, in turn, means that, if the normativity of the master rule is made to rest on its status as a co-ordination convention, it will be difficult to remain faithful to the Hartian project of explaining the normativity of law as being fundamentally *social*, in a way that is insulated and conceptually distinct from moral normativity. Thus, an institutional theorist who configures the master rule as a co-ordination convention must consequently accept to part ways with Hart's account of the normativity of law.[42]

One might reply here that this does not really pose a dilemma for an advocate of the institutional theory of law. After all, MacCormick had recently insisted that the trajectory of his legal thought has been away from some elements of the legal positivism expounded by H.L.A. Hart [. . .] that formed the backcloth to the argument in *Legal Reasoning and Legal Theory*,[43] so much so that he has described his legal theory as "post-positivistic".[44] This suggests that he would not necessarily object to a move which severed the institutional theory from Hart's legal theory.[45] However, this conclusion should not be taken for granted. MacCormick does not quite say that, in putting forward his institutional theory, he intended to break with Hart's jurisprudence altogether and pave the way for a non-positivistic concept of law. In fact, the very expression "post-positivistic" carries the ambiguity of an umbrella term referring to a range of legal theories whose only common denominator lies in their stemming from legal positivism while simultaneously distancing themselves from it. The term thus describes a theory that continues to bear a connection to legal positivism, even though the connection is not so strong as to make the theory entirely traceable to legal positivism. This is quite different to what happens when reliance is placed on the model of co-ordination conventions: the model marks a drastic departure from the Hartian origins of the institutional theory, for it cannot be reduced to the positivist tradition of legal thought pioneered by Hart, at least not as far as the account of normativity is concerned. This conclusion contradicts the widespread and traditional view that MacCormick champions a revised form of Hart's legal theory. And we should, accordingly, be cautious in constructing the

[42]For a discussion of the non-positivist outcome entailed by an account of the normativity of law based upon the idea of a co-ordination convention, see den Hartog, *Mutual Expectations*, note 31 *supra*, pp. 154–213.

[43]Neil MacCormick, *Rhetoric and the Rule of Law* (Oxford: Oxford University Press, 2005), p. 1.

[44]Ibid., p. 2.

[45]The same line of reasoning can be found in MacCormick's assessment that "the institutional theory in its present form, though originally developed within the strand of thought known as 'legal positivism', is not now a 'positivist' theory. Whether or not anyone chooses to class it as belonging within the tradition of 'natural law', it is certainly post-positivistic"; *idem*, *Institutions of Law*, note 5 *supra*, p. 5.

institutional theory of law as set clearly apart from the Hartian tradition. In short, if we follow the critique that there is no real dilemma involved in an institutional theorist relying on the idea of a co-ordination convention to explain the normativity of the master rule, we must also consider the deep implications that this has for the nature and the classification of institutional theory itself.

5.3.3 The Master Rule as a Constitutive Convention

A third conventionalist account of the master rule's normativity invokes the idea of a constitutive convention, in terms of which the master rule and its normativity are defined. It is argued on this account, which can be found, in particular, in the work of Andrei Marmor, that Hart's rule of recognition ought to be construed not as a co-ordination convention but as a constitutive one.[46] Constitutive conventions are conventions that define, or constitute, what a practice is and how to participate in it. Conventions of this kind emerge in response to various social problems and reflect deep and complex human needs. A typical example of this type of convention – an example that can help us to understand better the nature, structure, and function of constitutive conventions – is provided by the set of rules that define the game of chess and tell us how chess is played. The rules of chess cannot be reconstructed as co-ordination conventions, because the activity which they set up only came into being with the rules themselves, and thus there was no co-ordination problem of any kind that might have pre-existed the introduction of chess. The rules of chess are not primarily there to co-ordinate, then, but, instead, to define a practice born in response to a pervasive human need, namely, the need for games, a need that people in different societies at different times have felt and responded to by designing a variety of games. Similarly, constitutive conventions are conventional rules that set up a practice arising in response to a range of human needs. This is something these which rules do by framing the practice around some basic values and criteria of success or excellence, and ultimately by defining the structure and nature of the same practice. And, as much as constitutive conventions do not exhaust the practice which they define, they are, nonetheless, essential to it and thus lie at its foundation. It is Marmor's argument that Hart's rule of recognition is best interpreted as the convention by which the practice of law is constituted. In fact, the rule of recognition defines what the law *is* in a given society, sets out the fundamental legal values, and has a decisive part in establishing the very structure and nature of law. This makes the rule of recognition a typical example of a constitutive convention: it is, in particular, the convention constitutive of the law.[47]

---

[46]See Marmor, *Positive Law and Objective Values*, note 37 *supra*, pp. 1–24; *idem*, "How Law is Like Chess", note 2 *supra*, pp. 353–363.

[47]See Marmor, "How Law is Like Chess", note 2 *supra*, p. 368, for a paradigmatic statement to this effect.

Marmor's theoretical framework carries a twofold advantage: it explains the primary function of the rule of recognition, widely thought of as the device which establishes the boundaries of the legal domain; and it enables one also to acknowledge that the law serves more functions than just making social co-ordination possible. This twofold advantage over alternative conventionalist models might tempt an institutional theorist to rely on Marmor's account of constitutive conventions to explain in what sense the master rule can be regarded as normative, arguing that the master rule's normativity essentially boils down to the normativity of a constitutive convention, to wit, that the master rule is normative as a constitutive convention of the law. But this, too, is an account that falls short of expectations.

In fact, there are important normative features of constitutive conventions that Marmor's account leaves unexplained, and these shortcomings are bound to carry over into the institutional theory if it should rely on that account to explain the normativity of the master rule. There are, in particular, two related questions which Marmor leaves unexplained that arise out of two basic characteristics which his account ascribes to constitutive conventions and their normativity. The first of these characteristics is that constitutive conventions do not only constitute or *define* certain practices, but also *guide* the behaviour of those who take part in them.[48] If we apply this dual function to law, we will see that only in so far as we have a reason to participate *ab ovo* in this practice (the practice of law) will we have a legal obligation to behave in accordance with the directives emanating from or validated by the master rule. This legal "ought" thus appears to be conditional: it is an obligation which we ought to acknowledge on the condition that we accept to take part in the practice of law. But, if this is the case, the legal "ought" arising under the master rule does not differ in kind from the duties which we incur by taking part in other more circumscribed practices, such as games, which we typically take part in upon a voluntary basis, which makes the duties so incurred conditional to our accepting to play the game as willing participants. Marmor's account of the legal "ought", thus, is ultimately based upon the assumption that the law as a practice is akin to and conceptually continuous with games. The second characteristic which Marmor ascribes to the normativity of constitutive conventions applies specifically to the master rule itself: this rule sets up an obligation only for persons who already have, from the outset, a reason to participate in the practice of law;[49] there is nothing to explain why someone should have such an obligation, aside from the fact of his or her being such a participant to begin with. On Marmor's account, then, the reasons for participating in the practice of law – or in the "game" of law, if we are to follow the logic of the account – are not provided by the master rule or by any other legal

---

[48] As Marmor puts it, constitutive conventions "have a dual function: they both determine what constitutes the practice, and prescribe modes of conduct within it". It is the second function that bears directly on normativity, in that constitutive conventions are regarded as normative by virtue of their ability to prescribe certain modes of conduct; *idem*, "How Law is Like Chess", note 2 *supra*, p. 350. See, also, *idem*, *Positive Law and Objective Values*, note 37 *supra*, pp. 29–30.

[49] This second characteristic is outlined in Marmor, *Positive Law and Objective Values*, note 37 *supra*, pp. 25–34.

standard, but, instead, derive from moral and political considerations. Because the "ought" that comes with our participation in the legal realm is not itself legal, but is, in contrast, moral and political, it cannot be grounded in the master rule, and, indeed, it goes beyond the scope of this rule, which is a legal device, not a moral and political construction. The obligation to follow the law, in other words, comes not from the convention that constitutes what the law is, but from external practices whose nature is not necessarily conventional. In sum, the master rule constitutes the legal domain and grounds the duties of participants in the law, but it does not establish reasons why we should be participants therein in the first place.

These characteristics of the master rule in Marmor's account are such that his framework will not help the institutional theory make much progress in explaining the normativity of the rule. In fact, Marmor assumes that law and games are conceptually continuous, thereby making it so that the obligations to which the law gives rise (much like the ones a game does) turn out to be conditional, rather than categorical. This is not what MacCormick thinks, for whom legal obligations are, instead, categorical.[50] And he has good reasons for taking this view: conceiving the law as a game and modelling its normativity on that of games does not do justice to the normative claims the law makes on us. Aside from disregarding that law affects our lives in a much deeper and more encompassing way than any game can, this analogy is also problematical because it implies that we – precisely as participants in a *game*, the game of law – are bound to follow the directives of law only on the condition of our being *willing* to do so, and so (on this analogy) we can step outside the law just as easily as we can call ourselves out of a game. This does not square with the practice of law as we know it. The law concerns everyone within a territory, whether or not this or that person wants to be subject to the law and is willing to take part in the practice; it is not our choice, in other words, to decide for ourselves individually whether or not we will comply with the law, whose prescriptions apply regardless of any reluctance anyone may have regarding whether they fall under the scope of the law. The obligations the law claims to create for us as persons subject to the law are thus distinctively different from the ones a game sets up for its players. There is no such escape from the obligations of law as there is from those of a game, whose normativity is conditional upon our decision to get into the game and our willingness to keep playing it, in such a way that nothing will prevent us from leaving the game at any time (in most games anyway) and thus from relieving ourselves of the obligations incurred under the constitutive rules of the game. We do not *choose* to be bound by the law, as we, instead, typically choose to take part in a game: the law is *categorically* binding, not conditionally so, meaning that it applies regardless of what we may each think about a given provision. For these reasons, it seems misleading to model legal obligations on the kinds of obligations that we come under by way of the rules constitutive of a game. For the same reasons,

---

[50]See MacCormick, *Institutions of Law*, note 5 *supra*, pp. 51–55 & 103–199.

it seems that Marmor's account of the legal "ought" cannot be imported into the institutional theory of law in an effort to explain the normativity of the master rule, because, in that case, the theory would have to let go of one of its basic insights, namely, that the law binds categorically and not just conditionally: an institutional theorist must either put Marmor's account aside or revise one of the pillars of the institutional theory itself.

Likewise problematical is the fact that Marmor does not deal exhaustively with the question of what it is that makes it obligatory for us to take part in the practice of law: his remarks on this question are not specific enough to give us any true insight into the grounds of the normativity of the master rule; he simply comments that our obligation to follow legal standards, including those contained in the master rule, are grounded in certain moral and political considerations. But these remain unspecified and thus do not really help us to explain the normativity of law, especially as we do not know what it is that confers moral and political value on the law, or how it is that moral and political values can generate reinforced reasons for action. So, while Marmor's inquiry into constitutive conventions accounts – in an interesting way – for the social existence of the master rule, it does not go sufficiently far to clarify the normativity of the master rule: it only hints at what might account for our obligation to follow the law. For this reason, drawing on Marmor's work to interpret the master rule as a constitutive convention will not advance in any significant way an effort to explain how the rule can become normative: such a research avenue will not make it possible to tackle the very question that MacCormick leaves open. It is thus a distinctively limited contribution that Marmor's work can offer to the institutional theory in its attempt to explain the normativity of the master rule.

5.4 Conclusion

This chapter has taken a critical look at MacCormick's account of the normativity of law. We started out by observing that his institutional theory attributes a central role in this regard to the master rule, viewed as a social convention which lies at the foundation of law. This makes the institutional theory a variant of legal conventionalism. But as a conventionalist account of the normativity of law, the institutional theory faces the abiding problem of explaining how facts can become normative, considering that the master rule, posited as the cornerstone of the normativity of law, is, in essence, a social fact, and facts do not, in themselves, have anything normative about them. It was argued that MacCormick does not address this problem exhaustively, and so we are left with the task of finding an account of the normativity of law that holds its own and also coheres with the basic tenets of the institutional theory of law. The most logical place to turn to for help in this effort is the conventionalist approach, where at least three markedly different accounts of the normativity of law can be found.

It was argued that none of these accounts is of genuine help to MacCormick's institutional theory. On the first of these accounts, the normativity of the master rule is based upon our acceptance of the law. The problem here is that few of us can be expected to actually accept the law in full, and so we end up saying (on this account) that only those parts of the law are normative that gain acceptance, and for only those people who do happen to accept that the law is normative or binding. And at the same time – owing, in part, to the limited scope that this account allows for normativity in law, with its exclusive focus on the *officials*' endorsement of the law – normativity as acceptance really misinterprets the legal enterprise as a whole.

Next, we looked at the conception of the master rule as a co-ordination convention. One consequence of this approach is that it entails a break with the Hartian tradition of legal thought, and this is something which MacCormick might be reluctant to do. But, aside from this, there are three related problems involved in conceiving the master rule as normative in the way that a co-ordination convention is normative: we end up obscuring the constitutive role that the master rule plays in relation to law; we get an impoverished view of the functions of law; and we reduce the task of the master rule to that of identifying and validating the relevant standards within a specific legal system, thereby disregarding the essential role that the rule plays in shaping the concept of law.

The final account discussed understands the master rule as a constitutive convention, and it, accordingly, derives the normativity of law from that of constitutive conventions. What is normative about constitutive conventions is that, in constituting the practice to which they apply, they at the same time regulate the behaviour of those who take part in the practice. But then two related problems arise, which do not seem to have an adequate answer. For one the account analogises law to games (these being typical examples of constitutive practices), but the analogy yields a picture that distorts the practice of law by its very description of law as a practice, which is to say that games are practices which we typically choose to take part in and can just as freely withdraw from, in contrast to the law, which comes into our lives in a much more pervasive way, even intrusively, and is generally not something whose regulation we can avoid or put on hold. This analogy (by its suggestion of an opt-out scheme) puts pressure on the account to explain how it is that we come to have an obligation to obey the law, and this is where the second problem arises, since at this point the account invokes moral and political considerations generally. Here, one would expect an analytical treatment of the question, but none is offered, and thus the institutional theory ends up providing an account of the normativity of law which is as loose as the account that can be obtained by relying on the idea of a constitutive convention, with its important, albeit inarticulate, relation to morality, which we are left to work out for ourselves.

The overall assessment here is that we have yet to see a satisfactory way to account for the normativity of law on a conventionalist approach. Nor does MacCormick's institutional theory, for its part, offer an exhaustive account of such normativity. This means that the institutional theory is not yet a comprehensive theory of law: there is at least one gap the theory has not filled, since it still needs to thrash out the crucial question of why and how the law comes to be normative. But even with this shortcoming, the institutional theory, in the version defended by MacCormick in his recent work, offers an insightful approach upon which to tackle some of the more debated issues in jurisprudence today. And so, as much as MacCormick's theory may be partial and may not fully penetrate the question of the ground of the normative force of law, a critical reflection on the theory may just be the way to proceed in working toward such an objective.

Part IV
Jurisprudence

Chapter 6
Some Reflections on the Relationship Between Law and Morality – Neil MacCormick's Point of View

Marina Lalatta Costerbosa

6.1 On Labels: Distinguishing Natural Law from Positivist Theories

I will start with a general, trivial premise: labels are only labels. And it is necessary "to identify the real meaning of concepts – as Antonio Gramsci wrote in his *Quaderni del carcere* – because, under the same hat, different heads can be hidden".[1]

In his paper, *"Natural" Law Revisited*[2] Ronald Dworkin underlines the irrelevance of labels and, in particular, the controversial and notorious label of "Natural Lawyer". The *incipit* of the paper is clear:

> Everyone likes categories, and legal philosophers like them very much. So we spend a good deal of time, not all of it profitably, labelling ourselves and the theories of law we defend. One label, however, is particularly dreaded: no one wants to be called a natural lawyer.

But, Dworkin goes on:

> If the crude description of natural law I just gave is correct, that any theory which makes the content of law sometimes depending on the correct answer to some moral questions is a natural law theory, then I am guilty of natural law.

My thesis is that the same statement can, in a certain sense, describe MacCormick's philosophy of law. Provided, of course, we do not assume that what defines iusnaturalism is the claim that a true law both exists and is accessible to human knowledge, and that it expresses transcendent and objective values: values independent of

M. Lalatta Costerbosa (✉)
Department of Philosophy, Università di Bologna, Bologna, Italy
e-mail: marina.lalatta@unibo.it

[1]See A. Gramsci, *Quaderni del carcere*, critical edition of the Istituto Gramsci, vol 2, edited by Valentino Gerratana, (Turin: Einaudi, 1975), p. 1411.

[2]R. Dworkin, "'Natural' Law Revisited", (1982) 34 *University of Florida Law Review*, pp. 165–188, now collected in J. Finnis (ed), *Natural Law*, vol. II, (New York: New York University Press, 1991), pp. 187–210.

A.J. Menéndez, J.E. Fossum (eds.), *Law and Democracy in Neil MacCormick's Legal and Political Theory*, Law and Philosophy Library 93,
DOI 10.1007/978-90-481-8942-7_6, © Springer Science+Business Media B.V. 2011

human will and interest.[3] But if we agree with Dworkin's general definition of iusnaturalism, it is possible, in my opinion, to see a convergence of the two philosophers in this respect. But this is a generic assumption which needs more explanation, if only because the boundary between iusnaturalism and legal positivism has, through time, become more and more difficult to draw.[4]

With this in mind, this chapter will focus on the relationship between law and morality from Neil MacCormick's point of view. I will summarise some aspects of his theory of law with specific regard to this topic. Then, I will concentrate on some elements which, in this respect, seem to me to be problematical. Later on, I will deal with the concept of *reasonableness* in order to show the relevance and non-relativistic character of the conceptual connection between law and morality in Neil MacCormick's thought. His self-definition as "post-positivist" is, perhaps, compatible with the above-mentioned weak definition of the "natural lawyer", and this not simply because it rejects too austere a version of "legal positivism": a legalistic idea of "legal positivism". My thesis is that MacCormick accepts the idea of a conceptual connection between law and morality, but he considers morality in a relativistic way and, at the same time, maintains the principle of reasonableness as a principle of correctness for the law. These two statements about morality, however, cannot go together. We must choose either one or the other. And I am convinced that morality implies a claim of universalisability, otherwise it is not morality at all. Furthermore, "brutal relativism" – to borrow Bernard Williams' expression – must be rejected. In this light, if morality also means reasonableness (as MacCormick himself seems to suggest), the connection between law and morality is necessary and has a normative force: it is not true, any more that it is legitimate, to identify every sort of ethical or ideological content with the demands of morality as such.

These initial considerations on labels are, in part, an *excusatio non petita*, but perhaps they are also helpful indications about the content of this chapter and do not necessarily mean that one is looking at labels rather than theories. On the one hand, it is true: we must be careful, as reflection on labels can be a great waste of time. On the other hand, such reflection can tell us something which is not so irrelevant. The debate on the distinction between natural lawyers and legal positivists is a debate on the concept of law and on its relationship with morality. If labels are an outcome and not merely the main object of reflection, they can be a way of clearing up ideas and positions.

MacCormick tells us something in this perspective. Every label always has vague applications, to wit, we first of all have to define the concept, and only *then* can we apply it to different cases. This is true for the labels "natural law theory" and "legal positivism".[5] For this reason, one may argue that these two theories can be interpreted as being convergent, even if differences still remain (*ibidem*, 178). On this

---

[3]N. MacCormick and O. Weinberger, *Il Diritto come Istituzione*, translated and edited by Massimo La Torre, (Milan: Giuffrè, 1990), p. 7.

[4]Ibid., p. 178.

[5]Ibid., p. 159.

revisional perspective, MacCormick defines the "law's 'positive' character as nothing other than this very characteristic that is laid down through intentional human acts aimed at regulating human conduct. For *jus positivum* means 'law laid down', and 'positive law' is *jus positivum* translated into English".[6] And goes on to say that:

> The school of thought known as 'legal positivism', at any rate in its more austere and rigorous forms, absolutely excludes the possibility that there is any moral minimum that is necessary to the existence of law as such. The positive character of law is all there is to it. Conversely, the question of the moral value of obedience to law is always an open one. According to that conception of legal positivism, the present version of institutional theory is non-positivist, or, if you wish, 'post-positivist'. Conversely, if the universe of human thought is necessarily divided into two mutually exclusive camps, such that anyone who admits any moral minimum to be essential to the existence of law belongs outside the positivist camp and in that of its rival, this theory belongs in that rival camp. Believers in this two-way-divided universe of jurisprudence assign to the category 'natural law' any theory that fails their austere test for positivism. Such believers will therefore characterize the present work [MacCormick's work] as a form of 'natural law'.[7]

And he further adds that:

> It is perhaps most sensible to say that (...) it is post-positivist, if not anti-positivist.[8]

I will try to defend this conclusion, but not in the same sense. Or what is the same, the reason for defining MacCormick's concept of law as a form of natural law theory lies *not exclusively* in the assumption that it is not an austere version of legal positivism. This sort of definition is not so decisive by itself, but *can* be significant if it indicates a deeper comprehension of the relationship between law and morality, and, above all, of the idea of morality as such. I have the impression, in other words, that there is a more relevant reason – not only a negative reason, but also a conceptual one, too – for saying that this theory of law is a particular and very interesting form of natural law theory. My idea is that if we try to discover what is behind the fight for (about?) labels, we will find that MacCormick is a iusnaturalist, and not just a post-positivist. Naturally, he rejects a trivial form of positivism, but, in his theory, it is also possible, I think, to find some points which make him not so relativist as he declares himself to be. He argues for a particular concept of correctness, a conceptual connection between law and morality, and a principle of reasonableness (Section 6.2), which corresponds to a principle of rationality that is necessary if we do not want to abandon the attempt to pursue freedom as an end (Section 6.3). But I think that he is not so close to Finnis on what concerns the priority of what is good over what is right (as MacCormick himself underlines in his review of Finnis' masterpiece) (Section 6.4).

These three points go in the direction of iusnaturalism instead of moderate positivism or post-positivism. And, above all, in this perspective, MacCormick's view of the connection of law and morality seems to me necessary and critical, because

---

[6] N. MacCormick, *Institutions of Law*, (Oxford: Oxford University Press, 2007), p. 243.

[7] Ibid., p. 278.

[8] Ibid., p. 279.

it tells us something crucial for defining the concept of law. Notwithstanding this, with regard to the relationship between law and morality, MacCormick's work does present some ambiguities; and this is what I will proceed to elucidate.

6.2 Law and Morality

I think that it is true that debates on labels and discussions grounded on rigorous dichotomies "are rarely revealing of any important truth".[9] But, in this case, I suspect that one important truth is at issue. The relationship between law and morality, the problem that is at the bottom of this whole discussion, is a central one, or even *the* central one, when one is talking about law and the concept thereof. This is the theoretical question hidden underneath the labels. Law and morality have important characteristics in common. First of all, both concern obligations: they are normative orders. However, their nature is conceptually different. Morality has a non-institutional structure, while law is an institutional fact. The normative order of morality has to do with individual autonomy, with choices and sets of principles elaborated by self-governing individuals. The normative order of law is sustained by political authority, namely, the state and its coercive power.[10] In this respect, we can underline that, while morality is autonomous, law is heteronomous:

> It confronts each moral agent with categorical requirements in the form of duties, obligations, and prohibitions that purport to bind the agent regardless of the agent's own rational will as an autonomous moral being. The law's demands of the autonomous agent purport to bind the agent in a heteronomous way. Law is (in this sense) heteronomous, as well as authoritative and institutional; it thus stands in clear conceptual contrast to morality, which is autonomous, discursive, and controversial.[11]

This conceptual divergence is also related to a simple circumstance. Authoritative texts play a key role in legal argumentation, given that they are a fixed starting-point for interpretation, adjudication, deliberation and so on. Morality as autonomy recognises no authoritative texts at all.[12] But this does not mean that the two spheres (law and morality) do not overlap at a significant point. The point is reasoning, practical reasoning, to wit, that what constitutes their common source of correctness. As we read in *Institutions of Law* (on this point very close to Alexy's *Theorie der juristischen Argumentation*):[13]

---

[9]Ibid., p. 278.

[10]Ibid., p. 4.

[11]Ibid., p. 255. See, also, MacCormick, "The Concept of Law and *The Concept of Law*", in: R. P. George (ed), *The Autonomy of Law. Essays on Legal Positivism*, (Oxford: Clarendon Press, 1996), pp. 163–193, at 170–171.

[12]MacCormick, *Institutions of Law*, note 6 *supra*, p. 259.

[13]MacCormick, *Legal Theory and Legal Reasoning*, (Oxford: Clarendon Press, 1978), p. 304; *idem* & Weinberger, *Il Diritto come Istituzione*, note 3 *supra*, p. 234; MacCormick, *Rhetoric and the Rule of Law*, (Oxford: Oxford University Press, 2005), p. 99; and *idem*, *Institutions of Law*, note 6 *supra*, p. 260.

> That legal reasoning is a sub-species of practical reasoning, and hence either strongly analogous to, or even a specialized form of, moral reasoning, is true (. . .) To produce justifying reasons for one's decision, although these include legal norms and precedents, requires one to interpret the norms and precedents in the light of background principles and values, hence the interpretative reasoning is also in part moral reasoning. (. . .) All this is highly important, and a necessary corrective to a merely narrow legalism. (. . .) The more we take legal decision-making to be a public matter drawing on public sources, the less we force agents into the position of having to knuckle under the moral decisions of particular judges and other legal officials. (. . .) Law, by virtue of the way in which it addresses the moral agent *ab extra* is always at least relatively heteronomous. That is why law and morality are conceptually distinct.[14]

This is a very important point for my argument. The fundamental idea is that law implies a claim of moral correctness that has a procedural and contingent nature: it depends, according to certain standards of equality, on both the community and its principles. Here, the idea of an objective morality is rejected and the idea of a discursive and interpersonal morality is defended. Moreover, this sort of morality has a necessary connection with law in itself. Against moral realism, on the one hand, and legalism, on the other, the two domains go hand in hand if we define morality as critical morality and think that law implies a claim of not merely methodological correctness. The basis of the claim to correctness of the law is, ultimately, practical reason, with both its limits and its capabilities. In this sense, MacCormick defends a mid-way and partial relativistic position between the two extremes of Dworkin and Alf Ross. From MacCormick's perspective, Dworkin is ultra-rationalist because of his "one-answer" thesis, whereas Ross is anti-rationalist, because he thinks that justice is not a normative question, but a question of force. According to Ross, making laws or justice is like beating upon the table; it is only a question of efficiency.[15] The "space" between Dworkin and Ross is what interests MacCormick more, since it is there that we find the law and the possibility of its *correctness based upon the idea of practical reasoning.*

MacCormick (with Alexy) points out that law implies a claim to correctness, and therefore it involves a performative self-contradiction if it implements an unjust conduct of agency.

> The idea of legislation passed without even a pretension to correctness is a kind of absurdity.[16]

But what does correctness mean in this case?

These considerations on morality are not as univocal as they seem to be, because, according to MacCormick, they are consistent with other (and I think, very different) statements. I am referring to his essay on *Natural Law and the Separation of Law and Morals*, in which MacCormick underlines that this "necessary connection

[14] MacCormick, *Institutions of Law*, note 6 *supra*, pp. 260–261.

[15] A. Ross. *On Law and Justice*, (London: Steven & Sons, 1958), Italian translation edited by Giacomo Gavazzi, *Il Diritto e Giustizia*, (Turin: Einaudi, 1965), p. 297.

[16] MacCormick, "The Separation of Law and Morals", in: Robert P. George (ed), *Natural Law Theory. Contemporary Essays*, (Oxford: Clarendon Press, 1992), pp. 105–133, at 112.

between law and morality (...) does not *protect us from very much*",[17] and adds that:

> the fact that there are certain moral aspirations which are conceptually intrinsic to law (though not conditions of its validity) *could never stop perverted opinions about relevant values being transformed into perverted laws.* A stark warning is provided by the fact that some of the leading jurisprudential ideologues of Nazism in Germany were denouncers of positivism, and some even took themselves to be propounding a purified version of natural law doctrine (involving, inter alia, such obscenities as assertion of the natural human and moral superiority of the Aryan race and other such nonsense). The mistake they made was not that of thinking morality relevant to law-making; it was that of identifying their hideous views about the healthy sentiments of the people with the demands of justice and morality.[18]

This is a crucial point, but it is only true if we take away the core meaning of the idea of correctness and morality, only if we think that a claim to morality can imply any values, for example, even racist values. But is this correct? What does morality mean? What is consistent with the concept of practical reasonableness which is essential in the moral discourse?

MacCormick himself tells us that morality goes together with universality or universalisability, that it has to do with the concept of impartiality as used by Adam Smith:

> Smith perhaps has the most complete and almost convincing view, because his device of the ideal impartial spectator supplies for us a common inter-subjective yardstick against which to adjust and objectify our particular passionate responses to cases.[19]

But if that is so, how can we say, at the same time, that everything could go? "Everything" cannot go. If morality is reduced to emotions or personal and arbitrary preferences, it is true that the connection between law and morality is a totally open question, and, theoretically, open to the worst injustice. Here, it is clear that morality has no chance of being universalised. But is a morality that is far removed from the possibility of being conceptually universalised- *i.e.*, is a morality that is not rationally universalisable still a morality? I do not think so. And MacCormick also seems to be convinced that morality means universalisability, so the claim to correctness implicit in law is incompatible with evident injustice. He talks about reasonableness, and if reasonableness means something, it means universalisability; indeed, even more than that: public and discursive universalisability. The claim to correctness is the point of connection between law and morality. Correctness means, before all else, practical reasonableness.

---

[17]Ibid., p. 113.

[18]Ibid., p. 114, my italics.

[19]MacCormick, *Rhetoric and the Rule of Law*, note 13 *supra*, p. 87; see, also, idem & Weinberger, *Il Diritto come Istituzione*, note 3 *supra*, p. 277.

6.3 The Principle of Practical Reasonableness and the Claim to Correctness in the Law

The concept of reasonableness is a central one in MacCormick's work. It is its main normative principle. MacCormick gives us an articulated definition of "reasonableness" in *Reasonableness and Objectivity*[20] and in Chapter 9, entitled "Being Reasonable", of his *Rhetoric and the Rule of Law*.[21] The starting-point of the definition is an empirical observation, a concept which he uses in very different contexts[22]:

> Reasonable doubt is not the same as reasonable decision-making nor is either the same as reasonable care in driving.[23]

All the same, there is, nonetheless, a distinct common character.

> That common thread (...) lies in the style of deliberation a person would ideally engage in, and the impartial attention he would give to competing values and evidences in the given concrete setting.[24]

In general, and not merely in the limited field of law and institutional matters, the reasonable choice is not derived from our reasoning faculty as such, it is the outcome of a process, the application of a procedure: "It is not a job for the computer."[25] The search for reasons for action, that is, for what would make an action rational, is a complex procedure.

"Reason is inevitably involved in any attempt to constitute momentary ends into some coherent system or order, enduring through time and availing in common among persons. Reason is involved in the universalization and checking of particular projects, and weighing them in the setting of an aspirationally coherent way of life."[26] Reasonableness, in general, deals with *prudentia* in the classical sense of the term. "It is a virtue that is incompatible with fanaticism or apathy."[27] It implies moderation and responsibility towards risks and consequences of actions. It takes interests, different points of views, relevant positions and the principles involved

---

[20]MacCormick, "Reasonableness and Objectivity", in: F. Atria and N. MacCormick (eds), *Law and Legal Interpretation*, (Aldershot: Ashgate-Dartmouth Publishing, 2003), pp. 527–555.

[21]MacCormick, *Rhetoric and the Rule of Law*, note 13 *supra*.

[22]MacCormick, "Reasonableness and Objectivity", note 20 *supra*, pp. 532–533; MacCormick, *Rhetoric and the Rule of Law*, note 13 *supra*, p. 162.

[23]Ibid., p. 533.

[24]Ibid., p. 533.

[25]N. MacCormick, "Natural Law Reconsidered", in (1981) 1 *Oxford Journal of Legal Studies*, pp. 99–110, at 100.

[26]MacCormick, "The Separation of Law and Morals", note 16 *supra*, p. 119.

[27]MacCormick, "Reasonableness and Objectivity", note 20 *supra*, p. 531.

in action seriously. It tries to find reconciliation among divergent perspectives and opinions. It is a form of impartiality in a Smithian sense:

> reasonable persons resemble Adam Smith's 'impartial spectator' (...) For they seek to abstract from their own position to see and feel the situation as it looks and feels to others involved, and they weigh impartially their own interests and commitments in comparison with those of others.

I will continue the quotation, because this passage is very clear and crucial, and reveals an interesting continuity with regard to the Scottish enlightenment tradition and a still relevant influence of the work of Hume and Smith, in particular.

> They are aware that there are different ways in which things, activities, and relationships can have value to people, and that all values ought to be given some attention, even though it is not possible to bring all to realization in any one life, or project, or context of action. Hence, they seek to strike a balance that takes account of this apparently irreducible plurality of values.[28]

In short, "universalization [is] essential to justification within practical reasoning",[29] and legal reasoning is a special case of practical reasoning. In the context of this argument, reasonableness means the ability to find the relevant interests and values involved in an action; these have to prevail and to direct the actions which we want to be reasonable and universalisable. Reasonableness in deliberation has three ground features. It is "public",[30] "procedural", and is "a matter of degree", because it corresponds to a public and argumentative process of evaluation of the relevancy of the different risks, consequences, interests, values, and so on, involved in the case being considered. So, we may summarise, with MacCormick that:

> the final judgment is one attained by 'weighing' and 'balancing' to decide whether, all things considered, they constitute not merely good and relevant reasons in themselves for what was done, but adequate or sufficient reasons for so doing even in the presence of the identified adverse factors. (...) At best we ascribe greater or less weight to some reasons or factors than others, and the question is what are the grounds of such ascription.[31]

On legal reasoning, the conclusion of Chapter XI in MacCormick and Weinbergers' *Institutional Theory of Law* is very important.

6.4 The Supremacy of the Good upon the Right (on Finnis' Natural Law Theory)?

At this point, MacCormick's reflections on Finnis' Natural Law Theory take on relevance. However, in this context, I will only concentrate on the notion of *the good* and its relationship with the notion of *the right*. In the background, Rawls' dichotomy

---

[28] Ibid., pp. 531–532.

[29] MacCormick, *Rhetoric and the Rule of Law*, note 13 *supra*, p. 78.

[30] Ibid., p. 100.

[31] MacCormick, "Reasonableness and Objectivity", note 20 *supra*, p. 554.

between teleological and deontological theories of justice may be useful. The former presuppose the priority of the good over the right, while the latter presupposes the contrary. The idea is that, in the first group, we find theories which are perfectionist and assume that we need a true and substantive concept of the good, in order to be able to understand what is the right thing to do at every level, the institutional and the deliberative level. Here, the concept of what is right is subordinate to the concept of what is good. In the second group, in contrast, the starting point is right in its formal and weak – and, for this reason, universalisable – nature. The concept of good is a plural concept (it is always plural). Here, it is impossible to find any convergence, because different people have different ideas of what is good (and of what "good actions" are); moreover, it is contradictory to pretend otherwise, because, in such cases, the concept of right (and the related principle of autonomy) would collapse. MacCormick declares that he is sympathetic towards Finnis' conception of good, that is, to the former group (leaving aside all judgement on the ontological assumptions of Finnis).[32] As MacCormick writes in paragraph 5 ("The good and the right") of "Natural Law and the Separation of Law and Morals":

> If we had no sense of the good, we should have no sense of direction for the pursuit of any steady ends or aims; equally, no sense of what to shun or avoid as bad. Thus we should have no sense of right and wrong, for the wrong is precisely that which ought to be shunned; the right, that which may, or in some cases must, be done.[33]

I think the opposite to be true, and when MacCormick talks about "good", what he seems to have in mind is the concept of "right". The pattern, the legitimate (respectful) structure of agency is delimited by the concept of right, our different courses of action following these formal guidelines are, in a *radical* manner, personal expressions of the concept of good. This is confirmed, from my point of view, by the fact that MacCormick is sceptical about the determinate list of "goods" proposed by Finnis, and thinks that he can find a better solution in the theories of Habermas and Alexy. He says,"I remain uneasy with the ipsedixitism of [Finnis'] claim of self-evidence tied to a bald listing of seven basic goods".[34] And continues by saying that:

> the ideas of Jürgen Habermas and Robert Alexy on rational practical discourse here seem to me helpful, in suggesting how we might abstract out of concrete aims and wishes general categories of the good in terms of ends whose adoption would satisfy felt needs and interests in a potentially universalizable way.[35]

My impression is that Habermas and Alexy are talking about the concept of right, and not about the concept of good; they take sides with Rawls' second group of justice theorists, not with the first one. Moreover, this is confirmed by the fact that

---

[32]MacCormick, *Institutions of Law*, note 6 *supra*, p. 116.

[33]MacCormick, "The Separation of Law and Morals", note 16 *supra*, p. 125.

[34]Ibid., p. 128.

[35]Ibid.

the normative principle is, from MacCormick's perspective, procedural, and corresponds to the principle of reasonableness (rightness), and not to a set of substantial values.

In this sense, in MacCormick's interpretation, the distinction between the good and the right fades away. If we accept that MacCormick gives priority to the good, how can we talk about universalisability starting from a controversial and substantive (partial and determined in its content) idea of good? My idea is that, as MacCormick claims, we have to take the principle of universalisability as fixed, and that, at the same time, we should reject the perfectionist (above all Finnis') interpretation of the "hierarchical" relationship between the good and the right. On this point, MacCormick does not differ much from Dworkin or in general from authors who may be defined as procedural natural lawyers. This is even more significant if we do not forget the implications of the Finnisian priority of the good over the right from a specific political point of view; in other words, if we do not underestimate the practical consequences of Finnis' theory of political authority.

This is my first observation, but, for the moment, I will leave it aside, because I have briefly to focus on two other aspects of MacCormick's theory, before reaching a provisional conclusion.

6.5 Two Further Observations

6.5.1 Reasonableness and Freedom

The idea of reasonableness and the connected idea of rationality is not a choice, but a necessity, because of the conceptual connection between rationality and freedom. This is, for example, clearly explained by Amartya Sen in his introduction to *Rationality and Freedom*. As I have already stated, for MacCormick, "reason is inevitably involved in any attempt to constitute momentary ends into some coherent system or order, enduring through time and availing in common among persons. Reason is involved in the universalization and checking of particular projects, and weighing them in the setting of an aspirationally coherent way of life".[36] But if it is so, how can he defend the thesis that the rational discourse and the effort to be rational are only questions of preference – open questions – and that they do not "protect us from very much"?[37] I think that that claim necessarily deals with the possibility of being moral agents. I agree with Amartya Sen (and John Rawls), who tells us that rationality is conceptually-related to freedom, because it means the ability to elaborate one's own life-project, and that rationality presupposes freedom as free choice and self-determination; in other words, there is a dual link between rationality and freedom. This conviction sheds new light on, and perhaps questions, the

[36] Ibid., p. 119; and *idem* & Weinberger, *Il Diritto come Istituzione*, note 3 *supra*, Chapter XI.

[37] MacCormick, "The Separation of Law and Morals", note 16 *supra*, p. 113; see, also, *idem*, *Legal Theory and Legal Reasoning*, note 13 *supra*, p. 301.

middle-ground concept of law defended by MacCormick, placed half way, as if it were between Dworkin's and Ross'. If my claims are true, or at least plausible, then MacCormick is closer to Dworkin than to Ross. Rationality is an end, and there is a pull towards it in the case of Dworkin, too. The thesis of the "one-right answer" in its ideal character is not so far away from a position in which the idea of rationality and the idea of reasonableness are so important and normatively significant. And the review of Finnis' *Natural Rights and Natural Law* by MacCormick seems to me to be distant from his *Legal Reasoning and Legal Theory*.

6.5.2 Balancing and Compromise

The idea of balancing involved in applying the virtue of reasonableness, which, in the end, consists of a Smithian idea of universalisability, shows how balancing, by itself, is more than mere compromise. Balancing among different positions under the directive of reasonableness means trying to redeem a claim to correctness for this operation, assuming, for instance, that it is impartial. But if this is so, and I think it is, once again, MacCormick's position here is closer to Dworkin's "one-right answer" thesis, than to Ross' anti-rationalism. Dworkin does not talk about truth in an objective sense, but in an inter-subjective one, connecting it to impartiality and to *hic et nunc* universalisability. He has a procedural and empirical, weak but rational, concept of correctness, nothing to do with a transcendent or self-evident idea of truth *à la* Finnis. Here, we can find one more reason for the convergence between MacCormick and Dworkin in the critique of the theory of the "strong discretion" of judges.[38] Why, otherwise, does MacCormick believe that "every judge, after all, to be up to the job, will have to possess some small share of Solomon's wisdom?"[39] I will not defend the idea that MacCormick and Dworkin have the same theory, not even on this important point. Nevertheless, both defend the view that justification requires universalisation, because it "involves propounding good rational grounds for what one does".[40] They share the idea that "judges have to universalize rulings as best as they can within the context of an existing and established legal order".[41] I know that, in this way, adjudication can become compatible with moderate relativism and never-ending reflexivity, but I think that, in part, the same happens to Dworkinian judges, and for both of them this occurs within certain limits. Very unjust law is not law: "provisions which are unjustifiable by reference to any reasonable moral argument should not be considered valid as laws".[42] On this point MacCormick subscribes to Radbruch's thesis on inequality.[43]

---

[38]MacCormick, "Reasonableness and Objectivity", note 20 *supra*, p. 536.

[39]MacCormick, *Rhetoric and the Rule of Law*, note 13 *supra*, p. 81.

[40]Ibid., p. 149.

[41]Ibid.

[42]MacCormick, *Institutions of Law*, note 6 *supra*, p 242.

[43]Ibid., p. 271.

> If it is true that in the conception of law as institutional normative order we must include the idea that the proper purpose of such an order is the realization of justice and the common good, this has certain consequences.[44]

First of all, it implies a critical attitude towards the *status quo* about state, law, society, and also towards the duty to obey authority,[45] and, furthermore, it takes a stand on the moral quality of deliberations and sentences.

The thesis of impartial balancing (see Section 5.2 *supra*) and the former one about the connection between rationality and freedom (see Section 5.1 *supra*) are two foundational premises. If they are correct, the connection between law and morality is not so contingent and weak. The procedural character of correctness in law may be open, but it is strongly (albeit not substantively) normative, and perhaps (I hope) it may "protect us from" outright injustice, something that is relevant from a moral point of view.

At this turn in my argument, it comes, in part, as a surprise to read that MacCormick considers himself very close to Finnis and that the differences between the two theories appear to him irrelevant.[46] The self-definition of "post-positivist" with which Neil MacCormick labels himself, in contrast, shows that MacCormick's idea of morality being connected to the concept of law is close to a relativistic view of morality. But if this is consistent with some of his statements, for example, that law can "never stop perverted opinions being transformed into perverted laws", is in conflict with other of his statements, and, perhaps most importantly, with the implications of the principle of reasonableness which MacCormick both accepts and emphasises in his philosophy of law. For this last reason, his legal theory seems to me to have fundamentally much in common with a procedural idea of natural law such as Alexy's and Habermas', and this contrasts with moral relativism, on the one hand, and with the ontological and intuitive idea of natural law held John Finnis, on the other. Indeed, the structure of Finnis' theory is conceptually incompatible with a discursive theory.

In conclusion, our question is only apparently a question about labels. It is a question about concepts; a question about justifying the possibility of having a representation of a connection between law and morality which, perhaps, "does not protect us from very much", but at least protects us from very perverted ideologies.

---

44 Ibid., p. 264.

45 Ibid., p. 257.

46 MacCormick, "Natural Law Reconsidered", note 25 *supra*, p. 106; and *idem*, *Institutions of Law*, note 6 *supra*, p. 271.

Chapter 7
Legal Judgment and Moral Reservation

Jeremy Waldron

7.1 Neil MacCormick on Moral Judgement

In the fourth book of his quartet on "Law, State and Moral Reasoning" – in *Practical Reason in Law and Morality*[1] – Neil MacCormick considered the interplay of moral opinions and legal judgments. Much of that consideration was focused on an inquiry into the nature of moral reasoning, in the company of philosophers such as Adam Smith and Immanuel Kant. "What is moral judgement like?" they asked, and MacCormick echoed the question. What is moral judgement like? Is it, as Kant thought, like legislation (for example, legislation for the kingdom of ends)?[2] No, MacCormick argues, it is more like common law judgment, working from and elaborating already given principles. "Nobody comes to reflection about right and wrong in the context of practical deliberation save in the context of a learned and inherited practical code"(19–20). True, there is "no single authoritative rule-book",[3] which we interpret and apply. But there is no such canonical rule-book in common law, either: judges elaborate and apply norms of various sorts that are kind-of given but also kind-of open to further development in the hands of the very people who are applying them, particularly as new and challenging cases come up; and that, MacCormick reckons, is a better analogy to moral reasoning than the idea that we confront all situations with either a quasi-legislative capacity or with something like the sort of canonical rule-book that an umpire has in his back pocket in a football match or in cricket.

J. Waldron (✉)
New York University, New York, NY, USA; All Souls College, Oxford University, Oxford, UK
e-mail: jeremy.waldron@nyu.edu

[1] N. MacCormick, *Practical Reason in Law and Morality*, (Oxford: Oxford University Press, 2008). All page references in the text are from this work.

[2] Kant, *Grounding for the Metaphysics of Morals*, p. 39 (James Ellington trans., 1981), orienting morality to the concept of a rational being "as one who must regard himself as legislating universal law by all his will's maxims, so that he may judge himself and his actions form this point of view". See *Practical Reason in Law and Morality*, note 2 *supra*, pp. 19–20.

[3] *Practical Reason in Law and Morality*, note 2 *supra*, pp. 20, 189 and 197.

A.J. Menéndez, J.E. Fossum (eds.), *Law and Democracy in Neil MacCormick's Legal and Political Theory*, Law and Philosophy Library 93,
DOI 10.1007/978-90-481-8942-7_7, © Springer Science+Business Media B.V. 2011

Is morality, in the end, a matter of sympathy and sentiment, as Adam Smith thought? Yes, says MacCormick, provided we recognise the role accorded to reason in Smith's philosophy, in generalising one's sympathetic responses to others and in disciplining our response by impartial attention to every aspect of a given situation that might elicit sympathy for one person or another.[4]

> What I immediately feel, either as victim or by sympathy with the victim, is, so to say, recalibrated in accordance with an imagined common point of view, impartial between doer, sufferer, and interested or disinterested bystander. (62)

Once again, this encourages the judicial analogy: this impartiality is exactly what we require of the judge. Indeed, MacCormick toys with the idea that this is something the law learns from morality: it is "plausible to think that the good moral agent is the model that well-designed judicial systems seek to institutionalise" (66).

7.2 Moral Reservations

All three thinkers accepted that humans are capable of morality – capable of serious moral reflection and capable of monitoring and moderating their own behaviour and their relations with others upon the basis of the judgements formed upon the basis of such reflection. But they did not think moral judgement was enough for social life: "[W]e do not and cannot simply rely on people's moral self-command or self-restraint" (123). This is partly because "not all persons seem willing to exercise such self-command as is necessary in order to keep them from breaching the basic duties of mutual co-existence" (123). This is surely true, though, if it, alone, is given as the reason, it suffers from what I think of as the "righteous philosopher" syndrome – the syndrome that goes,

> If only all people were as thoughtful and self-controlled as me (the philosopher) and my friends and colleagues, then morality would be all we needed. But because we co-exist with another class of people – ruffians of one sort or another who are incapable of reflecting on their actions as we do and incapable of controlling their actions on the basis of thoughtful reflection as we are – we have to rely on 'laws and institutions of law such as police forces, criminal prosecutors, courts of criminal jurisdiction and prison, and probation services' as bulwarks against "tidal waves of crime and bad behaviour (123).

Maybe, it is an excess of self-insight; maybe, it is the impression that was made on me by Richard Posner's observation about "[h]ow odd it is to think that people who have never left school should be society's moral preceptors";[5] or, maybe, it is simple irritation at the posturing of many of the moral philosophers I know, who aim, in their writing, to convey, through the examples they use, how delicate their own moral sensibility is, or how respectable their intuitions are (and how congenial

[4]Ibid., pp. 57–66.

[5]Richard A. Posner, "The Problematics of Moral and Legal Theory", (1998) 111 *Harv. L. Rev.*, p. 1637, at 1688. See, also, Jeremy Waldron, "Ego-Bloated Hovel (a review of Posner, The Problematics of Moral and Legal Theory)", (2000) 94 *Nw. U. L. Rev., p. 597, at 620.*

those intuitions are likely to be to the others found around High Table) – but I find explanations for the necessity of law predicated on this sort of contrast unappealing. Suppose there were no such contrast, no lowlifes incapable of moral thought or moral self-restraint. Suppose we were to grant that everyone is as capable of thinking morally as the philosopher is, and capable, too, of the sort of moral self-restraint that the philosopher displays. Surely, we would still need positive law. Kant thought so:

> [H]owever well disposed men might be,. . . individual men, peoples, and states can never be secure against violence from one another, since each has its own right to do what seems right and good to it and not to be dependent upon another's opinion about this. So, unless it wants to renounce any concepts of Right, the first thing it has to resolve upon is the principle that it must leave the state of nature, in which each follows its own judgment, unite itself with all others (with which it cannot avoid interacting), subject itself to a public lawful external coercion, and so enter into a condition in which what is to be recognized as belonging to it is determined by law.[6]

Good moral reasoners disagree, and the better and more high-minded we are at moral reasoning, the more of an affront it will seem to us when someone tries to govern an area of common concern with *their* moral intuitions and judgements rather than ours. Sometimes, these disagreements are so serious and so potentially disruptive that they need to be superseded by a charter of officially-stated norms that can stand in the name of us all.[7] This is the case for positive law, and this case would stand even if we did not face what MacCormick referred to as "tidal waves of crime and bad behaviour" (123).

We need law, and we cannot have law unless some or all of us are prepared to make the moral judgements that law-making requires and offer them through a political process for the whole society to endorse. Moral judgement is an indispensable input into law-making, whether it is direct and explicit law-making (such as legislation) or oblique law-making (law-making under some other description, such as adjudication).[8] However, it is obvious that not all the moral judgements offered up in a society can become law: you think an estate tax is just, I think it is unjust; but we need a view on this matter which can stand in the name of us all; so one of the judgements must give way. The person whose moral judgement "loses out" in the political process (for example, because a majority of representatives do not support it) will think the resulting law wrong.[9] But the Kantian point is that such a person must recognise the need which we have in this matter to abandon the situation in which each follows his or her own judgement, and move into a condition in which what is to be acted upon officially as right or wrong, just or unjust, is determined by

[6]Immanuel Kant, "Metaphysical First Principles of the Doctrine of Right", in: *The Metaphysics of Morals*, §44, p. 124 (Mary Gregor trans., Cambridge: Cambridge University Press 1991).

[7]See, also, the discussion in Jeremy Waldron, "Kant's Legal Positivism", (1996) 109 *Harv. L. Rev.*, p. 1535 (1996); see, also, in Jeremy Waldron, *The Dignity of Legislation*, (Cambridge: Cambridge University Press, 1999), Chapter 3.

[8]The phrase "oblique law-making" is Austin's: see JW on principles of legislation.

[9]For MacCormick's reflection on this in the context of Kant's legislative analogy, see *Practical Reason in Law and Morality,* note 2 *supra*, p. 65.

positive law. And nothing about the high-minded way in which such a person forms his or her own judgement exempts him or her from this discipline.

I do not think Neil MacCormick would have disagreed with this, though it is not the version of Kant's account of the relation between legal and moral judgement that he pursues.[10] MacCormick accepts that people must, by and large, submit themselves to comply with what the law requires even when it is not a law whose enactment or whose imposition through adjudication they would have supported.[11]

But one thing that MacCormick did insist on was this: the citizen always reserves the right to make his own judgement on the matter that the law addresses even if he or she accepts that his or her behaviour must follow the law. He says:

> What never happens is that legal change (or legal stasis), by judicial decision or legislative enactment, cancels the validity of the conscientious judgment of any issue by a moral agent. Autonomy in moral judgment means that each person is responsible for her/his view of what is good and bad, right and wrong and can never be overruled on that issue. (181)

In *Practical Reason in Law and Morality*, he illustrates this with a case study, which considers the way in which the Court of Appeal in Britain dealt with a case concerning the surgical separation of conjoined twins, a procedure that would certainly kill one of them, though it was a necessary condition in order to avoid the death of them both.[12] The court required the separation to take place even over the objections of the parents (who refused to authorise what was, in effect, the killing of one child to save the other). MacCormick disagreed: "I cannot see any sufficient reason... to override the parents' view.... To impose a decision about the children over the head of the parents is morally unacceptable" (178). But the official decision was not entrusted to MacCormick; it was entrusted to a judge, Lord Justice Ward, who was constrained to say:

> It gives me no satisfaction to have disagreed with [the parents'] views of what is right for their family.... It may be no great comfort to them to know that, in fact, my heart bleeds for them. But if, as the law says I must, *it is I who must now make the decision*, then whatever the parents' grief, I must strike a balance between the twins and do what is best for them.[13]

Once this decision was given by the Court, then, as MacCormick says, "necessarily the legal judgment rendered anyone's moral judgement inoperative as far as concerned the actual performance of the operation" (180). A National Health Service hospital must operate as directed by law. MacCormick briefly mentioned the possibility of conscientious refusal by a doctor who might share MacCormick's and the

---

[10] He comes close to it in *Practical Reason in Law and Morality*, note 2 *supra*, p. 204.

[11] See ibid., pp. 20–21.

[12] *Re A (children) (conjoined twins)* [2001] Fam 147, [2000] 4 All ER 961 – discussed in *Practical Reason in Law and Morality,* note 2 *supra*, pp. 173–181.

[13] [2001] Fam at 193, [2000] 4 All ER at 1010, quoted in *Practical Reason in Law and Morality* note 2 *supra*, p. 179 (my emphasis). Lord Justice Ward was one member of a three-judge panel deciding the case; the panel decided unanimously, and Lord Justice Ward wrote the Court's opinion.

parents' moral view, though he said that, in a case like this, that "is not a serious possibility, nor a desirable course of action" (180).

Still, he said, it is important that each person reserve – and not abandon or compromise – his or her own autonomous judgement in this matter. There may be an appeal at a later date or an overturning of the implications of this decision in a subsequent case; or there may be a campaign to change the law on this matter; in either case, people need to maintain their own sense of right and wrong as possible inputs into these future legal or political processes. And I suspect MacCormick believes, too, that, even apart from the prospect of legal change, it is simply important from a moral point of view that people retain a sense of their own autonomous judgement in matters like these.[14] Of course, as he acknowledged, "people can and should reflect deeply whether their minority opinion on some matter is an aberrant eccentricity rather than a clearer insight than that of the majority, or of the judiciary, into a moral truth" (181). But they should not abandon their opinion just because the contrary view has, for the time being, the status of positive law.

7.3 The Connection with Autonomy

All this seems to add up to an attractive and familiar position, engaging, as it does, Kant's principles of responsible enlightened citizenship: "Make public use of one's reason in all matters" and "[A]*rgue as much as you want and about whatever you want, but obey!*",[15] and also Jeremy Bentham's insistence on complementing the role of the expositor of the laws with the role of the censor of the laws, along with his motto of good citizenship: "*To obey punctually; to censure freely.*"[16] We owe a duty to the law (not an absolute duty, but, as MacCormick argues, a substantial and, in most cases, a conclusive duty).[17] But we also owe it to our society as citizens and to ourselves as autonomous moral-reasoners to form and hold a critical view of our own on the matters which the law addresses so that, in due time, we can participate, if necessary, in campaigns for the laws' reformation:

> Thus much is certain; that a system that is never to be censured, will never be improved: that if nothing is ever to be found fault with, nothing will ever be mended: and that a resolution to justify every thing at any rate, and to disapprove of nothing, is a resolution which, pursued

---

[14]Later in the book (*Practical Reason in Law and Morality*, note 2 *supra*, p. 199), he says: "human beings in the territory of a state are heteronomous in face of the state's law and the commandments it imposes on them, but they are autonomous as moral agents. This gives each person the final say as to whether or not it is right to knuckle under to legal norms where one considers them to be morally unacceptable."

[15]Immanuel Kant, "What is Enlightenment", in: *Toward Perpetual Peace and Other Writings*, (New Haven CT: Yale University Press, 2006), p. 17, at 18 & 23, (Pauline Kleingeld ed., 2006). Emphasis in original.

[16]Jeremy Bentham, *A Fragment on Government*, pp. 98–99 & 101 (F.C. Montague ed., 1891).

[17]MacCormick, *Practical Reason in Law and Morality*, note 2 *supra*, p. 187.

> in future, must stand as an effectual bar to all the additional happiness we can ever hope for; pursued hitherto would have robbed us of that share of happiness which we enjoy already.[18]

A similar position is associated with modern English legal positivism, which insists on disentangling our own moral sense from our understanding of what the law requires. Only this, it is said, can keep alive the spirit of healthy criticism and prevent undue submissiveness to wrong-headed law. But for the moderns, as, perhaps, not for Bentham, the reservation of independent moral judgement is essential also to solve the question of obedience. So, for example, in the view of H.L.A. Hart:

> So long as human beings can gain sufficient co-operation from some to enable them to dominate others, they will use the forms of law as one of their instruments. Wicked men will enact wicked rules which others will enforce. What surely is most needed in order to make men clear sighted in confronting the official abuse of power, is that they should preserve the sense that the certification of something as legally valid is not conclusive of the question of obedience, and that, however great the aura of majesty or authority which the official system may have, its demands must in the end be submitted to a moral scrutiny. This sense, that there is something outside the official system, by reference to which in the last resort the individual must solve his problems of obedience, is surely more likely to be kept alive among those who are accustomed to think that rules of law may be iniquitous, than among those who think that nothing iniquitous can anywhere have the status of law.[19]

True, as Hart acknowledges, the big issue of obedience is not the only issue for which the citizen needs to reserve his or her moral judgement on the matter that law addresses.[20] There are all sorts of other detailed modes of engagement with a law's requirement – ranging from submission to punishment in the wake of disobedience, to dealing later with the legacy of what we judge to be injustice resulting from the operation of a law that we judge to have dealt wrongly with some issue – which require us to come to reflection and decision with our moral sense intact and uncompromised by the law.

For MacCormick, and, perhaps, also for Hart, the underlying idea of moral autonomy seems to be crucial. MacCormick puts this forward as a general proposition:

> As a person of self-command, or an autonomous agent, it can only be your own judgement that you apply in coming to a decision and acting on it. Sometimes, this can feel lonely and unpopular, but persons of independent mind have to put up with that. ... Perhaps, the weight of what you think is popular opinion, or peer-group opinion, scares you off, and you decide to go along with an opinion you truly consider misguided or downright wrong. In one sense, that is still your decision, and you are answerable for it; but it is not your authentic will. ... It is all down to self-command in the end.[21]

Talking of debates about the law on abortion or policies on nuclear weapons, *etc.*, MacCormick says:

---

[18] Bentham, *Fragment on Government*, note 17 *supra*, p. 101.

[19] H.L.A. Hart, *The Concept of Law*, (Oxford: Clarendon Press, 1994), pp. 210–211.

[20] Ibid., p. 211.

[21] *Practical Reason in Law and Morality,* note 2 *supra*, p. 68.

> The idea that everyone as a moral person has her or his own autonomy lends a particular character to discussions of this kind. No one may lay down the law to anyone else. Each is responsible for her or his own opinions and decisions.[22]

And so each person is entitled to – indeed, morally required to – form and reserve his or her own moral position on any matter that the law addresses.

One cannot push this too far, of course, or else it leaves no room for positive law to operate at all in a universe of autonomous agents. MacCormick cannot literally mean that "[n]o one may lay down the law to anyone else", for that is precisely what law does and MacCormick is not an anarchist. The point must be that law has its moral claims on us – which, themselves, can be apprehended morally – but that this fact does not diminish our responsibility to judge the matter for ourselves. This already indicates a more complicated picture and we shall consider these complications in detail in Section 7.9, below.

7.4 Hobbes vs. Moral Reservation

I said that the position which MacCormick adopts on the importance of our reserving the right of independent autonomous moral judgement in the face of a contrary legal norm is a respectable one. It is familiar and attractive. But it is not universally embraced in our tradition of political philosophy.

Consider the position of Thomas Hobbes. In *Leviathan*, Hobbes famously defined positive law in terms of the commands of a sovereign. But that is not all that he said about it in his definition. He said:

> I define civil law in this manner. Civil law is to every subject those rules which the Commonwealth hath commanded him, by word, writing, or other sufficient sign of the will, *to make use of for the distinction of right and wrong....*[23]

In Hobbes' view, laws are not just rules which we are commanded to comply with, in the spirit in which MacCormick thinks the NHS doctors were commanded to comply with the decision of the Court of Appeal in the case we considered above. Hobbes' requirements of compliance are demanding enough. Law is a command, and a command presents itself as something to be obeyed peremptorily:

> Command is where a man saith, 'Do this,' or 'Do not this,' without expecting other reason than the will of him that says it.[24]

But the Hobbesian definition of law goes way beyond behavioural compliance. We are to use the commanded rule for distinguishing between right and wrong; we are not to draw distinctions of right and wrong upon any other basis. To abide by law, Hobbes implies, is to renounce the reservation of autonomous moral judgement

[22] Ibid., p. 93.

[23] Thomas Hobbes, *Leviathan*, (Richard Tuck ed., 1996), Chapter 27, p. 183. (My emphasis.).

[24] Ibid., Chapter 26, p. 176.

that MacCormick cherishes so much. I will call this position of Hobbes' "the non-reservation principle" (though you can probably think of unkinder terms for it, such as "the authoritarian principle" or "the principle of heteronomy").

We may not like "the non-reservation principle" but the reason for it is clear in Hobbes' system. Our judgements of right and wrong, considered apart from law, are notoriously subjective and divisive. They start fights: people's disparate moral judgements offend and threaten one another. And they are likely to continue starting fights even if we submit our *behaviour* to a sovereign command that stands in the name of us all. So, submitting our behaviour to sovereign command is not enough for peace; we need to submit our judgement to it as well, our judgement of right and wrong. We need to discipline ourselves so that once the sovereign or his or her authorised agents (for instance, judges) have spoken, their judgments become our judgements and any vestige of contrary judgement that we have in the depths of our conscience (or however one describes one's moral sensibility in a Hobbesian world) is abandoned. One can also put this into the language of initial authorisation. Everything the sovereign judges, every command he or she issues, is something he or she has authorised and "owned" in advance; that is what submission to the sovereign amounts to.[25] And it is not only that each subject is required to behave as if these commands were his or her commands, but also he or she is required to judge as if these judgments were his or her own judgements. The subject is not to think of himself or herself as reserving an independent right of judgement.

I have no doubt that Hobbes intended the non-reservation view literally, though whether it is a viable position in his system is something that requires further thought (in a paper about Hobbes not MacCormick). Briefly, four other positions which he held might undermine it.[26] First, Hobbes believed that the subject necessarily reserves a right of final judgement about matters imminently related to his or her own immediate survival[27]; some of his contemporaries believed this undermined the sovereign authority which he sought to establish.[28] Secondly, he expected those charged with the interpretation of the sovereign's commands and judgements to treat them, when in doubt, as though they were in conformity with the law of nature.[29] This surely supposes that they must reserve an ability to make judgements about the law of nature, if only as an interpretive device. Thirdly, he seems to have toyed with the idea that, on religious matters, Christians and (for slightly different reasons) Jews

[25]Ibid., Chapters 17–19.

[26]I am most grateful to Richard Tuck for discussion of this aspect of Hobbes's philosophy.

[27]Ibid., Chapter 21, p. 151: "If the sovereign command a man, though justly condemned, to kill, wound, or maim himself; or not to resist those that assault him; or to abstain from the use of food, air, medicine, or any other thing without which he cannot live; yet hath that man the liberty to disobey."

[28]See the discussion in: Jean Hampton, *Hobbes and the Social Contract Tradition*, (Cambridge: Cambridge University Press, 1988). On this ground, Bishop Bramhall called Hobbes' view an "anarchist's charter."

[29]Hobbes, note 24 *supra*, Chapter 27, p. 188.

cannot give up the right to figure out for themselves what God requires of them.[30] Fourthly, he certainly thought that, in the context of contemporary sectarian disputes, good statesmanship, if not compelling principles of political theory, required the sovereign to limit his or her demands to external conduct, and to refrain from scrutinising people's private judgements. Fifth and most important: Hobbes believed that all the duties of the subject must be predicated on a deep and transparent understanding of the need for sovereignty and the need for subordination and obedience. There is no room for any legitimating myth or noble lies in Hobbes's system. It is against the sovereign's duty "to let the people be ignorant or misinformed of the grounds and reasons of those his essential rights".[31] So, if they are required to treat the sovereign's judgements as their own judgements, they are also required to have a full and transparent understanding of the reasons for this requirement; and it is not clear (to me at any rate)[32] that the replacement of their own autonomous judgements of right and wrong by the sovereign's judgement can survive this transparent understanding unshaken.

These (except, perhaps, the last) are all technical matters of Hobbes'craft, and thus not apt for discussion here. But even if "the non-reservation principle" could be made viable in a Hobbesian theory of politics, what should we think about it from a moral point of view? Is it not offensive to require people to abandon their moral judgement in the face of the law's judgments? Does not this concede altogether too much to the law? Should we not value the moral reservation that MacCormick cherishes and that Hobbes seemed to want to discredit?

I guess the answer to all these questions is "Yes", Silly old Hobbes. Of course, we should all want to reserve the right of moral judgement. Not that we want to disobey the law in every case in which we disagree with it, but at least we want to keep our moral *judgement* intact. That seems right. And we may want to congratulate ourselves for taking this stand in favour of moral autonomy and against legal authoritarianism. But before we start celebrating, we might want to give a moment's thought to whether there is anything – or whether there should be anything – in our own mature attitude to positive law, which might match, however imperfectly, the Hobbesian "non- reservation principle".

7.5 Disrupting Co-ordination

I guess if there is anything to be said for the Hobbesian position, it might be said in regard to situations which have the following two features: (i) it is much more important in the given situation that there be a rule which is generally followed than that it be the right rule; and (ii) concentration on an alternative rule (i.e., an

---

[30] Ibid., pp. 343–345.

[31] Ibid., Chapter. 30, p. 232. See, also, Jeremy Waldron, "Hobbes and the Principle of Publicity", (2001) 82 *Pacific Philosophical Quarterly*, p. 447.

[32] In conversation, Richard Tuck has indicated that he disagrees with me here.

alternative to the one that is laid down and generally followed) is likely to be a distraction from following the rule laid down.

Condition (i) is exemplified by the rule of the road – the rule that says we drive on the right (i.e., two cars approaching each other on a road from different directions each move to the driver's right) or, in Britain and New Zealand, the rule that says we drive on the left (i.e., two cars approaching each other on a road from different directions each move to the driver's left). Indeed, this is such a good example of (i), that it is not clear that the idea of "the right rule" makes much sense. Maybe there is an innate psychological disposition to veer right; or maybe we should strive for uniformity (and, since the right-hand rule is more commonly followed in the world, we should adopt that); or maybe, as Les Green once suggested, we should drive on the right because mnemonically that is the "right" side to drive on. But these paltry considerations shrink almost to nothingness compared to the importance of just having one rule or the other generally accepted on a given network of roads. Either rule is much better than none, much better than confusion.

But this is not really a good example for Hobbes, because it is not clear what it would be to go on believing, for example in America, that the left-hand-side was the right side to drive on, even though the right-hand rule is laid down and generally followed. Someone who said that they wanted to reserve the right of independent judgement on this matter, even though they, of course, intended to comply with the American rule, would probably strike us as a sort of lunatic. Maybe that is Hobbes' point. Anyway, the difficulty of imagining what it would be to reserve one's judgement on this matter means that we hardly even get to condition (ii) – *viz.*, imagining that the reserved judgement is distracting.

Here is a slightly different case, also a traffic example. In England, traffic at intersections is often controlled by traffic circles (roundabouts). They are used less frequently in the United States. For a traffic circle to work, there has to be a rule about right-of-way: who yields to whom, for example, when a driver is coming on to the circle. The English rule is "*Circle prevails*": traffic already on the circle always has right of way over traffic entering the circle, unless there are traffic lights controlling it like the circle where Headington Road meets the Oxford Ring Road. "*Circle prevails*" is highly efficient: it enables the circle to operate as a valve open to the heaviest flow, and so it allows more traffic through the intersection than any alternative. In Berkeley, California, there is a traffic circle where Marin Avenue meets Los Angeles Avenue and Arlington Avenue. Marin Avenue is a major street; plus it enters the traffic circle downhill from the east and continues westward on the other side of the circle. But there are four other entry points to the circle. When I lived in Berkeley, I discovered that the prevailing convention for this intersection (and, for all I know, the local traffic ordinance applying to it) was not "*Circle prevails*" but "*Marin prevails*": traffic already on the circle yields to traffic entering from Marin.

When I lived in Berkeley, I used to give people lectures on what an inefficient convention this was, and how Americans did not understand roundabouts. I knew perfectly well what the convention was, and, by and large, I obeyed it; but I reserved the right of independent judgement. I thought the local rule was wrong. This reserved judgement would flare up in my mind every time I approached this circle from any direction. Sometimes, I was tempted to yield to traffic on the circle even when I was coming down Marin Avenue; other times, I was tempted to assert a right-of-way on the circle even against oncoming Marin traffic. Usually, I did not do that, but, every time I entered the circle, these thoughts would enter my head. At the very least, I would fulminate, which is not a good driving practice. I never caused an accident, but my reserved judgement was definitely a distraction.

It would have been better if I had taken a Hobbesian approach once I discovered what the local rule was. Someone might say, "Well, you needed to reserve your judgement so that it would be there and available to use when you drove in England". But this is not so; I can drive ambidextrously so far as left-side and right-side are concerned; I just switch over into the relevant Hobbesian posture depending on what country I am in. I do not reserve any judgement; I do not fulminate; I just switch. I am sure that I could have done that for the Marin Circle, too, and then switched back easily to follow the English rule whenever I was in England. I did not need to reserve judgement in a MacCormick fashion when I was driving in Berkeley. But I did. I reserved judgement, telling myself on every occasion that, despite the local rule, "*Circle prevails*" would have been better. I was a fulminating menace as a result.

7.6 Fragile Rules and Institutions: The Rule About Civilians

But these are fairly trivial cases: let us try a serious one.[33] There is a rule about the use of armed force – a rule of *ius in bello* -that is known as the principle of distinction or the principle of discrimination. I will call it PD_1. PD_1 requires those engaged in war to distinguish or discriminate among targets: they may fire upon combatants (people in uniform or people openly carrying weapons), but they may not fire upon civilians.[34] It is not always complied with: but it continues to be regarded as an important rule, and most countries have it incorporated into their military law and doctrines.

---

[33]What follows is adapted from my paper *Civilians, Terrorism, and Deadly Serious Conventions*, available at http://ssrn.com/abstract=1346360 and also as Chapter 4 of my book, *Torture, Terror, and Trade-offs: Philosophy for the White House*, (Oxford: Oxford University Press, 2010).

[34]The basic legal principles are set out in Articles 48 and 51 of the First Protocol to the Geneva Conventions. Article 48: "In order to ensure respect for and protection of the civilian population and civilian objects, the Parties to the conflict shall at all times distinguish between the civilian population and combatants and between civilian objects and military objectives and accordingly shall direct their operations only against military objectives." Article 51: "(1) The civilian population and individual civilians shall enjoy general protection against dangers arising from military operations. To give effect to this protection, the following rules, which are additional to other applicable rules of international law, shall be observed in all circumstances. (2) The civilian population as such, as well as individual civilians, shall not be the object of attack. Acts or threats of violence the primary purpose of which is to spread terror among the civilian population are prohibited. (3) Civilians shall enjoy the protection afforded by this Section, unless and for such time as they take a direct part in hostilities."

Some political philosophers are on record as saying that PD_1 is a bad rule, since it exposes to deadly attack many people who are morally innocent (such as conscripts fighting in a just war against an aggressor) and immunises against attack many people who are guilty (such as civilian politicians and voters who instigated and supported unjust aggression). This is what Jeff McMahan thinks. He thinks that one could make a moral case for saying that certain civilians are liable to intentional attack - example, civilians who share responsibility for an unjust war. This is because he believes that"it is moral responsibility for an unjust threat that is the principal basis of liability to [be the target] of defensive (or preservative) force". Our principle of distinction should not be PD_1, it should be PD_2:

> The requirement of distinction should hold that combatants must discriminate between those who are morally responsible for an unjust threat, or for a grievance that provides a just cause [for war], and those who are not. It should state that while it is permissible to attack the former, it is not permissible intentionally to attack the latter. . .[35]

In some contexts, this might make an important difference. McMahan believes, for example, that the American capitalists who persuaded the Eisenhower administration to organise a *coup* in Guatemala in the 1950s so that they could get back some land that had been nationalised would have been legitimate targets for Guatemalan forces resisting American aggression.[36]

McMahan knows that PD_1 remains the law and is likely to remain the law so long as there are viable laws of war. But, he says,

> [T]he account I have developed of the deep morality of war is not an account of the laws of war. The formulation of the laws of war is a wholly different task, one that I have not attempted and that has to be carried out with a view to the consequences of the adoption and enforcement of the laws or conventions. It is, indeed, entirely clear that the laws of war must diverge significantly from the deep morality of war as I have presented it.[37]

The laws of war, he says, are conventions established to mitigate the savagery of war.[38] McMahan emphasises that when we move from what he calls the deep morality of warfare to these conventions, we are still in the realm of the moral.

> It is in everyone's interests that such conventions be recognized and obeyed. . .. Given that general adherence to certain conventions is better for everyone, all have a moral reason to recognize and abide by these conventions. For it is rational for each side in a conflict to adhere to them only if the other side does. Thus if one side breaches the understanding that the conventions will be followed, it may cease to be rational or morally required for the other side to persist in its adherence to them. A valuable device for limiting the violence will thereby be lost, and that will be worse for all.[39]

He is suggesting, in other words, that the situation satisfies Hobbesian condition (i): it is better that we lay down, adopt, and follow one rule to mitigate the savagery of

---

[35] McMahan, "The Ethics of Killing in War", (2004) 114 *Ethics*, p. 693, at 722–723.

[36] Ibid., pp. 725–726.

[37] Ibid., p. 730.

[38] Ibid., p. 730.

[39] Ibid.

warfare. It could be PD_1 or it could be PD_2; PD_2 may be the better convention; but since PD_1 is the established rule, we should stick with that. As another philosopher has commented:

> [T]he results of acting in conformity with a preferable convention which is not widely observed may be much worse than the results of acting in conformity with a less desirable convention which is widely observed.[40]

However, in true MacCormick fashion, McMahan wants to reserve his moral judgement in favour of PD_2. He believes, for example, that the moral arguments that he has given can provide a basis "for the reevaluation of the rules we have inherited".[41]

A couple of small points, which we can push to one side. (1) Notice that McMahan's approach is a little like my approach to the Marin traffic circle. He does not think that there is nothing to choose between PD_1 and PD_2. He does not think they are arbitrary alternatives; they are not like driving on the left and driving on the right. However, he thinks the basic logic is that of convention. In his view, the superiority of PD_2 over PD_1 is not so great as to justify running the risk of having no convention at all while we tried to replace PD_1 with PD_2 in international law and military doctrine and training. I think he is wrong about the logic of convention for this case, however. PD1 is not a Lewis-convention.[42] Unlike either the traffic circle case or the rule of the road case, it may make sense for me to follow (say) PD_1 even when nobody else is. My following it would still mitigate the savagery of war *pro tanto*, just not as much as it would be mitigated if others also followed this course.[43] (The equivalent makes no sense for the rule of the roads and next to no sense for the traffic circle example). However, for various other reasons, it may well be that a principle of distinction in warfare has little chance of being viable unless it is adopted by all or most armed organisations. Even though defecting while others follow it can make sense, and even though following it while others do not can also make sense, people are still unlikely to follow it for very long in the terribly fraught circumstances of warfare unless they are convinced that their opponents are going to follow it, too. Following a principle of distinction is costly; it is a handicap in relation to unrestrained indiscriminate warfare, and it may be a handicap that will be shouldered only by those who think it is being shouldered fairly on the other side. (Or there may be other mechanisms of reciprocity/retaliation that explain why the behaviour of some in this regard is likely to be sensitive to the behaviour of others.)

(2) A second point, also off to one side, is that McMahan's suggested alternative is a spectacularly inappropriate principle, for a couple of reasons. First, a principle

---

[40] Mavrodes, "Conventions and the Morality of War", (1975) 4 *Philosophy and Public Affairs*, p. 127.

[41] McMahan, "The Ethics of Killing in War", note 36 *supra*, p. 731.

[42] See David Lewis, *Convention – a Philosophical Study*, (New York: Wiley-Blackwell, 2002).

[43] So I think McMahan is wrong to say that "if one side breaches the understanding that the convention[...] will be followed, it may cease to be rational or morally required for the other side to persist in its adherence to [it]."

of discrimination (like all rules of *ius in bello*) has to be administered among people who almost certainly disagree (or pretend to disagree) about justice and guilt in relation to the armed conflict in question. It may be impossible to administer norms using words like "just" and "guilty" in their traditional moral senses, or to impose tests about whose application there is likely to be irresolvable disagreement, particularly because most administration of the laws of war is self-application. McMahan acknowledges this:

> the fact that most combatants believe that their cause is just means that the laws of war must be neutral between just combatants and unjust combatants, as the traditional theory insists that the requirements of *jus in bello* are.[44]

Laws *in bello* have to use simple categories, such as the distinction between members of the organised military forces and civilians, even though these categories are certainly over- and under-inclusive by moral standards. But the moral standards by which we judge them to be so could not possibly be administered effectively in these circumstances of dissensus.

Anyway, laws designed to govern conduct in the fog of war cannot possibly take account of every detail that a deep moral theory will take account of. Most rules of *ius in bello* are self-administered by individual soldiers and their unit commanders. A refined moral principle might require of our combatants a delicate inquiry into the guilt and moral status of every person or unit fired upon. But that would be utterly unworkable. Even if it is crude by moral standards, some criterion such as the wearing of uniforms has to be used, instead. No doubt, these criteria are conventional in character. They place what may seem to a philosopher undue emphasis on trivialities such as uniforms, or insignia, and the open (visible) carrying of weapons, and they denounce, again with what must seem like uncalled-for vehemence, the perfidious use of flags and signage of various sorts. But these conventional criteria are indispensable for the administration of any norm like the rule about civilians in the circumstances in which they have to prevail.

McMahan suggests that these points are less important for his deep moral inquiry than they would be if he were making a legal proposal. He seems to suggest that the moral judgement that he has reserved in favour of PD_2 is not vulnerable to all these irritating points about administrability. But then it is not clear to me what the point

[44]McMahan, "The Ethics of Killing in War", note 36 *supra*, p. 730. Perhaps, the laws *ad bellum* can afford to use criteria whose application is more controversial; perhaps they have to. But in their modern form even they strive to avoid the difficulty we are discussing by orienting themselves not to disputable questions of justice but either to authoritative political determinations (for example, UN Security Council determinations) or to circumstances that are thought to be patent and indisputable (like the imminence of attack). The 1967 war in the Middle East and the American invasion of Iraq in 2003 show that we have not wholly succeeded in this: the import of an array of Security Council resolutions can be a matter of dispute and the imminence of attack, justifying a resort to self-defence without authorization, can be a contested matter of judgment. So we do get some irresolvable disagreement over *ius ad bellum* too, which makes the administration of these norms quite difficult. But imagine the havoc that would result if the administration of the norms *in bello* were as contestable as this; that might well be the price of making the norms morally more refined along the lines that McMahan suggests.

of McMahan's moral inquiry is, or what function is served by his MacCormick-style reservation.[45] If his deep moral inquiry and its results stand quite apart from the laws of war, if they do not even represent a proposal to change the laws of war, then they may seem fatuous. The vaunted reservation of moral judgement in the face of a contrary law is still be sustained, but to what point? McMahan says that, even if his moral judgement does not represent a practical proposal, reserved for a propitious legislative opportunity, it can still provide a basis "for the reevaluation of the rules we have inherited".[46] But it will be an odd sort of "inactive" evaluation.[47]

We can factor this concern back into the main argument. If the reserved moral judgement is just an idly spinning wheel, then what is the big deal about moral autonomy and the reservations that it sponsors? Is it just a sort of game? That was not how Kant or Bentham or MacCormick presented it.

In one passage, McMahan acknowledges that his reserved deep moral criticism may not be so innocuous. He wonders, in fact, whether it might not be appropriate to suppress his and others' moral criticisms of PD_1:

> Suppose... that... if combatants are to be sufficiently motivated to obey certain rules in the conduct of war, they will have to believe that those rules really do constitute the deep morality of war. If it is imperative to get them to respect certain conventions, must we present the conventions as the deep morality of war and suppress the genuine deeper principles? Must the morality of war be self-effacing in this way? I confess that I do not know what to say about this.[48]

This toys with idea of a legal convention's being sustained by a sort of noble lie. If the troops become aware of the serious moral reservations that the philosophers (and perhaps the general officers) have about PD_1, they may be less inclined to follow it. Following it is already very demanding: they have to refrain from firing on civilians even when that would make the soldiers safer in a situation of terrible danger. They may not be disposed to incur this risk, suffer this cost, unless they are sure PD_1 represents what morality really requires, perhaps unless they internalise it as such. On the other hand, they may not think of themselves as competent to figure out the principle's moral status; they may defer implicitly to their betters in this regard. Knowing that their betters doubt its moral force may undermine their willingness to follow it. And even a little bit of undermining may cause the convention to collapse. This is really an instance of Hobbesian condition (ii): the reserved moral judgement may distract, not necessarily, those who hold it, but those who become aware of it. And so it may be better not to let on that PD_1 is morally objectionable. And if we cannot keep our moral inquiry secret from the other ranks, it may be better to act in a Hobbesian fashion – taking the legal norm as our moral norm, rather than

---

[45] Perhaps McMahan thinks that an administrable approximation to PD_2, whatever that was, would still be different from PD_1.

[46] McMahan, *The Ethics of Killing in War*, note 36 *supra*, p. 731.

[47] See, also, the "Endnote" at the conclusion of this chapter.

[48] Ibid., p. 732.

embarking on an inquiry which envisages the possibility of a divergence between the judgement of lawfulness and the judgement of right.

Notice how the danger in this case is different in character from the traffic circle case. In those cases, the danger of distraction is that moral fulmination will lead to collision. Being distracted by my reserved judgement about the traffic rule and by my irritation at its not being the law, I may have less self-control; and an accident may be caused as a result. But I am unlikely to shake the convention itself. Drivers coming down Marin Avenue will still enter the circle confidently and those on the circle will still yield to them. In the case of the rule about civilians, some soldiers' moral doubts about PD_1 may be the last straw so far as their own compliance is concerned, and their own war-making may be less restrained as a result: they may kill more civilians. This is the equivalent of me crashing into another car on the traffic circle. But, in addition, any sort of widespread failure on part of soldiers or military units to observe the conventional rule may actually shake or undermine the convention itself. Unlike the Berkeley rule about the Marin traffic circle, the rule about killing civilians is very precarious already. Quite apart from moral reservations, it is honoured often in the breach, and sometimes defied by whole units (indeed, by whole military organisations).

Any convention can stand a certain amount of defection and still survive; but the amount that it can stand and still survive may be quite limited. In the case of the laws of war, the environment in which they operate is such that they are inevitably close to this threshold most of the time. They are observed imperfectly at best and sometimes not at all. Violations here are not like individual contributions to pollution: a drop in the ocean, so to speak, making little discernable difference on their own. Quite the contrary, any significant number of violations may bring us close to the tipping-point where the convention simply collapses.

Remember, too, that these norms rely for their viability for the most part, on self-application, on the part of individual soldiers and unit commanders. There are sporadic *post facto* prosecutions for war crimes, and these may become more common with the institution of the International Criminal Court. But, for the immediate application of the rules protecting civilians, we rely on the discipline and military doctrines of the world's armed forces. So anything which distracts from a sustained willingness to observe the rule voluntarily is a danger to the rule itself.

These worries are amplified when we consider the prospect that a norm such as PD_1 is a norm of *international* law (international humanitarian law) and thus applies, in the first instance, to states, as well as secondly and indirectly to the individual soldiers that we have been considering so far. States are bound by it, and they are supposed to embody it in their military doctrine and enforce it among their troops. Now, presumably, the MacCormick privilege of reserved moral judgement applies to the submission of states to international law as well as to the submission of individuals to national law. But state allegiance to the legal norm may also be precarious and liable to upset in times of stress, anger, and danger; and a reserved national judgement (or a reserved moral judgement among high officials) that the norm probably does not have any real moral basis, anyway, lurks around awaiting an opportunity to break out in national decisions to violate the international norm and pursue some other approach as to who to fire upon. (We saw something like this happen in the United States with various policies about the treatment of captives in the war against terrorism and the wars in Iraq and Afghanistan in 2001–2008.) We know that in the recent past, PD_1 has been seriously violated at the level of national decisions, even amongst the most civilised and best organised armed countries: the use of fire-bombing and weapons of mass destruction against civilian areas in Germany and Japan by the United Kingdom and the United States are appalling examples. Thankfully, the nations that perpetrated these atrocities do not seem to have repudiated PD_1 altogether. Since 1945, they have reaffirmed it in their practice (to a certain extent), in their international commitments, and in their military doctrine. But the events of 1943–1945 showed how fragile the law in this area is. Doubtless there will always be violations, even when doctrine is firm.

As I said before, a convention can stand a certain number of violations and not collapse. But the distance from "a certain number of violations" to the tipping point may be quite small. We need to remember that, despite the large numbers of people actually engaged in combat, the numbers of individual states and armed organisations with military doctrines is quite small (numbered in the hundreds, not the millions).[49] Also, the knock-on effects of perceived violations, especially if these seem like acts of policy, are likely to be extensive. Terrorist organisations now routinely repudiate PD_1 and everything like it. In the name of "asymmetric warfare", they have organised a whole way of fighting around the repudiation of the laws and customs of armed conflict; they have adopted institutionally and doctrinally the principle of acting as though the viability of this body of law did not matter or as though it mattered only as something to exploit, via acts of spectacular violation. The temptation on the part of lawful states to respond in kind – with actions that are lawless and violent – is evident. Because of what is at stake for any group in an armed conflict, because of the problem of the costs of compliance, because of the temptations of positional advantage and the fear of being taken advantage of, any sense that others are securing an advantage in armed conflict by violating these norms is likely to lead to others violating them as well. And the rule may simply cease to be viable as a result (without it being quickly replaced by any other rule to mitigate the savagery of war.)

It may seem a bit much to saddle Jeff McMahan with all this. Jeff was just engaging in a harmless deep moral inquiry, and all he did was reserve the right to reach his own judgements on the matter of distinction in warfare – non-plussed by existence of contrary legal norms, by their fragility, and by the importance of their being upheld. He was not urging anyone to disobey PD_1 or to open fire on guilty civilians, *etc.* Still, a moral criticism of an existing legal rule can have an effect on it even when the critic does not urge disobedience. Legal rules are sometimes insecure; sometimes, they rest on little more than opinion. A reservation of moral criticism can make a difference to the climate of opinion in which the legal norm wilts or

---

[49] I do not just mean the numbers with regard to any given war, but even the numbers with regard to wars in general.

flourishes. A lot will depend, of course, on what other supports there are for the norm in the culture, or what other pressures it is under. It is perhaps ironic that the sort of moral challenge that McMahan's critique represents does tend to be mounted at precisely the times when the convention being evaluated is at its most insecure. It is when the country is challenged by a terrorist attack, and when the norms of war are under pressure from the anti-terrorist side as well, that the philosophers think the opportunity is right to hold conferences and publish proceedings on the deep morality of war.[50]

7.7 Legal Resilience

We have been exploring the significance of moral reservation, represented in Neil MacCormick's dictum to the effect that the law being thus-and-so should never be thought to "cancel[...] the validity of the conscientious judgment of any issue by a moral agent" (181). MacCormick's idea was that, even when the law settles an issue one way, it is never inappropriate for a person to form a contrary moral view – to the effect that the issue ought to have been settled in a different way. It may be wrong for a person to act on his or her reserved moral judgement; it may be necessary or right for him or her to follow the law; but he or she cannot surely be required to abandon his or her own moral judgement. We have been exploring this in the company of Thomas Hobbes, who thought that the proposition MacCormick has adopted is generally wrong. Hobbes thought that law is something which we should use to make our judgements of right and wrong, rather than reserving a power of judgement of right and wrong distinct from the law. He thought that moral reservation, as I have been calling it, would be disruptive. We have explored a couple of cases in which it seemed Hobbes might be right. By insisting on the reservation of his right of deep moral criticism, Jeff McMahan is not urging the violation of PD_1; by insisting on my right to criticise the rule that "Marin prevails" at the Berkeley traffic circle, I am not asking anyone to follow the norm embodied in my reserved moral judgement. It is not a question of incitement. However, we have seen how there might be pathways between a reserved moral judgement and law-breaking nonetheless – dangerous law-breaking or, worse still, jurispathic law-breaking, i.e., law-breaking that leads to a collapse of the norm. To that extent, Hobbes may be right and MacCormick wrong as to the general proposition.

Can we say anything in general about what distinguishes these cases from the general run of cases for which, it would seem, MacCormick's proposition is true? In

[50]The same is true of the rule about torture. Moral philosophers did not begin holding conferences on torture or manufacturing a prodigious number of "ticking-bomb" hypotheticals to challenge the existing law on torture and to put into circulation their own moral reservations about an absolute prohibition on torture until the prohibitory norm came under pressure. That got the philosophers excited, and although many of them would disavow any intention to destabilize the legal norm, it was inevitable that their discussions and their moral reservations would contribute to the atmosphere in which it came disgracefully close to being abandoned.

the case that he tells us about – his own moral dissent from the decision in the case of the conjoined twins -it looks unlikely that the legal ruling in *Re A (children) (conjoined twins)* or the underlying legal principles will be shaken by MacCormick's moral criticism or by such moral criticism in general, even if it is widespread. Law is robust enough in this area so that particular legal orders can command general respect, and be complied with, even in the face of significant moral criticism. Those who have a duty of compliance (and those responsible for supervising or enforcing it) – nurses, surgeons, hospital administrators, and health boards – are unlikely to be distracted by even their own moral reservations (in the way that I was in the Marin circle case) or by the moral reservations of others, as I imagined in the case of the rule about civilians. This is because compliance is largely incorporated into existing routines and institutional processes, which form part of the fabric of everyday life, and which provide something of a buffer between a legal order's inherent vulnerability to moral criticism, and the order being carried out and complied with in the usual way. I do not mean that we have made disobedience impossible. But one has to go out of one's way to do this and make an effort to tear apart the fabric of the ordinary routines of institutions, bureaucracy and professionalism, in which routine compliance is embedded.[51]

Ideally, military doctrine and military professionalism would serve this purpose, too, in the case of PD_1. But it is more difficult for that case. True, military training can establish in a person a whole form of life in which military principles and doctrines become internalised as routines, with layers of strict, even microscopic supervision, making the routines relatively impervious to whatever moral reservations about them a given soldier entertains wide awake in his barracks in the small hours of the morning. But *still*, the circumstance of *combat* is so stressful and so extraordinary – extraordinarily liberating (from regular constraints such as the constraint on killing) but, above all, extraordinarily dangerous – that it is very difficult for PD_1 to establish itself resiliently in the sort of environment in which it actually has to operate.

The same is true in respect of the international-law requirement that PD_1 be firmly established in a country's military doctrine. One would think that institutions like State Departments would be so lawyer-ridden and so institutionalised – so oriented in their whole routine structural- and bureaucratic-outlook to being regarded as institutional citizens in good standing in international law – that it would be hard for a well-established norm of international law such as PD_1 to be shaken. But it turns out that these structures and routines are vulnerable too, vulnerable to national panic and political opportunism in times of emergency, which puts everything up for

[51] Or if it is shaken, it will be shaken in an orderly fashion through the House of Lords' decision coming to be seen in due course as non-viable, and replaced (again in an orderly fashion) by a contrary precedent or by legislation. We have legal processes that can channel moral criticism in this way. Such processes not only reduce the threat to effective legal regulation in this area, actually (as MacCormick emphasised) they presuppose and draw on the moral reservations which people have established in relation to the legal *status quo*. As Bentham put it in the passage quoted earlier, "if nothing is ever to be found fault with, nothing will ever be mended".

grabs; and vulnerable, too, to the sudden evaporation of implicit moral support in the community once the time seems ripe for the moral philosophers to start grabbing a bit of the action.

We saw earlier that Neil MacCormick associated moral reservation not just with the possible vindication of moral objectivity (objective right and wrong), as against the contingencies and arbitrariness of positive law, but also with individual autonomy. We owe it to ourselves – we say – as autonomous agents and thinkers, to figure out the moral right and wrong for ourselves. We see this as admirable, and our self-admiration may be enhanced by the sense that this ability is, by and large, exercised in a way that does not have the destructive impact that Hobbes predicted. People are not as irresponsible, *we* are not as irresponsible, as Hobbes portrayed us, we may say. The inherent responsibility and respectability of our powers of autonomous moral judgement and our ability to manage our moral reservations responsibly – that, we may say, is what allows law to do its work in the sort of atmosphere of moralising that Hobbes regarded as so unpropitious.

In fact, the ability of law to flourish resiliently in spite of people's moral reservations may have more to do with the way in which law is established among us, than with any particular responsibility on our part so far as moral judgements is concerned. Law flourishes when it takes on a life of its own and becomes, as positivists portray it, something that, in large part, can be understood separately from the moral judgements that legal interpreters and the makers of legal argument bring to it.[52] It flourishes when it becomes routine, internalised in the lives of individuals as habit and training, or into the life of a society through institutionalisation.[53] It flourishes resiliently when we have set up effective and routinised enforcement systems, not just in the sense of good policing, but in the way in which we structure ordinary transactions. Also, although law cannot work without relying on self-application as its basic mode of administration,[54] it becomes resilient when it no longer has to rely on self-administration as the primary mode of applying serious sanctions.[55]

---

[52] In a footnote to the passages that we quoted above, Bentham said this: "There is only one way in which censure, as upon the Laws, has a greater tendency to do harm, than good; and that is when it sets itself to contest their validity." (*A Fragment on Government*, note 17 *supra*, note 103). He goes on to say this harm is least problematic in the case of written laws, most problematic in the case of unwritten laws, in as much as their identity and authority is never clearly established anyway.

[53] See, also, Aristotle's observations on the relation between law's constancy and law's role in habit formation in *Politics*, Book 2 and the last chapters of *Nichomachean Ethics*, Book X.

[54] For the idea of self-application, see Henry M. Hart & Albert Sacks, *The Legal Process: Basic Problems in the Making and Application of Law*, (Westbury NY: Foundation Press, 1994), pp. 120–121 (William N. Eskridge & Philip P. Frickey eds., 1994): "[E]very directive arrangement which is susceptible of correct and dispositive application by a person to whom it is initially addressed is self-applying. Overwhelmingly, the greater part of the general body of the law is self-applying, including almost the whole of the law of contracts, torts, property, crimes and the like."

[55] In the *Crito*, Socrates was able to imagine the Laws reproaching him for an escape attempt, saying: "Can you deny that by this act which you are contemplating you intend, so far as you have the power, to destroy us, the Laws, and the whole State as well? Do you imagine that a city can continue to exist and not be turned upside down, if the legal judgments which are pronounced in it have no force but are nullified and destroyed by private persons?" This was because once

So, to conclude, we may venerate our moral autonomy and flatter ourselves that we can exercise it in ways that are not self-indulgently destructive of social order. But the reality of the matter may be that the hard work in this regard has been done on the side of law. Law has made itself resilient so that it can withstand the mischievousness and self-indulgence of our vaunted moral autonomy

7.8 Is Waldron Becoming an Authoritarian?

I find myself vaguely embarrassed by all of this. What I am doing, defending the claims of positive law against the claims of moral judgment? How dare I use terms like "self-indulgent" and "irresponsible" to describe the autonomous exercise of the individual moral capacities of persons! Why am I worrying so much about the possible disruption to the legal order of people reserving the right of moral judgement to themselves? In short, what sort of authoritarian talk is this?

Maybe it is the company I am keeping. Not just Thomas Hobbes but Immanuel Kant,[56] and not just Kant, but Kant in his dotage,[57] Kant with his late authoritarianism, his insistence that defiance of the legislature "is the greatest and most punishable crime in a commonwealth".[58] Why have I distanced myself so far from an earlier Kant, that I regard moral autonomy as a menace? After all, an earlier generation of students in political theory saw Kant through the eyes of Robert Paul Wolff, as someone sceptical of all claims to legal authority, insisting, instead, on the responsibility of each person to figure out for himself or herself what he or she ought to do. The true moral agent, said Wolff, never does what another tells him or her *because* he or she has been told to do it:

> For the autonomous man there is no such thing, strictly speaking, as a *command*.[59]

Since submission to legal authority involves doing certain things precisely because the legislature tells us to, the burden of Kantian autonomy seems to be that we

---

a legal order was issued, its administration was still primarily in the hands of those to whom it was issued: Socrates was supposed to remain and administer his own execution tonic. Athens had no well established enforcement mechanisms, and it was therefore much more vulnerable to high profile acts of defiance than law is among us. See, also, Kraut, *Socrates and the State*, (Princeton NJ: Princeton University Press, 1987).

[56]See Waldron, "Kant's Legal Positivism", note 7 *supra*, and also *Kant's Theory of the State*, in: Immanuel Kant*: Toward Perpetual Peace and Other Writings on Politics, Peace and History*, (Pauline Kleingeld ed., 2006), p. 179.

[57]In Kant's declining years, as Hannah Arendt puts it, "the decrease of his mental faculties, which finally led to senile imbecility, is a matter of fact." (Arendt, *Lectures on Kant's Political Philosophy*, (Chicago IL: Chicago University Press, 1989)), p. 9.

[58]Kant, "On the Common Saying: That may be True in Theory, But it is of no Use in Practice", 8: 299 (in Mary J. Gregor (ed.), Applied Philosophy, Cambridge: Cambridge University Press, 1996, p. 298).

[59]Wolff, *In Defense of Anarchism*, (Berkeley CA: University of California Press, 1998), pp. 14–15 (emphasis in original).

are required, in principle, to reject legal authority – to become, as Wolff puts it, philosophical anarchists.[60]

True – the discussion in this chapter has not been about the legitimacy of civil disobedience or resistance, but only about the possible destabilising effects of the citizen's reservation of autonomous moral judgement in the face of the law. But even this concern seems excessive, with its laboured account (in Sections 7.5 and 7.6) of the possible pathways from moral autonomy to legal disruption.

Any answer to these worries must focus not on a denigration of moral judgement as such, but on a moral concern for the health and resilience of positive law. The idea is that law in areas of common concern – even law in areas of severe moral disagreement – is something we need. We need it as a resilient and effective force in social life for co-ordination, for the possibility of justice, and for the securing of public goods and the common good generally. We cannot do without it. If we do not have law, we have a natural duty, as Kant and modern thinkers such as Rawls and Finnis have emphasised, to play our part in bringing legal institutions into being.[61] And if our legal institutions are fragile and precarious, in general, or in some particular domain of importance (such as in the case of the laws of war that I dwelt on in Section 7.6), we have a duty either to play our part in making them more resilient, or at least to refrain from undertaking action or striking attitudes that may possibly undermine them.

All this is something that we can, and should, figure out autonomously, applying our moral judgement to the circumstances of our lives together. These considerations are not opposed to moral autonomy; instead, they are the upshot of its exercise.

7.9 Chipping Away at the Importance of Moral Reservation

But then MacCormick's position on moral reservations threatens to unravel in another way. Once a law has been passed in an area in which law is necessary, then its existence will attract favourable moral judgement in and of itself; and the fact that we ought to preserve it (or, at least, preserve the possibility of law in this area) will be the most important moral judgement which we can make for ourselves. If this is granted, is there room left for an additional moral reservation along the lines of: "I judge that the law ought to be, or to have been, different"?

It may seem obvious that the answer is "yes". But consider whether the reserved moral judgement then does any work in the moral life of the person who makes it. So

---

[60]Ibid., 18: "Insofar as a man fulfills his obligation to make himself the author of his decisions, he will resist the state's claim to have authority over him. . .. [H]he will deny that he has a duty to obey the laws of the state *simply because they are the laws*. . .. [I]t would seem that anarchism is the only political doctrine consistent with the virtue of autonomy."

[61]John Finnis, *Natural Law and Natural Rights*, (Oxford: Clarendon Press, 1980), Chapter 9; John Rawls, *A Theory of Justice*, Revised edition (Cambridge MA: Harvard University Press, 1999), p. 99.

far as his or her external actions are concerned, it seems that they should be governed by the moral principles that favour the law, i.e., they should be governed by:

(1a) Law or legal settlement is morally necessary for this domain, Δ, of conduct and interaction; and
(1b) The law that has been laid down for Δ requires me to do φ; and so
(1c) I ought to do φ in Δ.

Our reserved moral judgement, which may take the form either of:

(2a) I ought to do ψ ($\neq \varphi$) in Δ; or
(2b) The law ought to require me to do ψ (instead of φ) in Δ.

This should play little or no role in my practical moral thinking, at least until such time as I have the opportunity to present it as an input into the political process ("How should what the law requires in Δ be changed?"). At least until an appropriate political opportunity presents itself, insisting on one's right to reserve allegiance to moral judgements (2a) and (2b) seems like playing. It is no longer clear why the moral reservation has the importance that McCormick and others say it has.

None of this is strictly incompatible with what I quoted MacCormick and Bentham as saying in Sections 7.2 and 7.3 above. What they emphasised was precisely the utility of moral reservation for the sake of possible political reform of the laws. But there was also a strong hint in MacCormick's account that the reservation of autonomous moral judgement was important, both in and of itself, as something that an autonomous being owed to his or her moral faculties, quite apart from its utility in later revisiting of the processes by which law is made for the domain in question. If there is no immediate prospect of the law being changed or overturned, is there any practical point to such reservation? MacCormick hints that one ought to maintain one's moral autonomy, so that one can ultimately decide for oneself as to whether to obey the law that requires φ:

> [H]uman beings in the territory of a state are heteronomous in face of the state's law and the commandments it imposes on them, but they are autonomous as moral agents. This gives each person the final say as to whether or not it is right to knuckle under to legal norms where one considers them to be morally unacceptable.[62]

Fair enough. But, in this regard, it is worth noting two things. First, the judgement that follows (1a), (1b), and (1c) will already reflect the impact of a moral judgement that the law in question is not too wicked to serve in domain Δ, i.e., not so wicked that it would be better to have no norm at all than to follow *this* one. Like the judgement that we need law in this area, this will be part of a person's moral judgement in the (1)-series, as it were. Secondly, a law requiring φ in Δ can be thought unjust (and an alternative, requiring ψ, more just), even though it is rightly-judged morally-better to have a law requiring φ than no law at all. On this assumption, we may ask again: What is the practical importance of judgements (2a) and (2b)?

---

[62] *Practical Reason in Law and Morality*, note 2 *supra*, p. 199. See, also, note 2 *supra*, and the accompanying text.

Take this one step further. (1b) leaves entirely unexplained *how* it came to be that the law requires φ in Δ. Given the contingency of positive law, we may think: it just happened that way. But the processes by which it happened may, themselves, be morally significant. Suppose the relevant law was enacted in a properly elected representative assembly: that surely is a fact about it that has moral weight in addition to the straightforward necessity of having some law, any law, in this domain. Given the democratic credentials of the law requiring φ, in what sense can we continue to reserve our judgment (2b)? I guess (2b) might have functioned as my input into the morally significant process that yielded the law requiring φ, and when I lose out on this process, I may polish it and put it on the shelf for use in any future vote that there might be on this question. But, that apart, and for reasons familiar to *aficionados* of Wollheim's paradox of democracy, judgement (2b) may have little practical work to do.[63]

The case that Neil MacCormick presented us with – the English case of *Re A (conjoined twins)* from 2000 – was a case involving a legal order issued by a court, rather than a law enacted by a democratic assembly.[64] Is the moral centre of gravity less likely to be shifted to the law side of the equation in a case like this than in a case in which the morality of the democratic process of legislation comes into play? I am not sure. Maybe, there is little more to be said in favour of the decision made in that case (by Lord Justice Ward and the judges that voted with him) than that a decision was needed, and any authoritative decision is better than none in this area: maybe, there is nothing more to add to (1a), (1b) and (1c), in terms of the moral elements of the legal process, than that. But there might be.

The Court's decision in *Re A (conjoined twins)* might have drawn on precedents and it might, in Dworkinian terms, represent the best and most attractive fit of any possible outcome with the existing legal materials.[65] Most defenders of the use of precedent cite moral reasons for following decisions in past cases (such as the importance of established expectations and the importance of treating like cases alike), and Dworkin's theory of integrity is no exception. They are not simple or straightforward moral reasons – and we are certainly not going to go into them here – but they are moral reasons, nonetheless. So it is possible that a sophisticated moral thinker addressing this situation, with his or her moral autonomy intact, would think it appropriate to factor these reasons into his or her analysis of what it was right to do about this case. Certainly, such a thinker would think it a mistake to accord any great importance to (2a) or (2b) if they were predicated on *not* taking reasons of this kind into account. On this account, *legal judgment is a kind of moral judgement*, only a kind that takes the moral significance of more facts into account

---

[63] Richard Wollheim, "A Paradox in the Theory of Democracy", in: Peter Laslett & W.G. Runciman (eds), *Philosophy, Politics and Society*, Second Series, (Oxford: Basil Blackwell, 1969).

[64] *Re A (children) (conjoined twins)* [2000] 4 All ER 961 – discussed in *Practical Reason in Law and Morality*, note 15 *supra*, pp. 173–181. See text accompanying note 13 *supra*.

[65] Ronald Dworkin, *Law's Empire*, (Cambridge MA: Harvard University Press, 1986), Chapters 6 & 7.

than the usual sophomoric exercise of "moral autonomy" on the part of the legally unlettered.[66]

Now, such a sophisticated moral thinker might not exactly reach the decision that the court reached. He or she might think a legal order requiring ψ was a better fit with the existing precedents than a legal order requiring φ. At this stage, what this analyst might think of himself or herself as reserving would be a contrary view of what the relevant law was, not a contrary view sponsored by his or her moral judgement in opposition to the law.

(Much of Ronald Dworkin's early work on civil disobedience proceeds in this spirit, not by saying that morality sometimes dictates resistance to law, but by arguing that a good citizen is entitled to follow his or her own sincere figuring of what the law requires rather than a court's determination of that:

> A citizen's allegiance is to the law, not to any particular person's view of what the law is, and he does not behave unfairly so long as he proceeds on his own considered and reasonable view of what the law requires.[67])

Of course, a thinker who believes a court has got the law wrong may have to mobilise an additional layer of argument, along the lines of (1a) through (1c), to explain why it is sometimes, or always, better to allow a mistaken order of the highest court to take effect, at least for the case in hand, than to leave a situation unsettled. And this, too, will be a moral judgement. So, once again, it seems as if all the real moral action is on the side of the discussion in which we determine what the law requires; and there is very little of importance on the side of the reserved moral judgement if this is understood apart from the judgement of what the law is.

Note

In all of this, I have been assuming that the moral reservation thesis is uninteresting unless the reserved moral judgement has practical work of some kind to do. This may seem like an objectionable concession to prescriptivism,[68] as though moral judgements cannot just register interesting (moral) facts about laws and legal determinations. I plead guilty to closet prescriptivism. But even if there are non-prescriptive senses available for (2a) and (2b), I just fail to see what the big deal would be about respecting and reserving space for their autonomous production.

---

[66]Notice that this does not in any way draw on MacCormick's point, noted in Section 7.1, that moral reasoning is like adjudicative reasoning in various ways. That may or may not be true. The point here is that respectable moral reasoning must actually be a version of adjudicative reasoning, taking into account the moral significance of the same facts that judges take into account (like precedents) and taking them into account in the same way.

[67]Ronald Dworkin, *Taking Rights Seriously*, (Cambridge MA: Harvard University Press, 1977), p. 214. Certainly, this is the attitude that our judges often take. They persist with their dissent from one case to another; they do not simply knuckle under to the majority view.

[68]I mean the kind of theory discussed in R.M. Hare, *The Language of Morals*, (Oxford: Oxford University Press, 1952), and R.M. Hare, *Freedom and Reason*, (Oxford: Oxford University Press, 1963).

Chapter 8
Are We Beyond Sovereignty? The Sovereignty of Processes and the Democratic Legitimacy of the European Union

Tanja Hitzel-Cassagnes

8.1 Introduction

Neil MacCormick has, on different occasions, contributed to debates about the *sui generis* character of the EU in conceptual, analytical as well as in normative terms, and he has critically reflected upon the claim that transnational law comprises structural elements of law generation, institutional engineering and polity-building, which are without precedents in a strong sense. While *sui generis* perspectives have guided endeavours to find a new language to capture Europeanisation, to frame its internal structure of fragmentation, diversification and differentiation, to explain its modes of allocating binding-authority and of resolving normative conflicts, MacCormick acknowledged that reflections on the EU – like those more broadly directed towards transnational legalisation – do not really escape the normative and analytical terminology that has accompanied national and international legal developments, institution-building and social integration, more generally, since the early Enlightenment. In this respect, the emancipatory glance of individual autonomy and human dignity, combined with a philosophy of pluralism, structures concepts of political authority, public coercion and its legitimate sources, as well as concepts of the autonomy-enforcing power of society – be it society at the sub-national, national, transnational or universal level of "world-society".

This starting-point can be illustrated by the fact that the various discourses about an emerging European polity which challenge traditional understandings of law and democracy are systematically embedded in broader discourses of modern legal developments at the sub-national, national and international level. Although frequently not made explicit, European discourses mirror transformations of national *and* of international law in a twofold way: in phenomenological terms, the politico-legal system of the EU has often been paradigmatically taken as a litmus-test for "state-centred" notions and concepts, which start by questioning the status of European law as "law" in systematic terms, and end up by inquiring whether

T. Hitzel-Cassagnes (✉)
Leibniz University, Hannover, Germany
e-mail: t.hitzel-cassagnes@ipw.uni-hannover.de

A.J. Menéndez, J.E. Fossum (eds.), *Law and Democracy in Neil MacCormick's Legal and Political Theory*, Law and Philosophy Library 93,
DOI 10.1007/978-90-481-8942-7_8, © Springer Science+Business Media B.V. 2011

incremental processes of European constitutionalisation are resulting in a constitution proper. This is even more obvious with regard to normative questions: debates about the need, the conditions and the prospects of democratic legitimacy intensified; the emphasis of the status of the individual legal-subject called for an embedment of "a right to have rights", i.e., for "European citizenship", which shifted the focal point towards identifying "statehood" qualities of the European polity and towards reflections about the place and appropriateness of sovereignty.[1] In this regard, the conceptual challenges of political and legal theory are mainly derived from the institutional and structural changes resulting not just from pluralisation of law, but more radically from the disintegration of legal orders, the fragmentation of legal regimes, the disaggregation of institutions and the decentring of legitimate sources of law.

Beyond this background, however, the most serious challenge is to preserve the feasibility of an overall perspective of law as a purposive (legal) system, i.e., as a "kingdom of ends". In systematic, as well as in normative, terms, it is a question of describing the grammar of law as a medium of social co-operation that points towards universality. And this universal drive is not just a side-effect of the predominance of the "nation state", but is inherent in the language of rights and in the notion of "binding by law", which necessarily relies on a kind of monistic order. Law is still the ultimate medium for solving co-ordinative and co-operative problems, not just within, but also beyond, the nation state and in contexts of trans- and supranational integration (in political and legal as well as in sociological terms). Even if we can observe that law is fragmented into partial, functionally- and/or regionally-differentiated legal regimes, and that pluralisation and contestation in this respect are rising, law still embodies an emancipatory, equality-enforcing promise and supplying a language of normative universals. I would like to illustrate the intuition that there is a universalistic drive in legal developments which are not a side-effect of a concrete institutional configuration – such as those traditionally embodied in a "sovereigntist" nation-state paradigm – but constitutive for law as a means and medium of social integration in the following (Section 8.2). If we take law as a medium of social integration seriously, it provides us with a language which facilitates the justifications of the autonomy of agents in terms of rights. Beyond this, it seems quite natural that reflections about transnational and supranational legalisation end up by considering law not only in terms of a universalistic proclivity, but also in terms of legitimacy and democracy. We can call this a constitutional perspective of legalisation, which is not just integrating the structural universalistic proclivity of law (formal monism), but also a normative universalistic proclivity (democratic inclusion). To unfold a constitutional perspective on legal integration, I will proceed in three steps (Sections 8.3 and 8.4). I start with the assumption that, firstly, legal integration is possible only by establishing

[1] See N. MacCormick, "Liberalism, nationalism and the post-sovereign state", (1996) 44 *Political Studies*, pp. 553–567; *idem*, *Questioning Sovereignty: Law, State and Nation in the European Commonwealth*, (Oxford: Oxford University Press, 1999). See N. Walker, "Constitutionalising Enlargement, Enlarging Constitutionalism", (2003) 9 *European Law Journal*, pp. 365–385, and *idem*, (ed), *Relocating Sovereignty*, (Aldershot: Ashgate-Dartmouth Publishing, 2006).

the structures of a formal system; that, secondly, this embedded formalism is a normatively rich one, i.e., an ethical formalism which aspires to universal (and hence reciprocal) justification; thirdly and accordingly, it can be qualified as a formalism which acquires constitutional quality that is open for proceduralisation, reflexivity and democratic contestation: at the baseline, the universalistic drive of law is directed at the idea of law as a *formally* coherent system with an immanent monistic structure guiding its institutional reproduction. In so far as law is imbued with a universalising "ethos" – this is the case because the very language of law is responsive both to resolving and mediating norm-collisions and to rights-talk –, it is more than a structural monism in terms of a pure formalism that is constitutive for law, but a normative formalism. In other words, law as a universality-aspiring system is characterised by a Kantian, rather than by a Kelsenian, formalism. In Kantian terms, the (purely) formal structure of law is translated into a procedural scheme in which the normative quality of (a merely) structural formalism is secured by reflexive procedures. Reflexive procedures, in turn, suggest a notion of constitutionalisation which is not just contingently, but internally, linked to the idea of transformation though democratic self-determination and the public use of practical reason.[2]

A constitutional perspective of law shares a very general starting-point with MacCormick, in that legal integration is a reaction to the requirements of cooperation under the auspices of plurality and equality-claims, but, in contrast to his view, it envisages a procedural meta-scheme of mediation that is neither a "contingent matter",[3] nor beyond the formal notion of a monist system. I will suggest that the normative qualities of law as a mode and medium of integration can be derived from two sorts of principles which constitute the idea of law. The first relates to the formal characteristics of law as an agency-centred concept, and argues that law is necessarily universalistic in aspiration, and hence an inclusive and cooperative concept (Section 8.3). The second relates to the procedural second-order mechanisms, and argues that they are constitutional in aspiration, and, hence, reflexively-structured in order to proceduralise conflicts of supremacy (Section 8.4). In this regard, my aim is to find a way out of the dilemma, so that the *factum brutum* of pluralism can - in normative terms - be preserved (equality-securing), but, at the same time, and with regard to its negative consequences (norm-collisions and hegemonic norm-interpretation), be resolved only by neutralising and abrogating pluralism at a higher level. By taking Kant's reflections about the "provisional" nature of law as a heuristic perspective, I will argue for a scheme of institutionalising a meta- or second-order level to proceduralise the constitutive paradox of

---

[2] I owe this specification to Agustin José Menendez and John Erik Fossum.

[3] I would like to question his altogether sceptical conclusion "that the correct understanding of the interaction between different normative systems is a contingent matter, not one that flows from the very concept of normative order" (Neil MacCormick, "Risking constitutional collision in Europe", (1998) 18 *Oxford Journal of Legal Studies*, pp. 517–532, at 532, see, below, Sections 8.3 and 8.4). Even if this remark is interpreted in sociological and pragmatic terms, it neglects the fact that the "very concept of normative order" is addressed to structure interactions between normative systems reflexively, and in so far it is directed at counter-balancing what I would like to term the "structural ignorance of pluralism".

pluralism, i.e., collisions of validity-claims under conditions of equality. In this sense, I will approach the question of sovereignty indirectly – by asking when, and under which conditions, it might - in normative terms – be better to suspend sovereignty, i.e., to be anti-sovereigntist (but not necessarily anti-monist). Although I do share MacCormick's diagnostic starting-point which emphasises that we have to take egalitarian pluralism seriously, and that we should hence be sceptical about sovereignty-centred (and as such plurality-denying) forms of conflict resolution,[4] I would like to draw different conceptual consequences with regard to the subsequent idea of a constitutive plurality of law(s) and legal order(s), and accentuate the necessity of the unity of law as an overarching system of normative integration.[5] In order to secure equality and reciprocity, law has to supply procedural remedies for normative conflicts, but this is possible only if we do not lose an overall perspective on the law and its reflexive mechanism.

8.2 Ambiguities of Legalisation

A sketchy look at how modern developments of transnational and international law are interpreted in diagnostic terms, reveals comparable analytical problems and conceptual questions as with regard to European integration. In the light of current debates on governance beyond the nation state, legalisation and juridification seem to be the ultimate and irreversible trends of domesticating anarchy, injustice and the factual hegemonies of particular "sovereign" nation states. However, binding by law in transnational and international relations is rather ambiguous: The binding and implementing force of principles, rules and normative standards is contested, the status of norms and the subjects of the law are indistinct, processes and practices of juris-generation are highly inconsistent, and legacies are fragmented according to standards and fields of jurisdictions. Various normative spheres such as *lex humana*, *lex mercatoria*, *lex elextronica* evolve without yet being embedded in an overarching "order". We are confronted with specialisations of transnational and international law in different legal regimes *in res* and with formations of regionally-differentiated transnational regimes that have not just led to fragmentations of law, but also to a "reversal" of legal hierarchies.[6] Transnational and international law can neither rely

[4]See N. MacCormick, "Risking constitutional collision in Europe", (1998) 18 *Oxford Journal of Legal Studies*, pp. 517–532; *idem*, *Questioning Sovereignty,* note 1 *supra*; *idem*, "Some observations about sovereignty", in: ELSA International (ed), *International Law as we enter the 21st century*; and *idem*, "Questioning Post-Sovereignty", (2004) 29 *European Law Review*, pp. 853–863.

[5]N. MacCormick, "Argumentation and interpretation in law", (1993) 6 *Ratio Juris*, pp. 16–29, at 18; *idem*, "The Ethics of Legalism" (1989) 2 *Ratio Juris*, pp. 184–193; and *idem*, "Liberalism, nationalism and the post-sovereign state", note 1 *supra*.

[6]M. Koskenniemi, "The fate of public international law: Between technique and politics", (2007) 70 *The Modern Law Review*, pp.1–30. International Law Commission (2006) Fragmentation of International Law: Difficulties Arising from the Diversification and Expansion of International Law. Report of the Study Group of the International Law Commission, Finalized by Martti Koskenniemi, (Fifty-eighth session Geneva, 1 May – 9 June and 3 July – 11 August 2006, A/CN.4/L.682).

on a clear-cut hierarchy of norms such as *lex superior derogat lex inferior*, nor on an institutional hierarchy between constitutional and lower courts. As a consequence, conflicts of jurisdiction arise, especially with regard to the question of which legal regime is (legitimately) the point of reference to resolve a normative conflict. Quite similar to the problems associated with the fragmented structural elements of the EU-internal politico-legal order, questions of allocating and balancing institutional remedies to solve subsequent conflicts over jurisdictions come to pass.

On the other side of the coin, we can reconstruct a generic process of an "ethos of universal law" that has been affecting the coordinates of "sovereignty". Starting from a very broad and general observation, we can observe that legal regimes beyond the nation states have challenged territorial premises of sovereignty and particularistic presumptions about rights based, in a strong sense, upon national belonging. Most human rights lawyers, for instance, point out that the post-World War II emergence of international human rights law represents one of the most profound challenges to the notion that state sovereignty is irreducible and impermeable.[7] By the same token, the emergence of cosmopolitan norms has been accompanied by various debates about refugee-, immigrant- and asylum-statuses,[8] and the transformations of citizenship-concepts[9] have lead to a de-coupling of rights and identity – not least by invoking human rights conventions and demanding the recognition of rights for particularly vulnerable, discriminated or minority groups.[10] These de-couplings of rights and national belonging challenged the claim that nation-states are the ultimate source of normative authority and the exclusive allocators of individual, social and political rights.

If we take a look at the historical processes of embedding and codifying "universal" individual rights in an international legal order, the caesura of Word-War II and the European experiences with fascist regimes is of paradigmatic relevance. The post-World War II period was marked by the need to deal with the legacy of the Nazi-regime and the unprecedented genocidal scope of the Holocaust, which nurtured the idea of universal law (and justice) in a twofold way, in terms of universal law as a compulsory legal code (a prospect leading to the *Universal Declaration of Human Rights*) and in terms of universal jurisdiction (leading to

[7] H. H. Koh, "Complementarity between International Organisations and human rights. The rise of transnational networks and the third globalization", (2000) 21 *Human Rights Law Journal*, pp. 307–111. S. B. Twiss, "History, human rights, and globalization", (2004) 32 *Journal of Religious Ethics*, pp. 39–70; for a critical account, see T. Schilling, "On the constitutionalization of general international law", 2006 *Jean Monnet Working Paper*.

[8] S. Benhabib, "Twilight of sovereignty or the emergence of cosmopolitan norms? Rethinking citizenship in volatile times", (2007) 11 *Citizenship Studies*, pp. 19–36.

[9] See, about the notion of flexible citizenship, A. Ong, *Flexible citizenship. The cultural logic of transnationality*, (Durham NC-London: Duke University Press, 1999); about citizenship of residency, Benhabib, *The rights of others. Aliens, citizens and residents. The John Seeley Memorial Lectures*, (Cambridge: Cambridge University Press, 2004); about transformations in general, see S. Sassen, *Territory, authority, rights. From medieval to global assemblages*, (Princeton NJ-Oxford: Princeton University Press, 2006).

[10] Y. N. Soysal, *Limits of citizenship: Migrants and Postnational Membership in Europe*, (Chicago IL: University of Chicago Press, 1994); G. Delanty, *Citizenship in a Global Age*, (Buckingham: Open University Press, 2000).

International Tribunals for crime-prosecution, and, more recently, to the establishment of the *International Criminal Court*). In particular, the drafting of the *Universal Declaration of Human Rights* was inspired by the need to prevent uncivilised and barbaric state-behaviour from stripping citizens of civil and legal protection, subjecting them to inhumane practices and denying them the basic necessities for survival. A parallel course of action was related to the judicial prosecution of Nazicrimes, which, for the first time, recognised individual responsibilities and rights against the presumption of the auspice of national sovereignty: The *London Agreement* concerning the charter of the *International Military Tribunal*, for instance, lists a number of crimes which were previously not part of international law, and explicitly recognised the "individual subject" with rights and accorded them responsibilities. In this respect, it emphasises the jurisdiction of the *Tribunal* by dealing with individual responsibility "whether or not in violation of domestic law". For the first time in the history of international law, political accountability and criminal responsibility have been determinately interwoven into judicial procedures. This *caesura* provided the foundation and created important precedents to push the Nuremberg concept of crimes against humanity into a global arena.[11]

Interestingly enough, we can discern that the project of modern international law was also one of emancipating - in dogmatic terms - from domestic law by constructing it as a legal system on equal stance with national law – even more striking is the fact that this endeavour had already played a role with regard to the nascent international *corpus juris* during the inter World-War-period. In the 1930s, textbooks about cases and precedents, as well as methodologies for treaty-interpretation, were systematically edited. The literature on international law included reflections about the "superior" character and status of universal law in normative terms, among others projections of the *League Covenant* as "higher law" comparable to domestic "constitutional law",[12] and inter-war lawyers argued a good deal for the systematic nature of public international law.[13] One notion that is, indeed, foundational for the

[11] About the fact that memories of past injustice are successively articulated through cosmopolitan legal frames and refer to supranational principles, see S. Coliver, "Bringing Human Rights Abusers to Justice in U.S. Courts: Carrying Forward the Legacy of the Nuremberg Trials", (2006) 27 *Cardozo Law Review*, pp. 1689–1701; Y. Danieli, "Reappraising the Nuremberg Trials and Their Legacy: The Role of Victims in International Law", (2006) 27 *Cardozo Law Review*, pp. 1633–1649; S. Golob, "The Pinochet Case: Forced to be free abroad and at home", (2002) 9 *Democratisation*, pp. 25–57; Hirsch, *Law against Genocide: Cosmopolitan Trials*, (London: Glasshouse Press, 2003), D. Levy and N. Sznaider, "Sovereignty transformed: a sociology of human rights", (2006) 57 *The British Journal of Sociology*, pp. 657–676; R. Nagy, "Post-apartheid Justice: Can cosmopolitanism and nation-building be reconciled?", (2006) 40 *Law and Society Review*, pp. 623–652; and R. Teitel, "Transitional Justice: Postwar Legacies", (2006) 27 *Cardozo Law Review*, pp. 1615–1631.

[12] H. Lauterpacht, *The function of law in the international community*, (Oxford: Clarendon Press, 1933); G. Jellinek, *Die rechtliche Natur der Staatenverträge. Ein Beitrag zur Construction des Völkerrechts*, (Vienna: Hölder, 1880); and M. Koskenniemi, *The gentle civilizer of Nations: The rise and fall of international law (1870–1960)*, (Cambridge: Cambridge University Press, 2001).

[13] See H. Kelsen, *Das Problem der Souveränität und die Theorie des Völkerrechts*, (Tübingen: Mohr Siebeck, 1928); A. Verdross, *Die Verfassung der Völkerrechtsgemeinschaft*, (Vienna-Berlin:

idea of modern universal law is the formal notion of a "quasi-constitutional" quality of international law, i.e., the conviction that an international rule of law which creates a system of law is intrinsic to the idea of international law (in so far as it is intrinsic to juridical thought) and that it constitutes general law, i.e., general principles of law as structurally given in international law.

Another aspect of potential sovereignty-transcending developments concerns what is referred to as the cosmopolitanisation of jurisdiction. The cosmopolitanisation of jurisdiction or judicial globalisation is, itself, a complex field of different practices and institutional structures, relating to the spread in transnational, especially regional human-rights courts, international human-rights agencies on the one hand, and to a broadening of the institutional application of universal jurisdiction, on the other. Part of what is frequently referred to as phenomena of "judicial globalisation" is not only the spread of transnational and international judicial bodies of various kind (tribunals, arbitration bodies, courts), material scope (human rights law, trade and economic law, environmental law, *etc.*) and area of jurisdiction (transnational, for instance, European, Asian, pan-American or global), but also a spread of interpretative schemes which transcend national-statist jurisprudence. That is to say, national judiciaries take recourse to transnational and international legal sources as well as to comparative methods which consider the decisions and the jurisprudence of foreign (especially constitutional) and transnational courts.[14] Part of this trend is a growing international network-structure and co-ordinating practices of different national jurisdictions in international litigation. These practices of judicial borrowing of legal sources beyond their respective national system does not just result from functional imperatives and structures of interdependence, it is, to a certain extent, the result of "global mirror" justifications which hold that, where a global consensus in terms of customary international law or *jus cogens*, for instance, exists, international and comparative legal materials presumptively reflect commitments that are held domestically, as well as internationally, especially with regard to fundamental rights.[15] So, in constitutional and human rights issues, national courts frequently cite the human rights jurisprudence of such transnational tribunals as the European Court of Justice and its Inter-American counterpart. If we regard the more concrete idea of universal jurisdiction for human rights violations in the sphere of crimes

Springer, 1926); W. G. Grewe, *Epochen der Völkerrechtsgeschichte*, (Baden-Baden: Nomos, 1988); and, also, A. Eyffinger, *The Palace: Residence for Justice: 1913–1988*, (The Hague: Carnegie Foundation, 1988).

[14]A.-M. Slaughter, *A New World Order*, (Princeton NJ: Princeton University Press, 2004); M. S. Flaherty, "Judicial globalization in the service of self-governance", (2006) 20 *Ethics and International Affairs*, pp. 477–503; D. F. Donovan and A. Roberts, "The Emerging Recognition of Universal Civil Jurisdiction", (2004) 100 *The American Journal of International Law*, pp. 142–163.

[15]M. S. Flaherty, "Judicial globalization in the service of self-governance", *4 17 Princeton Law and Public Affairs Working Paper*; *idem*, "Judicial globalization in the service of self-governance", note 14 *supra*; and S. H. Cleveland, "Our international constitution", (2005) 31 *Yale Journal of International Law*, pp. 1–125.

against humanity, the practical implementation by national courts has – and still is – particularly difficult and thorny. However, apart from the failure to effectively guarantee individual plaintiffs access to judicial remedies and to incorporate the possibility of universal jurisdiction into national codes of criminal procedure, the cases and the public resonance to the proceedings, in particular, illustrate a growing concern with the global enforcement of individual and human rights.[16]

The development of concepts of international justice is definitely embedded in a longstanding debate between legal and moral cosmopolitanism and their sceptical counterparts, sovereignty and state centred views – and this debate has greatly influenced reflections about the EU as a transnational regime, too.[17] Broadly speaking, the "family" of contemporary cosmopolitanists[18] draw upon ideas of world citizenship and inclusion, of, more or less, Kantian principles of universal rights which rely on the assumption of the moral dignity and equality of all human beings as individuals and legal subjects, regardless of their ethical self-interpretation, culture or nationality. At the diagnostic level, they share the intuition that transnationalisation and globalisation go beyond mere functional interdependencies and co-ordinative schemes established and maintained by self-contained nation-states, and that globalisation is about co-operative problem-solving concerned with the moral space of general humanity and acknowledging individuals as agents of justice. In programmatic terms, they envision a global order which is able to establish universally-justified and applicable principles and norms. These perceptions run counter to statist views of the international order, in so far as they deny the strict notion of nation-states as the ultimate source of legal and moral authority, and the strict notion of the integrity of nation-states, which is guaranteed by the principles of non-intervention and national sovereignty. Statists, be it in the shape of republican or nationalist approaches, are not just concerned with the protection of ethical and cultural plurality, but also share the conviction that the state or the nation provides the best context in which rights and obligations, political self-determination, reciprocity, trust and solidarity is conserved: shared values, loyalties, common concern

[16]For a good overview, see J. Kokott, "Der Schutz der Menschenrechte im Völkerrecht", in: M. Lutz-Bachmann et al. (eds), *Recht auf Menschenrechte. Menschenrechten, Demokratie und internationale Politik*, (Frankfurt aM: Suhrkamp Verlag, 1999), pp. 176–198; J. Davis, "Justice Without Borders: Human Rights Cases in U.S. Courts", (2006) 28 *Law and Policy*, pp. 60–82; Nagy, "Post-apartheid Justice: Can cosmopolitanism and nation-building be reconciled?", note 11 *supra*; and R. McCorquodale and P. Simons, "Responsibility beyond borders: state responsibility for extraterritorial violations by corporations of international human rights law", (2007) 70 *Modern Law Review*, pp. 598–625.

[17]See for instance E. O. Eriksen and J. E. Fossum and A. Menéndez (eds), *Developing a Constitution for Europe* (London and New York: Routledge, 2004) and U. Beck and E. Grande, *Das kosmopolitische Europa* (Frankfurt am Main: Suhrkamp, 2007).

[18]For an overview about the debates, see P. Cheah and B. Robbins (eds), *Cosmopolitics: Thinking and feeling beyond the nation*, (Minneapolis MN: University of Minnesota Press, 1998), T. W. Pogge, "Cosmopolitanism and Sovereignty", (1992) 103 *Ethics*, pp. 48–75; C. Lu, "The one and many faces of cosmopolitanism", (2000) 8 *Journal of Political Philosophy*, pp. 244–26; S. Vertovec and R. Cohen (eds), *Conceiving Cosmopolitanism. Theory Context and Practice*, (Oxford: Oxford University Press, 2002); G. Brock and H. Brighouse, *The Political Philosophy of Cosmopolitanism*, (Cambridge: Cambridge University Press, 2005); and K. A. Appiah, *Cosmopolitanism: Ethics in a World of Strangers*, (New York: Norton, 2006).

and identity are conditions of political authority that can neither – so the assumption – be reproduced in a global order without borders, nor be directed at "general humanity.[19]

With regard to current political and legal philosophical discourses, there seems to be a revival of sovereignty-centred approaches and a growing scepticisms towards the idea of a *societas generis humani*[20] which is accompanied by a rather defensive withdrawal of universalistic aspirations with regard to the constitutive principles of transnational politico-legal orders – notwithstanding a broad body of studies analysing the cosmopolitan reference points in transnational juris-generation.[21]

---

[19]R. Rorty, "Human Rights, Rationality, and Sentiments", *idem, Truth and Progress – Philosophical Papers vol. 3* (Cambridge: Cambridge University Press,1998); C. Chwaszcza and W. Kersting (eds), *Politische Philosophie der Internationalen Beziehungen*, (Frankfurt aM: Suhrkamp Verlag, 1989); see, also, J. Bohman and M. Lutz-Bachmann (eds), *Weltstaat oder Staatenwelt? Für und wider die Idee einer Weltrepublik*, (Frankfurt aM: Suhrkamp Verlag, 2002).

[20]See, paradigmatically, Benhabib, "Twilight of sovereignty or the emergence of cosmopolitan norms? Rethinking citizenship in volatile times", note 8 *supra*, and *idem*, *The rights of others. Aliens, citizens and residents*, note 9 *supra*; Cohen, "Sovereign equality vs. imperial right: The battle over the new world order", (2006) 13 *Constellations*, pp 485–505; T. Nagel, "The problem of Social Justice", (2005) 33 *Philosophy and Public Affairs*, pp. 113–147; M. Canto-Sperber, "The normative foundations of cosmopolitanism", (2007) 106 *Proceedings of the Aristotelian Society*, pp. 267–283; O. Dahbour, "Advocating sovereignty in an age of globalization", (2006) 37 *Journal of Social Philosophy*, pp. 108–126; t. Christiano, "A democratic theory of territory and some puzzles about global democracy", (2006) 37 *Journal of Social Philosophy*, pp. 81–107, D. Heyd, "Justice and solidarity: The contractarian case against global justice", (2007) 38 *Journal of Social Philosophy*, pp. 112–130, and A. Sangiovanni, "Global justice, reciprocity, and the state", (2007) 35 *Philosophy and Public Affairs*, pp. 3–39; see, earlier examples, D. Rieff, *A bed for a night: Humanitarianism in crisis*, (New York: Simon and Schuster, 2002), D. Miller, *Citizenship and national identity*, (Cambridge: Polity Press, 2000); M. Cosnard, "Sovereign equality – the Wimbledon sails on", in: M. Byers and G. Nolte (eds), *United States Hegemony and the Foundations of International Law*, (Cambridge: Cambridge University Press, 2003), pp. 117–134.

[21]About the regulative vision of universal rights, see K. Günther, "Rechtspluralismus und universaler Code der Legalität als rechtstheoretisches Problem", in: K. Günther and L. Wingert (eds) *Die Öffentlichkeit der Vernunft und die Vernunft der Öffentlichkeit. Festschrift für Jürgen Habermas*, (Frankfurt aM: Suhrkamp Verlag, 2001), pp. 434–455; T. Hitzel-Cassagnes and N. Meisterhans,"Konstitutionalisierungsperspektiven eines fragmentierten Weltrechts", in: H. Brunkhorst (ed), *Demokratie in der Weltgesellschaft*, (Baden-Baden: Nomos, 2009), pp. 159–185; about the integration of human rights into the law(s) of worldwide organisations, see E.-U. Petersmann, "Time for integrating human rights into the law of Worldwide Organizations. Lessons from European Integration Law for Global Integration Law" 7 *Jean-Monnet Working Paper* 2001, and *idem*, "State Sovereignty Popular Sovereignty and individual Sovereignty: From constitutional Nationalism to Multi-Level-Constitutionalism in International Economic Law?", *EUI Working Paper* 2006; about the ideal of a global social contract, see B. He and H. Murphy, "Global social justice at the WTO? The role of NGOs in constructing global social contracts", (2007) 83 *International Affairs*, pp. 707–727; A. D. Smith, *National Identities*, (London: Penguin, 2004); about transnational associational solidarity and networks, see D. della Porta, "Multiple belongings, tolerant identities, and the construction of another politics: Between the European social forum an the local social fora", in: D. della Porta and S. Tarrow (eds), *Transnational protest and global activism*, (Lanham MD: Rowman and Littlefield, 2005), pp. 175–202; D. della Porta and L. Mosca, "In movimento: Contamination in action and the Italian global Justice movement", (2007) 7 *Global Networks*, pp. 1–27; M. Giugni and F Passy (eds), *Political altruism? Solidarity movements in international perspective*, (Lanham MD: Rowman and Littlefield, 2001); and about global civil society, see K. Anheier, M. Glaius and M. Kaldor (eds), *Global Civil Society*,

Whether it is inspired by democratic and republican motives or by social and anti-hegemonic intuitions, the sovereignty of states or of peoples is being revived as the normative cornerstone of contemporary order(s). Even within the European Union, especially in the context of the various enlargement debates, issues of sovereignty, supremacy and identity again turn out to be a focal point of normative reflections about integration and the constitutionalisation of the European polity.[22]

Neil MacCormick's work is, in this respect, a very consequent and instructive exception, because he has always taken in a critical stance and seriously been engaged with the question of how post-sovereignty might be thinkable. As I understand many of MacCormick's writings, the conceptual and normative background is - at the baseline - an empathetic philosophy of pluralism – be it in relation to the institutional theory of law,[23] in his constitutional studies about federalism and subsidiarity,[24] in his version of republicanism,[25] in his methodological

(Oxford: Oxford University Press, 2001); see, also, G. Teubner, "The Anonymous Matrix: Human Rights Violations by 'Private' Transnational Actors", (2006) 69 *Modern Law Review*, pp. 327–346; and A. Fischer-Lescano, *Globalverfassung. Die Geltungsbegründung der Menschenrechte im postmodernen ius gentium*, (Weilerwist: Velbrück, 2005).

[22]The intensification of political and scholarly debates on the Eastern enlargement and on the criteria of accession during the 1990s challenged anew the status of European Integration and constitutionalisation; see V. Breda, "A European Constitution in a Multinational Europe or a Multinational Constitution for Europe?", (2006) 12 *European Law Journal*, pp. 330–344; A. Albi and P. van Elsuwege, "The EU Constitution, National Constitutions and Sovereignty: An Assessment of a 'European Constitutional Order'", (2004) 29 *European Law Review*, pp. 741–765; Walker, "Constitutionalising Enlargement, Enlarging Constitutionalism", note 1 *supra*, W. Weiss, "Eastern Enlargement and European Constitutionalism", (2005) 1 *Queen's Papers on Europeanisation*; and J. Pribán, "European Union Constitution-Making. Political Identity and Central European Reflections", (2005) 11 *European Law Journal*. pp. 135–153. Not just opponents of enlargement raised various questions about the "integrative capability" of potential new Member States and the compatibility of their political and legal systems; see Blanco Sio-López, "The Europe of the Citizens vs. The Fortress Europe: Inclusion and Exclusion in the Integration Model of the Eastward Enlargement of the EU", *Conference-Paper: 6th Biennial Conference of ECSA-C* 2006, Breda, this note *supra*; D. L. Ellison, "Divide and Conquer: The EU Enlargement's Successful Conclusion?", (2005) 161 *Hungarian Academy of Sciences Working Paper*; D. Gosewinkel, "Europäische Konstruktionen der Staatsangehörigkeit. Gibt es einen west- und einen osteuropäischen Entwicklungspfad" in: J. Alber and W. Merkel (eds), *Europas Osterweiterung: Das Ende der Vertiefung?*, (Berlin: Edition Sigma, 2005), p. 281; B. Kitous, "Protectionism, Interventionism, Nationalism: Does 'Economic Patriotism' present a risk to Europeanisation?" *Conference-Paper: 6th Biennial Conference of ECSA-C* 2006; G. Pridham, "European Union Accession Dynamics and Democratization in Central and Eastern Europe: Past and Future Perspectives", (2006) 41 *Government and Opposition*, pp. 373–400; and Smith, *National Identities*, note 21 *supra*.

[23]N. MacCormick, *Institutions of Law*, (Oxford University Press: Oxford, 2007).

[24]N. MacCormick, *Who's Afraid of a European Constitution*, (Exeter: Imprint Academia, 2005); *idem*, "The European constitutional process: A theoretical View", (2005) 29 *Anales de la Cátedra Francisco Suárez*, pp. 299–319.

[25]N. MacCormick, "Liberalism, nationalism and the post-sovereign state", note 1 *supra*.

studies,[26] or in his work on transnational law, sovereignty and "post-sovereignty".[27] Beyond this background of a philosophical pluralism which guides his reflections on institutions, political authority and legal systems, MacCormick was able to urge us to be aware of the multi-layered and diffuse structure of sovereignty, on the one hand, and of the contested nature and declining performative power of sovereignty, on the other. I will take these two insights as a starting-point for some reflections on the normative qualities of law as a mode and medium of integration. In a first step, I will take MacCormick's insight that constitutive pluralism structures both, modern societies in general and co-operative and integrative second-order systems in particular. If we take pluralism seriously, he insists, we have to take the fact that equality is the basic structuring principle of cooperation and integration into account – be it in the sense of equal respect and concern, or in the sense of mutual acknowledgement and recognition.[28] I will take this issue of equality to unfold that law is also an inclusive, i.e., a democratic, project, and that it is necessarily universalistic in aspiration. In presenting an ethical formalism that is - with respect to the idea of universality - departing from MacCormick's version, I hope to capture the procedural principles of law as an agency-sensitive mode of co-operation. I will then consider MacCormick's sovereignty-critical stance, which, among others, hints at the fact that sovereignty is not just a constructive principle, but also a negative concept. It is negative and closing due to its potential to exclude and deny sources of normative claims: claiming to "be" sovereign frequently implies mis-recognition, in the sense that the recognition of conflicting validity-claims is denied. In this latter quality, sovereignty is a pre-reflexive concept. Alternatively, I would like to unfold a Kantian-inspired argument for reflexivity, which aims at the proceduralisation of supremacy-conflicts.

8.3 Law's Ethical Formalism

A very general starting-point for elaborating law as an inclusive medium of integration is the idea that once the language of law is used, agents are trapped in its particular grammar, and they necessarily strive towards a formal universalist alignment. The underlying idea is that law *in nuce* already relies on an ethos of universality, and that this reliance is not arbitrary, in so far as any kind of legality is

[26] N. MacCormick, "Argumentation and interpretation in law", note 5 *supra*; *idem*, "The concept of law and 'the concept of law'", (1994) 14 *Oxford Journal of Legal Studies*, pp. 1–23; *idem*, *Institutions of Law*, note 23 *supra*.

[27] N. MacCormick, "Liberalism, nationalism and the post-sovereign state", note 1 *supra*; *idem*, *Questioning Sovereignty: Law, State and Nation in the European Commonwealth*, note 1 *supra*; *idem*, "Some observations about sovereignty", note 4 *supra*; *idem*, "Questioning Post-Sovereignty", note 4 *supra*.

[28] MacCormick, "Argumentation and interpretation in law", note 5 *supra*; *idem*, *Who's Afraid of a European Constitution*, note 24 *supra*; *idem*, "The European constitutional process: A theoretical View", note 24 *supra*.

constitutively structured by an inherent logic that strives for (principled) unity and coherence – despite factually-existing differentiation and fragmentation. Even if we emphasise the differentiation, diversification and fragmentation of law and its subsequent interpretative conflicts, norm collisions and conflicts about jurisdictional competences, the very language of law has to take recourse to a kind of "universal code"[29] which hypostates a regulative vision of universal right. This structural aspect, in turn, renders law responsive both to individual demands of justice and to the participatory inclusion of agents of justice. Such a reference to a "universal code" is a *conditio sine qua non* of rights-talk, and, in this way, it is far from being an arbitrary or contingent matter to refer to a universal "rule" of recognition as a point of orientation. What is left if we depart from the idea of a universal scheme for reconciling normative conflicts is the contingency and hazard of autonomous "legal" regimes? In this light, we show that factually-fragmented multi-level and multi-institutional arrangements are not antithetical to the idea of a "universal" legal framework aligned by an abstract rule of recognition. In a way, this is a version of Kelsen's reading of law's internal logic, i.e., of his assumption that there is a necessary relation between legal "meanings", in the sense that legal norms (however fragmented, decentred or disaggregated they might *prima facie* be) cannot evolve independently, but that they are embedded in a system of inter-related and coherence-driven processes of interpretation. Here, too, the point is to acknowledge that, if one chooses the language of law, one cannot withdraw from its inherent structure, which basically follows a monistic alignment. A monist alignment, in turn, implies that legal regimes are neither adversary to a universal legal framework, nor detached from a *Stufenfolge* of law. The idea is that legal meaning can only be generated by reference to some broader, already established, interpretative scheme that renders this meaning meaningful. There must be some kind of universal principle from which validity can be derived. This basic *Grundnorm* or rule of recognition might be vague and abstract, but is still an indication of unity and coherence.[30]

---

[29]Günther, "Rechtspluralismus und universaler Code der Legalität als rechtstheoretisches Problem", note 21 *supra*.

[30]Although MacCormick's terminology is very much inspired by a kind of Hartian, i.e., sociological and pragmatist, understanding of the rule of recognition, I would still read his conceptual and normative reflections as a way of upholding the idea of conflict management and resolution on the base of a "universal" notion of reciprocity and inclusion, on the one hand, and as a search for institutional structures and mechanism that establish a cooperative scheme of conflict management, on the other hand; see, also, his methodological reflections: MacCormick "The Ethics of Legalism", note 5 *supra*, *idem*, "Argumentation and interpretation in law", note 28 *supra* and *idem*, "The concept of law and 'the concept of law'", note 26 *supra*; more recently, *idem*, *Rhetoric and the rule of law*, (Oxford: Oxford University Press, 2005). C. Joerges, "Deliberative Supranationalism. A Defence", (2001) 5 *European Integration Online Papers* and *idem*, "Rethinking European Law's Supremacy: A Plea for a Supranational Conflict of Law", 2 *EUI Working Paper*, 2005, is another proponent who works out that the idea of reciprocal recognition as equals (implying that conflicting normative claims have to be accepted, *prima facie*, as justifiable, i.e., as open to a reciprocal game of reason giving and reason taking) has to be taken as a premise in order to resolve conflicts by recourse to meta- or second-order rules acceptable to all parties concerned; Ch. Joerges, "Deliberative Supranationalism. A Defence", this note *supra*, p. 4; see, also, C. Joerges and

At this point, however, I would like to argue for a normative,[31] instead of a functional as in Kelsen, reading of coherence, which is restricted to a structural, i.e., "pure" understanding of the universalistic monist ethos of law. The structural elements of law are not just derived from the idea of law as a system unified at a very general level by a rule of recognition, but from the idea of law as an inclusive system

---

J. Neyer, "Vom intergouvernementalen Verhandeln zur deliberativen Politik, Gründe und Chancen für eine Konstitutionalisierung der europäischen Komitologie", in: B. Kohler-Koch (ed), *Regieren in entgrenzten Räumen. PVS Sonderheft*, (Opladen: Westdeutscher Verlag, 1998), pp. 207–234. *Unitas in diversitas* is his formula for integrating dis-aggregated and fragmented legacies into a meta-scheme of shared co-ordination. Especially with regard to the EU, quite a lot of scholars draw from the political and democratic theory of Habermas, *Faktizität und Geltung. Beiträge zur Diskurstheorie des Rechts und des demokratischen Rechtsstaats*, (Frankfurt aM: Suhrkamp Verlag, 1998) and Rawls, *Law of the Peoples*, (Oxford: Oxford University Press, 1992) and *idem*, *Politischer Liberalismus*, (Frankfurt aM: Suhrkamp Verlag, 1998), putting an emphasis on the feasibility of inclusive and discursive procedures capable of both rationalising and legitimising normative conflict resolution. In this light, the emphasis lies on the institutionalisation of practices of reciprocal justification and on the establishment of a "logic of appropriateness" that can provide the base for balancing conflicting legacies. See, about debates on transnationalisation in legal and democratic terms and for attempts to conceptualise a normative ideal of "deliberative supranationalism", R. Schmalz-Bruns, *Reflexive Demokratie. Die partizipatorische Transformation moderner Politik*, (Baden-Baden: Nomos, 1995), *idem*, "Deliberativer Supranationalismus: Demokratisches Regieren jenseits des Nationalstaats", (1999) 6 *Zeitschrift für internationale Beziehungen*, pp. 185–244, and *idem*, "Demokratisierung der Europäischen Union – oder Europäisierung der Demokratie jenseits des Nationalstaats", in: M Lutz-Bachmann and J Bohman (eds), *Weltstaat und Staatenwelt. Für und wider die Idee einer Weltrepublik*, (Frankfurt aM: Suhrkamp Verlag, 2007), pp. 260–307, Joerges, "Deliberative Supranationalism. A Defence", this note *supra* and *idem*, "Rethinking European Law's Supremacy: A Plea for a Supranational Conflict of Law", this note *supra*. See J. Bohman, "Democracy Across Boarders, From demos to demoi", (2005) 18 *Ratio Juris*, pp. 293–314, about the idea of a shared understanding of deliberative conflict management in the sphere of transnational constitutionalisation. About constitutional conflicts in the European Union, see Habermas, *Die postnationale Konstellation und die Zukunft der Demokratie*, (Frankfurt aM: Suhrkamp Verlag 1998), *idem*, "Der interkulturelle Diskurs über Menschenrechte", in: H. Brunkhorst et al. (eds), *Recht auf Menschenrechte, Menschenrechte, Demokratie und internationale Politik*, (Frankfurt aM: Suhrkamp Verlag, 1999), pp. 216–227, and *idem*, "Towards a Cosmopolitan Europe", (2003) 14 *Journal of Democracy*, pp. 86–100, J. Bohman, "Constitution Making and Democratic Innovation: The European Union and Transnational Governance", (2004) 3 *European Journal of Political Theory*, pp. 315–337; C. Closa, "Deliberative Constitutional Politics and the Turn toward a Norm-Based Legitimacy of the EU Constitution", (2005) 11 *European Law Journal*, pp. 411–431; O. Gerstenberg, "Expanding the Constitution Beyond the Court: The Case of Euro-Constitutionalism", (2002) 8 *European Law Journal*, pp. 172–192; E. O. Eriksen (ed), *Making the European Polity. Reflexive integration in the EU*, (London-New York: Routledge, 2005), and A. J. Menendez, "Between Laeken and the Deep Blue Sea: An Assessment of the Draft Constitutional Treaty from a Deliberative-Democratic Standpoint", (2005) 11 *European Public Law*, pp. 105–144.

[31]See Habermas' Tanner-Lectures on Weber's functional formalism and his elaboration of a normative, i.e., ethical formalism of law which greatly shaped his material reflection about the democratic rule of law in "Between facts and norms"; Habermas *Faktizität und Geltung. Beiträge zur Diskurstheorie des Rechts und des demokratischen Rechtsstaats*, note 30 *supra*.

of self-determination[32] – both requisites can be applied to juris-generative processes of transnational law in order to ameliorate these processes for the sake of effectuating the stake of "agents of justice". The assumption is that legal systems (however fragmented and contested they are) essentially depend on a universal alignment in order to meet their own pretensions (or rather, in order to fulfil the hope that they raise by claiming to be a legal system) for overcoming exclusiveness, arbitrariness and hegemonic distortion. Although, at first sight, the plurality of legal regimes seems to be antithetical to universal and monist interpretations of law, at second sight, we can identify law's inherent normativity, which is able to guarantee equal treatment and normative coherence.[33] In this respect, the fragmentation of legal regimes impairs the transparency, responsiveness and representativeness of a legal system, but it does not alter the internal legal perspective which supplies its universal and inclusive grammar. References to an abstract legal code are – despite fragmentation and decentralisation – ineluctable, and the internal logic is, accordingly, not to produce fragmented, exclusive rationalities alien to universality, but to organise diversity by a universal meta-code. In the name of legal justice, legal certainty and legal fairness, plurality has to be organised by an abstract, but shared reference to a code of fair and co-operative conduct: What is otherwise at stake is that specialised and partial regimes of jurisdiction become de-coupled and independent from justification and public deliberation, and, accordingly, from "reciprocal recognition". MacCormick's version of an ethical formalism (or legalism) embodies a similar notion when he states that "autonomy and independence within interdependence are the deepest justifying grounds for legalism".[34] With regard to the characterisation of legalism, however, he takes principles that are too substantial and concrete for granted:

> "[A]s the stance in legal politics according to which matters of legal regulation and controversy ought so far as possible to be conducted in accordance with predetermined rules of considerably generality and clarity, in which legal relations comprise primarily rights, duties, powers and immunities reasonably clearly definable by reference to such rules, and in which acts of government however desirable teleologically must be subordinated to respect for rules and rights."[35]

---

[32] I. Kant, "Beantwortung der Frage, was ist Aufklärung", in: W. Weischedel (ed), *Werke in zwölf Bänden. Theorie-Werkausgabe vol. XI Schriften zur Anthropologie, Geschichtsphilosophie, Politik und Pädagogik*, (Frankfurt aM: Suhrkamp, 1964), pp. 53–65; *idem*, "Grundlegung zur Metaphysik der Sitten", in: W. Weischedel (ed), *Werke in zwölf Bänden. Theorie-Werkausgabe vol. VII & VIII Schriften zur Ethik und Religionsphilosophie*, this note *supra*, pp. 11–107, at 33 *et seq.*; *idem*, "Kritik der praktischen Vernunft", in: W. Weischedel (ed), *Werke in zwölf Bänden. Theorie-Werkausgabe vol. VII & VIII Schriften zur Ethik und Religionsphilosophie*, this note *supra*, pp. 107–309, at 119 *et seq.*; *idem*, "Die Metaphysik der Sitten", in: W. Weischedel (ed), *Werke in zwölf Bänden. Theorie-Werkausgabe vol. VII & VIII Schriften zur Ethik und Religionsphilosophie*, this note *supra*, pp. 309–637.

[33] K. Günther, "Rechtspluralismus und universaler Code der Legalität als rechtstheoretisches Problem", note 21 *supra*, p. 541.

[34] N. MacCormick, "The Ethics of Legalism", note 5 *supra*, p. 192.

[35] Ibid., p. 183.

A more abstract and generalised version of formalism would account for a truly universalistic account of formalism, and would be more open to matters of proceduralisation.

If we specify law's inherent logic as a normative one, legal practices have to be considered as being essentially co-operative and necessarily inclusive, and in order to assure co-operation and inclusion, a broader understanding of procedural justice has to be taken into account: firstly, law and legal arrangements are not just conflict-solving or conflict-resolving devices, but co-operative arrangements from the outset. Even if we take the functional interests of actors as a starting-point, juridical procedures have to transcend these partial and exclusive interests – by referring to neutral reference points, by principled considerations such as *audiatur et altera pars* or *ius respicit aequitatem*, by considering their side-effects and negative externalities to third parties, and by reacting responsively to externalities. Secondly, in order for co-operation and, subsequently, mediation to work, reciprocal recognition has to be assured. The original legal parties, the arbiter or judicial agent as well as those concerned, i.e., potential third parties or agents of justice, have to acknowledge themselves as equal legal subjects mutually. This recognition as equals is a premise of the idea of reconciliation through law. Thirdly, and this leads to procedural questions, the realisation of reciprocal recognition relies on notions of inclusion – not least because reciprocal recognition can be guaranteed only if it includes all agents of justice concerned. However, the decision about who is to be included (in order to include all those concerned) is not to be predetermined, but left open to challenges, i.e., to revisable processes of justification. This implies that procedural remedies to grant access responsively to the potential agents of justice are vital for any legal order to function properly. The normative expectations just sketched lead to the conclusion that – in systematic and institutional terms – a constitutional order, i.e., an order able to assure an inclusive second-order scheme, has to be established. In one way or another, one can then sustain that it is a "moral" duty following from law's inherent normative promises to engineer second-order mechanisms institutionally. Concepts of transnational legalisation frequently neglect the potential self-blocking and arbitrary structures of normative regimes that are not embedded in a second-order system of mediation: firstly, in so far as legalisation implies the differentiation and fragmentation of legal regimes that highly rely on partial and contractual agreements, these arrangements are vulnerable to arbitrariness, hegemony and exclusion, on the one hand, and vulnerable to fragmentation of, and conflicts about, jurisdiction, on the other. Secondly, access to law-generation is exclusive and not responsive to different "agents of justice". Accordingly, contestation and societal inclusion can neither be structurally-embedded nor procedurally-guaranteed, but can, at best, be granted in a mode of benign *ad-hocism*.

The overall assumption is hence that legal integration can be acceptable in normative terms only if it is rooted in a broader scheme of proceduralisation, and that such a scheme has to involve a second-order system of mediation and inclusion (essentially relying on the notion of a universalistic monist idea of law). European integration and European constitutionalisation, in particular, should be understood in this light, as a procedural scheme enabling conciliation between conflicting principles, norms and rules, ensuring results that are acceptable to all those concerned and affected, and preventing hegemonic self-interpretation in negligence of conflicting demands. Constitutionalism can be taken as a systematic articulation of the idea of inclusive (and democratic-procedural) legalisation guaranteeing juris-generative and jurisprudential practices of mutual self-restraint. The remaining question is how to capture the idea of constitutionalisation as a system of mutually self-restrained norm-generation and -application, i.e., as a procedural system of horizontal checks and balances at institutional level, and how to guarantee reciprocal recognition and inclusion within such a constitutional second-order scheme. One answer could be to render legal regimes more sensitive to justificatory practices, to the normative demands of various "agents of justice" and to the need to establish institutional reflexivity.[36] In a final step, I would like to employ the Kantian idea of "provisional law [*provisorisches Recht*]" to make an argument for a more coherent proceduralisation of supremacy-conflicts, which is, at the same time, an anti-sovereigntist argument.

8.4 Law's Provisional Structure

The contestedness of the corpus of European law, especially with regard to the *acquis communautaire*, has, to a certain extent, been driving European integration. Looking back, it seems that the development of the European Union has been characterised by continuous conflicts about the substantial content and scope of law that can be considered being part of the *acquis*.[37] As such, the *acquis* itself has always been a contested concept, its acknowledgement by the national legal orders

---

[36] The hope is hence that European law can be organised by an inclusive constitutional (not just legislative) infrastructure and can organise practices of institutional self-observation that reach beyond partial responsiveness. About institutional justification and reflexivity; see R. Forst, "Das grundlegende Recht auf Rechtfertigung. Zu einer konstruktivistischen Konzeption von Menschenrechten", in: H. Brunkhorst, M. Lutz-Bachmann et al. (eds), *Recht auf Menschenrechte. Menschenrechte, Demokratie und Internationale Politik*, (Frankfurt aM: Suhrkamp Verlag, 1999), pp. 66–106, on the idea of rationalisation through deliberation, see K. O. Apel, "Auflösung der Diskursethik? Zur Architektonik der Diskursdifferenzierung in Habermas' Faktizität und Geltung, Dritter transzendentalpragmatisch orientierter Versuch, mit Habermas gegen Habermas zu denken", in: P. Niesen and R. Schomberg (eds), *Zwischen Recht und Moral: Neuere Ansätze zur Rechts- und Demokratietheorie. Mit Grundtexten von Karl-Otto Apel und Ingeborg Maus*, (Münster: LIT-Verlag, 2002), pp. 61–177; J. Habermas, *Erläuterungen zur Diskursethik*, (Frankfurt aM: Suhrkamp Verlag, 1991), *idem*, Faktizität und Geltung. Beiträge zur Diskurstheorie des Rechts und des demokratischen Rechtsstaats, note 30 *supra*; *idem*, Die postnationale Konstellation und die Zukunft der Demokratie, note 30 *supra*, *idem*, *Die Einbeziehung des Anderen. Studien zur Politischen Theorie*, (Frankfurt aM: Suhrkamp Verlag, 1999).

[37] See already P. P. Craig and C. de Búrca, *EU Law – Text, Cases, and Materials* (Oxford: Oxford University Press, 1998); *idem*, *The Evolution of EU Law* (Oxford: Oxford University Press, 1999); J. Shaw, *Law of the European Union* (Houndsmills: Palgrave Law Masters, 2000); C. de Búrca and J. H. H. Weiler (eds), *The European Court of Justice* (Oxford: Oxford University Press, 2002).

in particular hesitant and disputed,[38] and there have always been conflicts about the material content and meaning of the "*acquis*" as a body of law. The reasons are of various kinds:[39] (a) the *acquis communautaire* is fragmented into quasi-constitutional principles of law (supremacy and direct effect, on the one hand, basic and individual rights, and proportionality, on the other), procedural and administrative statutes, and material codes in different areas (from purely economic-, competition- and market-law to social and political or citizenship rights), (b) the legal instruments of the *acquis* are differentiated according to range and binding effect, depending on different kinds of legal source (treaty-law, regulations, directives, or precedents); and (c) what might be the most crucial aspect is that the structure of the *acquis* highly depends on a broader definition of the European Union as a functional, social or political community. These background orientations about the general scheme of the Union determine the concept of rights associated with them, for example, negative rights of (economic) freedom on the one hand versus positive (social, political, and procedural) rights on the other, and they structure concrete conflicts about the legal status quo of the European Union. In all these areas, processes of the EU's incremental "constitutionalisation" have been contested.

In normative terms, the idea of constitutionalising the European Union is ambiguous in several aspects, at least when compared to the standards traditionally associated with constitution-making proper: first of all, there is a lack of a factual foundational moment, including something like a constitutional assembly and, in particular, a visible *pouvoir constituant* able to articulate and execute a general, constitutionalising will. The basic features of the development of the European legal system (i.e., supremacy, direct effect, the incorporation of human and fundamental individual rights, the establishment of a system of judicial review and appeal)

---

[38] See, for example, S. Bertea, "Looking for Coherence within the European Community", (2005) 11 *European Law Journal*, pp. 154–172; A. von Bogdandy, "European Integration: Doctrine of Principles", (2003) 9 *Jean Monnet Working Paper*; P. Dann, "Thoughts on a Methodology of European Constitutional Law", (2005) 6 *German Law Journal*, pp. 1453–1474; P. Dann and M. Rynkowski, *The Unity of the European Constitution* (Berlin: Springer, 2006); A. Wiener and G. Schwellnus, "Contested Norms in the Process of EU Enlargement: Non-Discrimination and Minority Rights", (2004) 2 *ConWEB Papers*.

[39] A lot of insights about contested issues can be found in studies dealing with the evolution of European law and constitutionalisation. See, especially, P. Craig, *The Evolution of EU Law*, (Oxford: Oxford University Press, 2002), A. Bodnar, M. Kowalski, K. Raible and F. Schorkopf (eds), *The Emerging Constitutional Law of the European Union. Beiträge zum ausländischen öffentlichen Recht und Völkerrecht 163*, (Berlin: Springer, 2003), A. von Bogdandy and J. Bast (eds), *Principles of European Constitutional Law*, (Oxford: Hart Publishing, 2006); J. H. H. Weiler and M. Wind (eds), *European Constitutionalism Beyond the State*, (Cambridge: Cambridge University Press, 2003), T. Christiansen and C. Reh, *Constitutionalising the European Union*, (Houndsmills: Palgrave, 2005); C. Church and D. Phinnemore, *Understanding the European Constitution: An Introduction to the EU Constitutional Treaty*, (London: Taylor and Francis, 2006), C. Barnard (ed), *The Fundamentals of EU Law Revisited. Assessing the Impact of the Constitutional Debate*, (Oxford: Oxford University Press, 2007); see, also, A. Williams, *EU Human Rights Policies. A Study in Irony*, (Oxford: Oxford University Press, 2004).

have frequently been characterised as being part of a process of constitutionalisation, despite the fact that, in normative terms, these qualifications have always been subject to disagreement. Even if one is willing to accept the factual and incremental development of the European legal system as a process of constitutionalisation, serious questions about the justification and legitimacy of this constitution arise – questions which the European Union has, itself, tried to tackle by establishing such fora as the Charter of Fundamental Rights and the European Convention. However, in normative terms, the –mainly informal and élite-driven –constitutionalisation can be legitimised only if it is subsequently exposed to processes of justification, because public processes of justification can promise to generate *–ex post facto–*reciprocal understanding as well as mutual recognition and acceptance. [40] Legitimate processes of justification, in turn, have to meet two sets of normative criteria. On a general level, such processes have to be essentially discursive and inclusive: a reciprocal game of reason-giving and reason-taking, which is open for contestation and revision, has to be established. This implies the notion of equal concern and respect, which has to be realised by securing the equality of voices, on the one hand, and the potential inclusiveness of all stakes, on the other. In formal terms, these processes of justification have to be characterised by transparency, openness and reversibility. Along these lines, constitutionalisation can be regarded as legitimate only if it is able to meet normative standards of deliberation, but, in order to

[40] I cannot *in extenso* outline and justify this normative starting point that is basically relying on conceptual notions of discourse theory and deliberative democratic theory. For further and principled elaboration, see J. Habermas, Faktizität und Geltung, note 30 *supra* and*idem*, "Über den internen Zusammenhang von Rechtsstaat und Demokratie", in: U. Preuss(ed), *Der Begriff der Verfassung*, (Frankfurt aM: Suhrkamp Verlag, 1994); R. Forst, "Das grundlegende Recht auf Rechtfertigung. Zu einer konstruktivistischen Konzeption von Menschenrechten", note 36 *supra* and *idem*, *Das Recht auf Rechtfertigung. Elemente einer konstruktivistischen Theorie der Gerechtigkeit*, (Frankfurt aM: Suhrkamp Verlag, 2005), Schmalz-Bruns, *Reflexive Demokratie. Die partizipatorische Transformation moderner Politik*, note 30 *supra*, F. I. Michelman, "Law's Republic", (1988) 97 *The Yale Law Journal*, pp. 1493–1537, and*idem*, "Bringing the Law to Life", (1989) 74 *Cornell Law Review*, p. 256. For approaches relating to the supra-, trans- and international level, see Habermas, "Towards a Cosmopolitan Europe", note 30 *supra*; Bohman, "Constitution Making and Democratic Innovation: The European Union and Transnational Governance", note 30 *supra*, Closa, "Deliberative Constitutional Politics and the Turn toward a Norm-Based Legitimacy of the EU Constitution", note 30 *supra*: Gerstenberg, "Expanding the Constitution Beyond the Court: The Case of Euro-Constitutionalism", note 30 *supra*; O. Gerstenberg and C. Sabel, "Directly-Deliberative Polyarchy. An Institutional Ideal for Europe?", *Working Paper* available at: http://www.law.columbia.edu/sabel/papers.htm; Eriksen, *Making the European Polity. Reflexive integration in the EU*, note 30 *supra*;T. Auberger and T. Hitzel-Cassagnes, "Bedingungen und Kontexte von Diskursivität", in: T. Hitzel-Cassagnes and T. Schmitt (eds), *Demokratie in Europa und Europäische Demokratie*, (Wiesbaden: Verlag für Sozialwissenschaften, 2005); Joerges, "Deliberative Supranationalism –Two Defences", note 30 *supra*, Menéndez, "Between Laeken and the Deep Blue Sea: An Assessment of the Draft Constitutional Treaty from a Deliberative-Democratic Standpoint", note 30 *supra*, and R. Schmalz-Bruns, "An den Grenzen der Entstaatlichung: Bemerkungen zu Habermas Modell einer'Weltinnenpolitik ohne Weltregierungen'", in: B. Herborth and P. Niesen (eds), *Anarchie der kommunikativen Freiheit. Jürgen Habermas und die Theorie der Internationalen Politik*, (Frankfurt aM: Suhrkamp Verlag, 2007), pp. 269–293.

realise these normative standards, processes of justification have to be embedded in an institutional structure which is capable of embodying these principles and of ensuring the normative acceptability of deliberative outcomes.

This line of thought leads back to the argument which underlies the idea of a monist second-order scheme and which endeavours to tackle the problem of conflicting claims of supremacy and sovereignty. Kant's regulative ideal of a democratic generation of law and of self-legislation within the framework of *civitas* or *res publica* is strongly linked to a fallibilist intuition, i.e., an awareness of deficiency, an awareness that keeps in mind the precarious prospects of procedurally and institutionally realising the "dignity of a rational being, obeying no law but that which he himself also gives",[41] or, in other words, of guaranteeing the co-originality of democracy and law. On the one hand, factually existing institutional structures are expected to be deficient, but, on the other, institutions are obliged to acknowledge democracy-enhancing and democracy-enforcing principles. What I would like to take up and clarify in a twofold way is Kant's concept of the provisional, *i.e.*, his idea that law and, accordingly, institutions are provisional in nature. For him, freedom and self-determination is based upon reason(ing) as a faculty that enounces laws which are imperative, "or objective laws of freedom and which tell us what ought to take place, *even if this might never happen* [*ob es gleich vielleicht nie geschieht*]".[42] In my reading, this afterthought about the precarious prospect of factual realisation is constitutively built into the architecture of his thinking, and I would like to take this critical consciousness seriously in order to plea for an idea of proceduralisation as a permanent, provisional and reflexive structure of legislation. In his epistemological groundwork "*Metaphysics of Morals*" he specifies that:

> "all legislation, whether relating to internal or external action, and whether prescribed a priori by mere reason or laid down by the will of another, involves two elements: First, a law which represents the action that ought to happen as necessary objectively, thus making the action a duty; second, a motive [*Triebfeder*] which connects the principle determining the will [*Bestimmungsgrund der Willkür*] to this action with the mental representation of the law [*Vorstellung des Gesetzes*] subjectively, so that the law makes duty the motive of the action [*dass das Gesetz die Pflicht zur Triebfeder macht*]."[43]

His "categorical imperative" most prominently reflects the idea that an articulation of the condition of freedom is possible only in the form of a universal law [*allgemeines Gesetz*], which is, at the same time, a litmus test for our reasoning:

> "For reason brings the principle or maxim of any action to the test [*der Probe unterwerfen*], by calling upon the agent to think of himself in connection with it as at the same time laying down a universal law, and to consider whether his action is so qualified as

[41] See I. Kant, "Kritik der praktischen Vernunft", note 32 *supra*; *idem*, "Die Metaphysik der Sitten", note 32 *supra*. This and the following quotations of Kant are my own translation.

[42] I. Kant, "Kritik der reinen Vernunft" in: W. Weischedel (ed), *Werke in zwölf Bänden. Theorie-Werkausgabe vol. I & II*, (Frankfurt aM: Suhrkamp Verlag, 1956), p. 657 emphasis added.

[43] I. Kant, "Kritik der praktischen Vernunft", in: W. Weischedel (ed), *Werke in zwölf Bänden. Theorie-Werkausgabe vol. VII & VIII Schriften zur Ethik und Religionsphilosophie*, note 32 *supra*, p. 323.

> to be fit for entering into such a universal legislation [*durch denselben sich zugleich als allgemein gesetzgebend zu denken, er sich zu einer solchen allgemeinen Gesetzgebung qualifiziere*]."[44]

At first sight, this phrasing seems strange in so far as it is not obvious how these insights can – in the light of the rigid and final character of formality – lead to proceduralisation, reflexivity and reversibility. A procedural conceptualisation is accessible when considering two further, but related, arguments, firstly, the argument that we ought to differentiate between a hypothetical and constitutive status of regulative ideas, and, secondly, that processes of a public use of reason are the ultimate litmus test for formal legislation. In the chapter "*Of the regulative employment of the ideas of pure reason*" of his book *Critique of pure reason*, he introduces the thesis that transcendental ideas, i.e., those ideas which reflect upon the conditions of the possibility of reasoning, cannot be of constitutive use or employment.[45] They do not supply us with material concepts which define objects, but they do order, structure and, at best, enlighten in character. In this sense, Kant talks of the regulative and hyphothetical status of regulative ideas.[46] They are – in very general terms – a touchstone of rules of reasoning (and truth) where reason touches upon the conditions and borders of its realisation.[47] This regulative structure is the same with regard to the realisation of autonomy, self-determination and freedom, i.e., with regard to the law of freedom:

> "I term all that is possible through free will, practical. But if the conditions of the exercise of free volition are empirical, reason can have only a regulative, and not a constitutive, influence upon it".[48]

Kant's notion of personality, i.e., of persons as ends in themselves, strongly relies on a model of (rational) accountability. Thus, the idea of the free will, or of freedom more generally, is intrinsically related to the concept of individuals as both moral

---

[44]Ibid., p. 331.

[45]I. Kant, "Kritik der reinen Vernunft", in: W. Weischedel (ed), *Werke in zwölf Bänden. Theorie-Werkausgabe vol. I & II,* (Frankfurt aM: Suhrkamp Verlag, 1956), p. 565.

[46]It is important to notice that the idea of proceduralisation is not just elaborated in Kant's practical philosophy dealing with the moral, ethical and legal realms of society and with the different modes of self-determination in concrete but also in his theoretical philosophy mainly dealing with epistemological reflections. In the chapter on the differences between "*Opining, knowing, and believing*" in the *Critique of pure reason*, he elaborates procedural modes of solving epistemological questions. The basic assumption is that agreement and consensus is the best possible appropriation of fulfilling 'truth-conditions'. The motive for proceduralising epistemological questions is threefold: firstly, there is a constitutive mismatch or discrepancy between the ideal truth-conditions and their realisation. secondly, we have to take into account the necessarily subjective structure of "holding a thing to be true" and thirdly, individual judgements are vulnerable to deception and illusion; see Kant, note 42, supra, p. 687.

[47]I. Kant, "Kritik der reinen Vernunft", in: W. Weischedel (ed), *Werke in zwölf Bänden. Theorie-Werkausgabe vol. I & II,* note 45 *supra*, p. 567.

[48]Ibid., p. 673.

and legal subjects, who are responsible and accountable, and whose actions are, in principle, imputable:

> "A person is a subject who is capable of having his actions imputed to him. Moral personality is, therefore, nothing but the freedom of a rational being under moral laws [...] Hence it follows that a person is properly subject to no other laws than those he lays down for himself, either alone or in conjunction with others."[49]

By way of unfolding the idea of the law of freedom within a framework of social co-operation, the positive characteristics of law as a legal order can be derived; by the same token, it can be argued that any kind of institutional order is internally linked to the formal inclination of reason and law. The law is the "embodiment" [*Inbegriff*] of those conditions which enable citizens to be united by a universal law of freedom which respects the free will of all and the common will.[50] In this context, Kant is quite empathetic and extensive with regard to the spheres of social co-operation, which implies a duty to inaugurate a *status civilis*. In order to avoid arbitrary and hegemonic structures, social co-operation has to be legally embedded and law-bound. This perspective has institutional consequences: "Be a person bound by the idea of law" [*Sei ein rechtlicher Mensch*],[51] i.e., "act to treat yourself not

[49] I. Kant, "Die Metaphysik der Sitten", note 32 *supra*, p. 329.

[50] In the original it reads: "Das Recht ist also der Inbegriff der Bedingungen, unter denen die Willkür des einen mit der Willkür des anderen nach einem allgemeinen Gesetze der Freiheit zusammen vereinigt werden kann"; I. Kant, "Die Metaphysik der Sitten", in: W. Weischedel (ed), *Werke in zwölf Bänden. Theorie-Werkausgabe vol. VII & VIII Schriften zur Ethik und Religionsphilosophie*, note 32 *supra*, p. 337.

[51] I. Kant, "Die Metaphysik der Sitten", note 32 *supra*, p. 344. Elsewhere, he specifies the duties following from this requirement: "For all rational beings come under the law that each of them must treat itself and all others never merely as means, but in every case at the same time as ends in themselves. Hence, results a systematic union of rational being by common objective laws, i.e., a kingdom which may be called a kingdom of ends, since what these laws have in view is just the relation of these beings to one another as ends and means. It is certainly *only* an ideal" (Kant, "Grundlegung zur Metaphysik der Sitten", note 32 *supra*, p. 66, emphasis added). To my mind, the phrasing "it is only an ideal" should be interpreted as a hint to the regulative nature of the ideal, not as a redemption of the claim that the ideal is categorically justified and morally grounded. That Kant's version of the Hobbesian command *exeundum esse e statu naturali* is not prudentially or pragmatically founded is also well elaborated in his essay "Perpetual Peace: A Philosophical Sketch", where he states, for instance, "that reason, from its throne of supreme moral legislating authority, absolutely condemns war as a legal recourse and makes a state of peace a direct duty", Kant, "Die Metaphysik der Sitten", in: W. Weischedel (ed), *Werke in zwölf Bänden. Theorie-Werkausgabe vol. VII & VIII Schriften zur Ethik und Religionsphilosophie*, note 32 *supra*, p. 211 *et seq.*, also Kant, Kritik der reinen Vernunft in W. Weischedel (ed), *Werke in zwölf Bänden. Theorie-Werkausgabe vol. I & II*, note 45 *supra*; 'Kritik der praktischen Vernunft' in W. Weischedel (ed), *Werke in zwölf Bänden. Theorie-Werkausgabe vol. VII & VIII Schriften zur Ethik und Religionsphilosophie*, note 32; "Erste Fassung der Einleitung in die Kritik der Urteilskraft", in: W. Weischedel (ed), *Werke in zwölf Bänden. Theorie-Werkausgabe vol. IX & X Kritik der Urteilskraft und Schriften zur Naturphilosophie*, (Frankfurt aM: Suhrkamp Verlag, 1957), pp. 173–237; 'Kritik der Urteilskraft', in: W. Weischedel (ed), *Werke in zwölf Bänden. Theorie-Werkausgabe vol. IX & X Kritik der Urteilskraft und Schriften zur Naturphilosophie*, (Frankfurt aM: Suhrkamp Verlag 1957), pp. 237–623; and "Die Metaphysik der Sitten", in: W. Weischedel (ed), *Werke in zwölf*

merely as a means to others but aim to be an end for them" [*mach dich anderen nicht zum bloßen Mittel, sondern sei für sie zugleich Zweck*][52] is a regulative idea with two implications: on the one hand, the normative expectation that citizens of a *res publica* should understand themselves as both, authors and addressees of the law, is raised. On the other hand, public institutions are expected to ameliorate and realise the conditions of freedom and self-determination. This duty of institutional engineering[53] is backed up by procedural and organisational principles of which the most important ones structure "democratic" juris-generation and the system of institutional checks and balances (the system of separation of powers). To highlight and qualify the separation of powers principle within an institutional order of *civitas* is important because it specifies one condition for realising laws of freedom and self-determination, i.e., reflexivity. Within a framework of checks and balances, *nemo judex in causa propria* is the structuring principle for establishing a mutual system of self-restraint and for guaranteeing reflexivity.

Apart from this procedural juris-generic aspect which is supposed to guarantee the democratic production of law and the congruency between subjects of the law, the legal and institutional order is, in another way, responsive to the claims of self-determination embedded in *civitas*. By way of the public use of reason, *civitas* has the potential to legitimise as well as to de-legitimise and challenge public institutions. Considering the idea of a public use of reason as a procedure of testing institutional performance with regard to the realisation of (the conditions of) freedom advances the claim that the institutional order of a *res publica* necessarily embodies reflexive and provisional structures. For Kant, the freedom of public reasoning and judgement is not only both the base and the main source of approaching the idea of autonomy and self-determination; but it is also the base and the main source of ameliorating democracy-enhancing and democracy-enforcing institutions, and of establishing legal principles and norms apt to guarantee freedom. He is quite explicit in this regard, among others in elaborating the constitutive status of the principle of free speech and public will-formation:

> "This freedom will, among other things, permit of our openly stating the difficulties and doubts which we are ourselves unable to solve, without being decried on that account as turbulent and dangerous citizens. This privilege forms part of the native rights of human reason, which recognises no other judge than the universal reason of humanity; and as this [freedom] is the source of all progress and improvement."[54]

Bänden. Theorie-Werkausgabe vol. VII & VIII Schriften zur Ethik und Religionsphilosophie, note 32 *supra*, p. 422 *et seq.*

[52] I. Kant, "Die Metaphysik der Sitten", in: W. Weischedel (ed), *Werke in zwölf Bänden. Theorie-Werkausgabe vol. VII & VIII Schriften zur Ethik und Religionsphilosophie*, note 32 *supra*, p. 344.

[53] T. Hitzel-Cassagnes, "Der EuGH im Spannungsfeld von Konstitutionalisierung und Demokratisierung", in: M. Becker and R. Zimmerling (eds), *Politik und Recht. PVS Sonderheft*, (Baden-Baden: Nomos, 2005).

[54] I. Kant, "Kritik der reinen Vernunft", in: W. Weischedel (ed), *Werke in zwölf Bänden. Theorie-Werkausgabe vol. I & II*,, note 45 *supra*, p. 640.

To conclude: the public use of reason can potentially lead to changes in the *status civilis* itself and in the institutional structure of *res publica* – which is, after all, desirable because it might be a way of closing legitimacy-gaps, of diminishing democratic deficits, and of strengthening reflexivity and responsiveness. This perfectionist, but hypothetical and regulative, ideal is directed at the factual imperfections of institutional and legal orders, thereby imposing reflexive responsiveness. To my mind, a Kantian notion of a basically formal structure of reflexive institutions can also inspire a conceptualisation of law, democracy and constitutionalisation within the EU. To elaborate the formal structure of law in normative, not just functional, terms, the universalistic, equality-securing and inclusive potentials of formalism can be explicated. Beyond that background, the formal structure of law and institutions can be qualified in a twofold way, on the one hand, it is embedded in a broader conception of proceduralisation – in particular, democratic jurisgeneration, public justification, mutual self-restraint and reflexivity –, and on the other hand, institutional orders and legal systems are provisional in nature in order to preserve the idea of progress (under reserve with regard to a better state).[55] The Kantian idea of the provisional is very well equipped to conceptualise constitutionalisation as a meta-scheme of co-operation, reciprocity and reflexivity, which replace partiality and arbitrariness of juris-generation and conflict-resolution. If constitutionalisation is, in this light, seen as a systematic articulation of a procedural ideal directed at establishing an inclusive system of juris-generation, which is responsive towards different agents of justice, it entails an organisational ideal: a monist ethos of law. Within such a monist scheme, pluralism is taken not just as a starting-point, but also taken seriously all the way down (or up) in normative terms, i.e., captured within an institutional system of mutual self-restraint and equal respect.

Beyond this background, one can argue that it is not so much the notion of sovereignty or supremacy that keeps the inherent promise of law (autonomy and self-determination) in mind, but open, accessible and revisable procedures. In this regard, there would be no need to worry about the permeability or withering away of sovereignty because law as a *proviso* will take the edge off the expectation that it is possible to justify supremacy-premises (except in the above mentioned version of a universalist aspiration). Claiming supremacy or sovereignty would, in justificatory terms, be rather counter-productive; it would deny the idea of reciprocal recognition of agents of justice as equals. If law is understood as a reflexive medium of social co-operation, it has to proceduralise supremacy-conflicts, and thus sovereignty could only be attributed to (constitutional) processes, to second-order procedures which secure autonomy and self-determination.

[55] With regard to a better state, see I. Kant, "Die Metaphysik der Sitten", in: W. Weischedel (ed), *Werke in zwölf Bänden. Theorie-Werkausgabe vol. VII & VIII Schriften zur Ethik und Religionsphilosophie*, note 32 *supra*, p. 463.

Part V
Legal Argumentation

Chapter 9
Coherence and Post-sovereign Legal Argumentation

Flavia Carbonell

9.1 Introduction

The renaissance of the practice of giving reasons was nearly contemporaneous with the linguistic turn. As an echo of the rise of argumentation theories in the philosophy of language, and strongly influenced by the harsh reactions and criticisms towards legal positivism that followed the Second World War, argumentation theories soon appeared in legal theory, most of them considering, on the one hand, that legal argumentation shared some features with practical or moral reasoning, and, on the other, highlighting the specificities that reasoning acquires in this field of human knowledge.[1]

In the mid- to late-1970s, three different scholars – Alexy, Aarnio and MacCormick – coming from three different legal traditions,[2] pinned down in their writings a common concern about argumentation in law that was up in the air, without knowledge of the parallel work of each other. Despite some differences, these theories shared the prominent place that argumentation should have in law, and included, though with differing intensity, references to the role of coherence in legal thinking.[3]

MacCormick's theory of legal argumentation has to be understood with regard to his wider reflections on the concept of law and legal pluralism. With regard to the

F. Carbonell (✉)
Universidad Alberto Hurtado de Santiago de Chile, Santiago, Chile
e-mail: flocarbonell@yahoo.es

[1] Alexy's special-case thesis is the main reference here. See R. Alexy, *A Theory of Legal Argumentation: The Theory of Rational Discourse as Theory of Legal Justification*, (Oxford: Clarendon Press, 1989); "The Special Case Thesis", (1999) 12 *Ratio Juris*, pp. 374–384.

[2] These are, roughly speaking, and without accounting for the particularities that they present in Germany, Finland and Scotland, the Civil-law tradition, the Scandinavian tradition and the Common-law tradition respectively.

[3] A further product of the joint concern on this topic were the meetings held between Aarnio, Alexy and Peczenik between 1979 and 1980, which resulted in the well-known collective article by these authors "The Foundation of Legal Reasoning", (1981) 12 *Rechtstheorie*, pp. 133–158, pp. 257–279 and pp. 423–448.

A.J. Menéndez, J.E. Fossum (eds.), *Law and Democracy in Neil MacCormick's Legal and Political Theory*, Law and Philosophy Library 93,
DOI 10.1007/978-90-481-8942-7_9, © Springer Science+Business Media B.V. 2011

former, a relevant feature of law is, according to this author, its practicality. Norms are guides for action, and, in this respect, a central question arises about how norms function in practice, or to put it differently, how the institutional normative order is operationalised. Law adjudication, as the main way in which norms are applied to concrete cases, is mediated by argumentation. In this process of justifying decisions, there are also reasons beyond rules that should bc included – for example, principles, values, maxims and the claim to correctness – albeit always within the limits of the rule of law. With regard to legal pluralism, the fact that, together with state law, there is also law between states, and law ordering the functioning and the powers of international and supranational organisations, reveals the co-existence of different interacting institutional normative orders. In addition, the pluralistic approach to law conceives these legal orders as independent and distinct from one another.

Coherence, then, plays a role both in the conceptualisation of an institutional normative order as a legal system and in legal reasoning. In the latter, coherence displays its force as a general guideline when justifying legal decisions – overall coherence – and as a particular argument concerning facts and norms. But what happens with these types of coherence when they are confronted not just with one but with multiple interacting and independent legal systems?

This chapter will critically reconstruct MacCormick's conception of coherence in legal reasoning when it interplays with legal pluralism, and examine both how and to what extent both ideas factor into the case-law of the European Court of Justice (ECJ). For this purpose, I will first deal with MacCormick's argument of coherence, framing it inside the general theoretical debate about the concept and value of this argument in legal reasoning (Section 9.2). Secondly, attention will be given to legal reasoning in the European Community, with special focus on the way in which the ECJ uses coherence, and on the possibility of rendering this argument compatible with a pluralistic approach to Community law (Section 9.3). The final section will offer some concluding remarks (Section 9.4).

9.2 Coherence in Legal Justification: MacCormick's Theory

The idea of coherence seems inherent in legal thinking,[4] and is considered as a significant value of law.[5] Connecting these general statements with legal argumentation, everyone would accept that coherence is a positive and desirable feature of legal reasoning. Moreover, it is commonly acknowledged that it is a criteria of its

---

[4]A. Aarnio, 'Why Coherence – A Philosophical Point of View', in: A. Aarnio (ed), *On Coherence Theory of Law*, (Lund: Juristfoerlaget, 1998), pp. 28–40, at 34. In a different sense, Bobbio refers to coherence as a "legal virtue". Legal coherence, for this author, is the respect of the legality principle (*pacta sunt servanda*). N. Bobbio, *Studi sulla teoria generale del diritto*, (Torino: Giappichelli, 1950), p. 149 *et seq.*

[5]N. MacCormick, "Arguing about Interpretation", *Rhetoric and the Rule of Law: A Theory of Legal Reasoning*, (Oxford: Oxford University Press, 2005), p. 132 and p. 139.

soundness, or even a component of justice according to law.[6] Put negatively, the lack of coherence is considered to be a failure to make sense.[7]

However, this initial agreement would probably disappear if one tried to ascertain what each potential participant in it actually meant by coherence. This is not the place to give an account of all of them, but only to recall the ambiguity of the concept of coherence, its diverse uses, and the different theories developed around the idea of coherence.[8] A basic preliminary notion, though, both in coherence theories of truth[9] *and* in the role of coherence in law, acknowledges that the idea of coherence has to do with elements or parts sticking or hanging together, or with something (for example, an object) being in harmony with another thing.[10]

MacCormick's interest in coherence in law is already present in his first essays on legal reasoning, in which he emphasises its important position inside the structure of legal justification and the idea of law as a system.[11] As a starting-point, he remarks that logical consistency, or the absence of contradiction between legal propositions[12] is not a sufficient criterion for understanding or achieving coherence, since, for the latter, it is the content of the premises, and not just the formal

---

[6]N. MacCormick, "Being Reasonable", ibid., p. 188.

[7]N. MacCormick, "Coherence, Principles and Analogies", in: *Rhetoric and the Rule of Law*, note 5 *supra* p. 189.

[8]As for the role of coherence in legal reasoning see R. Alexy, 'Coherence and Argumentation or the Genuine Twin Criterialess Super Criterion' in Aarnio, note 4 *supra*, pp. 41–49; R. Alexy and A. Peczenick, "The Concept of Coherence and Its Significance for Discursive Rationality", (1990) 3 *Ratio Juris*, pp. 130–147; S. Bertea, "The Arguments from Coherence: Analysis and Evaluation", (2005) 25 *Oxford Journal of Legal Studies*, pp. 369–391; K. Günther, "A Normative Conception of Coherence for a Discursive Theory of Legal Justification", (1989) 2 *Ratio Juris*, pp. 155–166; J. van Dunné, "Normative and Narrative Coherence in Legal Decision Making", in: F. Atria and N. MacCormick (eds), *Law and Legal Interpretation*, (Aldershot: Ashgate-Dartmouth Publishing, 2003), pp. 409–429; L. Moral Soriano, "A Modest notion of Coherence in Legal Reasoning. A Model for the European Court of Justice", (2003) 16 *Ratio Juris*, pp. 296–323. For wider views of coherence in legal science, see Nerhot, "Interpretation in Legal Science. The notion of narrative coherence", in: Nerhot (ed), *Law, Interpretation and Reality. Essays in Epistemology, Hermeneutics and Jurisprudence*, (Dordrecht: Kluwer, 1990), pp. 193–225, and A. Peczenik, "Coherence in Legal Doctrine", in: E. Pattaro (ed), *Scientia Juris. Legal Doctrines as Knowledge of Law and as a Source of Law. A Treatise of Legal Philosophy and General Jurisprudence, volume 4*, (Dordrecht: Springer, 2005), pp. 115–165; J. Raz, "The Relevance of Coherence", in: *idem*, *Ethics in the Public Domain. Essays in Morality of Law and Politics*, (Oxford: Clarendon Press, 1994.

[9]N. Rescher, *The Coherence Theory of Truth*, (Oxford: Oxford University Press, 1973); J. Young, "The Coherence Theory of Truth", *Stanford Encyclopedia of Philosophy*, available at: http://plato.stanford.edu/entries/truth-coherence (accessed 20 June 2010).

[10]S. J. Pethick, "An Investigation of Coherence and Coherence Theory in Relation to Law and Legal Reasoning", (DPhil thesis, University of Oxford, 2000), p. 18. Etymologically, the word comes from the Latin *cohærere* ("cohere") that means to stick (*hærere*) together (*com-*).

[11]N. MacCormick, "Formal Justice and the form of Legal Arguments", in: C. Perelman (ed), *Études de logique juridique*, (Brussels: Bruylant, 1976), pp. 103–118, pp. 114–115.

[12]This distinction is kept also in his recent writings, for example, in MacCormick, note 6 *supra*, p. 190.

inexistence of contradiction alone, which matters. He remarks that complete consistency is not a necessary condition for coherence, because coherence is a matter of degree, unlike consistency,[13] and can be predicated not only on statements, but also on forms of behaviour. In this last case, coherence seems to be related to instrumental rationality.[14] Finally, coherence is complex, as it depends on the interaction between the different arguments and on the interpretation of the applicable norms and system.

On the other hand, coherence can be distinguished from universalisation that consists of the judge's obligation of extending the rationale of the present decision to future similar cases.[15] Justification of legal reasoning requires the universalisation of the reasons for realising formal justice or the egalitarian character of the rule of law.[16] In turn, equal treatment among similar circumstances, is only possible if the system is conceived coherently.[17]

Legal reasoning uses both the idea of overall coherence as a general guidance in justifying decisions and as a particular and well-defined argument. However, let us first say a few words with regard to overall coherence.

9.2.1 Overall Coherence in Legal Reasoning

When arguing in favour of a particular interpretation of a legal text, together with presenting different types of arguments – be they linguistic, contextual, teleological – the interpretation should be shown to be an acceptable understanding of the norm as part of the legal system. It is within this systemic context that the legal material acquires its significance. Therefore, the ideal of overall coherence governs the view of the legal system as a system, and helps to make sense, to bring together and to order the multiplicity of the different kinds of norms that comprise the whole legal system.[18] Accordingly, coherence steps into the idea of system of law when conceived as a set of inter-related norms which have a common ground of formal validity and which cohere or hang together purposively. In this sense, law can be

[13]Gianformaggio considers this distinction, together with the one between weak and strong derivability, of fundamental importance. L. Gianformaggio, "Legal Certainty, Coherence and Consensus: Variations on a Theme by MacCormick" in: Nerhot, note 8 *supra*, pp. 402–430, at 420.

[14]P. Comanducci, "Osservazioni in margine a N. MacCormick's 'La congruenza nella giustificazione giuridica'", in: P. Comanducci and R. Guastini, *L'analisi del ragionamento giuridico*, (Torino: Giappichelli, 1987), pp. 265–272, at 272.

[15]N. MacCormick, 'Universals and Particulars', in: *Rhetoric and the Rule of Law*, note 5 *supra*, pp. 98–99, p. 78 and p. 89.

[16]MacCormick, 'Legal Narratives', in *Rhetoric and the Rule of Law*, note 5 *supra*, pp. 230–231.

[17]MacCormick, 'Formal Justice...', note 11 *supra*, pp. 114–115. This is the link also pointed out by M. La Torre, *Constitutionalism and Legal Reasoning. A New Paradigm for the Concept of Law*, (Dordrecht: Kluwer, 2007), pp. 63–64.

[18]MacCormick, "Arguing about Interpretation" note 5 *supra*, pp. 127–132.

considered as "an expression of reasonably tenable values of principles concerning human social interaction".[19]

On the other hand, the systemic character of law is partially ideal, since it is – at least in part – realised when the law is implemented or applied to practical problems. As Bengoetxea claims, even when law is treated by legal agents as if it were a system in the formal sense – and for this reason, has the features of completeness, consistency and decidability which characterise it – a more realistic picture shows that these features cannot be assured *a priori*, but only *a posteriori*, in a post-interpretative stage.[20]

9.2.2 Coherence as a Specific Argument: Normative and Narrative

In MacCormick's theory, coherence is an argument that acts in the second-order justification, consisting of the material justification of the normative and factual premises. This second-order justification follows the deductive syllogism (first-order justification) when the latter is insufficient to solve a hard case, or similarly, when there is a problem of interpretation, relevance, proof or classification.[21] At this second level, three elements have an important role to play: consistency, coherence, and the consequences of the alternative decisions.[22]

In the context of legal justification, coherence applies both to matters of law (normative coherence) and to matters of facts (narrative coherence). First, normative coherence can be described as a matter of common subservience by a set of laws to a relevant value or values, and avoidance of conflict with other relevant values or principles.[23] Put differently, "a set of rules is coherent if they satisfy or are instances of a single more general principle". The observance of principles is an intrinsic "means of realising values", and values are, in turn, the product of a system of practical reason. In short, principles and values are extensionally equivalent.[24] However, this extensionality does not mean that every value is operationalised as a legal principle in the system.[25]

---

[19]MacCormick, 'Legal Narratives', note 16 *supra*, p. 231.

[20]J. Bengoetxea, "Legal System as a Regulative Ideal", (1994) 53 *Archiv für Rechts – und Sozialphilosophie*, pp. 59–88.

[21]The first two have to do with the major premise (law), and the others with the minor premise (facts). See N. MacCormick, *Legal Reasoning and Legal Theory*, (Oxford: Clarendon Press, 1978 – quoted from the second edition of 1994), pp. 65–72 and pp. 87–97.

[22]Ibid., p. 132. The first two are requirements of the decision making sense within the given system, while the latter looks for the decision to make sense with the perceptible world.

[23]MacCormick, "Coherence, Principles...", note 7 *supra*, p. 192.

[24]N. MacCormick, "Coherence in Legal Justification", in: A. Peczenick, L. Lindhal and B. van Roermund (eds), *Theory of Legal Science*, (Dordrecht: Reidel, 1984), pp. 235–251, at 236–238.

[25]MacCormick, "Coherence, Principles...", note 7 *supra*, p. 192.

The test of normative coherence implies justifying legal rulings or normative propositions in the context of a legal system which is conceived as a normative order.[26] Coherence is a character of systems viewed synchronically, at the time of the judgment or of decision-making. What is significant, however, is not formal derivability, but that the relevant norm is shown to be axiologically congruent with the values and principles from which it derives. The coherence of the set of higher principles or values, in turn, depends on their ability to express as a whole a satisfactory form of life akin to that promoted by Aarnio.[27]

In order to achieve normative coherence, a judge must ask himself or herself about the possible values or principles underlying the relevant set of rules and rulings, and their adjustment or adequacy with the pre-established body of law.[28] Principles, then, provide guidance in interpretation of statutory texts, and, in this interpretative activity, coherence shall include the (theoretically fictitious) intention of the legislator to legislate coherently.[29]

However, I have been presupposing the "relevance of normative coherence" (an expression coined by Raz), in the sense that coherence justifies an interpretation or decision, or plays a relevant role in that justification.[30] MacCormick tackles this possible objection pointing out that legal systems have a particular hierarchical structure of derivability from general principles to particular and specific rules. This chain is, at the same time, a validity test and a justification test, since the detailed provisions should stand as subservient to a more general set of coherent principles, and can therefore be justified by appealing to them. Understood in this sense, coherence has only weak justificatory force, given that it only assures derivability, but does not evaluate the goodness or badness of the higher principle from which the rule derives. Nevertheless, normative coherence functions as a negative test, in the sense that judges must at least comply with this weak derivability of a decision or a ruling from the pre-existent body of law, and explaining the law in this way is an important "formal" judgment in legal reasoning.[31]

On the other hand, narrative coherence deals with facts. It is a test of truth or of the probability of the facts of the case and it is their evidence that has to do with the justification of the findings of facts and the drawing of reasonable inferences from

---

[26]Ibid., p. 189.

[27]Ibid., p. 194. Concerning A. Aarnio, see *On Legal Reasoning*, (Turku: Turun Yliopisto, 1977), pp. 126–129; and *The Rational as Reasonable. A Treatise on Legal Justification*, (Dordrecht: Kluwer, 1987).

[28]Justification through principles has been distinguished from justification through consequences. See J. Wróblewski, "Justification through principles and justification through consequences", in: C. Farrali and E. Pattaro (eds), *Reason in Law*, (Milan: Giuffrè, 1984), pp. 129–161, at 161.

[29]MacCormick, "Coherence in Legal Justification", note 24 *supra*, p. 242.

[30]For a contrary view, see Pethik, note 10 *supra*, p. 315 *et seq*, who claims that MacCormick does not really explain why coherence justifies, since he treats what is necessary to justify but not what is sufficient for the law to be a complete or finite coherent set.

[31]MacCormick, "Coherence, Principles...", note 7 *supra*, pp. 203–204.

the evidence.[32] Since legal disputes generally concern past facts, and in the absence of direct proof, facts and courses of actions must be reconstructed, and narrative coherence must be observed in doing so.[33]

Narrative coherence uses two principles of explanation: the principle of universal causation (all that happens can be *prima facie* explained in terms of some cause occurring before or simultaneously with the event to be explained), and the principle of rational motivation (human decisions or actions are based upon different reasons, such as principles, values, plans or purposes). However, human decisions are a partial exception to the principle of universal causation, in the sense that, if you explain the former through reasons, there is no need to explain it through causes.[34]

When a problem of proof is at stake, or in other words, when the question is how to establish an acceptable account of past events, narrative coherence "provides a test as to the truth or probable truth of propositions about unperceived things and events", explaining the proposition within the ordinary explanatory schemes. The relative probability and coherence of a proposition which relates unperceived events depends on a number of other events which are supposed to have occurred.[35] Thus, the more coherent story is the one that involves fewer improbabilities, the one that justifies beliefs or perceptions by trying to make the phenomenal world intelligible, rational. Yet, in the establishment and reconstruction or the proof of facts, a moderate scepticism should remain, such as that which stands behind the formulae "intimate conviction", "balance of probabilities", or proof "beyond reasonable doubt". These kinds of formulae require the subjective exercise of judgment; that is, they do not operate objectively and do not lead to absolute certainty. In this sense, narrative coherence is a "necessary but not sufficient condition for real-world credibility".[36]

With regard to the temporal dimension of narrative coherence, MacCormick states that it is located in analytical time, in the sense that events are presented in a temporal sequence of before-simultaneously-after.[37] Linked with this, narrative coherence has a diachronic character because its appreciation is made through time, taking into account interconnected events that occur in different temporal moments.

The main common feature between normative and narrative coherence lies in the idea of rationality, significant both in the construction of social systems as the legal one, and in the interpretation of the perceived events of the natural and human

[32] Ibid., p. 189.

[33] Dealing with the problems of proof and evidence, MacCormick linked explicitly narrative coherence with a coherence theory of truth. N. MacCormick, "The Coherence of a Case and the Reasonableness of Doubt", (1980) 2 *Liverpool Law Review*, pp. 45–50, at 46.

[34] MacCormick,, 'Legal Narratives', note 16 *supra*, p. 222.

[35] This resembles the supportive relations and mutual consistency as fundamental elements of the theory of coherence exposed by Alexy and Peczenik, note 8 *supra*, p. 131.

[36] MacCormick, "Legal Narratives", note 16 *supra*, pp. 226–227.

[37] The difference delineated here is between perspective or real time (past, present and future) versus analytical time (before, simultaneously, after). These dimensions are inter-related, since "the capacity for thought in analytical time is a condition for acting in real time". Ibid., p. 216.

world. Thus, the rational normative order and the rational world-view as expressions of coherence are rooted in this overarching idea of rationality.[38]

On the other hand, coherence is not a complete argument that can justify a decision on its own. In the case of normative coherence, for example, the decision-maker has to justify that the principles from which the norm is an instantiation (i.e., those that support the norm) are the correct ones, and that they operate within the specific branch of law or within the whole legal order. On other occasions, arguments that emphasise the aims of the norm, or the consequences of the decision, will reinforce or complete the justification of the decision. Similarly, narrative coherence is only part of the external justification of the minor premise of the syllogism, since the factual assertion and the causal nexus also need justification, and because the factual statement comes together with its normative qualification.[39] In this respect, the consideration of law as an argumentative practice needs to attend to different types of argument, and to how they fit together.

Finally, as has been suggested in the previous reflections, MacCormick's legal theory of coherence is not only a criterion of justification, but also the building method of the practical system of law proposed by him.[40] This hierarchically-constructed system of rules, principles and values is universalised when applied to a specific case. At the top of the pyramid, one can find the ultimate principles that express a "satisfactory form of life". In this framework, normative and narrative coherence are not only operative criteria for justifying (judicial) decision-making (coherence of adjudication), but are also the ideal value (integrity) that guides the reconstruction of the system as a set of coherent rules derived from higher and more general principles (the coherence of the system).

9.3 Legal Reasoning in a Post-sovereign Constellation

9.3.1 Institutional Theory of Law and Integrity in a Post-sovereign Constellation

Until now, I have focussed principally on the argument of coherence within legal reasoning. However, the ideas of law as integrity and of system related with this argument connect the spectrum of analysis with the concept of law and with the notion of system underlying it. MacCormick's concept of law as *institutional normative order* is the legal framework under which legal argumentation should be understood. To simplify, a normative order is a kind of ideal order that guides choices and which necessarily involves judgment. When this normative order is formalised through validly enacted rules, one can speak of institutional normative order. Both legislation and adjudication are institutionalised, and both legislators

---

[38] MacCormick, "Coherence, Principles...", note 7 *supra*, p. 189.

[39] Comanducci, "Osservazioni in margine", note 14 *supra*, pp. 274–275.

[40] Ibid., p. 272.

and judges should develop the law bearing in mind the idea of a systemic (coherent) whole.[41]

It is interesting to note, and an important purpose of this chapter, that the concept of law as institutional normative order, the notions of system and integrity, and the theory of legal argumentation elaborated by MacCormick are not constrained by the nation-state conception, but can be applied to other entities, such as a post-national constellation.[42]

The European Community (EC) is one of the representative entities of this post-national constellation. In MacCormick's opinion, this is a post-sovereign polity or commonwealth which comprises "no-longer-fully-sovereign states", and in which the relationships of the various parts depend on a "still-to-be-elaborated" principle of subsidiarity and not on a zero-sum game of competition for sovereignty.[43] In this "post-sovereign" Europe, sovereignty is now parcelled between different organs and powers. This new entity and the way of understanding the interactions of the legal and political powers can be called a "commonwealth", in the sense of a group of people that looks consciously towards a common good, and, to that end, envisages their representatives or authorities to come into a new form of political structure and to engage in common constitutional arrangements.[44]

From a legal point of view, the main problem here is the interaction between the nation-state law systems and the Community law as a new *sui generis* legal order, each of which has its own validity mechanisms. This co-existence of distinct genuinely institutional normative legal orders, called legal or juridical pluralism, renders it necessary to look for a way to achieve common legal standards between the states, and, at the same time, to settle the boundaries in the interaction of the Community legal order and the state-law of the Member States.

Moving these ideas into the realm of judicial decision-making process, the interaction between systems has to deal with the problems of how the ECJ and the national courts interpret and apply Community Law, how to harmonize the interpretations and correct application of that body of law,[45] how to guarantee the coherence and integrity of a certain branch or of the whole Community law system, and how

---

[41] N. MacCormick, *Institutions of Law. An Essay in Legal Theory*, (Oxford: Oxford University Press, 2007), p. 304; N. MacCormick, "The Legal Framework: Institutional Normative Order", in: *idem*, *Questioning Sovereignty: Law, State and Nation in the European Commonwealth*, (Oxford: Oxford University Press, 1999), p. 7.

[42] J. Habermas, *The Post-National Constellation*, (Cambridge MA: The MIT Press, 2001).

[43] N. MacCormick, "A Very British Revolution?", in: *idem*, *Questioning Sovereignty: Law, State and Nation in the European Commonwealth,* note 41 *supra*, p. 95; idem, "After Sovereignty: Understanding Constitutional Change", (1998) 9 *The King's College Law Journal*, pp. 20–38, at 38.

[44] N. MacCormick, "Democracy and Subsidiarity in the European Commonwealth", in: *idem*, *Questioning Sovereignty: Law, State and Nation in the European Commonwealth,* note 41 *supra,* p. 143.

[45] In this sense, the norms should be not only formally operative in the different Member States, but also operative in the same sense. This is the purpose of the preliminary rulings put before the ECJ by the national courts, to obtain a common or uniform interpretation of the norms, focusing on the principles that underlie them. MacCormick, "Legal Narratives", note 16 *supra*, p. 231.

all these tasks can be compatible with the content and understanding of national legal orders. The construction of European law, it has been argued, should be influenced both by its interpretation by the ECJ and by the way in which it is interpreted and applied by the national European courts. A coherent EU legal order would require both vertical discourse (between the ECJ and national courts) and horizontal discourse (between national courts). The problem would then be how to manage non-hierarchical relations between the different legal orders and institutions, and how to integrate the validity claims of national and EU constitutional law. This is precisely the difficulty which Maduro tries to solve through his principles of "contrapunctual law", which aim at harmonising these different legal levels and promoting discourse and mutual influence.[46] Within these principles of contrapunctual law, vertical and horizontal coherence have the role of ensuring the uniform and coherent application of the EU law, guaranteeing, at the same time, the constitutional pluralism of Europe.[47] A similar reasoning can be found in MacCormick's theory when he affirms that the interactive and pluralistic character of the systems under analysis would need the mutual respect of the national interpretative judgments in order not to fragment the Community law by unilateral judicial or legislative decisions on the part of the states, on the one hand, and it would require the ECJ to reach its decisions by taking into consideration their potential impact on national constitutions, on the other.[48]

9.3.2 Legal Reasoning in the European Community

Only few scholars have engaged in translating the main questions of contemporary legal philosophy into the Community legal debate.[49] Among them, some have indicated that the analysis of the judicial decision-making process should centre on the

---

[46] M.P. Maduro, "Contrapunctual Law: Europe's Constitutional Pluralism in Action", in N. Walker (ed), *Sovereignty in Transition*, (Oxford, Hart Publishing, 2003), pp. 501–537, at 518–519.

[47] Ibid., pp. 527–529. Different concepts of horizontal and vertical coherence are proposed by S. Besson, "From European Integration to European Integrity: Should European Law Speak with Just One Voice?", (2004) 10 *European Law Journal*, pp. 257–281, at 262 *et seq*. See, also, C. Tietje, "The concept of coherence in the Treaty on European Union and the Common Foreign and Security Policy", (1997) 21 *European Foreign Affairs Review*, pp. 224–231.

[48] MacCormick, "Juridical Pluralism and the Risk of Constitutional Conflict", in: *idem, Questioning Sovereignty: Law, State and Nation in the European Commonwealth,* note 41 *supra*, pp. 118–121.

[49] The book of Joxerramon Bengoetxea is still the leading text on this topic, providing an interesting and complete account of the legal reasoning of the Court. See J. Bengoetxea, *The Legal Reasoning of the European Court of Justice*, (Oxford: Clarendon Press, 1993). A previous attempt from the point of view of the interpretation methods was made by A. Bredimas, *Methods of Interpretation and Community Law*, (Amsterdam: North-Holland, 1978). Besides Neil MacCormick, whose important contributions are being examined here, it is worth mentioning the work of Frank Dowrick, René Barents, Ian Ward and Mattias Kumm, and the articles by Bertea and Moral referred in note 8.

justifying reasons that support its judgments, rather than on the Court's ideology in interpreting Community law.[50]

As well as national courts, the ECJ uses different types of arguments to justify its decisions, such as linguistic or semiotic, systemic or contextual, and dynamic arguments.[51] In general, the Court has followed both a systemic and teleological approach to interpretation, attempting to show that the decision fits, on the one hand, with the norms and principles of Community law or of a specific branch of it (as authoritative reasons), and, on the other, with the *telos* or purpose of a provision or set of provisions of the Treaties, taking into account in this way the common objectives, policies and aims of the European integration process.[52] This has pushed the ECJ to act as a vehicle for integration, both by contributing to represent Community law as a coherent whole, and by promoting the objectives and principles of Community law.

The principles of Community law are either contained in the Treaties[53] or they are unwritten principles recognised by the ECJ,[54] and they are generally used as standards of interpretation or review of national and Community acts.[55] The latter principles are part of what has been called the "material constitution" of the European Community.[56]

---

[50]The reference is to Rasmussen's approach. See J. Bengoetxea, N. MacCormick and L. Moral Soriano, "Integration and Integrity in the Legal Reasoning of the European Court of Justice", in: G. de Búrca and J.H.H. Weiler (eds), *The European Court of Justice*, (Oxford: Oxford University Press, 2001), pp. 43–85, at 43–44.

[51]Ibid., pp. 57–58. For this classification, see Z. Bankowski and N. MacCormick, "Statutory Interpretation in the United Kingdom", in: N. MacCormick and R. Summers (eds), *Interpreting Statues. A Comparative Study*, (Aldershot: Ashgate-Dartmouth Publishing, 1991), pp. 364–373; J. Bengoetxea, *The Legal Reasoning of the European Court of Justice*, note 49 *supra*, pp. 233 *et seq.*; J. Bengoetxea, "Una defensa del consecuencialismo en el Derecho", (1993) 2 *Telos (Revista Lationoamericana de Estudios Utilitaristas)*, pp. 31–68, at 34–35; J. Bengoetxea, "Legal System as a Regulative Ideal", note 20 *supra*, p. 76.

[52]Bengoetxea calls this combination "systemic-cum-dynamic interpretation". *Idem*, *The Legal Reasoning of the European Court of Justice*, note 49 *supra*, p. 234.

[53]These general principles are the ones prescribed in Article 6 TEU: liberty, democracy, respect for human rights and fundamental freedoms, and the rule of law. To these, one should add the principle of solidarity, ruled in Article 1(3) TEU and Article 2 EEC Treaty.

[54]Bruno de Witte defines the principles of supremacy-primacy of EC law, direct effect and direct applicability as "unwritten principles, recognised by the European Court of Justice, which possess a high law status by the fact that they may be invoked as a standard for the review of Community acts". B. de Witte, "The Role of Institutional Principles in the Judicial Development of the European Union Legal Order", in: F. Snyder (ed), *The Europeanisation of Law. The Legal Effects of European Integration*, (Oxford: Hart Publishing, 2000), pp. 83–100, at 83.

[55]See the classification of principles of EU law proposed by Bengoetxea, note J. Bengoetxea, *The Legal Reasoning of the European Court of Justice*, note 49 *supra*, pp. 76–79, and p. 225 *et seq.* A further classification is given by P. Pescatore, "Los principios generales del Derecho como fuente del Derecho Comunitario", (1988) 40 *Noticias C.E.E.*, pp. 39–56; and by J. Raitio, *The Principle of Legal Certainty in EC Law*, (Dordrecht: Kluwer, 2003), p. 94 *et seq.*

[56]J. E. Fossum and A.J. Menéndez, "The Constitution's Gift", (2005) 11 *European Law Journal*, pp. 380–410, at 390 *et seq.*; A.J. Menéndez, "Some elements of a Theory of European Fundamental

The relevance of principles in the legal reasoning of the ECJ is considerable, since they are used to instil coherence into the system. But this kind of coherence is not a strong normative one, because it does not claim the derivability of the system from universal rules (and does not presume a pre-established priority order between reasons), and because, rather than assuming coherence as a present or actual value, it instructs judges to reconstruct the legal system coherently. Thus, before considering colliding legal principles, the Court will firstly have to assign a content or meaning to them, and to determine their sphere of application; secondly, it will have to see what the value or force of that principle is in order to decide the case; and thirdly, it will have to decide the conflict by favouring one of the colliding principles, and justifying that the one adopted is more coherent with the rest of the norms of the system considered as a whole than others. This set of operations is commonly called "balancing" of arguments or principles.[57]

9.3.3 Coherence in the Reasoning of the ECJ and Legal Pluralism

One of the duties of the ECJ is to guarantee the unity and consistency of Community law (Article 225 EEC, Article 62 Statute ECJ), and to ensure the correct interpretation and application of it by the Member States (Article 220 EEC).[58] Unity and consistency can be understood here as coherence. The ECJ, it could be argued, uses the argument of coherence in order to comply with this legal duty in several ways. A complete panorama of these uses would call for a detailed study of all of the case-law of the Court, searching for implicit references to coherence, or for explicit references to this argument under a different terminology. The purpose here is a much more modest one: to identify some of the uses that the Court gives to the notion "coherence", to determine how these uses fulfil the duty to ensure the unity and consistency of Community law, and to analyse these results in the light of the theoretical framework provided by MacCormick. In addition, I will present

---

rights", in: A.J. Menéndez and E.O. Eriksen (eds), *Arguing Fundamental Rights*, (Dordrecht: Springer, 2006), pp. 155–184, at 156 *et seq*.

[57] J. Bengoetxea, N. MacCormick and L. Moral Soriano,"Integration and Integrity in the Legal Reasoning of the European Court of Justice", note 50 *supra*, pp. 64–65. They identify three criteria that play an important role in the balancing of reasons made by the Court: the rule of reason, the test of proportionality, and the principle of non-arbitrariness (pp. 67 *et seq* & 79). Even if here the notion of balance is used in this collective article, MacCormick thinks that it is inappropriate to use the idea of weight in relation to choice among legal principles, since principles do not always make the same contribution to every act or judgment in which they count as a reason. MacCormick, 'Universals and Particulars', note 15 *supra*, p. 87.

[58] For a discussion on three judgments in which the Court of Justice tries to remedy the incoherencies produced by the disobedience of national courts to follow the ECJ's interpretation, see J. Komárek, "Federal Elements in the Community Judicial System: Building Coherence in the Community Legal Order, (2005) 42 *Common Market Law Review*, pp. 9–34.

and criticise the author's conception of legal pluralism and the tensions between this notion and the argument of coherence.

The following paragraphs will analyse the uses of the argument of coherence by the Court, grouping them according to the effects that coherence has in extending or restricting the scope of Community law: 1) the use of this argument as a means of increasing the coherence of Community law, and by this way, extending its scope; and 2) the use of coherence as a way of establishing limits to the scope of Community law, in so far as what prevails or aims to be protected is coherence at the national level.[59]

A. Coherence as a means of consolidating and extending the scope of Community law

MacCormick's notions of coherence, overall coherence and, with some differences, normative coherence, are both used by the ECJ as a way of strengthening and extending the scope of Community law. The following account of some cases will illustrate this point.

(i) Overall coherence or integrity

The idea of the overall coherence or integrity of legal systems has been frequently applied to the European legal order.[60] The European Community has been considered as a community of principles – written and unwritten – that come either from Community law and its interpretation, or from the common constitutional traditions of the Member States. The value of integration as the *telos* or core idea of both the European project and the scheme of the Treaties stands as a guiding principle for interpretation of Community law by the Court. Moreover, integration requires integrity, which can be understood as creating connections between the different elements of the European legal order and the values and policies that support them.[61]

---

[59]These different attitudes, indeed, reflect a much deeper issue, specifically the diverse conceptions of the European Community as a democratic polity. One important theoretical framework is the proposal of conceiving the European Union as a functional (problem-solving) international organisation, as a federal state based upon a collective identity, or as a rights-based post-national union with an explicit cosmopolitan imprint. See the papers by E.O. Eriksen and J.E. Fossum, "Europe in Transformation. How to Reconstitute Democracy?", RECON Working Paper No. 01/2007, available at: http://www.reconproject.eu/main.php/RECON_wp_0701.pdf?fileitem=5456091 (accessed 30 October 2010); and "A Done Deal? The EU's Legitimacy Conundrum Revisited", RECON Working Paper No. 16/2007, available at:http://www.reconproject.eu/main.php/RECON_wp_0716.pdf?fileitem=16662534, (accessed 30 October 2010).

[60]At the legislative level, reference to integrity is made in Article 299 (3) TEU. Case C-282/00, *Refinarias de Açúcar Reunidas SA (RAR)* v *Sociedade de Indústrias Agricolas Açoreanas SA (Sinaga)* [2003] ECR I-4741 refers to this last disposition. "Consistency and continuity" prescribed by Article 3 TEU have been considered as expressions of the principle of European integrity. Besson, 'From European Integration to…', note 47 *supra*, p. 262 *et seq*

[61]J. Bengoetxea, N. MacCormick and L. Moral Soriano, "Integration and Integrity in the Legal Reasoning of the European Court of Justice", note 50 *supra*, pp. 48 and 82–85.

Focus on integrity in legal reasoning, to wit, on how the Court uses the idea of overall coherence in its case-law, one can find that the Court refers to coherence with different formulations, such as "coherence of the community system", "coherence of the community law", "coherence of the community legal order", and "coherence of the community legal system". Thus, the Court has ruled that the principle of coherence of the supranational legal order must be taken into account when interpreting the provisions of directives. For example, it has been ruled that "secondary Community legislation [has] to be interpreted in accordance with the general principles of Community law".[62] In a similar vein, the failure to recognise the jurisdiction of the Court to ensure a uniform interpretation of the rules deriving from the ECSC Treaty is "contrary to the objectives and the coherence of the Treaties and irreconcilable with the continuity of the Community legal order".[63]

Even if the formulation of this systemic argument does not connect explicitly the applicable norm or norms with the principles underlying them, the ECJ generally makes reference to principles of Community law in justifying its decisions.[64] In other cases, this systemic argument adopts the form of appeals to the scheme, spirit, or system of the Treaty.[65]

By using these types of justificatory reasons, the ECJ is preserving and emphasising the particular coherence of Community law conceived of as a new logic derived from the purpose and aims of the founding Treaties. At the same time, this coherence takes the constitutional traditions common to the Member States into account, as a way of rescuing some sort of common European rationality.

Both attitudes not only consolidate and reinforce a kind of European identity, but they also privilege one specific type of coherence, that which the ECJ considers to be operating inside the Community legal order. The use of this interpretation of coherence has the clear purpose of placing limits on national competencies, and, in this way, of posing limits on their sovereignties. In stressing the idea of the coherence

---

[62] Case C-499/04, *Hans Werhof* v *Freeway Traffic Systems GmbH & Co. KG*, [2006] ECR I-2397; Case C-1/02, *Privat-Molkerei Borgmann GmbH & Co. KG* v *Hauptzollamt Dortmund* [2004] ECR I-3219.

[63] Case C-119/05, *Ministero dell'Industria, del Commercio e dell'Artigianato* v *Lucchini SpA*, [2007] ECR I-6199; Case C-221/88 *European Coal and Steel Community* v *Acciaierie e Ferriere Busseni SpA*, [1990] ECR I-495. See, also, Case 283/81, *CILFIT e Lanificio di gavardo SPA* v *Ministero della sanità*, [1982] ECR 3415.

[64] These principles, it has been argued, are the result of a selective choice of the best or most suitable principles and traditions that operate in the constitutional systems of the Member States. M. Cappelletti and D. Golay, "The Judicial Branch in the Federal and Transnational Union: Its Impact on Integration", in: M. Cappelletti, M. Seccombe and J.H.H. Weiler (eds), *Integration through law: Europe and the American federal experience*, (Berlin: Walter de Gruyter, 1985), pp. 261–351, at 351.

[65] Case 193/85, *Cooperativa Co-Frutta Srl* v *Amministrazione delle finanze dello Stato,* [1987] ECR 2085. In a different field, the Court has decide that excluding measures adopted by the European Parliament from the action for annulment would lead to results contrary both to the spirit of the Treaty and to its scheme. See Case 294/83, *Parti écologiste 'Les Verts'* v *European Parliament,* [1986] ECR 1339.

of Community law, the Court does not incorporate the diversity of national legal orders to the legal order that coherence aims to protect, but, instead, either imposes the primacy of the supranational system or stresses the convergence of national legal traditions.

(ii) Normative coherence in particular branches of Community law

Community law can be thought of as different sub-systems of rules which are interconnected under several common values, principles or goals. The construction of one particular sub-system can be conceived as the process of identification of specific common principles that operate in that area of law. These particular principles should be respected when interpreting and applying its provisions, and, in this sense, maintaining its own internal coherence.

Normative coherence is used here to support decisions that respect the particular coherence of the corresponding branch of law.[66] A first example can be found in cases regarding the conservation of nature and natural resources within the framework of the Habitats Directive adopted by the European Community (*Natura 2000*).[67] This directive aimed to ensure bio-diversity through the conservation of natural habitats and of wild fauna and flora in the European territory of the Member States, and, at the same time, aimed to set up "a coherent European ecological network of special areas of conservation".

Within these regulations, the ECJ uses the argument to favour decisions that protect a coherent European ecological network,[68] or simply the coherence of *Natura 2000*,[69] which is an objective legally-required in implementing environmental national policies. Here, coherence seems to stand not only for the need to adjust

---

[66]Bengoetxea has suggested that this sub-systemic coherence could resemble a way of institutional thinking according to MacCormick's theory. The idea of coherence used by the Court would be appealing to the system logic present in these different areas or case studies, and much closer to a regulative ideal than to coherence as a discursive argumentative tool. It could also match with the local coherence in the sense used by Bertea: see S. Bertea, "Looking for Coherence within the European Community", (2005) 11 *European Law Journal*, pp. 154–172, at 157–158.

[67]Council Directive 92/43/EEC of 21 May 1992 on the conservation of natural habitats and of wild fauna and flora, OJ L 206, 22.7.1992, pp. 7–50.

[68]Case C-371/98, *The Queen* v *Secretary of State for the Environment, Transport and the Regions*, [2000] ECR I-9235; Case C-508/04, *Commission* v *Republic of Austria*, [2007] ECR I-3787.

[69]Case C-304/05, *Commission* v *Italian Republic*, [2007] ECR I-7495; Case C-239/04, *Commission* v *Portuguese Republic* [2006] ECR I-10183; Case C-209/04 *Commission of the European Communities* v *Republic of Austria*, [2006] ECR I-2755; Case C-117/03, *Società Italiana Dragaggi SpA and Others* v *Ministero delle Infrastrutture e dei Trasporti and Regione Autonoma Friuli Venezia Giulia*, [2005] ECR I-167; Case C-127/02, *Landelijke Vereniging tot Behoud van de Waddenzee and Nederlandse Vereniging tot Bescherming van Vogels* v *Staatssecretaris van Landbouw, Natuurbeheer en Visserij*, [2004] ECR I-7405; Case C-324/01, *Commission* v *Kingdom of Belgium*, [2002] ECR I-11197. See, also, Case C-220/99, *Commission* v *French Republic*, [2001] ECR I-5831; Case C-71/99, *Commission* v *Federal Republic of Germany*, [2001] ECR I-5811; Case C-67/99, *Commission* v *Ireland*, [2001] ECR I-5757.

the decision to a certain pre-established environmental system of norms and principles, but also to a value or a principle itself. In some other cases, coherence seems to imply the need of conscientious work in the determination of the protected areas.[70] However, the Court does not explicitly grapple with the meaning and content of coherence in this field.

A different matter in which the Court uses this intrasystemic argument of coherence concerns remedies. As Bertea points out, the ECJ has come forward several times to clarify and to fill the gaps in the Treaty provisions regarding remedies in judicial review, thereby shaping Community law. Thus, in doing so, the Court has often invoked the notion of coherence.[71]

In fact, in a large number of decisions, the ECJ has solved several remedies issues by appealing to the coherence criterion. In these cases, the path that the Court follows is to identify some vacuum in the regulation of the Treaties and to apply a solution in accordance with the general framework of the system of remedies built up by the Court. In the same way in which the Court appeals to some "general system of Community Law",[72] the Court has created a special order in the "system of legal remedies"[73] or in the "system of judicial protection".[74] In this way, the Court provides an universalisable argument for solving other cases, namely, the respect of the general system of remedies. A good example of this use of coherence can be seen in the field of preliminary rulings procedure.

Article 234 EEC states that any court or tribunal of a Member State can request the Court of Justice to give a preliminary ruling when it faces specific problems of interpretation. However, the ECJ has ruled that, according to European law, it is not mandatory to send the request if the judges have no real doubt about the application of European law.[75] If the judges consider that the norm or provision is clear, or if the question is irrelevant for solving the case, or if it has already been previously solved, they can interpret the European legal order themselves, following the guidelines provided by the Court.[76]

---

[70] Case C-244/05, *Bund Naturschutz in Bayern eV and Others* v *Freistaat Bayern*, [2006] ECR I-8445; Case C-371/98, *The Queen* v *Secretary of State for the Environment, Transport and the Regions*, [2000] ECR I-9235.

[71] S. Bertea, 'Looking for Coherence within the European Community', note 66 *supra*, p. 162.

[72] Joined Cases 3, 4 and 6/76, *Cornelis Kramer and others*, [1976] ECR 1279; Case 185/73, *Hauptzollamt Bielefeld* v *Offene Handelsgesellschaft in Firma H. C. König*, [1974] ECR 607; Case 22/70, *Commission of the European Communities* v *Council of the European Communities*, [1971] ECR 263.

[73] *Les Verts*, note 65 *supra*.

[74] Case C-461/03, *Gaston Schul Douane-expediteur BV* v *Minister van Landbouw, Natuur en Voedselkwaliteit*, [2005] ECR I-10513.

[75] The *acte claire* doctrine was first established in *CILFIT*, note 63 *supra*.

[76] See H. Schermers and D. Waelbroeck, *Judicial Protection in the European Union*, (The Hague: Kluwer, 2001) (6th edition), p. 57 *et seq*.

But the Court found problems in applying this principle in a case involving the validity of an act of the Community institutions (Article 234 b). A general permission enabling national judges to declare the invalidity of those acts when the ground of invalidity is clear was considered inadequate. Alternatively the Court ruled that:

> the possibility of a national court ruling on the invalidity of a Community act is likewise incompatible *with the necessary coherence of the system of judicial protection* instituted by the EC Treaty.[77]

Explaining this argument, the Court claimed:

> it is important to note in that regard that references for a preliminary ruling on validity constitute, on the same basis as actions for annulment, a means of reviewing the legality of Community acts. By means of arts 230 EC and 241 EC, on the one hand, and art 234 EC, on the other, the Treaty established a complete system of legal remedies and procedures designed to ensure review of the legality of acts of the institutions and has entrusted such review to the Community Courts.

The same solution was adopted in the leading case *Foto-Frost* v *Hauptzollamt Lübeck-Ost*,[78] in which the inability of national courts to invalidate the acts of the institutions was premised on "the necessary coherence of the system of judicial protection established by the Treaty". The Court further argued that the Treaty established a complete system of legal remedies and procedures designed to enable the Court of Justice to review the legality of measures adopted by the institutions. Accordingly,

> [S]ince article 173 gives the Court exclusive jurisdiction to declare void an act of a community institution, the coherence of the system requires that where the validity of an act is challenged before a national court the power to declare the act invalid must also be reserved to the Court of Justice.

In these cases, especially on what concerns remedies, the use of the idea of coherence as a way of fostering the supremacy of the European legal order acquires special force. What the Court does through this case-law is to create sub-systems endowed with their own internal coherence, and, having these sub-systems as parameters, it rules out divergent solutions which are incompatible with the particular sub-system. As has been pointed out above,[79] the problem here is that, as coherence is an incomplete argument, there is a further need to justify the principles governing such a sub-system, because they cannot be taken for granted. Put differently, once the Court uses the idea of a particular coherence of a certain legal branch, then the justification of its decisions is made by appealing to that coherence, but the content of the coherence of the sub-system or the justification of the sub-system itself has not been necessarily spelt out.

The same expansive attitude is at stake when the Court, facing conflicts between Community law and European institutions, ruled that it had exclusive competence

---

[77] *Schul*, note 74 *supra* (emphasis added).

[78] Case 314/85, *Foto-Frost* v *Hauptzollamt Lübeck-Ost*, [1987] ECR 4199.

[79] See the text that follows in note 38 supra.

to resolve them. By using the argument of the coherence of the system of remedies, the Court stresses the hierarchical character of its interpretation and understanding of Community law.

B. Coherence as a means of strengthening national systems and limiting the scope of Community law

There are a few cases in which the Court is interested in strengthening and protecting the coherence of national systems, or, more accurately, of the sub-systems within them, and, in this way, limiting the scope of Community law. A clear example is the case-law concerning taxes.

The EEC Treaty constrains tax systems design since it prescribes the abolition of all tariff and non-tariff barriers at intra-EC borders (Articles 23–31) One of the exceptions to these constraints, which was created by the Court, is the *rule of reason,* by which a restrictive national measure is acceptable if (i) it is necessary to protect a legitimate public interest, (ii) it does not distinguish in any way between domestic and imported goods, and (iii) its restrictive effects do not go any further than necessary to protect that legitimate interest (proportionality).[80]

In relation to different or restrictive tax treatment of/in cross-border situations compared to similar domestic situations, the Court has accepted only three justifications under the rule of reason, one of which is the need to protect the *coherence* of the national tax system (fiscal coherence). Fiscal coherence was accepted for the first time in the *Bachmann case.*[81] This case was about the possibility of deducting from personal income tax the amounts paid on account of insurance policies subscribed with companies established in other Member States. The Court observed that, if these deductions were forbidden, the measure could be against the interests of non-nationals, because, normally, they would take their policies with foreign insurers. But, at the same time, the Court accepted the argument that this prohibition would be better in order to maintain the coherence of the national tax system. In fact, in Belgium, which favours this prohibition, there is a direct link between the deductibility of contributions and the taxation of future benefits. This link makes the system coherent. And this coherence could have been disrupted if it had been accepted that Belgium was obliged to deduct all insurance payments.[82] It can be seen from this judgment that the reasoning of the Court took the special link between deduction and taxation of future benefits into account, gave it the treatment of a system, and protected this special linkage from possible breaches.

After *Bachmann*, however, the ECJ regretted its acceptance of fiscal coherence as a mechanism to justify fiscal restrictions, and began to make the features of the link between the tax benefit and the subsequent taxation more precise. This link, ruled

[80]For a wider discussion concerning the rule of reason in case-law on taxes, see B. Terra and P. Wattel, *European Tax Law*, (The Hague: Kluwer, 2005) (4th edition), pp. 41 et seq.

[81]C-204/90 *Hanns-Martin Bachmann* v *Belgian State*, [1992] ECR I-249.

[82]B. Terra and P. Wattel, *European Tax Law*, note 80 *supra*, p. 108.

the Court, has to be immediate,[83] concern the same tax, the same taxpayer and the same contract.[84]

According to the case just described, the aim of the Court is to understand integration by respecting the solutions given by each legal system in this specific matter. This could be considered to be a kind of legal pluralism, since the Court recognises that the formation of a Community common legal order may be the result of strengthening the internal legal coherence of its units, even when the latter hold different legal solutions for the same matter.

Similarly, it can be concluded that the Court includes, in interpreting its duty to ensure the effectiveness of, and compliance with, the provisions of the Treaties and its duty to enhance integration, the respect of the particular coherence of national (sub-) systems. Nevertheless, this attitude of self-restraint, which consists of not interfering or affecting national legal systems in areas excluded from the scope of Community law, is a marginal tendency, and is, in fact, gradually decreasing.

C. Coherence and Legal Pluralism

The reason why an account of law as institutional normative order leads to a pluralistic conception of law is to be found, in MacCormick's theory, in the fact that the conceptualisation of law as an institutional normative order implies denying any analytical nexus between law and state.[85] It is not just that the concept of law is detached from the figure of the sovereign, but that law can exist independently of entities which have the features of a state (for example, in organisations or associations without jurisdiction over a well-defined territory, or without having the monopoly of coercive power).

Institutional normative order, however, needs to entrust in some organ the competence of conclusively determining what counts as authoritative norms of the system. In other words, it requires the institutionalisation of judgments on the validity of the norms of the system which is in the hands of the legislative and judicial bodies. The complex legal reality at the present shows, in MacCormick's opinion, that there are different valid normative orders which interact, each of which has its own ground of validity, with none of them subordinating their validity to a different system.

The result of applying this conceptual framework to EC law is that both the Member State and the Community legal orders have their own criteria of validity for recognising norms as binding rules ("Community-validity", and "Member

---

[83]Opinion of Mr Advocate General Mischo delivered in Case C-324/00, *Lankhorst-Hohorst GmbH* v *Finanzamt Steinfurt*, [2002] ECR I-11779.

[84]B. Terra and P. Wattel, *European Tax Law*, note 80 *supra*, p. 120. See Case C-484/93, *Peter Svensson and Lena Gustavsson* v *Ministre du Logement et de l'Urbanisme,* [1995] ECR I-3955; Case C-251/98, *Baars* v *Inspecteur der Belastingen Particulieren/Ondernemingen Gorinchem,* [2000] ECR I-2787.

[85]In the exposition of MacCormick's ideas, I mainly follow the article "Juridical Pluralism...", note 48 *supra*.

State-validity")[86]. In the case of the Member States, this criterion can be found mainly in the Constitution, while, in the case of Community law, this criterion consists of the norms of the founding Treaties (material constitutional) together with the interpretative principles acknowledged by the ECJ. To express it differently, legal pluralism denies the constitutional dependency of states on each other or of the Member States on the Community.

Furthermore, a legal pluralistic reading of the principle of primacy of Community law holds that Member States have amended their criteria of recognition to include domestically the principles of direct effect and the primacy of EC law. In this regard, it is claimed that EC law validity criteria is not superior to the constitutional validity criteria of the Member States. The same can be argued concerning the ultimate character of the highest decision-making authorities of the different systems. The ECJ authoritatively interprets the norms of Community law as a court of law resort, while the higher courts of the Member States interpret the norms of their legal orders and the interaction between EC law and their constitutional norms.

It seems to me, however, given the duty assumed by the Member States to accept and incorporate the interpretations of the ECJ (Article 234 EEC) in their reasoning, it is not clear whether there is a sharp independence, or an absence of some sort of hierarchical relation, among the ECJ and national higher courts, or ultimately, between EC law and Member States legal orders. The argument that the Member States voluntarily amended their validity criteria is not a strong one, since, if states do not incorporate Community law and its authoritative interpretation by the ECJ into their legal orders, they would be in a situation of lack of compliance and would eventually incur liability.

It is certainly correct not to understand the doctrine of supremacy of Community law as a "kind of all-purpose subordination of member-state-law to Community law", and it would also be hard to accept a thesis that holds "that accession to the Community or Union necessarily entails subordinating the state's constitution as a whole package to Community law".[87] Indeed, there is a relevant range of topics excluded from Community law or which belong to areas which are beyond the reach of integration purposes or agreements. But, in my contention, the important thing here is, firstly, to determine the domains where there is interaction and overlap, or from a different perspective, to identify the existence of a conflict relevant to EC law. The second problem consists of determining if there is, and if there should be, a mechanism to solve the conflict. The third problem is whether all conflicts should be judicially solved or else if there is space, within the framework of European integration, to maintain unresolved issues and/or to resolve them through different

[86]MacCormick, "Juridical Pluralism. . .", note 48 *supra*, p. 113; see, also, p. 103; N. MacCormick, "On Sovereignty and Post-Sovereignty", in: *idem*, *Questioning Sovereignty: Law, State and Nation in the European Commonwealth*, note 41 *supra*, p. 132.

[87]MacCormick, "Juridical Pluralism. . .", note 48 *supra*, pp. 116–117.

channels. And here the answer given by the Court seems to me conclusive: the Court does not look kindly upon leaving conflicts unresolved, and whenever there is a conflict, it engages in its resolution. In this latter process, the ECJ has ruled that it is the one entitled to interpret Community law and to determine the way in which certain national norms breach EU law.

Some of these difficulties are well-known by MacCormick. He acknowledges that understanding the interlocking legal systems as being hierarchically independent has some problems, and more specifically, that the application of a pluralistic legal view to the relations between the state-law systems of the Member States of the EC and the Community legal order brings ongoing challenges. At the same time, he has moved from a position of "radical pluralism" to what he calls "pluralism under international law". Both types of pluralism stress that the Member State and the Community legal orders have independent validity rules and that there is no hierarchical relation among them, but an interactive one, and that each system has its own decision-making final authorities. They only differ in the nature of the relations between the states and Community law, on the one hand, and international law, on the other. According to pluralism under international law, international law establishes a framework for the interaction between national and Community law systems, while radical pluralism considers these conditions only as a third perspective, but not as a hierarchically superior obligation. A consequence of this difference is that, under radical pluralism, there are legal problems that cannot be solved legally, but only through revolt or revolution, recalling Phelan's proposal. However, according to pluralism under international law, there always remains the possibility of recourse to international adjudication or arbitration in order to solve the conflict. This last view resembles, in fact, Kelsen's theory of legal monism, in the sense that international law governs the pluralistic relations between the law of the Community and the Member States. In other words, pluralism takes place under a monistic framework imposed by international law.

Together with the problems inherent in legal pluralism just mentioned, a further difficulty consists of articulating it with the overarching idea of coherence in law and in legal reasoning that inspires MacCormick's theory. For the simple image of coherence as the parts making the whole, or the idea that a coherent norm or decision is the one that is derived from a more general value or principle, seems to require hierarchical relations, or genus-species articulation. What does it mean, then, to promote coherence by respecting diversity? In my opinion, it can only mean that there are areas in which, though there are conflicting solutions to some problems given by diverse systems, there is no interaction or overlap. From this point of view, plurality would entail that there is no real conflict among diverse responses to the same question, because they exist in an area where the systems preserve independence of decision-making procedures. Coherence as making sense of the parts of a system implies the reconstruction of the relations between them, and, in this reconstruction, some prioritising criteria are generally present in order to decide which element should prevail, or some mechanisms are created to solve the collision between elements.

Grounding these ideas in the relations between Member State legal systems and Community law, legal pluralism can only account for a description of diverse legal sources that co-exist. But when law is applied to practical cases, there is a hierarchical rule that entrusts the problem-solving capacity to the ECJ when facing conflicting interpretations of Community law. Ultimate decision-making by this Court will inevitably imply options of principles, of values, and, in the end, of systems. And this point of view, internal to the law as a solving-problem instrument, responds to a monistic approach to law,[88] not to a pluralistic one.

Someone could object to this conclusion by saying that, frequently, if not always, the Court justifies its decisions by appealing to the constitutional traditions common to the Member States. In this sense, the Court could be recognising the plurality of orders interacting with Community law. The interesting point here is that these traditions, which are effectively used as guides for the coherent reconstruction of Community law, are the result of a convergence of common principles – though coming from the different Member States – rather than the expression of legal pluralism – which entails different solutions for the same legal problem.

9.4 Conclusion

Finally, I would briefly like to draw some conclusions concerning the theoretical model of the argument of coherence proposed by MacCormick, the way in which the ECJ uses this argument, and the relation between coherence and legal pluralism, both theoretically and in the Court's case-law.

Firstly, with regard to the theoretical model, both normative and narrative coherence are, though they have only weak justificatory force, an initial useful test in the justification of legal reasoning, since they imply an effort to best reconstruct the chain of axiological derivability of the principle that rules the case or the chain of relevant facts respectively. Overall coherence complements these specific forms of the argument of coherence, making further connections among the elements of the system, and enabling the decision-maker to reconstruct interpretatively the legal order as a coherent whole.

Admittedly, there are limits to the use of coherence in legal argumentation, of which MacCormick is aware. However, an incomplete or insufficient argument continues to be a criterion of justification, and these limits only mean that other arguments, such as teleological or deontological ones, will be needed to justify the decision. What is important for a sound argumentation is explicitly making the connections and pointing out the reasons underlying the decision, and showing why the given solution is the better or preferable one for the case in point. MacCormick

---

[88] This claim coincides with the one made by S. Prechal and B. van Roermund in the introductory essay to *The Coherence of EU Law. The Search for Unity in Divergent Concepts,* (Oxford: Oxford University Press, 2008), p. 1, stating that there is one single authority, and that this unity opposes pluralism.

himself contends that the best objectivity available in human sciences is that of an honest interpretation both open to the values it presupposes and alert to failures and successes of the system.[89]

Secondly, in the cases considered, the Court uses the argument of coherence in a twofold way: as a means of reinforcing the autonomy and extending the scope of Community law as a system, and as a way both of recognising particular national logics that operate within their legal systems or sub-systems and of posing limits to the application of Community law. However, the Court does not employ these different uses of the argument of coherence with equal force or frequency. Indeed, the general attitude is to use overall coherence or the coherence of Community sub-systems in order to highlight the *sui generis* character of the EC legal order, in order to bring into the province of Community law cases that, even if the matters to which they refer are not clearly within its scope, and in order to defend the primacy of Community law over national legal orders in the matters that fall within the scope of Community law. In contrast, the attitude of self-restraint – either by means of the creation of exceptions to previous decisions of the Court itself, or by protecting the coherence of national sub-systems on specific domains – is employed rather seldom.

Under MacCormick's theoretical framework, the notions of coherence used by the Court correspond, roughly speaking, to the author's idea of overall coherence and of normative coherence. Overall coherence operates in the Court's reasoning as a way of stressing the logic of Community law. The decision to be adopted must be that which fits better with the norms of this legal order, especially with its general principles or with its material constitution. However, this sole argument needs to be backed by a sound supportive structure of reasons, and it is not sufficient to make a mere appeal to the coherence of Community law in order to justify the decision. For this argument to be a persuasive one, the Court should show why a certain solution coheres with the system, and to what extent it is preferable to others. On the other hand, the way in which the Court uses the argument of normative coherence does not strictly correspond to that proposed by MacCormick. While he considers normative coherence to reconstruct the chain of derivability of the norm according to which the case is to be solved, the Court refers to coherence as the systematicity of certain specific spheres of law (environmental protection, remedies and taxation). In these cases, the ECJ first creates sub-systems at the European or the national sphere by attributing them a particular internal coherence, and then decides the case according to its compliance or not with this sub-systemic coherence. More than an argument, coherence here refers to the particular logic or principles governing these sub-systems. The problem arises when the Court does not clearly limit these sub-systems, does not explicitly mention the principles that operate within them, and falls short of explaining what coherence means for a particular sub-system. Again, mere appeals to coherence fail to justify the decision, and can lead to high degrees

[89] MacCormick, *Institutions of Law...*, note 41 *supra*, p. 305.

of discretion. Appeals to coherence should be, then, transformed into arguments of coherence by giving justificatory reasons that supports the particular decision.[90]

Thirdly, as I have tried to argue, there is an internal theoretical tension in MacCormick's legal theory between coherence and pluralism. Coherence within a legal system requires a hierarchical order among the system's elements or mechanisms, which enables reconstruction of this order *a posteriori*. For the connections that coherence pursues – in the form of derivability or others – are aimed at dissolving conflicting responses to the same problem, at eliminating inconsistency, and at furnishing a final answer to the problem concerned. Clearly, this is true only concerning the intersection of the different systems which regulate the same conflict, and not of all the different legal solutions to a problem in cases in which there is no interaction. Since pluralism claims independence and non-hierarchical relations among systems, the role that coherence could have inside interactive systems is difficult to figure out.

At the level of the case-law, it can be argued that, where the Court enhances the coherence of national legal sub-systems, a sprout of legal pluralism can be recognised, since the Court is tolerating the co-existence of diverse solutions within the legal orders of the Member States. But the expression of legal pluralism in the particular cases analysed seems to wither away when the Court changes its decision by restricting the scope of the application of the exception of internal coherence. One reason for this attitude could be the purpose of progressive convergence or the approximation of national legislation in the areas included or those which could affect Community law principles, freedoms and rights, and the expansion of the scope of Community law via the interpretation of ECJ.

The main use of coherence by the Court in order to increase the reach of Community law does not favour a legally pluralistic conception, but a rather monistic conception of the European legal order. The Court is the final decision-maker in charge of solving conflicting interpretations or the collisions of norms. In deciding these conflicts, the Court establishes a hierarchy among the competing principles or relations of priority among norms, and in this way, aims to reconstruct Community law as a coherent whole.

---

[90] Bertea highlights this difference between appeals to coherence and the argument from coherence ('The Arguments from Coherence: Analysis and Evaluation', note 8 *supra*, p. 378).

Part VI
The Constitution(s) of the European Union

Chapter 10
Legal Pluralism in the European Union

Martin Borowski

The great mystery of European Union law:[1] It is, we are told, original and supreme, but we are also told that the Union derives its powers from the Member States. The precise legal relation between the Member States and the European Community – now, after the Treaty of Lisbon, the European Union – has remained unclear and contested for more than five decades. Neil MacCormick's theory of legal pluralism represents the most sophisticated attempt to date to explain the "pluralistic" nature of European Union law, overcoming the simple confrontation of the "European view" and the "national view".

First (Section 10.1), these two conflicting views will be explained, before (Section 10.2) they will be put into the context of the debate on monism, dualism, and pluralism and common assumptions on the "hierarchy" in the legal system. Then (Section 10.3) MacCormick's theory of legal pluralism in the European Union will be analysed and evaluated against this backdrop. Finally (Section 10.4), an alternative legal reconstruction of the Union will be sketched – Union law as derived from national constitutional orders, but nearly unconditionally supreme.

10.1 Two Conflicting Views and the Dilemma

There are two views on the legal reconstruction of the Union, the European view and the national view.

M. Borowski (✉)
Birmingham Law School, College of Arts and Law, University of Birmingham, Birmingham, UK
e-mail: m.borowski@bham.ac.uk

[1] This article is devoted primarily to the analysis of the phenomenon that I might term "classic first-pillar supranationality", which was exhibited by European Community law rather than European Union law. However, the distinction between "European Community law" and "European Union law" was abolished by the Treaty of Lisbon, which has changed the fundamental legal architecture of the European Union. According to Article 1, paragraph 3, clause 3, Treaty on European Union (TEU) "[t]he Union shall replace and succeed the European Community". Although the nature of the classical problem of the re-construction of European Community law has not changed, it has become a problem of European Union law. In what follows, the expressions "Union" and "Union law" are used in the sense the Treaty of Lisbon has given them.

A.J. Menéndez, J.E. Fossum (eds.), *Law and Democracy in Neil MacCormick's Legal and Political Theory*, Law and Philosophy Library 93,
DOI 10.1007/978-90-481-8942-7_10,

10.1.1 The European View

In its case law, the European Court of Justice (ECJ) has developed the European view step by step.[2] To mention only four well-known milestones, the court stated, in *van Gend en Loos*, that the founding treaty "has created its own legal system", and that EC law cannot "be overridden by domestic legal provisions, however framed".[3] This was reaffirmed in *Costa* v *ENEL*, where the Court emphazised the "original nature" of EC law.[4] In applying this doctrine of supremacy of EC law, it held, in *Internationale Handelsgesellschaft*, that

> the validity of a Community measure or its effect within a Member State cannot be affected by allegations that it runs counter to either fundamental rights as formulated by the constitution of that state or the principles of a national constitutional structure.[5]

In *Simmenthal*, one reads that provisions of directly applicable EC law "not only by their entry into force render automatically inapplicable any conflicting provision of current national law but [...] preclude the valid adoption of new national legislative measures" of such nature.[6] This approach of Union law has been reaffirmed in many decisions.[7] The unconditional supremacy of Union law is complemented by judicial supremacy of the ECJ. According to the view of the ECJ, it is solely the ECJ itself, standing over and above the supremacy of Union law, that is empowered to invalidate or to forbear from applying Union law.[8]

10.1.2 The National View

According to the national view, the Member States are the source of all sovereign rights in the Union. The Union has only those powers that the Member States have transferred, and it has them subject to the conditions of derivation in the constitutions of the Member States. For this national view, the case law of the German Federal Constitutional Court (hereafter, FCC) is paradigmatic. The FCC held in *Solange I* that it would continue to review EC law by means of the yardstick of German constitutional rights "as long as" no comparable protection of fundamental

---

[2] Admittedly, the position of the ECJ is far more complex. A thorough and comprehensive analysis of the case law of the Court goes, however, well beyond the scope of this chapter.

[3] Case 26/62, *Van Gend en Loos* [1963] ECR 1.

[4] Case 6/64, *Costa* v *ENEL* [1964] 12 CMLR 425

[5] Case 11/70, *Internationale Handelsgesellschaft* [1970] ECR 1125, para 3.

[6] Case 106/77, *Simmenthal* [1978] ECR 629, para 17.

[7] See, in particular, Joined Cases C-13/91 and C-113/91, *Debus* [1992] ECR I-03617, para 32; Case C-158/91, *Levy* [1993] ECR I-04287, para 9; Case C-347/96, *Solred* v *Administración General del Estado* [1998] ECR I-00937, para 30; Joined Cases C-10/97 to C-22/97, *Ministero delle Finanze* v *IN.CO.GE'90 Srl et al* [1998] ECR I-06307, para 20.

[8] Cases 7/56 and 3/57 to 7/57, *Algera et al* [1957] ECR 39. See also Case 314/85, *Foto Frost* [1987] ECR 04199, para 17.

human rights in EC law is forthcoming.[9] Twelve years later, the FCC held in *Solange II* that a comparable standard of protection of fundamental human rights had been established in the interim by the case law of the ECJ. It declared that it would suspend review of Community law "as long as" this standard is upheld.[10] This does not count as an acceptance of the European view; rather, it is a statement to the effect that the conditions for review by the FCC – based on the national view – are not currently being fulfilled. This mere suspension for the time being has been confirmed in later decisions,[11] most recently in the decision of the FCC on the "constitutionality" of the Treaty of Lisbon.[12] What is more, passages in later decisions have been interpreted to mean that German public authority is empowered simply to disregard EC law that, in its issuance, has transgressed attributed competences.[13] This position of the FCC, reserving the competence to enforce national law against Community law and now Union law under certain conditions, has attracted the support of the highest courts of other Member States.[14]

10.1.3 The Dilemma and Its Importance

Both of these mutually exclusive views seem to have compelling arguments. The national view is correct in insisting that the national constitutions are the starting points of the derivation of the sovereign rights of the Union. To be sure, the European view emphasizes correctly the sheer need of "supremacy" of Union law. One has to accept, at least on principle, the "supremacy" of Union law and the proposition that the power to review Union law has to be left to the ECJ, lest a uniform application of Union law should remain an illusion. Union law would increasingly fragment, and the Union, in the end, would legally disintegrate.

Still, both views have serious problems in explaining the current practice in Union law to grant to Union law, on principle, supremacy. How can the European

[9]BVerfGE 37, 271 (285). English: *Internationale Handelsgesellschaft* [1974] 2 CMLR 540.

[10]BVerfGE 73, 339 (378-81). English: *Wünsche Handelsgesellschaft* [1987] 3 CMLR 225.

[11]BVerfGE 89, 155 (210). English: *Brunner* [1994] 1 CMLR 57. In the *Bananas Market* decision the Court reaffirmed explicitly the *Solange II* ruling, BVerfGE 102, 147 (167).

[12]BVerfGE 123, 267 (335). An English translation is available at: http://www.bundesverfassungsge-richt.de/entscheidungen/es20090630_2bve000208en.html.

[13]Beyond the field of fundamental rights, the FCC stated in the *Brunner* decision, where the compatibility of the Treaty of Maastricht with the German Basic Law was at stake, that Germany were not bound by an "interpretation" of attributed competences by EC institutions that would amount to an amendment of the treaties. See also the passages on the limits of the jurisdiction of the ECJ by Laws J in *R* v *MAFF ex parte First City Trading* [1997] 1 CMLR 250, p. 268.

[14]See Case 12/94 *Ecole Europèenne, CA*. 3 February 1994, B6 for Belgium; *Carlsen* v *Rasmussen* [1999] 3 CMLR 854 for Denmark; *Frontini* v *Ministero della Finanze* [1974] CMLR 386 for Italy; *Marks & Spencer* v *CCE* [1999] 1 CMLR 1152 for the United Kingdom. On more recent decisions of the Czech Constitutional Court, the Hungarian Constitutional Court and the Polish Constitutional Tribunal see W. Sadurski, "'Solange, Chapter 3': Constitutional Courts in Central Europe – Democracy – European Union", EUI Working Papers, Law 2006 No. 40, pp. 6–26.

view, apparently presupposing both the original sovereignty and the supremacy of the Union, be reconciled with the merely derived nature of the sovereign rights of the Union? How can the national view, insisting on national law as the starting point of all legal power of the Union, allow for the supremacy of Union law at all?

For the time being, the dilemma has been left unresolved. The pragmatic solution consists in treating Union law and its interpretation by the ECJ as, in principle, supreme – in the hope that the limits of this supremacy will not be put seriously to the test. Thus, one has to grant that the greater part of the everyday application of the law in Europe is not actually affected by this controversy. To be sure, the question of whether the supremacy of Union law and the exclusive power of the ECJ to review Union law will prevail without any exception is, without doubt, an important question for the proper understanding of the entity "Union". Given this importance, it strikes one as nigh astonishing that little effort has been made to enquire thoroughly into the legal relation between the Member States and the Community – now the Union.[15] It may well be that political implications bedevil the legal analysis here, for political supporters of European integration may feel strongly tempted to support the European view, regardless of whether they find convincing legal arguments. And, the other way round, Eurosceptics may in a comparable way feel compelled to take the national view. Still, even those who are tempted to dismiss the question of the precise reconstruction of the legal relation between the Union and its Member States as small-minded ought not to underestimate the importance of a convincing reconstruction, looking here to the success of the project of European integration.[16] Thus, there can be little doubt that – in Neil MacCormick's words – "deeper thought needs to be given to the question how we are to understand systems and linkages or interrelationships between them".[17]

10.2 The Implications of Monism, Dualism, and Pluralism

The ECJ claimed, in *van Gend en Loos*, that the EEC had created an "own legal system".[18] This is certainly true in the sense that the founding treaty had established the organs of the EEC and the processes for law-creation. The motif of an "independent" legal system of the Community or the Union has since become a commonplace. On closer inspection, however, it becomes clear that Union law interacts with municipal

---

[15]See, on this phenomenon, N. MacCormick, *Questioning Sovereignty – Law, State, and Nation in the European Commonwealth* (Oxford: Oxford University Press, 1999), p. 105.

[16]It is understood that excessive claims to sovereignty on the part of the Member States threaten the European project. The other side of the coin is, however, that excessive claims to supremacy on the part of the Union will inevitably trigger resistance on the part of the Member States. Those who politically support the European integration are well advised not to try to maximise the Union's supremacy at any cost. Rather, they ought to seek a reasonable course that secures the necessary degree of supremacy for the functioning of the Union but does not unnecessarily go beyond that.

[17]MacCormick, *Questioning Sovereignty*, note 15 *supra*, p. 106.

[18]Case 26/62, *Van Gend en Loos* [1963] ECR 1.

law in a very complex manner, which places the idea of the "independence" of Union law in perspective. This raises the question of the legal reconstruction of the European Union – do we have one legal system in the Union with several subsystems, or do we have a plurality of legal systems? And what is the relation between and among these independent legal systems or subsystems? To what extent does the answer to the first question determine the answer to the second?

10.2.1 Monism, Dualism, and Pluralism

The problem of whether there is a plurality of legal systems or a single complex system with several subsystems is well-known from the debate on the reconstruction of international law. Most notably, Hans Kelsen advocated a monistic reading of international law and municipal law on the basis of his idea of the "cognitive unity of all law".[19] He emphatically rejects a dualistic reading – which, according to him, is "better characterized as 'pluralistic', considering the multiplicity of state legal systems".[20] A monistic reading can be construed, however, either from the standpoint of the state legal system or from the international legal system. This gives rise to the distinction between two forms of monism: (1) monism with primacy of the state legal system and (2) monism with primacy of the international legal system. For Kelsen the decision on the form of monism is a political decision. For him there are no compelling arguments on behalf of one or the other form.[21]

It is tempting to apply this much discussed distinction in international law – (1) dualism, (2) monism with primacy of the international legal system, and (3) monism with primacy of the state legal system – to the phenomenon of supranationality in the European Union.[22] Whether and, if so, to what extent, this or that reconstruction supports either the national view or the European view depends on which assumptions on "supremacy" or "priority" are connected with these reconstructions.

10.2.2 The Hierarchical Structure of the Legal System

Both the decision (1) between dualism and monism and (2) between monism with primacy of the state legal system and monism with primacy of the international legal

---

[19] H. Kelsen, *Introduction to the Problems of Legal Theory*, transl B. Litschewski Paulson and S. L. Paulson (Oxford: Clarendon Press, 1992), p. 111; H. Kelsen, *Pure Theory of Law*, transl M. Knight (Berkeley CA: University of California Press, 1967), p. 328.

[20] Kelsen, *Introduction to the Problems of Legal Theory*, note 19 *supra*, p. 111; Kelsen, *Pure Theory of Law*, note 19 *supra*, p. 328.

[21] See, for example, H. Kelsen, *General Theory of Law and State*, transl A. Wedberg (Cambridge MA: Harvard University Press, 1945), p. 388.

[22] On such attempts, see T. Öhlinger, "Die Einheit des Rechts", in: S.L. Paulson and M. Stolleis (eds), *Hans Kelsen als Staatsrechtslehrer und Rechtsphilosoph* (Tübingen: Mohr Siebeck, 2005), pp. 160–73.

system are often – be it explicitly or implicitly – influenced by assumptions on the "hierarchical structure" in legal systems. If one assumes that law that is higher in the "hierarchy" takes priority over law that is lower in the hierarchy, the decision between (1) dualism and monism and (2) between the two forms of monism seems to have enormous legal and political implications. (1) Monism with primacy of the state legal system supports, on first glance, the "national view", (2) monism with primacy of the international legal system the "European view", and (3) dualism or pluralism appears to be somewhere in between. It is, however, far from clear whether these assumptions are justified. Kelsen for his part emphasizes that the choice of the form of monism has no implications at all for derogation between and among norms in municipal and international law.[23] He refers to his "doctrine of alternative provisions", according to which exercising a power-conferring norm can create a valid norm even outside the competence granted.[24] This doctrine is, to say the least, far from convincing. The decisive question is whether and, if so, to what extent "higher law" necessarily derogates from "lower law". Kelsen neither explicitly discusses this "hierarchy of derogation" nor its relation to the "hierarchy of conditions"; rather, he focuses on the latter hierarchy alone.[25] This lies, however, far beyond the scope of this chapter. It will suffice here to point out that the legal reconstruction of the European Union as dualistic or monistic and – if the latter is preferred, in which form – does not necessarily decide as to whether the 'national view' or the 'European view' is correct. What is needed is a thorough analysis of the relation between Union law and Member State law – which norms delegate to what extent legal power to whom, and which norms derogate from which other norms?

10.3 Neil MacCormick's Pluralistic Reconstruction of the European Union

Neil MacCormick has advanced the most sophisticated pluralistic reading of the European Union. Inviting attention here to only the three most important of MacCormick's writings on the theory he developed on legal pluralism and post-sovereignty,[26] there is an early statement of core ideas in the article "Beyond the

---

[23] Kelsen, *Introduction to the Problems of Legal Theory*, note 19 *supra*, pp. 118–119; Kelsen, *General Theory of Law and State*, note 21 *supra*, pp. 371–372; Kelsen, *Pure Theory of Law*, note 19 *supra*, pp. 330–301.

[24] Kelsen, *Introduction to the Problems of Legal Theory*, note 19 *supra*, pp. 71–75; Kelsen, *General Theory of Law and State*, note 21 *supra*, pp. 153–161; Kelsen, *Pure Theory of Law*, note 19 *supra*, pp. 267–278.

[25] On these two forms of hierarchies in legal systems, see M. Borowski, "Die Lehre vom Stufenbau des Rechts nach Adolf Julius Merkl", in: S. L. Paulson and M. Stolleis, note 22 *supra*, pp. 122–159, at pp. 141–153. On the relation between these two forms of hierarchies, see ibid., pp. 153–156; M. Borowski, "Balancing and Hierarchy", Ms. 2010.

[26] I shall not undertake a more detailed analysis of MacCormick's theory on sovereignty or "post-sovereignty" in this chapter. See Martin Borowski, "Neil MacCormick's Legal Reconstruction

Sovereign State", published in 1993.[27] The most comprehensive version of his theory is presented in his monograph *Questioning Sovereignty*, published in 1999.[28] Finally, key ideas from *Questioning Sovereignty* are reworked in the review essay "Questioning Post-Sovereignty", published in 2004.[29] According to MacCormick, the Member States of the Community – which has now been succeeded by the Union – are no longer sovereign. What is more, this is a welcome development.[30] "Universal sovereign statehood" has had a bloody history and was responsible for two world wars in the twentieth century.[31] Based on his "institutional theory of law", MacCormick proposes that neither the Member States nor the Community/Union has the final word. Rather, both meet on an equal footing. Both lay claim to an area in which they have supremacy, both claim to be originally empowered, that is, without thereby being empowered by some higher source of power. In the jargon of systems theory, national law and Community/Union law are described as self-referential systems that find no superior authority outside themselves.[32] MacCormick emphatically rejects the idea that national law and Community/Union law might be ordered hierarchically, such that one form of law would be rendered a subsystem of the other.[33] The result is juridical or legal pluralism, the Community/Union law and the law of the Member States being "distinct but interacting".[34] This theory is certainly by far the most sophisticated attempt to overcome the simple confrontation of the European and the national view and to establish a middle way that takes account of all legitimate interests.

Critical analysis can demonstrate, however, that MacCormick's pluralist reconstruction of the Union is less than convincing. A truly pluralist reading does not allow for legal decisions of conflicts between and among different legal systems. In addition, to assume that the Union and the Member States meet on an "equal footing" presupposes that the Union boasts of original sovereignty, a presupposition that cannot be reconciled with the Union's nature as derived from the Member States. In order to highlight certain features of MacCormick's theory and to illustrate aspects of my criticism, I shall sketch at the end of this chapter a legal reconstruction of the Union, according to which Union law counts as a subsystem of the law of the Member States, and, no less for that, enjoys nearly unconditional supremacy.

---

of the European Community – Sovereignty and Legal Pluralism", in: A. J. Menendez and J. E. Fossum (eds), *The Post-Sovereign Constellation – Law and Democracy in Neil MacCormick's Legal and Political Theory* (Oslo: Arena, 2008), pp. 191–231, at pp. 197–205.

[27] N. MacCormick, "Beyond the Sovereign State" (1993) 56 *Modern Law Review*, p. 1.

[28] MacCormick, *Questioning Sovereignty*, note 15 *supra*.

[29] N. MacCormick, "Questioning Post-Sovereignty" (2004) 29 *European Law Review*, p. 852.

[30] MacCormick, "Beyond the Sovereign State", note 27 *supra*, pp. 16–17; MacCormick, *Questioning Sovereignty*, note 29 *supra*, pp. 132–135 *et passim*.

[31] MacCormick, "Beyond the Sovereign State", note 27 *supra*, p. 17; see also MacCormick, *Questioning Sovereignty*, note 29 *supra*, pp. 126 and 142.

[32] See MacCormick, *Questioning Sovereignty*, note 29 *supra*, p. 7, p. 109 and p. 141.

[33] Ibid., pp. 116–117 *et passim*.

[34] Ibid., p. 118.

10.3.1 MacCormick's General Theory of Legal Pluralism

According to legal pluralism, different legal orders can exist independently in one territory. Two legal orders are independent if the one does not derive power from the other, which, if it did, would render the one order a mere subsystem of the other.[35] MacCormick's legal pluralism presupposes a specific concept of law. The crucial problem of this theory lies in the question of whether a convincing reconstruction of the decision of conflicts between different normative orders is available.

10.3.1.1 Legal Pluralism and the Concept of Law

According to MacCormick's "institutional theory of law", law is an institutional normative order. Characteristic was the effort to realize a certain kind of order:

> The will directed towards realizing a practicable, rationally coherent and humanly satisfactory ideal order constitutes it as normative order.[36]

This normative order has to be institutionalised to be law.[37] Of course, it would be difficult to find a legal philosopher who is prepared to deny that the law is at its core a consistent and coherent system of institutionalized norms. It is worth noting, however, that different understandings of "institutionalization" are possible.

MacCormick is very generous. According to him, the "tendency to take for granted the equation of 'law' with 'state-law'" has had "serious distorting effects for legal theory".[38] He emphasizes at several points that state law is not the only form of law,[39] and on his list of organizations creating law beyond the state one finds "churches, sporting organizations, commercial guilds, and leagues, international organizations, and agencies".[40] To be sure, the idea of law beyond and apart from state law is by no means an innovation. Scholars focusing on sociological aspects of the law, to mention only Eugen Ehrlich,[41] Max Weber,[42] and Hermann

---

[35]MacCormick, *Questioning Sovereignty*, note 15 *supra*, p. 75 *et passim*.

[36]Ibid., p. 4.

[37]Ibid., pp. 6–7, p. 13.

[38]Ibid., p. 9.

[39]Ibid., pp. 9, p. 15, p. 17, pp. 20–21, pp. 75–78 and p. 102; see also MacCormick, *Institutions of Law* (Oxford: Oxford University Press, 2007), p. 288 *et passim*.

[40]MacCormick, *Questioning Sovereignty*, note 15 *supra*, p. 7. See also *ibid*., 20: "law merchant", "canon law". On church law, see furthermore *ibid*., p. 104 *et passim*. Pluralism is also illustrated, with a variety of examples, in: K.I. Winston (ed), *The Principles of Social Order: Selected Essays of Lon L. Fuller*, 2nd ed. (Oxford: Hart Publishing, 2001).

[41]According to Ehrlich, "living law", the law which is effective in governing the different associations in society, has to be distinguished from "norms for decision", the legal norms courts use for deciding conflicts. On "living law", see E. Ehrlich, *Fundamental Principles of the Sociology of Law*, transl W.L. Moll (Cambridge MA: Harvard University Press, 1936), pp. 39–41, on "norms for decision", pp. 121–132, and on "state law", p. 132.

[42]M. Weber, *On Law in Economy and Society*, transl by E. Shils and M. Rheinstein (Cambridge MA: Harvard University Press, 1954), pp. 65–97.

Kantorowicz,[43] have emphasized that phenomenon. Such a broad understanding of "law" presupposes an equation of institutionalization with mere social efficacy of norms, that is, obedience to norms and sanctions imposed for their violation.[44] Corresponding to these two elements, different conceptions of social efficacy are imaginable. To be sure, all conceptions have in common the notion that the existence and validity of law become a matter of sheer facticity. For example, if church law is obeyed and sanctions are imposed for its violation, church law counts as law. The question of the legal authority to issue law plays no role at all.

It is by no means obvious, however, that law *is* sheer facticity. On the contrary, many would argue that this misses the essence of law, its specific normativity, completely.[45] The third element of characterizations of the concept of law, beyond social efficacy and moral correctness, is authoritative issuance. A norm is authoritatively issued if it has been "issued in a duly prescribed way by a duly authorized organ and does not violate higher-ranking law".[46] This leads to a narrower understanding of institutionalization, according to which only authoritatively issued and socially effective norms are law.[47] To illustrate the point: It may seem obvious that a church is entitled to regulate its own internal matters, but "church law" may well extend far beyond that. To use a drastic example, church law could impose the death penalty for apostasy. Do clergymen have the authority to issue such a decree as law? According to Hart's theory, one would have to ask whether the apostasy rule is identified as law by the rule of recognition. If the apostasy rule is not treated as valid law by state officials, particularly where it conflicts with state law, then, following the state's rule of recognition, it does not count as law at all. This means, however, only that the decree is not state law. Can we understand clergymen as officials of a self-standing legal system, accepting a church's rule of recognition from the internal point of view, according to which the apostasy rule does count as law? When Hart speaks of "revolution", "enemy occupation", the "simple breakdown of ordered legal control", and a colony cutting the cord to the colonial power, it is understood that the co-existence of two distinct legal orders in one territory is not the normal state of affairs.[48] The same applies to Kelsen, for whom the creation of law requires the empowerment by the state constitution. If, however, the church were empowered by

---

[43]H. Kantorowicz, *The Definition of Law* (Cambridge: Cambridge University Press, 1958), pp. 15 and pp. 82–89.

[44]However, Kantorowicz's approach is complex. Although he endorses the thesis of the existence of law beyond state law with vigour, he argued powerfully against the American Legal Realists' exaggerated reduction of the law to concoctions of fact; see H Kantorowicz, "Some Rationalism about Realism" (1933–1934) 43 *Yale Law Journal*, pp. 1240–1253.

[45]And one does not have to appeal to classical natural law theory to make the point, see, for example, Kelsen, *Introduction to the Problems of Legal Theory*, note 19 *supra*, pp. 33–35.

[46]R. Alexy, *The Argument from Injustice*, transl B Litschewski Paulson and S.L. Paulson (Oxford: Clarendon Press, 2002), p. 87.

[47]Non-positivistic concepts of law require, in addition, a certain connection between law and morality as necessary.

[48]H.L.A. Hart, *The Concept of Law*, 2nd ed. (Oxford: Clarendon Press, 1994), pp. 118–121.

the state constitution to create law, church law would be rendered a subsystem of state law, depriving church law of its independent status *vis-à-vis* state law.

For MacCormick, by contrast,[49] the plurality of legal orders in one territory is not an exceptional or problematic state of affairs. Rather, "[t]he theory of law as institutional normative order has built into it an inherently pluralistic conception of legal system. Distinct systems", he continues, "can co-exist without any one having to deny either the independence or the normative character of another". His theory could "fully endorse the normative quality of law while allowing for a radical pluralism such that objectively valid normative orders may give conflicting answers to the same point".[50] Owing to MacCormick's thesis of the existence of non-state law, the relation between the state and law is "imperfect identity, overlap without complete identity".[51]

10.3.1.2 Decision of Conflicts Between and Among Norms in Independent Legal Orders

To take socially established systems of rules seriously rather than insisting on a monolithic and hierarchical understanding of law strikes one as both realistic and tolerant. The important question, however, is how to resolve conflicts between and among norms in different legal orders. MacCormick distinguishes two perspectives.

(a) Officials

The first is the perspective of the officials of the respective system. The question which norm takes precedence is, MacCormick argues, "of course self-answering, for the system's agencies can never say other than that the system's norm ought to prevail".[52] An agency within the system is, first and foremost, if not only, committed to the norms of its legal system. MacCormick does not add, however, that norms of a legal system can – explicitly or implicitly – refer to norms of other systems. By reason of such a reference these norms can give rise to legal consequences in the former legal system. Intersystemic conflicts can acquire, thereby, an intrasystemic nature or dimension.

(b) Citizens

The second perspective is that of "citizens" or persons who experience conflicting claims. For them "the issue is which to respect, on grounds external to the self-referential answer provided by rival normative orders".[53] Are there legal criteria

[49]One hastens to add, however, that MacCormick claims, with reference to one article of Hart's, that his writings were sympathetic to a pluralist understanding of the law; see MacCormick, *Questioning Sovereignty*, note 15 *supra*, p. 76, footnote 35.

[50]MacCormick, *Questioning Sovereignty*, note 15 *supra*, p. 75.

[51]Ibid., p. 25.

[52]Ibid., p. 8.

[53]Ibid., pp. 8–9.

or methods determining which system's answer ought to prevail? In setting out his general theory of legal pluralism, MacCormick is quite clear that this is by no means necessary:

> [I]t is perfectly possible that conflicts will simply go unresolved, or that the solution may be a matter for political rather than legal processes.[54]

In the context of his analysis of the relation of the legal system of the Union and municipal law MacCormick speaks of a "superfluity of legal answers" that are "not logically embarrassing, because strictly the answers are from the point of view of different systems".[55] Even if one is willing to grant that such conflicts are not "logically embarrassing", there remains the problem that they are – as MacCormick explicitly concedes – "practically embarrassing".[56]

MacCormick's solution to the problem of intersystemic conflicts of norms is pragmatic in nature: Resolution or avoidance is "a matter for circumspection and for political as much as legal judgment".[57] To be sure, states, as everyone knows, tend to monopolize law, subjecting rival – in MacCormick's words – normative orders to their legal system.[58] On what does the state's decision to establish a monopoly depend? Is it simply a matter of policy? What is more, MacCormick concedes that

> the organizations need not in turn [. . .] acknowledge that primacy in the form in which it is asserted by one or another state.[59]

If these organizations are not supposed to acknowledge such primacy in whatever form it may take, is it a matter of policy for them, too? If one understands the law as "a determinate guide to conduct",[60] and if states are free to take political decision to subject non-state law, what sense does it make to term normative orders beyond state law "law" at all? And how can one say that different legal orders meet on an equal footing?

If one is inclined to agree that possible solutions of intersystemic norm conflicts have to be political in nature, the political bargaining position will depend very much on whether the association in question is large and politically powerful or merely something on the fringe. The former will be able to coerce the state to undertake far more favourable compromises than the latter, which will be entirely subject to state law. Substantive legitimacy and equality among associations play a role only to the extent that policy or prudence requires; they do not, as such, count as criteria.

The result is that the "law" dissolves into rival claims. Which claim will prevail becomes simply a question of politics and power. The outcome is hard to predict, a matter which ought to be taken seriously. There can be no legal certainty where a

---

[54] Ibid., p. 75.

[55] Ibid., p. 119.

[56] Ibid.

[57] Ibid. See, also, Ibid., p. 120.

[58] Ibid., p. 25. See also MacCormick, *Institutions of Law*, note 39 *supra*, p. 288.

[59] Ibid.

[60] See MacCormick, *Questioning Sovereignty*, note 15 *supra*, p. 102.

variety of legal answers lurk behind every question, with no established criteria for determining which of the answers is to be chosen. In the absence of legal certainty, law is scarcely in a position to fulfil its central task mentioned above, that of serving as a determinate guide to conduct.

Pluralism is also questionable from a substantive point of view. In liberal democracies the state guarantees democratic procedures and the fundamental rights of the individual. To call this into question through conflicting normative orders that may not be democratic and may not respect fundamental rights at all, and to resolve conflicts simply by appeal to political power does not seem to be an attractive solution.

(c) An Example: The "Crime" of Apostasy

The consequences of legal pluralism may be illustrated by the example of church law. According to "the law" of certain religious communities, "church law", "apostasy" can be forbidden on penalty by death. The judgment is taken by a designated court of the church, the penalty may be carried out by the faithful whenever and wherever they get hold of the "apostate". Assuming that the deviant is declared to be an "apostate" by the responsible authority of the church and subsequently killed by a fellow believer, what does the law require? The pluralist's question would be: Is it required that the person who killed the "apostate" be punished as a murderer, according to state law, or is it required instead that he be honoured for the exemplary execution of "the law", this according to "church law"?

(aa) The Pluralist's Solution

For a pluralist, the resolution to this conflict between state law and non-state law is a matter of politics, with all the problems adumbrated above. The only way out is to deny that one of the conflicting norms is valid law, thereby denying that there is any conflict at all. On the basis of a non-positivistic concept of law, one could claim that where law that does not respect fundamental rights, it does not deserve to be called law properly-so-called. This would mean that the "church law", imposing the sanction of death penalty for "apostasy", would not be law owing to the violation of religious freedom on the part of believers of that church. MacCormick seems to move somewhat in that direction. There remain, however, serious problems.

First, MacCormick explicitly acknowledges the importance of fundamental rights as constraints on state power;[61] this applies, however, not to organizations of non-state law and their power. After having emphasized the importance of fundamental rights, he writes:

---

[61] MacCormick, *Questioning Sovereignty*, note 15 *supra*, p. 24. See also MacCormick, *Institutions of Law*, note 39 *supra*, pp. 190–191, p. 201 and pp. 273–274.

> *Governmental* systems which fail in these regards fall short of some of the essential virtues of legal order, even if they succeed to in sustaining some form of institutional order, and to this extent of law.[62]

Why do fundamental rights count as constraints only for state law, and not for non-state-law? If one accepts the pluralistic reconstruction, legal authority beyond state authority can indeed seriously endanger and violate fundamental rights of individuals. A gap in the protection of these fundamental rights can only be avoided if this authority is (1) itself bound by fundamental rights (direct commitment) or (2) subjected to state law, which itself is bound by fundamental rights (indirect commitment, *mittelbare Drittwirkung*).

Second, MacCormick does not establish a clear connection between a violation of fundamental rights and the loss of the legal character of a norm. If one looks, for example, at the quotation above, fundamental rights are among the "essential virtues of a legal order". What is the import of this where they are absent?

Third, if MacCormick were to establish a clear connection between the legal character of a norm and the respect for fundamental rights, this would count as a strikingly thick conception of natural law. The precise content of fundamental rights is hotly contested even in liberal democracies. A natural law conception could only draw the outermost limits of the law.[63] It could not cover comprehensively the values in liberal democracies and protect them against conflicting normative orders.

(bb) The Integration Model

From a historical point of view, it counts as an achievement of the modern constitutional state that churches and believers are subject to state law.[64] Many people would argue that the example of the killings of "apostates" simply has one talking about murder, whatever the "judgments" of church courts may say. This implies that church law, at least beyond purely internal matters of the religious community, is indeed subject to state law. This view is based on the integration model, according to which norms count as law only if they are integrated into the state legal order. Against the backdrop of the analysis of legal pluralism thus far, three aspects of the integration model ought to be emphasized.

First, it should be apparent that to insist on the law as a consistent and coherent system of norms is by no means merely an end in itself or a utopian exercise in the logic of the law, it is rather a means of the protection of substantive values embodied

---

[62] MacCormick, *Institutions of Law*, note 39 *supra*, p. 201 (emphasis added). On fundamental rights as constraints on the exercise of state power, see also MacCormick, *Questioning Sovereignty*, note 15 *supra*), p. 24 and MacCormick, *Institutions of Law*, note 39 *supra*, p. 190 and p. 274.

[63] See, for example, MacCormick, *Institutions of Law*, note 39 *supra*, p. 270: "The duties of justice (according to some reasonable conception of justice) can properly be exacted under sanctions of law. Beyond that, law may not go without degenerating towards tyranny." "Some reasonable conception of justice" does not exclude much.

[64] See M. Borowski, *Die Glaubens- und Gewissensfreiheit des Grundgesetzes* (Tübingen: Mohr Siebeck, 2006), pp. 491–495.

in the constitution, in particular fundamental human rights of the individual along with democracy. From this standpoint it is fairly obvious that religious freedom does not give a church the definitive right to kill people whom it regards as "apostates".

Second, to understand church law or other kinds of systems as integrated into state law does not mean that from a substantive standpoint they are not taken seriously. Integration – or, to put a sharp edge on it, formal subjection – does not necessarily mean undermining of substantive import. To the extent that claims of respect for norms beyond state law are legitimate, state law ought to respect these norms. This is exactly what happens in modern liberal democracies, which grant freedom of religion. Church law regulating internal matters will deserve, as a rule, protection by means of special guarantees of the constitution, or through the greater dimension of religious freedom. Thus, in subjecting all other kinds of social system or law to state law, the state as the general compulsory association of all citizens can provide a neutral framework for reconciling all legitimate interests. This framework establishes authorities, state courts, whose decisions count as final. In balancing the rights of groups and individuals, all legitimate claims can be considered with due attention to their respective merits.

Third, the possibility of integration or incorporation of norms into state law shows that the "origin" of norms is ambiguous. This can be illustrated by a quotation from Kantorowicz, one of the early pluralists. The idea of incorporation struck him as absurd:

> [I]t would be equally reasonable to argue that every language spoken or every melody sung in the British Commonwealth originates from Whitehall or Westminster.[65]

To begin with, (1) "origin" or "originate" can refer to the social context of the genesis of norms. To use the example of church law again, it emerges socially in the religious community. It does not come as a surprise that an approach emphasizing "sociological realism"[66] prefers this reading. (2) "Origin", however, can also refer to the formal relation of being subject to conditions stemming from higher law.[67] If state law incorporates church law by reference in a constitution or a parliamentary statute, church law becomes formally a part of state law. This is not to say that church law "originates" in state legislation – this applies only to the norm incorporating church law, not to church law itself or its content. The distinction between the social context of the genesis and the formal relation of being subject to conditions imposed by higher law demonstrates that Kantorowicz's metaphor is mistaken – "language" and "melodies" do not exhibit the formal relation of being conditioned by higher entities, whereas this is indeed characteristic of the law.

Even these brief remarks suggest that the integration model – which will be taken up in a section below – is far more sophisticated and convincing than the pluralists would have us believe.

---

[65] Kantorowicz, *The Definition of Law*, note 43 *supra*, p. 15 (footnote omitted).

[66] MacCormick, *Questioning Sovereignty*, note 15 *supra*, p. 117.

[67] See Borowski, "Balancing and Hierarchy", note 25 *supra*.

10.3.1.3 Legal Pluralism in the European Union

From the summary of MacCormick's general theory of legal pluralism it ought to be clear that it must have seemed tempting for him to reconstruct European Union law along these lines. The Union, so it is said, boasts of its own legal system. Primary Union law creates the institutions and processes for legislation, administration and adjudication, and the institutions create secondary law. This seems indeed to be a clear example of non-state law.[68] The idea that the Union legal system is subject to conditions imposed by any particular state's constitution is dismissed quickly,[69] and MacCormick points out correctly that the Member States' constitutions do not owe their validity to Union law.[70] He characterizes the relation between the Union and the Member States as "interactive rather than hierarchical" and "distinct but interacting".[71]

(a) The Decision of Conflicts Between Union Law and Member States' Law

The analysis of MacCormick's general theory of legal pluralism has shown that a crucial problem lies in the fact that there are no legal criteria for conflicts between norms of different systems. This applies, on principle, to a pluralistic reconstruction of the Union, too – there are no legal criteria for conflicts between Member States' constitutions and Union law. One has to distinguish, however, between two conceptions, "radical pluralism" and "pluralism under international law". MacCormick, initially a proponent of "radical pluralism", later supported "pluralism under international law".[72]

(aa) Radical Pluralism

According to "radical pluralism" there are no legal criteria at all for resolving conflicts. This means that the "tragic solution" holds true, according to which "the constitutional court of a member-state is committed to denying that its competence to interpret the constitution by which it was established can be restricted by decisions of a tribunal external to the system". MacCormick continues:

> Conversely, the ECJ is by the same logic committed to denying that its competence to interpret its own constitutive treaties can be restricted by decisions of member-state tribunals.[73]

---

[68]However, on closer examination the Union is far from being paradigm for legal pluralism, because it is derivative in nature.

[69]MacCormick, *Questioning Sovereignty*, note 15 *supra*, p. 118.

[70]Ibid., p. 117.

[71]Ibid., p. 118.

[72]Ibid., pp. 118 and 120–121.

[73]Ibid., p. 119. See also Ibid., p. 95.

The lack of legal criteria for the resolution of intersystemic conflicts means that one has to resort to "political action".[74]

(bb) Pluralism Under International Law

MacCormick's later position, "pluralism under international law", "suggests that we need not run out of law (and into politics) quite as fast as suggested by radical pluralism".[75] The difference *vis-à-vis* radical pluralism is that legal pluralism among the Union and its Member States is embedded, he argues, into "'monism' in Kelsen's sense",[76] into a monistic system of international law.[77] In contrast to his general theory of legal pluralism and "radical pluralism", "pluralism under international law" provides legal criteria for the decision of conflicts between Union law and Member States law. Conflicts between Union law and national law, he states, do not occur in a "legal vacuum, but in a space in which international law is also relevant". Because of the "continuing normative significance of *pacta sunt servanda*", he continues, the Member States "owe each other obligations under international law".[78] He claims that, as a matter of last resort, even an international court could settle disputes.[79] Thus, a third system and a third court seem to be available to settle conflicts between two conflicting systems and courts. To begin with, it is far from clear which international court MacCormick has precisely in mind. What is more: Is MacCormick really referring to a third system? *Pacta sunt servanda* is, perhaps, the most important principle of international law, for treaty obligations are of utmost importance in international law. This principle is, however, a general legal principle with relevance in any legal system or field of law. It counts, too, as a principle of the law of the Member States and of Union law. To fulfil obligations arising from the Union treaties is, first and foremost, an obligation in Union law. If one distinguishes international law from supranational law (and if one emphasizes that international law is a different system *vis-à-vis* Union law and Member States law, one is using this narrower meaning), then *pacta sunt servanda* in international law refers to international treaties, not to supranational treaties. One can, however, use a broader meaning of "international law", embracing also supranational law, but in this case international law does not count as a "third system". Thus, it seems that MacCormick is in fact proposing that conflicts between Union law and Member State law be decided by the yardstick of Union law. This form of disguised supremacy of Union law would hardly be an expression of meeting on an equal footing.

Even more fundamental is the argument that "pluralism under international law" cannot be reconciled with characteristics of "pluralism" in the first place. If the law

---

[74] Ibid., p. 120.
[75] Ibid.
[76] Ibid., p. 121.
[77] Ibid., pp. 120–121.
[78] Ibid., p. 120 (emphasis in the original).
[79] Ibid., p. 121.

of the Member States and international law together form a "monistic system", and if Union law and international law also form a monistic system, then all three kinds of law – international law, Union law, and Member State law together form a monistic system. Monism, at least "in Kelsen's sense" – to which MacCormick refers – necessarily excludes dualism or pluralism among parts of the monistic system.[80] Every decision of a court applying legal criteria to a conflict of norms stemming from two "different systems" of norms necessarily integrates these two "different systems" into a complex system, rendering these "different systems" subsystems of a monistic greater whole – for the validity of all norms of both systems is now subject to the condition that the legal criteria applied by the relevant court in the case of conflicts of norms of different subsystems do not render the norm in question invalid.[81]

(b) Failing to Reconstruct the Derivative Nature of the EC

With his reconstruction of the Union as holding non-delegated powers along the lines of his general theory of legal pluralism, MacCormick inevitably becomes a victim of the paradox of Union law. The paradox consists in the fact that the ECJ and many scholars treat the Union – as they before treated the Community – as an original source of legal power, at least on an equal footing with the Member States. The Union is, however, a creation of the Member States and derives all powers from them. To be sure, from the *sociological point of view* the Union is certainly an entity distinct from the Member States. It is, however, hard to deny that the Union has been created by a treaty among the Member States and subsequent accession treaties and treaty revisions. It boasts only of the sovereign rights that have been transferred to it, and it has them only because they were transferred to or conferred upon it. Article 5(1) TEU expresses the principle of conferral, underscored by Article 5(2) TEU. Even in *Costa*, the ECJ concedes that, in founding the Community, a "transfer of powers from the States to the Community" had taken place.[82] This derivative nature cannot be depicted by a conception that understands the entities concerned as equally holding non-delegated powers.

To put a sharp edge on it, for legal pluralism the relation between the Union and the Member States would in principle be the same if the Union had not been established by a treaty of the Member States and subsequent accession treaties but had been created in the mid-twentieth century by means of the coercion of an

---

[80]Kelsen, *Introduction to the Problems of Legal Theory*, note 19 *supra*, p. 111; Kelsen, *General Theory of Law and State*, note 21 *supra*, p. 363; Kelsen, *Pure Theory of Law*, note 19 *supra*, p. 328.

[81]This applies also if the legal criteria applied in deciding the conflict is reconstructed in the form of a balancing exercise. In this sense balancing norms stemming from different legal systems necessarily integrates these legal systems into a greater whole, an integrated complex legal system.

[82]Case 6/64, *Costa* v *ENEL* [1964] 12 CMLR 425. Also, MacCormick explicitly mentions the transfer of sovereign rights from the Member States to the Community. See MacCormick, *Questioning Sovereignty*, note 15 *supra*, p. 107.

extra-European force that had grown weary of being called upon to help to settle wars that began in Europe and then spread to the whole world. We could think of this as a thought-experiment. The sovereign rights are not transferred by treaties among the Member States; rather, they are usurped by the institutions (comparable to the institutions the Union has now) created by the extra-European force. Of course, there is a psychological difference between a voluntary transfer of sovereign rights and someone usurping sovereign rights. It need not, however, be unrealistic to assume that such a form of paternalism might be successful. It could well be the case that the acceptance of Union law in the thought-experiment reaches an extent that one experiences nowadays on the basis of voluntary agreements. To be sure, such a thought-experiment might strike one as curious. It shows, however, that legal pluralism proper would see no decisive difference. The legal system of the EU would be existent, socially effective, and would lay claim to original power. Owing to its mere existence and the fact that it would be capable of restraining the Member States' law, one would have to state that there is a plurality of legal systems. Thus, for "legal pluralism" the difference between voluntarily transferred powers and usurped powers is not a decisive one. Such a conception cannot grasp the specific nature of Union law as derived.

MacCormick's turn towards "pluralism under international law", even if, for the reasons mentioned above, it is hardly convincing, can be read as an attempt to go beyond the mere facticity of "radical pluralism" – in the end, as an attempt to bring the treaties creating the Community and later the Union more into play than "radical pluralism" provides for. To be sure, as long as the legal originality of Union law is taken as an unquestionable and unconditional starting point of the analysis, there will be no way adequately to reconstruct the Union with its derivative nature.

10.4 The Non-pluralistic Alternative: Union Law Derived from Member States Law

The distinctive features of MacCormick's legal pluralism will become clearer if one contrasts it with the fundamental alternative, a reconstruction of Union law based on the integration model. MacCormick himself opposes his conception of legal pluralism to a conception according to which, in his words, "every normative order must be a part of a dynamically integrated whole".[83] This conception, thus characterized, is attributed to Kelsen. According to this model, the law derives its validity from state law, in particular from the state constitution. Authoritative issuance plays an important role, for it prevents merely socially effective norms from becoming "law" without an incorporation or integration by authoritatively issued norms. A comprehensive enquiry into the reconstruction of Union law based on the integration model goes well beyond the scope of this chapter. Still, an outline of the model will offer a first impression.

[83] MacCormick, *Questioning Sovereignty*, note 15 *supra*, p. 75.

The particular challenge of a reconstruction of Union law on the basis of the integration model is that state law had to integrate Union law, which is said to be supreme. This supremacy seems to be the main issue, rather than "originality". Originality, it appears, is not claimed to be an end in itself, rather, it is claimed to back up supremacy. If EC law or Union law is not original, it is necessarily derived, and derived law – this at any rate is the intuition – is necessarily inferior to the law from which it is derived. The idea of the necessary inferiority of derived law seems too obvious to require explanation. MacCormick shares this view: "For the constitution, however skeletal, is always 'above' the powers it confers."[84] That the idea of the necessary inferiority of derived law is taken to be obvious has stood in the way of according a serious reception to the integration model in the context of Union law. Taking the integration model seriously, however, gives rise to altogether new perspectives.

Granting that none of the attempts to justify original power or sovereignty of the Union has proved to be convincing, not MacCormick's legal pluralism either, the Union inevitably derives its powers from the Member States. The "supremacy" that is accorded to Union law in the integration model can be conditional or unconditional.

10.4.1 Derived and Unconditionally Supreme Union Law

Even in the integration model Union law can be unconditionally supreme. "Unconditionally supreme" means that Union law prevails *qua* form over national law. There are two ways to argue that the Union has acquired such unconditional or absolute supremacy. The first way claims that the Member States have transferred unlimited supremacy in the treaties, according to the second the Member States have accepted unconditional supremacy in the practice of Union law and its application.

10.4.1.1 The Transfer of Unconditional Supremacy in the Treaties

The first question is whether states can transfer sovereign rights to an entity to the effect that the law of this entity then enjoys unconditional supremacy over the states' law. It is often assumed that the hierarchy of the legal system provides only for a delegation of power to lower levels in the hierarchy of derogation[85], not to higher levels in this sense. My thesis is that the theory of the hierarchical structure of the legal system does indeed provide for a delegation of powers to higher levels in the hierarchy, to the effect that delegated law counts as formally superior. A comprehensive and thorough enquiry into this theory, however, lies well beyond the scope

[84] Ibid., p. 103.

[85] On the distinction between the hierarchy of conditions (or of delegation) and the hierarchy of derogation, see Borowski, "Balancing and Hierarchy", note 25 *supra*.

of this chapter.[86] Supposing that this theory does not rule out to transfer powers to institutions outside of and standing over a national state, the Member States of the European Union would be in a position to merge into a European Superstate whenever they wished. To be sure, the question is whether such a reconstruction of Union law as it currently stands is convincing. In particular, the question is of whether the Member States intended to transfer the highest competence to create and change norms to an entity outside of and standing over their legal systems. This would mean that they would cease to exist as independent entities, for they would be altogether subject to decisions outside their own legal system. Their legal system would become a mere subsystem of a new system – formally inferior to the highest levels in the new system.

There is a test question here, to determine, namely, whether the unconditional supremacy of Union law and the unconditional judicial supremacy of the ECJ qualify as correct characterizations of the current legal situation. If the ECJ were to decide, either explicitly or implicitly, that there are no limits to its jurisdiction, that in other words it is not committed to any legal constraints, would this count – the question of political prudence aside – as being *legally correct*? Does Union law boast of the *competence-competence* or *omnicompetence*? Just a quick look at the European Treaties shows, however, that the answer has to be "no". The principle of conferral in Article 5(1) TEU sets limits to the Union's powers. Of course, the ECJ is empowered to interpret primary law; this interpretive competence is not, however, without limits. One may quarrel about where the interpretive discretion of the ECJ ends; it is clear, however, that there is an end.[87] Decisions of the ECJ beyond this discretion are *legally defective*. In particular, the ECJ is not empowered to amend treaties as it wishes.

To sum up: The understanding of Union law as "derived" and unconditionally supreme was, from the point of view of legal theory, possible. This meant that one has to understand the European Treaties and the constitutional amendments made by the Member States in the course of the European Integration as transferring the unlimited power to derogate from any provision of the law of the Member States, and the ECJ had the final say regarding the validity of such law. One cannot interpret the European treaties, as they stand, however, to read that Member States have subjected themselves legally to the most serious misinterpretations of the those treaties.

10.4.1.2 Acceptance of Unconditional Supremacy by the Member States

If unconditional supremacy has not been transferred by the European treaties, one could argue that the Member States have simply accepted it. This would raise the question of how political practice ought to be transformed into Union law. To be

---

[86]On the reasons for the usual assumption of the parallelism between the hierarchy of conditions and the hierarchy of derogation, see *ibid*. To be sure, this parallelism only goes so far as good reasons are at hand.

[87]It is noteworthy that MacCormick distinguishes explicitly the "interpretive competence" from the "competence-competence", see MacCormick, *Questioning Sovereignty*, note 15 *supra*, p. 117.

sure, the acceptance of unconditional supremacy is, as a matter of fact, out of the question. Telling is the fate of Article I-6 of the Treaty Establishing a Constitution for Europe (TCE),[88] which was set to positivize the case law of the ECJ on the basis of the supremacy or primacy of Community law.[89] Of course, one might argue that the simple fact of transforming case law into a treaty provision does not change anything. This misses a decisive point, however, seen against the backdrop of Continental law. In short, in Continental law the primary source of law is the statute. Precedents do not count as a source of law at all.[90] This means that the Continental Member States, following their tradition, assume that "wrong" decisions of the ECJ – for example exaggerated claims to supremacy made by the ECJ – do not mark a change in Union law at all. There is no real need to react to the claim of supremacy as made by the ECJ. It is, however, different where supremacy has been set down in a treaty provision. Thus, to positivize the case law on supremacy changes the situation somewhat.[91]

It is not without reason that a provision comparable to Article I-6 TCE was omitted in the Treaty of Lisbon at the Intergovernmental Conference at the European Council in Brussels in June 2007. In turn, the Council Legal Service felt bound to publish an opinion contending that this omission does not mean that the principle of primacy and the existing case law of the ECJ is changed in any way.[92] This opinion was included into a declaration annexed to the Treaty of Lisbon, stating that "the Treaties have primacy over the law of Member States, under the conditions laid down by the said case law".[93] The declaration is not, however, legally binding, which is to say that one is still left with the case law of the ECJ.

In conclusion, unconditional supremacy has neither been transformed into a binding treaty provision nor tacitly accepted by the Member States.

10.4.2 Derived and Nearly Unconditionally Supreme Union Law

That the Member States have not transferred the power to derogate from their constitutions unconditionally does not mean that they can derogate from Union law as they wish. Rather, derogations are limited to extreme circumstances – where fidelity to

---

[88]This article reads: "The Constitution and law adopted by the institutions of the Union in exercising competences conferred on it shall have primacy over the law of the Member States."

[89]See "Declarations annexed to the Treaty Establishing a Constitution for Europe", Declaration (No. 1) on Art. I-6: "The Conference notes that Article I-6 reflects existing case-law of the Court of Justice of the European Communities and of the Court of First Instance", OJ 2004/C 310/420.

[90]See, for example, K. Larenz, *Methodenlehre der Rechtswissenschaft*, 5th ed (Berlin *et al.*: Springer, 1983), pp. 413–415.

[91]See, also M. Kumm and V. Ferreres, "The Primacy Clause of the Constitutional Treaty and the Future of Constitutional Conflict in the European Union" (2005) 3 *International Journal of Constitutional Law*, p. 477.

[92]Opinion of the Council Legal Service, European Council in Brussels, 22 June 2007, 11197/07, JUR 260.

[93]"Declarations Annexed to the Final Act of the Intergovernmental Conference which Adopted the Treaty of Lisbon", Declaration (No. 17) Concerning Primacy, OJ 2007/C 315/344.

Union law becomes unacceptable to the Member State. This is a very high threshold for derogation of Union law by Member States' law, and whether the threshold has been crossed is determined by balancing. This means that the supremacy of Union law is not formal superiority, it is rather created by deference to Union law's claim to supremacy whose extent has to be determined by balancing.[94]

10.4.2.1 The Legal Foundation of the Union in the Constitutions of the Member States

The appropriate starting point of this balancing model is the fact that the popular sovereignty of the peoples of the Member States is still the last point of attribution for the highest level of law. MacCormick is correct in emphasizing that the Member States retain "crucial attributes of sovereignty",[95] their legal power is non-delegated. In exercising power provided in their constitutions they created the Union and transferred sovereign rights. This renders Union law inevitably derivative. To be sure, Union law – primary and secondary law – is formally backed up by provisions of constitutions of the Member States. They have jointly embarked on the enterprise of creating the Union, and the aim of European integration is expressed in constitutional provisions (for example, Article 23(1) of the German Basic Law). These "European integration provisions" are on the same level in the hierarchy of legal norms as all other constitutional provisions. This means that Union interests, strictly speaking, are in a certain sense always national interests, too – the Union is an undertaking of the Member States, and the Member States are seriously interested in a functioning Union. This fact is often obscured by the simple confrontation of national interests and Union interests. It deserves to be emphasized that the "European integration provisions" in national constitutions serve as the legal foundation of the Union. They undergird the whole of Union law, and with it the supremacy of Union law and judicial supremacy of the ECJ.

10.4.2.2 Balancing Union Law against National Law – The Formal Principle

There can be no doubt that the Union, from a sociological and a political point of view, acts autonomously and independently of the Member States. From the legal point of view, it does so, however, within a very wide framework created by the law of the Member States. The key to understanding the nearly unconditional supremacy of Union law and nearly unconditionally supreme jurisdiction of the ECJ, granted by the Member States' constitutions, is the formal principle that figures in balancing

---

[94]Balancing presupposes the validity of the norms to be balanced despite the fact that these norms conflict (M. Borowski, *Grundrechte als Prinzipien*, 2nd ed (Baden-Baden: Nomos, 2007), p. 80 and p. 100). Norms to be balanced have to be on the same level in the hierarchy of the legal system. See also Borowski, "Balancing and Hierarchy'", note 25 *supra*.

[95]MacCormick, "Questioning Post-Sovereignty", note 15 *supra*, p. 863.

national law against Union law. Substantive principles require the optimal realization of certain fixed content, for example, freedom of religion. Characteristic of formal principles is their requirement of the optimal realization of the results of a process.[96] Formal principles create a margin, in which no conflicting substantive principle overrides any of the other.[97] Paradigmatic is the democratic process – whatever the outcome of the democratic process, it counts as important simply *because* it is the outcome of the democratic process. Union law as a whole is the result of processes, too. Primary law is the result of negotiating and agreeing upon treaty provisions, secondary law is the result of Union legislation as established by primary law, and the judgments of the ECJ are the result of judicial processes as defined in the treaties and inferior Union law.

The abstract weight of "European integration" as a constitutional aim is very high, and this integration requires nearly unconditional supremacy of Union law. That the Union cannot function without sufficient supremacy of its law is the empirical thesis from *Costa* v *ENEL*, and it is impossible to deny. In particular, respect of Union law is a mutual obligation of the Member States. Since every derogation from Union law on grounds of national law serves as a precedent for other Member States to claim derogations with an eye to their national interests, the fragmentation of Union law is a real and serious danger, threatening the project of European integration. This suggests that there is only a thin red line between a justified derogation from Union law where it has become unacceptable for Member States to be subjected to certain aspects of Union law and a fatal erosion of respect for Union law.

10.4.2.3 Derogations from Union Law as the Exception

To make exceptions from the supremacy of Union law and the supremacy of the jurisdiction of the ECJ by national courts will be the exception where vital interests of a Member State are seriously infringed upon and Union law provides no plausible solution. The *Solange* saga provides a good example. The Union's power to infringe on individual liberties without granting sufficient protection of fundamental rights is certainly a serious case. The ECJ did not ignore the FCC's ruling in *Solange I*, insisting on the unconditional supremacy of its rulings. Rather, it developed its jurisprudence on the protection of fundamental rights to get back to the point where Union law and the ECJ enjoy supremacy. Following Mattias Kumm's categorization, areas of serious conflicts between national law and Community law beyond fundamental rights are *ultra vires* acts, and particular provisions in national

[96] Borowski, *Grundrechte als Prinzipien*, note 94 supra, pp. 88 and 127–130; M. Borowski, "The Structure of Formal Principles", in: M. Borowski (ed), *On the Structure of Principles* (Steiner: Stuttgart, 2010), pp. 19–35. See also R. Alexy, *A Theory of Constitutional Rights*, transl J. Rivers (Oxford: Oxford University Press, 2002), pp. 414–425.

[97] On margins as a result of the consideration of formal principles in balancing, see Borowski, *Grundrechte als Prinzipien*, note 94 *supra*, pp. 128–129; Borowski, *Die Glaubens- und Gewissensfreiheit des Grundgesetzes*, note 64 *supra*, pp. 213–215.

constitutions,[98] for example, the protection of unborn life in Article 40(3)(3) of the Irish constitution. To take up here only the *ultra vires* constellation, the German FCC claimed in the *Brunner* decision that it would be empowered to review the question of whether legal acts of the Union go beyond attributed competences. Taken literally, this sounds like a rather brusque denial of the supremacy of Union law and the ECJ's supreme jurisdiction. Against the backdrop of the model developed here, it ought to be clear that this could be only the last resort. A decision of the ECJ had to be sought beforehand, and only if the ECJ did not redress the conflict and if the national interest is so serious that it overrides substantive Union interests plus the very weighty formal principle of supremacy of Union law, then national courts could set aside Union law. This will be the extraordinary exception, and the ECJ can avoid this in the first place if it takes legitimate national interests seriously. As a result, Union law enjoys nearly unconditional supremacy.

10.4.2.4 Is Nearly Unconditional Supremacy of Union Law Enough?

The integration model sketched above can explain how the constitutions of the Member States can remain, formally, the highest source of law, while Union law enjoys in nearly every case supremacy. Union law does not enjoy formal superiority; rather, it boasts of nearly unconditional supremacy, created by a huge margin in balancing Union law and national constitutional law.

Does this nearly unconditional supremacy suffice? One ought not to forget that it is nothing less than the existence of the Union that is at stake if derogations from Union law are allowed. Of course, everything turns on the reading of "nearly unconditional". The Union would be seriously endangered if derogations from Union law were not limited to very exceptional circumstances. To declare that even the mere possibility of a derogation of Union law in extreme circumstances reaches to the very root of Union life and to respond with a call for unconditional supremacy strikes one as extreme. A radical solution of this nature might have been necessary in the early years of the Community, when the phenomenon of supranationality had not yet been clearly developed, let alone commonly accepted. One ought always to be careful, however, when an "all or nothing"-argument is said to outweigh every possible counterargument. Union law has developed into a firmly established institution. That Union law is supreme on principle is not seriously challenged. A slight qualification of this supremacy, limited to extreme cases where it is apparent that it becomes unacceptable for a Member State to subject itself to certain parts of Union law, would nowadays not strike at the very root of the European integration.

[98] See M. Kumm, "The Jurisprudence of Constitutional Conflict – Constitutional Supremacy in Europe Before and After the Constitutional Treaty" (2005) 11 *European Law Journal*, pp. 264–267.

10.5 The Union as a Mere Bundle of Overlapping Laws?

It has become apparent that according to the approach developed here Union law is, strictly speaking, a legal extension of the law of the Member States. MacCormick dismisses such a conception quickly: Union law "would amount to no more than a bundle of overlapping laws to the extent that each state chose to acknowledge 'Community' [now: Union] laws and obligations."[99] Even if the formulation may sound a bit contemptuous, Union law is, indeed, technically backed up by nothing more than a "bundle of overlapping laws". This construction is the inevitable consequence if one takes the derivative nature of the Union seriously, accepting the notion that the Member State constitutions alone serve as sources of non-delegated legal power. It should have become apparent that this construction does not mean that the Member States can derogate from Union law as they wish. This would seriously endanger the project of European integration. The need for mutual respect for the Union in the form that has been agreed upon serves as a very strong unifying force. This explains why Union law as – to use MacCormick's words – a mere "bundle of overlapping laws" remains, as if by magic, nearly perfectly congruent.

10.6 Conclusion

It has been shown that legal pluralism is not convincing, neither as a general theory nor as the basis of the reconstruction of Union law. It fails to reconstruct the derivative nature of Union law and cannot provide an adequate framework for the decision of conflicts between Union law and national constitutional law. However, MacCormick's contribution to tackle the difficult and complex problem of the reconstruction of Union law remains invaluable.

Acknowledgments I wish to thank my colleague Stanley L. Paulson for valuable advice.

[99]MacCormick, *Questioning Sovereignty*, note 15 *supra*, p. 118.

Chapter 11
From Constitutional Pluralism to a Pluralistic Constitution? Constitutional Synthesis as a MacCormickian Constitutional Theory of European Integration

Agustín José Menéndez

11.1 Introduction

This chapter explores in a critical, but sympathetic, fashion Neil MacCormick's writings on European integration. It is structured in four parts and a conclusion. The first section explores the main constitutional implications of MacCormick's institutional theory of law. I consider how the breed of jurisprudence advocated by the Scottish philosopher created the theoretical space within which it is possible to make sense of legal and political phenomena below, above and beyond the nation-state. The second section offers a critical analysis of the standard constitutional theories of Community law. I claim that, because standard theoretical reconstructions of Community law are premised on the close relationship between law and nation-state, they turn out to be incapable of providing a satisfactory and simultaneous answer to three fundamental questions, namely (1) how a European constitutional law came about (the genesis riddle), (2) in what relation European constitutional law should stand *vis-à-vis* national constitutional law (the primacy riddle), and (3) what the sources of the stability of the Community legal order are (the stability riddle). The third section dwells on the many achievements of MacCormick's constitutional theory of European integration, hereafter referred to as European constitutional pluralism. I give an account of what seem to me to be the two main elements of European constitutional pluralism: the thesis that Community law can be approached from at least two differentiated, but equally authoritative, standpoints (the differentiated but equal standpoints thesis) and that the stability of the European legal order is rooted on non-legal bases that reveal the transformation of sovereignty in contemporary Europe (the stability beyond sovereignty thesis). I also consider the turn that the Scottish philosopher made towards a moderate pluralism under international law in the second half of the 1990s, a shift that is, in my view, decisive in order to understand the *problématique* of Community law and

A.J. Menéndez (✉)
Facultad de Derecho, Universidad de León, León, Spain; ARENA, University of Oslo, Oslo, Norway
e-mail: agustin.menendez@unileon.es

A.J. Menéndez, J.E. Fossum (eds.), *Law and Democracy in Neil MacCormick's Legal and Political Theory*, Law and Philosophy Library 93,
DOI 10.1007/978-90-481-8942-7_11,

the questions that MacCormick was struggling to solve. The fourth section contains the main elements of the theory of constitutional synthesis, a constitutional theory of European integration which aims to apply the key insights of MacCormick's European constitutional pluralism to solving the problems which were left open by the theory of the Edinburgh professor. By emphasising the singularity of the European path towards a democratic constitution, the theory of constitutional synthesis combines sensitivity towards the fundamental pluralistic traits of Union law with a commitment towards the idea of constitutional law as a monistic means of social integration. The fourth section contains the conclusion.

11.2 The Constitutional Implications of MacCormick's Institutional Theory of Law

As Massimo La Torre argues at length in his chapter in this volume, MacCormick's institutional theory of law is properly interpreted as the theoretical *deepening* of some of the key insights contained in the "classical" positivism of Hans Kelsen and H.L.A. Hart (and reflecting, I may add, a keen interest in Scandinavian Legal Realism). The key distinctive contribution of Neil MacCormick to jurisprudence is his emphasis on the *institutional* dimension of law as a normative order. As already argued in the Introduction to this volume,[1] MacCormick defended a pluralistic understanding of law, capable of accounting both for its normative underpinnings and its societal roots, and specifically aimed at clarifying the argumentative character of law.

For the purposes of this chapter, it is perhaps proper to consider in greater detail what MacCormick's institutional theory of law has contributed to the answering of three classical jurisprudential questions, namely, (1) the functions of law and the limits of its province; (2) the normative foundations of law; and (3) the pieces that make up law. A sequential and joint consideration of these issues is proper because it reveals the extent to which MacCormick's institutional theory of law has managed to mould legal theory in such a shape as to make it fit much better with the democratic and social state of law, or as Neil himself used to refer, the democratic and social *Rechtsstaat*.

Firstly, MacCormick made a major contribution to a nuanced and multidimensional understanding of the social functions of law which was at the same time conscious of the limits of law as a means of social integration and of its normative roots.

Kelsen made phenomenal contributions to legal theory, including the basic intellectual map with which we still approach positive law: the Kelsenian pyramid, which

[1] Indeed, MacCormick and Ota Weinberger are rightly characterised as the founding fathers of the "new" institutional approach to law. See MacCormick and O. Weinberger, *An Institutional Theory of Law: New Approaches to Legal Positivism*, (Dordrecht: Kluwer, 1996). On the two jurisprudential traditions that these two authors represented, see Massimo La Torre in this volume.

was, after all, perhaps not so much Kelsenian, but Merkelian;[2] Kelsen was also a ground-breaker when he pointed to the systemic character of law as a means of social integration,[3] structurally creating the intellectual space in which the multidimensional character of the societal functions of law could be thought of. However, there was a clear "prescriptivist" bias in Kelsen. Indeed, the insistence of the Austrian legal theorist on the "coercive" character of law was ambivalent at the very least,[4] and seems to have become even more so by the end of his life (especially in the *General Theory of Norms*, written by the so-called "second Kelsen").[5] So, for all the structural contribution, Kelsen still defined law as a coercive social technique. This was, in a way, the point of departure of Hart. When he criticised Hobbesian and Austinian legal positivism for its definition of valid norms as the commands of the sovereign, he was laying down the ground for a criticism of Kelsenian reduction of law to coercion and conflict-solving.[6] Hart found that such a reductionist approach failed to capture not only the fact that power was constituted by law, but also that law was also a key institution in the production of normative knowledge; the latter function being somehow autonomous (even if not independent) from the coercive side of law. As a result, Hart claimed that Hobbesian and Austinian theories of law failed to explain, in a coherent and economic fashion, the dynamicity and reflexivity of the legal order *beyond* the holder of coercive power, beyond the *sovereign*.[7] This prompted Hart to introduce his famous distinction between primary and secondary norms, including, among the latter, the rule of recognition.[8] The shift from norm to system also implied recharacterising the sense in which law was coercive, at the same time that it enlarged the view on the social tasks that law discharged as such a system. Hart could pay heed to the fact that law was expected not only to solve conflicts, but also to be the empowering grammar with the help of which individuals could construct their world of social relations (the typical function, indeed, of contract law and private law in general) and to be the supporter of collective action in the pursuit of collective goals (as, typically, public law is, at least in the *Sozialer*

[2] Ibid., p. 235 *et seq*. See, also, "Foreword to the Second Printing of Main Problems in the Theory of Public Law", in: S. L. Paulson and B. L. Paulson (eds), *Normativity and Norms. Critical Perspectives on Kelsenian Themes*, (Oxford: Oxford University Press, 1998), pp. 3–22, especially p. 11 *et seq*. The very metaphor of the pyramid seems to have been coined by the French translator of the *Pure Theory*. This was, for once, a clear added value resulting from the sensitivity of one national tradition to specific mental and architectural forms.

[3] H. Kelsen, *The Pure Theory of Law*, especially p. 193 and p. 201.

[4] H. Kelsen, "The Law as a Specific Social Technique", (1941) 9 *University of Chicago Law Review*, pp. 75–97.

[5] H. Kelsen, *General Theory of Norms*, (Oxford: Oxford University Press, 1991). See, also, S. L. Paulson, "Kelsen's Theory of Law: The Final Round", (1992) 12 *Oxford Journal of Legal Studies*, pp. 265–274.

[6] H.L.A. Hart, *The Concept of Law*, (Oxford: Oxford University Press, 1961), Chapters III and IV.

[7] Ibid.

[8] Ibid., Chapter V.

Rechtsstaat).[9] However, there was still a remnant of prescriptivism in Hart's theory, which was reflected in his characterisation of law by reference to the law of the nation-state. Not only were constitutional and legal pluralism depicted as the result of political pathologies,[10] but critically Hart (contrary to Kelsen) remained sceptical of the legal character of international law[11] (and a trifle Eurocentric in his consideration of non-Western legal orders).[12] MacCormick pushed the insights of both Kelsen and Hart further forward by clarifying the implications of a systemic approach to law, fully conscious of the social tasks that the legal order, as a whole, is expected to perform. In particular, the three-fold set of social tasks discharged by law as revealed by Hart should not only make us ponder over the extent to which legal systems should be defined by exclusive reference to one of the techniques through which they integrate society (coercion) to the exclusion of others (ensuring certainty of moral knowledge and enabling the decentralised shaping of the social fabric), but also over the degree to which law cannot but be the reflection of the normative and institutional imagination of human beings.[13] This moved MacCormick to re-characterise law as a social means of integration which complements critical morality in the task of integrating society when the complexity of societal relationships, the sheer number of those involved, or the speed at which social or environmental changes take place, make integration through spontaneous order reliant upon the normative and institutional genius of human beings simply insufficient, and incapable of guaranteeing stable social integration.[14] This not only reveals that coercion is only one of the legal techniques of social integration, but it also makes explicit the extent to which coercion cannot, by itself, found a legal system, or ensure the stability of the legal order (a conundrum that plagues the Hobbesian approaches to law, not to be thrown away in haste, as Waldron reminds us in his contribution to this volume). But after this is acknowledged, there is no good reason left to restrict the legal phenomenon to nation-state law.[15] Nation-state law may be the more relevant form of law in modern societies, but that still does not make it the *only* form of law.[16] If law is defined by taking the plurality of tasks that it discharges into account, and of the corresponding social techniques employed

---

[9]On this, see T. Honoré, "The Dependence of Morality on Law", (1992) 13 *Oxford Journal of Legal Studies*, pp. 1–17, and "On the Necessary Connection of Law and Morality", (2002) 23 *Oxford Journal of Legal Studies*, pp. 489–95. This also entailed a renewed understanding of the point of coercion. See Hart, note 6 *supra*, p. 198: "Sanctions are therefore required not as the normal motive for obedience, but as a *guarantee* that those who would voluntarily obey shall not be sacrificed to those who would not."

[10]See Hart, note 6 *supra*, pp. 117–121.

[11]Ibid., Chapter X.

[12]See P. Fitzpatrick, *The Mythology of Modern Law*, (London: Routledge, 1992).

[13]N. MacCormick, *Institutions of Law*, (Oxford: Oxford University Press, 2007), p. 24 *et seq*.

[14]Ibid., p. 21 *et seq*.

[15]N. MacCormick, "Law as Institutional Fact", (1974) 90 *Law Quarterly Review*, pp. 102–129; MacCormick and Weinberger, note 1 *supra*; and MacCormick, *Institutions of Law*, note 13 *supra*.

[16]Ibid., pp. 39–49.

to discharge such tasks, instead of a clear cut and binomic characterisation of institutional systems as legal and non-legal, we should draw the limits of the province of jurisprudence in gradualistic ("range") terms, and be open to the consideration and reconstruction of legal orders *above*, *below* and *beyond* the state.[17] This also resulted in MacCormick stressing the "constructed" character of the legal system, thereby reflecting not only its being posited (thus, our talk of *legal positivism* and *positive law),* but also, and perhaps crucially, the fact that the legal system is not a pre-given reality, but a regulatory ideal (as I will shortly claim a premise with a Kelsenian flavour).[18] Whether, in such a reconstruction, we emphasise or play down the national borders and the (alleged) unbound primacy of the national constitution becomes and open, not a given question. In this regard, MacCormick broke ranks more with Hart than with Kelsen. While the Austrian legal theorist was a child of the Austro-Hungarian Empire, and a committed internationalist,[19] Hart was (as already indicated) somehow defiant of international law,[20] and regarded the manifold constitutional problems resulting from decolonisation as temporal departures from the close and narrow attachment between law and the nation-state.[21] Indeed, the re-reading of Kelsen was rather influential in shaping the mature form of European constitutional pluralism.[22]

---

[17]MacCormick was existentially and politically interested in state forms different from that of the nation-state. The "utilitarian nationalistic" position Neil openly advocated in "Independence and Constitutional Change" was not so much interested in specific constitutional clothes as in the diversification of "real centres" of power. See "Independence and Constitutional Change", in: N. MacCormick (ed), *The Scottish Debate*, (Oxford: Oxford University Press, 1970), pp. 52–64. See, especially, p. 55: "Upon this view of the matter, the real question of principle is not whether Scotland should become wholly independent or not. It is whether or not we shall choose to establish some form of separate political institutions in Scotland, and shall take a pragmatic and utilitarian view in deciding which form would be most beneficial."

[18]J. Bengoetxea, "Legal System as a Regulative Ideal", (1994) 53 *ARSP*, [Supplement] pp. 66–80.

[19]On Kelsen and the underlying normative theory to the pure theory of law, see L. Vinx, *Hans Kelsen's Pure Theory of Law*, (Oxford: Oxford University Press, 2007).

[20]See Hart, note 6 *supra*, Chapter X on international law.

[21]See Hart, note 6 *supra*, pp. 119–23. The fact that the British philosopher labelled such situations as "pathological" may reveal that, while his legal theory was pluralist friendly, his political theory may not have been so. Indeed, Hart seems to have shared with Kelsen the belief that only a monistic legal order could properly ensure social integration trusted to it. This accounts for the implicit "creeping" in Hart's theory of a series of assumptions concerning a common "cultural" code shared by judges, which plays a key role both in ensuring that one and the same rule of recognition underlies the practice of all judges, and in framing their discretion in hard cases. On "cultural" codes and judicial application of law, see K. Tuori, "Fundamental Rights Principles: Disciplining the Instrumentality of Policies", in: A. J. Menéndez and E. O. Eriksen (eds), *Arguing Fundamental Rights*, (Dordrecht: Springer, 2006), pp. 33–52. What is probably lurking there is the "élitist" drive of which not even committed Labourites, such as Hart, were fully conscious at the time. See M. L. Torre, "The Hierarchical Model and H.L.A. Hart's Concept of Law", (2007) 93 *ARSP*, pp. 81–100.

[22]C. Richmond, "Preserving the Identity Crisis: Autonomy, System and Sovereignty in European Law", (1997) 16 *Law and Philosophy*, pp. 377–420, was perhaps the most influential piece on MacCormick's nuancing of his pluralistic position. See *infra*.

Secondly, MacCormick clarified the normative foundations of law and state. As has already been indicated when considering his analysis of the functions of law, MacCormick embraced the systemic and dynamic approach to law and jurisprudence introduced by Kelsen and Hart. But he was willing to explore the very foundations of law, questioning the implicit premise in both Kelsen and Hart, namely, the continued existence of the state. This prompted him to stress, as was already hinted, that law is, indeed, made possible by the normative and institutional imagination of human beings, and to claim "radically" that law must, indeed, be understood and theorised not from the standpoint of institutional actors, but from that of the addressees of the law, *i.e.*, citizens. Both Kelsen and Hart had fought the corner of legal autonomy against sociologists (later joined as advocates of a reductionist view of law by economists and critical legal scholars),[23] and had stressed that law could only be meaningfully understood from a standpoint internal to the law, which, indeed, takes the normative claim (or claims) of law seriously. This was famously phrased by Hart as the distinction between the internal and the external points of view, to which I have already referred.[24] However, both Kelsen and Hart were somewhat victims of the prevalent worldviews (even in their social-democratic political entourages), and tended to take the "state" (indeed, as we saw, the nation-state) as the founding block of law. This allowed them to set aside complex foundational questions, and to take for granted that law, as a means of social integration, was somehow intrinsic to this pre-given entity, the state. This is reflected in the tendency of both scholars to identify the internal point of view of law with that of institutional agents. Legislatures and judges were decisive in the process of defining the Kelsen's *internal point of view*, both in leading the process of the identification of the contents of the *grundnorm* (the historical constitution to which it pointed),[25] and of the Hart's socially-backed rule of recognition (defined by reference to the social practice of judges).[26] On his side, MacCormick problematised the very foundations of law as a means of social integration, and made it unequivocally clear not only that law was possible because of the normative and institutional imagination and proclivities of human beings, but also that the proper justification of law had to do with the potential of constitutional democratic legal orders to realise – to the largest possible extent- the autonomy of individuals.[27] This constitutes the background to MacCormick's breaking ranks with both Kelsen

[23]See Kelsen, "Una fundamentación de la sociología del derecho", (1993) 12 *Doxa*, pp. 213–256; Hart, "Scandinavian Realism", in: *idem*, *Essays in Jurisprudence and Philosophy*, (Oxford: Oxford University Press, 1983), pp. 161–169. See, also, Owen Fiss, "The Death of Law", (1986) 72 *Cornell Law Review*, pp. 1–16.

[24]Hart, *The Concept of Law*, note 6 *supra*, pp. 89–91 on the internal and external points of view on law.

[25]Kelsen, *The Pure Theory of Law*, note 3 *supra*, p. 196: "The dynamic type is characterised by this: the presupposed basic norm contains nothing but the determination of a norm-creating fact, the authorization of a norm-creating authority or (which amounts to the same) a rule that stipulates how the general and individual norms of the order based on the basic norm ought to be created."

[26]Hart, *The Concept of Law*, note 6 *supra*, pp. 100–109 and 116.

[27]See N. M. Cormick, "The Relative Heteronomy of Law", (1995) 3 *European Journal of Philosophy*, pp. 69–85.

and Hart by promoting a "norm-user" approach to legal theory, in which, at the end of the day, the internal point of view hinges on the social practices of *citizens at large*.[28] This is, indeed, why MacCormick came to affirm very clearly, in *Institutions of Law*, that all legal systems are based upon a constitutional convention, underpinned by citizens.[29] This shift has not only legal-dogmatic implications, but also contributes to the reconciliation of legal theory with democratic public philosophy, by democratising the very basis upon which the definition of the province of law rests.

Thirdly, MacCormick has made major contributions to our understanding of the structure of legal orders and legal argumentation. In particular, I would like to stress that his *Institutional Theory of Law* weighs up the role of principles in legal argumentation with the necessary rule-based character of modern systems. It is well-known that Hart shared with classical legal positivism the view that hard cases were not governed by law. The "penumbra" of legal norms required judges to act as legislators in deciding the case at hand, and establishing a precedent which would be part of the applicable law next time[30] (a characterisation very congenial to the *common* sense of *common* lawyers, one must add).[31] Clearly influenced by Scandinavian legal realists,[32] and dialectically motivated by the major implications of Dworkin's criticism to Hart's legal positivism,[33] MacCormick paid great attention to the processes through which norms were applied from his very first writings. *Legal Theory and Legal Reasoning*[34] was one of the handful of decisive books on

---

[28]MacCormick, *Legal Theory and Legal Reasoning*, (Oxford: Oxford University Press), 1978, pp. 275–292; *idem, H.L.A. Hart*, (Princeton NJ: Princeton University Press, 2008) (second edition), pp. 202–6; MacCormick, *Institutions of Law*, note 13 *supra*, p. 57, p. 61 *et seq.*, p. 238 and p. 286 *et seq.* This is closely associated to the central claim made by MacCormick that law is one of the many normative orders of society, and that state law is one of the many institutionalised normative orders in a given society. On the purity of the pure theory of law, MacCormick stated that "Law is not only an object of study for legal science, but it is in some form an element in the lives and actions of citizens and officials", in: Hart, *The Concept of Law*, note 6 *supra*, p. 23.

[29]*Institutions of Law*, note 13 *supra*, p. 287: "Obviously, what makes them [constitutions] work is the will of whichever people conceive the constitution to be their constitution, when there are enough people, sufficiently agreed (though certainly never unanimous) about the ideological underpinnings. What they agree on, however articulately or tacitly, is a common norm that they ought to respect the constitution thus underpinned, and that anyone purporting to exercise public power must do so only in the terms permitted by the constitution."

[30]H.L.A. Hart, "Positivism and the Separation of Law and Morals", (1958) 71 *Harvard Law Review*, pp. 593–629, at 609 and 614, on the discretion of judges in the area of penumbra.

[31]On how the artificial reason of law elucidated by judges was still said to be authored by the people, see A. Cromartie, "The Idea of Common Law as Custom", in: A. P. Saussine and J. B. Murphy (eds), *The Nature of Customary Law*, (Cambridge: Cambridge University Press, 2007), pp. 203–227.

[32]K. Olivecrona, *Law as Fact*, (London: Stevens, 1971) (second edition), Chapters III, IV and V. See, also, S. Castignone, *La macchina del diritto: il realismo giuridico in Svezia*, (Milan: Edizioni di Communità, 1974), and L. L. Hierro, *El Realismo Jurídico Escandinavo*, (Valencia: Fernando Torres, 1981).

[33]R. Dworkin, "The Model of Rules (I)", now in *Taking Rights Seriously*, (London: Duckworth, 1978), pp. 14–45.

[34]N. MacCormick, *Legal Theory and Legal Reasoning*, (Oxford: Oxford University Press, 1978).

legal reasoning coming from the positivistic tradition which highlighted the central role of reconstructive argumentation in the forging of law as a social reality.[35] While, in the first edition of the book, MacCormick was still engaged in figuring out how the central role of principles in legal theory could be accommodated within classical British positivism,[36] he progressively shifted away from Hart on this matter and came closer to what is generally labelled as a post-positivistic position close, but not identical, to Dworkin's.[37] To the claims of Dworkin concerning the texture of legal argumentation, the institutional theory of law added the point that principles make it possible to combine the authoritative collective regulation of social relations with the division of labour between social institutions in order to avoid overtaxing the capacities of any of them. In particular, they render it possible to split the production of collective action-norms between legislative and regulatory decision-making processes. While this entailed recognising that legal principles allowed the prospective regulation of social relations to be combined with the instillation of normative values into the law, MacCormick rightly insisted on the fact that the specific and unconditional character of rules is fundamental to the process of integration through law, as rules provide authoritative, non-contradictory and explicit (ready-made, if you wish) normative guidance, in the vast majority of cases in which this is needed to solve conflicts, to allow citizens to shape their lives in mutual agreement with others, and to pursue collective goals through co-ordinated collective action.[38] This implied the critique of Dworkin's argument characterising law as a matter of principle and the favouring of a depiction of law as a matter of rules and principles.

---

[35] In addition to MacCormick's, see R. Alexy, *The Theory of Legal Argumentation*, (Oxford: Oxford University Press, 1987); A. Peczenik, *On Law and Reason*, (Dordrecht: Kluwer, 1989); A. Aarnio, *The Rational as Reasonable, A Treatise on Legal Justification*, (Dordrecht: Kluwer, 1987).

[36] MacCormick, *Legal Theory and Legal Reasoning*, note 24 *supra*, pp. 152–194.

[37] MacCormick, "*The Concept of Law* and the Concept of Law", (1994) 14 *Oxford Journal of Legal Studies*, pp. 1–23, at 19 *et seq*; *idem*, *Rhetoric and the Rule of Law*, (Oxford: Oxford University Press, 2005), p. 189 *et seq*; See, also, MacCormick in this volume.

[38] MacCormick, *Rhetoric and the Rule of Law*, note 37 *supra*, p. 6. "Whether we hold a non-cognitivist or a cognitivist approach to morality, we will regard law as a necessary complement of moral reasoning in the integration of modern societies. The cognitivist will consider law necessary because even if there are objectively, or at the very least inter-subjectively valid moral principles, they are unfit to serve as common action norms in modern societies. As already observed, there may be a correct moral answer to each moral problem, but the limited moral faculties of human beings leave us uncertain concerning their actual content. Morality tends to be expressed in the language of principles (first and foremost, the principle of universalisability), while modern conditions call for integration through concrete rules attuned to concrete ethical and prudential questions. Furthermore, moral norms are fragile tools of social integration, given the fact that the inclination to comply with moral requirements may be undermined in absence of the insurance provided by institutions ready to coercively enforce common action norms, or, whether due to disagreement, weakness of will, or simply ignorance, substituted or replaced as a spring of action by the fear of being at the receiving end of the sanctioning power. The role of law as a means of social integration is even further stressed from a non-cognitivist standpoint, given the inexistence of objectively or even inter-subjectively valid moral principles. Under such a perspective, law is not so much a complement of morality, but the key medium which holds together a society."

MacCormick was led to this insight by his bottom-up reconstruction of law as a reflection of the normative and institutional imagination of human beings. Indeed, democratic law needs to be quantitatively an order of rules in order to ensure that law is applied in a decentralised manner by citizens; only then would it be able to discharge its task of complementing critical morality in the integration of society (just consider how the self-assessment of the income tax, characteristic of democracies, is dependent on the tax being defined by very precise and detailed rules, not principles). Moreover, if law is functionally a matter of rules, but argumentatively a matter of principles, there is less of an obstacle to come to terms with nascent legal orders beyond the state, based upon principles which are open to be progressively "thickened" by the production and derivation of rules (as, indeed, Community law can be fairly described to have been and, to a large extent, continues to be).

These three key contributions can be seen as a major step towards the exploration of the constitutional implications of positivism as a legal theory. MacCormick broke the allegedly necessary link between law and the nation-state, and suggested a less drastic contrast between law and other institutional orders, pushing the classical tradition of the general theory of law and the state *below*, *above* and *beyond the nation-state*. The Scottish philosopher *democratised* the underlying approach of positivism by placing the citizen, not institutional agents, at the core of legal theorising. Finally, the Edinburgh professor calibrated the relationship between the components of the legal order, rules and principles, by showing the close relation between a bottom-up legal order and rules, and also by rendering visible the critical mutual dependence of rules and principles. These constitutional explorations made positivism more self-conscious of its normative baggage, and helped the liberal and democratic public philosophy that propelled both Kelsen and Hart to become fully-reflected in positivistic legal theory. The hidden legacies of Hobbes (or, as some authors would have it, of natural law) were detected and abandoned in MacCormick's institutional theory of law.

11.3 The Intriguing (Legal and Political) Nature of the European Union and of Its Constitution

The process of political, economic and legal integration unleashed by the Treaty establishing the European Coal and Steel Community (and further refined and completed by a succession of additional Treaties, up to the Treaty of Lisbon of 2007) has resulted in the creation of a supranational level of government, framed by a constitutional legal order and equipped with an autonomous institutional structure. This is what is generally referred to as the European Union, as Union law (or still very frequently, Community law, as I will do in this chapter prey to nostalgia), and as "Brussels" (meaning the supranational institutional structure).[39]

[39]See, in general, J. E. Fossum and A. J. Menéndez, *The Constitution's Gift. A Constitutional Theory for a Democratic European Union*, (Lanham MD: Rowman & Littlefield, 2011).

In addition, Community law and European institutions play a key and, indeed, growing, role in shaping the legal and political orders of Member States of the European Union (and even of states which are not full members of the Union).[40] Whatever the concrete quantitative figures, it is a fact that the key constitutional principles and fundamental policies legally articulated at the supranational level (Community laws made in Brussels, if you wish) play a a decisive role in framing national politics.[41] Similarly, European integration has come hand in hand with the Europeanisation of national legal and political orders.[42] Furthermore, it has become almost self-evident that Community laws would prevail over clashing national legal provisions, with the sole, and rather theoretical, exception of the "core" principles of national constitutional law.[43] This is the basic content of the European constitutional practice, which acknowledges the primacy of Community law over conflicting national norms.

Having said that, all these developments have taken place within a constitutional structure which is *formally* characteristic of public international law. It is still the case that the European Union is, strictly speaking, an international organisation, Community law an international legal order, and the institutions of the Union tend to be reconstructed as purely intergovernmental, or, at most, supranational, agencies under the, more or less, direct control of their principals, the Member States. This is why national political actors and national constitutional judges claim that the European Union is an international organisation *sui generis*, and thus, that Community law should be constructed as an international legal order (at most, of a special and peculiar breed).[44] However, the characterisation of the European Union, its law and its institutional structure as "international" is overly conservative and flies in the face of the constitutional developments and practices that have just been referred to. This is why "supranational" political actors and supranational judges

---

[40] Including not only the EEA Member States (Norway, Iceland, Liechtenstein), but also Switzerland and the non-Member States which have adopted the euro as their unofficial (or even official) currency.

[41] There has been a "conflict of the statistics" concerning the percentage of the total number of new laws which are approved in Brussels and in national capitals. But the real issue is the substantive weight of Community law, its framing power of national political wills. On the socio-economic dimension, see R. Letelier and Agustín J. Menéndez (eds), *The Sinews of Peace*, (Oslo: ARENA, RECON Report 8/2009).

[42] Indeed, one of the leading research centres on European studies is called ARENA (Advanced Research on the Europeanisation of the Nation State). See, for example, Johan P. Olsen, "The Many Faces of Europeanization", (2002) 40 *Journal of Common Market Studies*, pp. 921–952 and *Europe in Search of a Political Order*, (Oxford: Oxford University Press, 2006). The reader should be informed that my judgment about the importance of the centre may be clouded by the fact of having been closely attached to it for a number of years.

[43] M. Kumm, "Who is the final arbiter of constitutionality", (1999) 36 *Common Market Law Review*, pp. 351–386, and "The Jurisprudence of Constitutional Conflict: Constitutional Supremacy in Europe Before and After the Constitutional Treaty", (2005) 11 *European Law Journal*, pp. 262–307.

[44] See, for example, D. Wyatt: "New legal order or old?", (1982) 7 *European Law Review*, pp. 147–166.

seem to have come to endorse the view that Community law is the constitutional law of a state (if not an actual nation-state) in the making, to wit, the European Union.[45] This would, to a large extent, explain the present constitutional practice, but it would also leave many questions unanswered concerning how it came about (who authorised this constitutional transformation and when?) and how it can be rendered compatible with the (decisive) primacy of the national constitutions and the persistence of the autonomous constitutional identity of each Member State and its respective national legal order. Such principles are part and parcel not only of national constitutional law, but also of Community law and of the Treaties of the European Union in particular.

In particular, the two standard approaches to the constitutional theory of European integration fail to provide a satisfactory and simultaneous answer to three basic problems or riddles: How did Community law come about? (the genesis riddle); How do supranational and national constitutional law relate? (as conflicts between norms require us to consider the position in which they stand to one another); and How can it be possible that such a fragile creature as Community law has not only been proved to be remarkably stable, but has also grown so exponentially (as stability is supposed to require a matching of the validity and legitimacy of legal norms, which is to be doubted in the case of Community law)?

How did the present supranational institutional set up and decision-making procedures come about? ("the genesis riddle"). The three original Communities constituted in 1951 and 1957 were established by means of three international treaties, and thus came into existence as a trio of classical international organisations.[46] This could be expected to have resulted in the creation of a new legal order of public international law. From the perspective of national legal orders, the Treaties would probably be granted the rank and status of statutes (albeit with a higher passive force within their scope), and the eventual secondary norms produced by Community institutions would be regarded as statutory instruments or administrative acts. But, in the present constitutional practice (even national constitutional practice), the Treaties are constructed as though they were the constitution of the European Union, while regulations and directives are constructed as though they were statutes. But how could such a transformation have taken place if the only "constituting" act of the European Union has been the ratification of the founding Treaties and the subsequent amendments to them? How could such a major constitutional change (the "constitutionalisation" of the Treaties and the "legalisation" of regulations and directives) have taken place without an explicit constitutional reform?

What is the relationship of Community legal norms vis-à-vis *national norms?* ("the primacy riddle"). European integration has resulted in the establishment of a

[45] The "constitutional" approach underpins the case law of the ECJ since the 1960s.

[46] They were partially consolidated into a single institutional structure through the 1965 Merger Treaty; structure which was re-configured in the 1992 Treaty of Maastricht and in successive amending treaties.

set of institutional structures and law-making processes, which seem, *prima facie*, to be autonomous from national ones, but whose breadth and scope of application essentially overlap with national ones. But, if this is so, what is the relationship between the normative outcome of national and supra-national law-making processes, or, in short, between national and Community laws? What should we do if the said norms seem to prescribe different normative solutions in concrete cases? Which norm should prevail? In order to answer this question, we need to clarify the criteria upon which we should decide the issue. Are the relevant conflict rules part and parcel of the national order? Or are they to be found in the Community order? Or should we invoke some kind of meta-norm external to both the national and the Community legal systems? Social legal practices clash in this regard. But it is far from clear which one should be regarded as the more promising. If we grant primacy to national norms, we run the risk of undermining the effectiveness of Community law, and thus, not only legal integration as such, but also the equality of all Europeans before their common law. But if we give primacy to supranational norms (which seems to be frequently done), are we setting aside what seem, *prima facie*, to be the norms invested with a higher democratic legitimacy in favour of those with less legitimacy. Should we re-think the democratic rationale upon the basis of which national constitutional norms are supposed to prevail over Community ones? Or should we draw a solution from the very fact that social practices are plural and come into conflict?

How can it be that European integration and the resulting supranational institutional set-up and decision-making procedures have proved remarkably stable even though the institutional structure of the Union is somewhat incomplete or even defective when compared to national and federal structures? ("the stability riddle"). Leaving aside the question of what type of polity the European Union is, it seems beyond doubt that the institutions of the European Union do not have, at their direct disposal, any means of direct enforcement or coercion by which they could supplement the motivation of European citizens and national legal actors to comply with the obligations imposed by Community law. Similarly, the institutions of the Union have very limited material resources at their disposal. Not only is the budget of the Union miniscule in comparison to that of the Member States, but the Member States retain control of the flow of the resources that accrue to the Union.[47] This leaves the existence and effectiveness of the Union literally at the mercy of national institutions, the selfsame institutions which have seen their powers either transferred to, or framed by, the European Union. And, notwithstanding this, the Union has not only proven to be a stable institutional creation, but has also acquired new competences and resources over time. How could this be? How could the Union not only be remarkably effective in the use of its powers, but also increase them when the (national) institutional actors losing their powers had the power to block this very process (as they are after all, supposed to be the "Masters of the Treaties")?

---

[47] A. J. Menéndez, "Taxing Europe", (2004) 10 *Columbia Journal of European Law*, pp. 297–338.

These three riddles reveal that we have a well-established constitutional practice which has (still) not been properly captured, explained, or justified by a coherent constitutional theory of European integration, by a public philosophy of European integration and Union law capable of accounting both for the democratic legitimacy of the Union, and of serving as the basic normative framework within which to solve basic questions of constitutional interpretation. The mechanical affirmation of the primacy of either national or Community norms, which derives from the "classical" theories, either fails to account for actual practice (in which Community norms always prevail, at least for the time being), or fails to go hand in hand with a solvent normative explanation of the actual primacy of Community norms (democratic legitimacy which seems to be poorer than that of national norms, and, as such, points to the opposite solution).

When law transcends national borders, as is clearly the case with Community law, our understandings of law, the constitution and politics reveal themselves to be inadequate. This is, indeed, one basic insight to which MacCormick returned to again and again. Indeed, he rightly claimed that:

> It is not only our theories of law, but also our theories of democracy, that are challenged by the new forms that are evolving among us in Europe.[48]

He was not only stating that our theories of law and constitutional theories could not come to terms with Community law as a law *above* and *beyond* national borders, but also (and critically) that any alternative constitutional theory of Community law should be grounded on a democratic public philosophy of European integration. And this is the challenge which the Scottish philosopher tried to meet with his European Constitutional Pluralism.

11.4 European Constitutional Pluralism

Both his legal theory (in the terms considered in Section 11.2) and his existential commitment to Scottish nationalism made Neil MacCormick's legal and political theory structurally interested in legal phenomena *below*, *above* and *beyond* the nation-state. These were the two *fait différentielles*, which worked their way into MacCormick's theory and made his approach a distinct one in the 1970s and 1980s. Indeed, MacCormick's rejection of the necessary connection between law and the nation-state (or more precisely, between the legal system and the nation-state) goes a long way to explain why he was naturally curious about the European Union and its emergent legal system.

This is, indeed, the existential and theoretical background of his path-breaking work entitled *Beyond the Sovereign State*, which appeared in the *Modern Law Review* in 1993. The text established itself rather rapidly as a *must read*, part and

[48] N. MacCormick, *Questioning Sovereignty*, (Oxford: Oxford University Press, 1999), p. 135.

parcel to this day of the compulsory readings of graduate and undergraduate courses on European Studies.[49]

In *Beyond the Sovereign State* and in the successive essays later gathered in the volume entitled *Questioning Sovereignty*, MacCormick claimed that the theoretical and practical flaws of standard constitutional theories of European integration could be traced back to the (wrong) assumption that the whole set of European norms could, and, indeed, should, be reconstructed from a single and final standpoint (that of the *master rule* of the legal order, be it located at national or supranational level).[50] This assumption reflected the hidden Hobbesian (if not natural law) inheritance in modern positivism, and significantly found resonance in the obsession with *the* sovereign.[51] MacCormick invited legal and political actors to recognise that European constitutional practice proves the possibility of the peaceful and fruitful co-existence of at least two of such *master rules (*the European and the national ones; in technical terms, of at least twenty-eight such norms at the time of writing).[52]

---

[49]MacCormick's theory may be said to have imposed itself as the standard theory of Community law among *European* scholars (although, as might be expected, not among *national* scholars studying European law). And even if it is improbable that the Court of Justice and the national constitutional courts will endorse it, given that their authority is closely dependent on affirming a monistic understanding of law, individual justices seem to have come to endorse pluralism in their academic writings, at the same time that pluralist scholars have become judges. Moreover, the implicit understanding of the relationships between courts seems to have come to be inspired by some form of pluralism; this is clearly reflected in the constantly repeated claim that European courts do not stand in a hierarchical relationship, but do, indeed, dialogue (or bargain) with each other.

[50]MacCormick, "Beyond the Sovereign State", (1993) 52 *Modern Law Review*, pp. 1–18, at 5: "One thing which is necessary for jurisprudence of the philosophy of law to do in the present state of affairs is to guard against taking a narrow one-state or Community-only perspective, a monocular view of these things"; p. 6: "Instead of committing oneself to a monocular vision dictated by sovereignty theory, one can embrace the possibility of acknowledging differences of perspective, differences of point of view"; and p. 17: "Can we think of a world in which our normative existence and our practical life are anchored in, or related to, a variety of institutional systems, each of which has validity or operation in relation to some range of concerns, none of which is absolute over all the others, and all of which, for must purposes, can operate without serious mutual conflict in areas of overlap?".

[51]In "The Benthamite Constitution", now in: *Questioning Sovereignty*, note 48 *supra*, MacCormick undertakes a very revealing historical research to show that the upholding of "monism" and the rejection of "pluralism" are but the hidden inheritance of "old" natural law theories to "modern" positivism. "Old" natural law theories affirmed that natural law was, indeed, authored by God. "Modern" positivist theories continue to hold the same, only they have "secularised" god by means of replacing it by a "secular" character, *i.e.*, the sovereign, the holder of raw power. This implies a full continuity in the assumption that a key feature of law is authorship by a concrete individual will (thus, the central role played by God, and now played by the sovereign), reflected in the tendency to reduce laws to "commands", and consequently, to characterise law as a tool to constrain and limit action, neglects the "constitutive" aspects of law. Similarly, this hidden heritage renders us blind to the close connection between law and practical reason, and consequently, to the necessarily collective authorship of any modern law.

[52]Of perhaps three, if it is claimed (as perhaps MacCormick, himself, would be inclined to do) that the regional legal order also has a relevant *grundnorm*.

Consequently, the reconstruction and the interpretation of Community law should be undertaken from the assumption that there are (at least) two equally-valid standpoints from which Community law can be, and actually is, reconstructed and interpreted in Europe.[53] Let us call it *the plural but equal standpoints thesis*. Legal pluralism was *thinkable* because the very idea of what the system of law is is the result of a process of reconstruction as the argumentative character of law made evident (if, as we saw, the legal system is a regulatory ideal, there is nothing *necessary* about the identification of the legal system and the legal order of the nation-state). And European constitutional pluralism was *possible* because the stability of a legal order is not dependent on the will of one single and omnipotent sovereign, but on the social practice, on the part of the citizens at large, of following the legal norms.[54] Let us call it the *legal stability beyond sovereignty thesis*.

The *plural but equal standpoints thesis* is coherent with the emphasis in MacCormick's institutional theory of law upon the social basis of law and its thorough cleansing of prescriptivism from legal theory. As considered in Section 11.2, while prescriptivist legal theories move from the assumption that law is constituted by the will of a sovereign to the conclusion that there must be one single viewpoint from which to reconstruct and interpret the legal system correctly, institutional theory is interested in gaining a proper understanding of how the human normative imagination leads to spontaneous order, and how the human institutional imagination results in the institutionalisation of normative practices. From the latter perspective, the obvious "pluralistic" traits of European constitutional practice are not aberrations to be left aside in any proper theoretical explanation of Community law; on the contrary, the mark of the plausibility of any European constitutional theory lies in its making sense of such pluralistic constitutional practice. It seems well-established that the understanding of European law of national constitutional courts, on the one hand, and the European Court of Justice, on the other, is far from being the same. How legal arguments about normative conflicts should be formed is not answered in the same way in Karlsruhe or Rome as it is in Luxembourg. To this, it must be added that these differentiated institutional practices reflect wider social practices. While most citizens may tend to share the practice of their national constitutional court, having been educated and socialised in a political system which accepted (and, in many cases, promoted) national constitutions as the supreme law of the land, some of them may share and even act upon the basis of the practice followed by the European Court of Justice, either due to the acceptance of an "existential" European political identity (a phenomenon related to the increasing numbers of citizens who spend a part of their lives in another Member State, or who acquire

[53]MacCormick, "Juridical Pluralism and the Risk of Constitutional Conflict", now in: *Questioning Sovereignty*, note 48 *supra*, p. 119: "A pluralistic analysis in either of these senses shows the systems of law operative on the European level to be distinct and partially independent of each other, though also partially overlapping and interacting."

[54]Ibid., pp. 119–121, especially at 119: "Resolving those problems, or, more wisely still, avoiding their occurrence in the first place, is a matter for circumspection and for political as much as legal judgment."

strong personal links with other Member States) or, perhaps more frequently, to the fact that European law promotes, to a large extent, the material interests of (some of) the citizens involved. Finally, the co-existence of overlapping social-legal practices both across and within the borders of a Member State does not undermine the capacity of law to solve conflicts and co-ordinate actions. This clearly indicates that the preconditions for reconciling legal pluralism with the effectiveness of law are, at the very least, for the time being, being met in Europe.

The equal, but differentiated, viewpoints thesis thus seem capable of dissolving both the genesis and the primacy riddles. Firstly, the genesis riddle becomes a non-problem. From the national constitutional standpoint, there is no riddle at all, because the validity of Community law continues to be dependent on the national constitution (to be more precise, on the national constitutional provisions upon the basis of which the foundational treaties of the Union and its successive amendments were ratified, the constitutionality of which has been aptly policed by national constitutional courts). From the European constitutional standpoint, the autonomy, if not the independence, of Community law can be presented as a necessary development in order to realise the very constitutional programme enshrined in European postwar constitutions. The *effective* integrative capacity of law in Europe was, and indeed remains, dependent on integration through supranational law (something which, one could argue, is the real moral lesson of the two World Wars). Secondly, European constitutional pluralism solves the primacy riddle by splitting it. Once there is no privileged standpoint to reconstruct Community law, it follows that constitutional conflicts can be solved in different ways from different standpoints. This is a far from surprising conclusion for the institutional theory of law, given that, if the idea of the legal system as a complete and coherent order is a *regulatory* ideal, it is bound to be realised *only to a certain extent* in real legal systems. As long as constitutional practice manages to preserve the integrative capacity of law, such divergences are only part and parcel of what a legal order is, and how it functions.

The stability beyond sovereignty thesis highlights the limits of supranational and national legal norms as a means of social integration, and reveals the necessary foundation of legal stability on something other than positive law or the naked power of one single, ultimate sovereign. By highlighting the connection between the normative and the institutional imagination of human beings and law, the institutional theory of law not only makes us see European constitutional conflicts as *normal,* but also stresses that integration cannot rest on law *de facto* providing one single authoritative answer to all legal problems. The stability of Community law does not depend so much on the provision of one right answer through one single *master rule*, as on the affinity of the legal systems and on political deliberation and bargaining, reasoning and decision-making.[55] This goes a long way to dissolving the stability riddle, as it reveals that the assumption that stability depends on the very

[55]The proposals to create specific, *ad hoc* bodies in charge of arbitrating European constitutional conflicts present clear pluralistic undertones. See, for example, Christoph Schmid, "From Pont

structure and character of law is an illusion. Law is only one of the means of social integration. Nation-state law and community law are not the only institutional normative orders available, and their integrative capacity is neither a reflection of their mere existence, nor of their having been established by a sovereign. If the ultimate foundation of Community law is the social practice of citizens (and not merely that of institutional actors), who solve conflicts and co-ordinate action by reference to Community law, then the stability of Community law *must* appeal to the normative and institutional proclivities of citizens. It is a *normative problem*, mediated not only by law, but also, and critically, by politics (and indeed by a concrete political tradition and setting, as Neil Walker reminds us when referring to the "comfort zone" of European integration in chapter 1.

While *Beyond Sovereignty* contains the core of European constitutional pluralism (and, as such, remains the centre of gravity of the theory, in the expanded version which one finds in several chapters of *Questioning Sovereignty*), MacCormick nuanced the theory in the second half of the 1990s and in the early years of the present century, heavily influenced by his re-reading of Kelsen.[56] In particular, he moved from a commitment to a "radical" form of European constitutional pluralism, to a "moderate" European constitutional pluralism, or pluralism "under international law". It seems to me that this is a change of critical importance, which increases, not diminishes, the coherence between MacCormick's overall legal-theoretical project and his European constitutional theory; while drastically reformulating the first premise of European constitutional pluralism.

The original "radical" constitutional pluralism of MacCormick was right to point out that legal monism, the claim that there is a need to reduce law to a system observed from one, and only one, legal viewpoint, is a rather flawed theory, if it stems from a prescriptivist conception of law, because the insistence on a mythical single sovereign is no solution to the key problems in legal theory, or, for that matter, in European constitutional law. However, this does not do away with the normative force of the regulatory ideal of the legal system. Indeed, there are very good *normative* reasons to hold fast to the Kelsenian attachment to the regulatory ideal of law as a monistic legal order, "imperially" prone to translate all social conflicts and co-ordination problems into one single language and find one single answer to such problems.[57] And such reasons include the close connection between law and the normative and institutional imagination of human beings. Indeed, it is only if we subscribe to the regulatory ideal of the single legal order that law can serve as an institutionalised alternative to spontaneous order in the very terms that MacCormick

d'Avignon to Ponte Vecchio. The Resolution of Constitutional Conflicts between the European Union and the Member States through Principles of Public International Law", (1998) 18 *Yearbook of European Law*, pp. 415–476 and "The neglected conciliation approach to the 'final arbiter' conflict", (1999) 36 *Common Market Law Review*, pp. 509–514.

[56] See note 41 *supra*, and "Questioning Post-Sovereignty", (2004) 29 *European Law Review*, pp. 852–863.

[57] See A. Somek, "Kelsen lives", (2007) 18 *European Journal of International Law*, pp. 409–451. See, also T. Hitzel-Cassagnes in this volume.

argued with gusto and brilliancy in all his writings. This, in my view, explains why he moved from radical pluralism to moderate pluralism. Both the insistence on the term "pluralism" and the choice of a "third" legal order, "international law", are clear indicators that MacCormick continued to think that there was something irrepressibly pluralistic about the European constitution. Unrestrained pluralism was no way out because it imperilled the integrative capacities of law, but a return to monism *simpliciter* would betray the basic intuition behind the institutional theory of law, and the imperative to make the theory capable of accounting for a social practice which had normative merit. In Section 11.5, I will argue that "moderate" constitutional pluralism is to be taken as both a perceptive diagnosis of a problem, and a provisional solution to it. This is why I will try to consider in more detail what is genuinely pluralistic about Community law (and claim that the European constitution combines a single law with a pluralistic institutional structure).

But, before doing so, it should also be stressed that the shift from radical to moderate constitutional pluralism is also indicative of the fact that European constitutional pluralism remains under-defined (as, it seems to me, Neil Walker claims in his contribution to this volume). The reference to "international law" as the "monistic" framework of a dual legal system renders it clear that the *stability beyond sovereignty thesis* remains too general and abstract, as it does not consider the *concrete* sources of stability of Community law. Would one conclude that international politics, international negotiation and deliberation are plausible sources of stability? How come they play such a function with regard to Community law, but fail rather patently to play a similar role at the world or global level?[58] Is this completely unrelated to the role played by law in European integration? The move from radical to moderate pluralism only highlights that, while *the stability beyond sovereignty thesis* points in the right direction, it is unsatisfactory because it fails to consider the sources of stability of Community law *in detail*. As I claim in Section 11.5, this can be done in pure MacCormickian spirit, by considering that not only is European politics highly mediated by national and supranational law in its contents, but it is also structurally framed by European constitutional law. Indeed, MacCormick hinted on several occasions at the close relationship between national and supranational constitutional law. However, he did not explore the issue in depth, but this *can* be done, and I will start to do so in the next section.

11.5 Constitutional Synthesis

MacCormick's European constitutional pluralism combines a brilliant and perceptive *critique* of "standard" constitutional theories of Community law (on

---

[58] As, indeed, the so-called "war on terror" has made abundantly clear, and as Neil with great civic courage reminded us from the European Parliament during the "dark years" in which the gloves came off and only a handful of just men in our institutions kept their pledge to liberty and democracy. See his Tercentenary Lecture, "On Public Law and The Nature of the Law of Nations", available at: http://www.law.ed.ac.uk/file_download/series/14_tercentenarylecturepubliclawandthelawofnatureandnations.pdf.

account of their being premised on the close relation between law and nation-state) and a perceptive reconstruction of the law of the European Union, which has come a long way to equip us with a theory capable both of guiding the solution of constitutional conflicts and controversies, and of being proposed as a public philosophy of European integration. In short, of being a democratic constitutional theory of Community law. However, in the previous section, I found that European constitutional pluralism was still a partially unfinished constitutional theory. The shift from radical to moderate pluralism revealed a major tension lurking behind the very term "pluralism". The characterisation of law as being necessarily "one", sometimes reflects a "prescriptivistic" bias, resulting from the close (and unjustified) association of law, the sovereign, and the nation-state. But the endorsement of legal system as a regulatory ideal is nonetheless required in order to carry out the integrative tasks assigned to law in modern societies. At the same time, constitutional pluralism insisted that the stability of Union law depended on sources other than the existence of a mythic and monolithic sovereign will to underpin it. But it failed to spell out the role played in this regard by the foundational relationship between national and Community law, and by the overall institutional design of the Union.

The theory of constitutional synthesis[59] builds on European constitutional pluralism, both on its major achievements and on its unfinished parts. In particular, the theory of constitutional thesis is premised on the assumption that the key insights of European constitutional pluralism (the differentiated but equal viewpoints and stability beyond sovereignty) are sound and correct. However, and, for the reasons already considered in Section 11.4 and briefly repeated now, constitutional synthesis draws (four) different implications from these two premises. Firstly, the "equal, but differentiated", standpoints thesis implies that any sound European constitutional theory must account *simultaneously* for the relevance of supranational and national constitutional law in the forging of European constitutional law. In other words, it must reduce law to a system in such a way that the relationship between the twenty-seven legal orders of the Member States and Community law is properly clarified. Secondly, the "equal, but differentiated" viewpoints implies that any sound European constitutional theory must take the fact that there is no institution, be it in European or in national law, which has been authoritatively granted the monopoly on the final word of the interpretation of Community law, seriously. The institutional pluralism of the Union is, in this regard, a fact which has to be reconciled with the claim to authority of both Community law and national constitutional laws. Thirdly, the differentiated approach to primacy must be constructed as requiring any European constitutional theory to account for the European constitutional practice which grants an almost complete primacy to Community law while explaining the continued adherence to the primacy of national constitutions (as the supreme law of the land), and, consequently, explaining the central role of national European constitutional clauses in the process of European integration. Fourthly,

[59] A first attempt at fleshing the theory of constitutional synthesis is to be found in my "Sobre los conflictos constitucionales europeos. Validez del derecho comunitario y legitimidad democrática de la Unión Europea", (2007) 24 *Anuario de Filosofía del Derecho*, pp. 139–196. This made its way, although in a much edited version, into Fossum and Menéndez, note 39, supra.

the plurality of stability sources alerts us to the fact that European constitutional theory must pay special attention to the principles of European constitutional law that have a structural effect and reduce the likelihood of a conflict, while providing a transfer of democratic legitimacy from national to European constitutional law, seriously.

11.5.1 The Core of Constitutional Synthesis in Three Theses

The basic idea behind synthesis is that the European Union and its legal order are the result of a process of constitutional synthesis, of an "ever closer" putting in common of national constitutional norms (normative synthesis) and of the "development" of a supranational institutional structure (institutional development).

This intuition can be specified by reference to three theses.

11.5.1.1 The Peculiarity of the Synthetic Path Towards the Establishment of a Democratic Constitution

The *first thesis* is that the constitutional law which frames and contributes to steer the process of European integration is neither revolutionarily established in a "Philadelphean" constitutional moment, nor the outgrowth or accumulation of "Burkean" constitutional conventions and partial constitutional decisions *à la anglaise*. On the contrary, constitutional synthesis is characterised by the central structuring and legitimising role played by the constitutions of the participating states (*seconded* to a new role as part of the collective constitutional law of the new polity),[60] or by the regulatory ideal of a common constitutional law, which is progressively recognised as the constitution of the new polity, and whose normative consequences are fleshed out and specified as the process develops further. To put it differently, instead of a revolutionary act of constitution-making, or the slow growth of constitutional conventions, constitutional synthesis is launched by an act

[60]The idea of a supranational constitutional law which is the result of seconding national constitutions was hinted at by the European Court of Justice in Case 11/70 *Internationale*, par 4 when claiming that the lack of a written bill of rights in the primary law of the Union came hand in hand with an unwritten principle of protection of fundamental rights, which was filled in by reference to the "constitutional traditions common to the Member States" properly spelled out in the context of European integration ("the protection of such rights, whilst inspired by the constitutional traditions common to the Member States, must be ensured within the framework of the structure and objectives of the Community"). In doing this, the Court was following a line of reasoning pioneered by P. Pescatore: see "Fundamental Rights and Freedoms in the System of the European Communities", (1970) 18 *American Journal of Comparative Law*, pp. 343–351. On the technical aspects of legal synthesis, it must be stressed that a critical comparative approach has underpinned the case law of the ECJ since its very inception. See K. Lenaerts, "Interlocking legal orders in the European Union and Comparative Law", (2003) 52 *International and Comparative Law Quarterly*, pp. 873–906. On the constitutional aspects of the idea of constitutional synthesis, see A. J. Menéndez, "The European Democratic Challenge", (2009) 15 *European Law Journal*, pp. 277–308.

which implies the secondment of national constitutions to the role of common constitutional law. This makes synthetic founding much more economical in political resources than revolutionary founding, and, at the same time, it is much quicker than evolutionary founding. The price to be paid is that, instead of an explicit set of constitutional norms, the founding Treaties reflect a scattered set of norms, while the bulk of the common constitutional law remains implicit, *a mere ideal* to be fleshed out as integration progresses.

European constitutional law was composed of, and, to a large extent, keeps on being composed of, the *common constitutional law* of the Member States. The establishment of the European Communities was thus akin to a foundational moment; but, contrary to what is the case in a revolutionary constitutional tradition (such as the French or the Italian one), the constitution of the Union was not written by *We the European People*, but was defined by implicit reference to the six national constitutions of the founding Member States. In this way, the French, German, Italian, Dutch, Belgian and Luxembourgeois constitutions were *seconded* to the role of being part of the constitutional collective of Europe. National constitutions started living a "double constitutional life". They combined their old role as national constitutions and the new role as part of the *collective* supranational constitution.[61]

Constitutional synthesis is grounded on the national constitutional provisions which not only authorise, but also mandate, the active participation of national institutions in the creation of a supranational legal order as the only way of fully realising the principles which underlie the national constitution (s). Thus, the "opening" clauses of post-war constitutions, and the explicitly European clauses of the more recent ones are constructed as reflecting the self-awareness of the national constitution(s) about the limits of realising constitutional values in one single nation-state.

Constitutional synthesis claims that there is a substantive identity between national constitutional norms and Community constitutional norms. In other words, European integration presupposes the creation of a new legal order, but not the creation of a new set of constitutional norms; a key source of the legitimacy of the new legal order is, indeed, the transfer of national constitutional norms to the new legal order. However, the process, by necessity, has major constitutional implications for each Member State. Firstly, the accession of a state to the European Union marks a new constitutional beginning for that state. Contrary to what is the case in most constitutional transformations, constitutional change is not mainly about the substantive content of the fundamental law, but concerns the *scope* of the polity (there is an implicit re-definition of who we acknowledge as the co-citizens of our political community) and the very *nature* of the new polity (as it actually aims at re-founding both the national and the international legal orders by means of transforming sovereign nation-states into parts of a cosmopolitan federal order). Secondly, the very essence

---

[61] The founding of the Communities implied that national constitutions abandoned their constitutional solitude as constitutions of the self-sufficient nation-state and placed themselves in the common European constitutional field. Constitutional autarchy was thus replaced by constitutional openness, co-operation and reflexivity.

of the process of constitutional synthesis is that of the progressive ascertainment of common constitutional standards which may eventually result in marginal changes in national constitutional norms *to align them* with the contents of Community constitutional law, which, in turn, is reflective of what is actually *common* to the Member States. In this regard, it should be noted that Community constitutional law is not defined by reference to individual sets of constitutional norms, but to what is common to *all* national constitutional norms. In those cases in which national constitutional norms point to different normative solutions, synthesis is not achieved by finding a common minimum denominator, but by means of considering which of the national constitutional norms is more congenial to Community law. This is to be decided by considering the underlying arguments for or against the competing national constitutional solutions, and, in particular, by considering the extent to which the national norm can be "Europeanised", both in the sense of fitting with European constitutional law as it stands (as already synthesised in the Treaties, the amendments to the Treaties or the legislation and case law of the Union), and with its consequences being acceptable in the Union as a whole.[62]

11.5.1.2 Synthetic Supranational Institutional Development

The *second thesis* is that the supranational legal order comes hand in hand with a supranational institutional structure. But the latter is only partially established at the founding, takes time to be rendered functional in a process in which different national institutional cultures and structures try to leave their mark at the supranational level, and its structure is necessarily rendered more complicated as new institutions and decision-making processes are added in order to handle new policies. This entails that constitutional synthesis can be described as the combination of normative synthesis and institutional development and consolidation, two processes that have very different inner logics. While normative synthesis exerts a centripetal pull towards homogeneity, institutional consolidation is a more complex process with strong built-in centrifugal elements – it serves as the conduit through which the constitutional plurality of the constituting states is wired into the supranational institutional structure.

Institutional development concerns the outgrowth and consolidation of the institutional structure of the supranational polity. Its logic is not exclusively *normative*. Institutional organisations are not exclusively about law. They occupy buildings, make use of objects with empirical existence, and are represented by very material (when not venial) beings. Institutional organisations cannot be brought into existence by a normative regulatory ideal; they have to be created, staffed and

[62] If all national constitutional norms converge, as in most cases they do, the common norm is easy to establish. The strong affinity between national and Community constitutional norms is due to the history of European integration, to the fact that all Member States are parties to the European Convention on Human Rights; moreover accession to the European Union is conditioned to candidate states indeed fitting in the constitutional paradigm defined by the common constitutional traditions.

funded, and develop their own institutional identity. In a constitutional union of already established constitutional states, this process is complicated by three factors. Firstly, constitutional synthesis presupposes the combination of a single constitutional order with a pluralistic institutional structure, to the extent that supranational and national institutions are not hierarchically organised or ranked. Secondly, constitutional synthesis at the regional-continental level of government (*i.e.*, in between global organisations and nation-states) tends to proceed in a far from crowded institutional space. In contrast to the constitution of a nation-state, which *de facto* relies upon an existing institutional structure, constitutional synthesis requires the creation of new institutional structures. This usually entails that institution-making proceeds in a fragmentary fashion, that the synthetic polity starts with bits and pieces of an institutional structure, instead of with a complete one. Thirdly, the derivative character of the synthetic polity implies that the *institutional void* is only formally a *void*, as the creation of supranational institutions consists of the *projection* (or at least, attempts at the projection) of national institutional structures and cultures to the supranational level. But because such structures and cultures are much more idiosyncratic than national constitutional laws, the probable result is that the creation of supranational institutions is the site of a bitter contest between different national institutional structures and cultures.

Upon such a basis, the *homogenising* logic of normative synthesis contrasts with the manifold pluralistic proclivities proper of institutional consolidation. This tension is aggravated over time, and a crisis emerges when the relationship between the two processes is polarised. As normative synthesis proceeds, it fosters some institutional convergence. But the synthetic process can also feed institutional pluralism and conflict, and thus produce a constellation incapable of solving institutional conflicts among the different levels of government. That is also part of the history of European integration.

11.5.1.3 The Pluralistic Character of Constitutional Synthesis

The *third thesis* is that the regulatory ideal of a single constitutional law comes hand in hand with the respect for national constitutional and institutional structures. This entails that, while supranational law is one, there are several institutions that apply the supranational law in an authoritative manner. The peculiar combination of a single law and a pluralist institutional structure results from the just mentioned fact that there is no ultimate hierarchical structuring of supranational and national institutions, and is compounded by the pluralistic proclivities of institutional consolidation at supranational level.

The fact that the synthetic constitutional path is one in which participating states retain their separate existence, as well as their separate constitutional and institutional identity, implies that constitutional synthesis is a peculiar breed of pluralistic constitutional theory. On the one hand, it *is not* pluralistic to the extent that it endorses the monistic logic of law as a means of social integration through the *regulatory ideal of a common constitutional law*. The integrative capacities of law (its role as a complement of morality in the solving of conflicts and the co-ordination of action by means of determining, in a certain manner, what the common action norms are) require law to be as conclusive as possible. Were law to be as inconclusive as morality, it would not add much to our practical knowledge, and thus it would not be capable of operating effectively as a means of social integration. Both autonomy and the motivational force of law require that we assume that law gives one *right* answer to all the problems to be solved through it. Legal argumentation breaks down if we assume that the same case can have different, even contradictory solutions. This may be the case *empirically*, but, from a perspective internal to law, this cannot be endorsed as part of the social practice of integration through law. Democratic legal systems are further pushed into this peculiar form of "monism" by the normative requirements of the principle of equality before the law.

On the other hand, constitutional synthesis is pluralistic in a double sense. First, the regulatory ideal of a common constitutional law co-exists with the actual plurality of national constitutional laws. The constitutional moment in synthesis only results in the endorsement of a regulatory ideal, and in the bits and pieces of the set of common constitutional norms enshrined in the founding document. Most constitutional norms remain *in nuce*, or better put, in several drafts, as many national constitutions participate in the process of integration. The regulatory ideal of a common constitutional law is fleshed out in *actual* common constitutional norms (and, in general, in common legal norms) only very slowly (and not without setbacks and backlashes). Furthermore, the regulatory ideal of a common constitutional law comes hand in hand with a pluralistic institutional setting. As already indicated, instead of a hierarchically-structured institutional set-up, a synthetic polity is characterised by the existence of a plurality of institutions all of which legitimately claim to have a relevant word in the process of applying the "single" constitutional legal order. This is, in my view, the proper implication to draw from the "differentiated, but equal" viewpoints thesis. Indeed, constitutional synthesis has not led (and is not expected to lead) to Member States losing their autonomous political and legal identity (which has been coined, in the European constitutional jargon, as the national constitutional identity).[63] This is so *thanks to*, and not *despite of*, integration. The constitutional pluralism that comes hand in hand with constitutional synthesis is

[63]The term "national constitutional identity" entered the European debate in the famous ruling of the German Constitutional Court *Solange I*, 1974 WL 42441 (BverfG (Ger)), [1974] 2 C.M.L.R. 540, par. 22: "Article 24 of the Constitution must be understood and construed in the overall context of the whole Constitution. That is, it does not open the way to amending the basic structure of the Constitution, which forms the basis of its identity, without a formal amendment to the Constitution, that is, it does not open any such way through the legislation of the inter-State institution". It was then propelled to the supranational level in Maastricht (resulting in Article 6.3 of the Treaty of European Union, where the principle of respect of national identities in general terms was affirmed). And in the Constitutional Treaty and in the Treaty of Lisbon, this principle was spelled out by reference to constitutional identity. On the academic debate following the Constitutional Treaty, see Armin von Bogdandy, "The European constitution and European identity: Text and subtext of the Treaty establishing a Constitution for Europe", (2005) 3 *International Journal of Constitutional Law*, pp. 295–315; M. Rosenfeld, "The European treaty–constitution and constitutional identity: A view from America", (2005) 3 *International Journal of Constitutional Law*, pp. 316–331; J. H. Reestman and L. F. M. Besselink, "Constitutional identity and the European

both rendered possible *and* stabilised by the new institutional structure and the growing substantive convergence between national constitutional orders. Constitutional synthesis could be seen as the political and legal counterpart to the common market of old (not the single market of the Single European Act!) in the objective of rescuing the nation-state;[64] in my view, it is more proper to consider it as a means of reconfiguring and redefining the state, and, thereby, at the very minimum, detaching the state from the nation; and perhaps even disposing of the idea of the sovereign state completely.[65]

Thus, constitutional synthesis articulates two key insights of the pluralist theory of Community law when (1) it stresses the open character of the process of constitutional synthesis (which accounts for the fact that no institutional actor has been acknowledged the power to solve, in an authoritative and final manner, conflicts between norms produced through Community and national law-making processes), and (2) it highlights the pluralist source of European constitutional law, the actual result of the process of constitutional synthesis of national constitutional norms. This not only provides the basis for the claim to the democratic legitimacy of Community law (transferred from the national to the European constitutional order when national constitutional norms become the core constitutional framework of the Union), but also reveals the complexity of constitutional conflicts in the European legal order, as they are, at the very same time, "vertical" conflicts between Community and national law, and "horizontal" conflicts between national constitutional laws, aspiring to define the common constitutional standard.

However, the theory of constitutional synthesis reconciles pluralism with the normative defence of a monist reconstruction of the European legal order, in part on account of the social integrative capacity of European law and the fostering of equality before the law across borders, in part on account of the substantive identity of European and national constitutional law. Moreover, it offers a limited, but comprehensive, explanation of the sources of stability of the European legal order, which, at the same time, accounts for the progressive weakening of the said sources.

11.5.2 How the Theory of Constitutional Synthesis Solves the Three Riddles

The theory of constitutional synthesis claims that the genesis riddle is solved once we realise that the establishment of the constitution of the European legal order has not been the result of either an act of revolutionary constitution-making or

courts", (2007) 3 *European Constitutional Law Review* 3, pp. 177–181. In more general theoretical terms, see the interesting reflections of Gary Jeffrey Jaconsohn, in "Constitutional Identity", (2006) 68 *The Review of Politics*, pp. 361–397.

64 A. Milward, *The Rescue of the European Nation-State*, (London: Routledge, 1992).

65 W. E. Scheuermann, "Postnational democracies without postnational states? Some skeptical reflections", (2009) 2 *Ethics & Global Politics*, pp. 41–63; Hauke Brunkhorst, "Reply: States with constitutions, constitutions without states, and democracy – Skeptical reflections on Scheuerman's skeptical reflection", (2009) 2 *Ethics & Global Politics*, pp. 65–81.

the outcome of a process of constitutional evolution, but is properly described as the transfer of the common national constitutional norms to the Community legal order as authorised and mandated by the national constitutions of the Member States themselves.

Firstly, the ultimate normative foundation of the present European constitutional practice is to be found in the "opening" clauses of national constitutions which authorise and mandate supranational integration as a necessary means to realise the constitutional principles of the fundamental law, given the impossibility of doing so within the confines of a closed national-constitutional order. The fundamental laws of three out of the six founding Members of the European Coal and Steel Community, and of five of the six founding Members of the European Economic Community and the Euratom contained radically innovative clauses concerning the relationship between the nation-state and the international community. Since then, general integration clauses have been replaced by specific European clauses, which have also been inserted in the constitutions of most of the states which have acceded to Union membership since then.[66] The constitutional importance of these clauses stems from the fact that they do not limit themselves to determining the procedure through which international treaties have to be negotiated, signed and ratified, or the place assigned to them in the system of the sources of law, as standard constitutional clauses on international affairs and external relations usually do. On the contrary, the supranational integration clauses mandate the active participation of the state in the creation and defence of multilateral international organisations, which implies a mandate to exercise some of their national sovereign powers collectively, and consequently, the transcendence of the *national* character of such public powers created and disciplined by the constitution itself. These clauses can be properly regarded as the positivisation of the moral duty to create common supranational institutions and to agree common norms capable of solving conflicts and co-ordinating common action in view of the common public interest. This grounds the claim that they must be seen as the late fruit of the cosmopolitan conceptions of democracy and law elaborated in the interwar period,[67] which explains the close relationship in which they stand to the normative foundation of the primacy of Community legal norms.

---

[66] K. Loewenstein, "Sovereignty and International Cooperation", (1954) 48 *American Journal of International Law*, pp. 222–244, especially at 233–234 (the European Coal and Steel Community), and at 237–238 (European Defence Community): Antonio Cassesse, "Modern Constitutions and International Law", (1985) 192 *Recueil*, pp. 331–476; T. M. Franck and A. K. Thiruvengadam, "International Law and Constitution-Making", (2003) 2 *Chinese Journal of International Law*, pp. 467–518. On European clauses in the Constitutions of Member States of the European Union, see M. Claes, "Constitutionalising Europe at its source", (2005) 24 *Yearbook of European Law*, pp. 81–125, and Christopher Grabenwarter, "National Constitutional Law Relating to the European Union", in: A. von Bogdandy and J. Bast, *Principles of European Constitutional Law*, (Oxford: Hart Publishing, 2006), pp. 95–144; on more recent clauses, see A. Albi, "'Europe' Articles in the Constitutions of Central and Eastern European Countries", (2005) 42 *Common Market Law Review*, pp. 399–423.

[67] H. Kelsen, "Les rapports de système entre le droit interne et le droit internationale public", (1926) 14 *Recueil des Cours*, pp. 227–331; J. G. Starke, "Monism and Dualism in the Theory of

Second, the establishment of a new common constitution by reference to already existing national constitutional norms offers a (temporary and provisional) alternative to the coupling of democratic agency and legitimacy characteristic of revolutionary constitution-making and to the progressive acquisition of democratic legitimacy characteristic of the evolutionary model. Because the new constitution is formed by national constitutional norms, it draws from them the democratic legitimacy of which they were invested in each national constitution-making process (either through revolutionary or evolutionary constitution-making processes). And because the validity of each and every European law depends on compliance with European constitutional law, then the derivative democratic legitimacy of Community constitutional norms is radiated to secondary Community norms when they are interpreted and constructed according to the basic principles of European constitutional law. This provides integration with democratic legitimacy in the absence of an explicit constitution-making process.[68]

When these two premises are properly considered, the present European constitutional practice reveals itself to be far less problematical than it may seem at first glance. The claim that European law is the supreme law of the European "land" is but another way of saying that the common constitutional laws of the Member States are the supreme law of the European "land". When one realises that such a transformation was authorised and mandated by national constitutions, the riddle is solved.

Constitutional synthesis claims that the primacy riddle is solved once we take the fact that European constitutional law and national constitutional law cannot be properly portrayed as two sets of differentiated constitutional norms into account. The

---

International Law", (1936) 17 *British Yearbook of International Law*, pp. 66–81; Boris Mirkine-Guetzévitch, "Droit International et droit constitutionnel", (1938) 38 *Recueil des Cours*, pp. 311–463; Umberto Campagnolo, *Nations et Droit*, (Paris: Felix Alcan, 1938); A. Rolin, *Les Origines de l'Institut de droit international (1873–1923): Souvenirs d'un témoin*, (Brussels: Vroment, 1923). A concrete application to Europe before the Second World War is documented in B. Mirkine-Guetzevicth and G. Scelle (eds), *L'Union Européenne*, (Paris: Librairie Delagrave, 1931). In the war period, see H. Kelsen, *Peace through Law*, (Chapel Hill NC: University of North Carolina, 1944); in the post-war period, see H. Kelsen, *The Law of the United Nations*, (London: Stevens and sons, 1950); Alf Ross, *Constitution of the United Nations*, (Copenhagen: Munksgaard, 1950).

[68] Integration through the explicit writing of a new federal constitution for the European Union may or may not have been a feasible alternative after the Second World War. It could be argued that the political conditions under which an explicit European constitutional general will could be forged were lacking, and that there was no clear idea of what the institutional and decision-making set-up of a supranational Union should look like. This was, indeed, the paradox of European integration before the European Communities were established. The need to overcome the nation-state was strongly felt for a rather long-time (stretching back to the Abbé Pierre and Kant at the very least) but an effective and democratic way of breaking away from the nation-state seemed not to be available. Indeed, the risks of opening an explicit constitution-making process were proven by the failure of the Defence and Political Communities in 1954. Synthetic constitution-making promises allow us to proceed with the process of European integration sufficiently far as to render the new supranational polity robust enough to be capable of undergoing an explicit constitution-making process. Because it has a solid (even if derivative) democratic legitimacy-basis, a synthetic constitution is one that would be expected to enact changes in the legal and political order of the political community which it constitutes.

collective of national constitutional norms *constitutes* the deep layer of European constitutional law. European constitutional law is not only *derivative*, in the sense of being a creature of national constitutional law, but is also *common*, its being *what is common to national constitutions*. Constitutional synthesis implies a particular form of, and understanding of, constitutional primacy. In other words, the shape of primacy under constitutional synthesis does not emanate from the elevation of one set of constitutional norms to the status of the supreme law of the land, but through one over-arching arrangement emanating from the synthesis of the many, instead. Once the initial legal-institutional structure is put in place, synthesis is not achieved by finding a common minimum denominator, but by means of considering which of the national constitutional norms is more congenial to Community law. This is no mere copying exercise, however, as I have underlined above. It is a reflexive process which considers the underlying arguments for or against the range of competing national constitutional solutions. It considers the extent to which the national norm can be "Europeanised", both in the sense of fitting with European constitutional law as it stands (as already synthesised in the Treaties, the amendments to the Treaties or the legislation and case law of the Union), and whether its consequences will be acceptable to the Union as a whole.[69] Numbers are relevant, but not decisive. The key question is one of critical comparison between national solutions, which is preferably settled through the Community law-making process. When a national constitutional norm is relegated, or trumped by the common constitutional standard, that solution is not incompatible with the national constitution, but can be justified by the reflexivity that is an implicit requirement of the national constitutional mandate of openness. Thus, in horizontal conflicts, there is only an apparent riddle in claiming that the derivative legal order (Community law) prevails over the original legal orders (national constitutional orders). The primacy of the derivative order is willed by each national constitution because it is a necessary requirement for the process of integration through constitutional law. From the national viewpoint, European legal integration leads to the "opening" of national constitutional norms to the fundamental laws of all the other Member States. As already hinted at, this "opening" may eventually trigger a process of reflexive change to reconcile the primacy of the national constitution with the constitutional mandate to integrate into supranational political structures. From the Community standpoint, this entails that the constitution of the Community be underpinned by a plurality of constitutional sources (each of the constitutions of the Member States), but that, at the same time, the constitutional aspiration of the Community is to forge a single and cohesive set of fundamental norms as integration proceeds.

[69] If all national constitutional norms converge, as, in many cases they do, the common norm is easy to establish. The strong affinity between national and Community constitutional norms is due to the history of European integration, to the fact that all Member States are parties to the European Convention on Human Rights; moreover, accession to the European Union is conditioned to candidate states fitting into the constitutional paradigm defined by the common constitutional traditions.

Primacy is less clearly justified in vertical conflicts. Indeed, the Court of Justice has still to substantiate good arguments for giving primacy to its "transcendental" understanding of the economic freedoms over national laws protecting overriding national interests. The right intuition behind the "counter-limits" and "national constitutional identity" of national constitutional courts, is precisely that all constitutional conflicts cannot be solved by reference to a one-size-fits-all standard. Indeed, it seems to me that what is wrong in the theoretical construction of national constitutional courts is the emphasis on the defence of the national constitution against the European one (even if this emphasis is easy to explain, given the national institutional identity of European constitutions). The best argumentative countermove would be to gain the supranational constitutional ground, and claim that limits to *vertical* primacy are not only required by the defence of the national constitution as national, but also of the collective of national constitutions, and thus, of the *deep* constitution of the European Union. Because Community law combines the regulatory ideal of one single constitutional order with a radical institutional pluralism, national constitutional courts should take their duty to guard not only the national, but also the European constitution, seriously.

The theory of constitutional synthesis shows that the primacy riddle is more easily solved once we realise that synthesis gives a distinct shape to the very notion of primacy, given the composite character of the supranational constitutional order. Acknowledging primacy to European constitutional norms is not demeaning to the overall primacy of the Constitution, but it does mainly contribute to realise it, and only marginally requires the revision of the national constitutional standard by reference to the collective of national constitutional standards. The derivative character of Community law comes hand in hand with its primacy in *horizontal conflicts* because primacy is the only way to realise the shared objective of integrating through constitutional law. Primacy is, indeed, only problematical when the vertical conflict is the result of the emancipation of Community constitutional standards from (and thus, against) the substantive contents of national constitutional standards (such was the case in the famous *Viking* ruling, and, in general, every time that economic freedoms overrule national norms on the grounds that they are obstacles to the maintenance of the single market).

The theory of constitutional synthesis claims that the key source of the stability of the European legal order resides in the foundational role played by national constitutional norms in both the Community and the national legal orders. It is because (and one could add, it will continue to be the case as long as) national constitutional norms play the same role in the domestic and in the Community legal orders that European legal integration is infused with the democratic legitimacy which provides decisive motivational force to citizens and institutional actors alike.

Moreover, the theory of constitutional synthesis shares with the national and pluralistic theories of Community law the notion that the stability of the European legal order is critically dependent on the internalisation of the double role which national constitutions play due to their dual function as supreme national law and as part of the collective of supreme Community norms. Because the substantive unity of European law comes hand in hand with a differentiated institutional structure and overlapping law-making processes, the way in which law is systematised and turned into a consistent whole plays a decisive role. Thus, the theory of constitutional synthesis finds the insights provided by pluralist theories on the relevance of the argument from coherence in ensuring the stability of the European legal order to be appealing. But it adds that the force of the argument does not merely come from its being a logical part of any theory of legal argumentation, but also from its implicit endorsement, both by the Community and by national constitutional courts, of provisions which impose a reciprocal obligation of constitutional loyalty.[70] In particular, national constitutional courts should assume their double identity as the guardians of both the national and the European constitution, as I have just argued. Because the said courts are no longer mere national institutions, but part and parcel of the overall European institutional structure, because their opinions are not only relevant to their citizens and permanent residents, but can also influence the way in which European constitutional law is constructed (as the synthesis of all national constitutional norms), their role as the defender of the national constitution cannot but include that of the guardian of the Community constitution. If the Constitutional Court of any Member State adjudicates upon a European constitutional conflict, both Community law and national Constitutional law require the Court to ground its decision *not only on a narrow set of constitutional arguments,* but on a *wider* set of constitutional arguments which takes the fact that the national legal order has become integrated, in application of its own constitution, into the European legal order, into account.

11.6 Conclusion

This chapter has emphasised the close relationship between Neil MacCormick's European constitutional theory and his major achievements as a legal theorist, and, in particular, his fundamental contribution to the establishment and the development of "modern" institutional jurisprudence. In Section 11.2, I sustained that MacCormick's reconciliation of legal positivism with the liberal and democratic public philosophy, which was endorsed, but not coherently followed, by the two foremost legal positivists of the last century (Kelsen and Hart), created the theoretical space within which it was possible to forge a constitutional theory *beyond the state*, and, in particular, a constitutional theory of the European Union. In Section 11.4, I claimed that MacCormick put forward some of the basic building-blocks of a sound constitutional theory of European integration. In particular, his emphasis on the co-existence of a plurality of equally authoritative standpoints from which to reconstruct and systematise Community law pointed to the structural "pluralistic" character of the European Constitution. Similarly, his underlining

[70]Or, to put it otherwise, the obligation is not merely moral, prudential or grounded on scholarly-constructed principles, but it is, indeed, a legal obligation which derives from the best possible interpretation of the law in force in each and every Member State.

of the limits of law, and, in particular, of the incapacity of any legal system to ensure its own stability, helped rebut claims which diminished the full-blown "legal" nature of Community law on account of the fact that it was not supported by an independent "sovereign" will. However, I also argued in Section 11.4 that MacCormick's own writings reveal his uneasiness with some of the implications of constitutional pluralism. Very significant in this regard is his shift from a radical to a moderate "pluralistic" standpoint. This led me to put forward, in Section 11.5, an alternative constitutional theory of the European Union: the theory of constitutional synthesis. Its key insight is that the constitutional path through which the European constitution has been democratically established is different from both that of revolutionary and evolutionary constitutionalism; and that such a path is what makes the Union intrinsically pluralistic from a legal standpoint. To say that the European Union is the result of a process of constitutional synthesis is the same as claiming that already constitutionally-established constitutional states *put their constitutions in common* and in a progressive, albeit piecemeal, process, developed a common and supranational institutional structure. I affirmed and now reiterate that constitutional synthesis is able to remain loyal to the key insights of MacCormick's institutional theory and European constitutional theory, but that it manages to ease some of the tensions underlying the constitutional theory of the author of *Legal Theory and Legal Reasoning*. But, even if it departs from MacCormick's European constitutional pluralism, the theory of constitutional synthesis is highly indebted to MacCormick's institutional theory and to his reflections on European constitutional history, and constitutional synthesis endeavours to be fairly MacCormickian in spirit. In that same spirit, this chapter is intended more as a move in (hopefully) the right direction, than as a definitive and final rendering of this very necessary European constitutional theory. If only Neil could still show us the way!

Part VII
Post-sovereign Nationalism

Chapter 12
Nation-States vs. Nation-Regions in the Post-sovereign European Polity

Joxerramon Bengoetxea

12.1 Introduction

It is an honour, a pleasure and a challenge to participate in a collective work aimed at analysing the work of my doctoral father, a legal and political theorist and philosopher I admire and persistently tend to agree with, who was always a dear friend. MacCormick's theories on legal reasoning, his institutional approach to theories on sovereignty and liberal nationalism, his defence of personal autonomy and social democracy are all essential items of my own intellectual make-up. Since the days I worked on my doctoral thesis under his guidance in Edinburgh, I have seen my own thinking about practical reason, in many significant ways, as an ongoing conversation with Neil MacCormick.

This chapter is an invitation to continue that dialogue in relation to the idea and theoretical implications of *internal enlargement*, a term coined by Neil MacCormick when he acted as alternate member of the Convention on the Future of Europe (2002–2004) representing the European Free Alliance group of the European Parliament, to refer to the possibility of Member States, such as the United Kingdom, dividing or splitting into new Member States. "Internal enlargement" is the EU side of the motto "Independence in Europe", a normative institutional aspiration of some citizens in some nations without their own state such as the Basque Country or Scotland. This concept not only raises many interesting questions of Public International Law, European Union law, constitutional law and theory, political philosophy, and practical philosophy generally, but it also challenges the political strategies of established states and of infra-state nationalist movements. More specifically, the strategic debate revolves around the options of full statehood, or independence, and regionalism or autonomy. In any case, the options presuppose the possibility of the choice of status, which requires analysing the difficult questions of sovereignty and self-determination.

J. Bengoetxea (✉)
Universidad del País Vasco/Euskal Herriko Unibertsitatea, Vitoria, Spain
e-mail: joxerramon.bengoetxea@ehu.es

A.J. Menéndez, J.E. Fossum (eds.), *Law and Democracy in Neil MacCormick's Legal and Political Theory*, Law and Philosophy Library 93,
DOI 10.1007/978-90-481-8942-7_12, © Springer Science+Business Media B.V. 2011

A shift of focus has been suggested[1] with regard to the understanding of the phenomenon of sovereignty and its normative implications from hard conceptions which stress power, independence and non-interference from other powers, to softer or lighter conceptions based upon co-decision-making capacity in a connected world of interdependence. In my contention, this shift of conceptions is leading to a new understanding of sovereignty, to a new concept which will also have an impact on law and state. However, this shift of focus is, for the moment, taking place mainly in the minds of scholars and some of the relevant actors, but is not yet being seen in the practice of international relations, or in international law. International law still clings to the harder conception of sovereignty and self-determination, as can be seen in the 2008 episodes of Kosovo, or in the South Ossetia and in the Abkhazia Oblasts and in the tensions between Georgia and Russia. The different notions of sovereignty used by the relevant states involved in these processes and the lack of coherence in the treatment of these situations all tend to show that new phenomena are shaping the understanding of traditional categories such as self-determination, respect for state and national structures, and the conditions for state recognition.

12.2 Neil MacCormick's Contribution to the Debate on Nation, Law and the State in Europe

Nationalism is behind the different motivations of the main players involved in such conflicts: nationalism is the driving-force for state formation in Kosovo and also the reason for denying Kosovo its own statehood in the larger Serbia. Nationalism is the driving-force towards re-unification of Ossetia, or towards support for such claims on the part of Russia or towards its rejection on the part of Georgia. Nationalism is, therefore, everywhere, but it might be cloaked in a different language such as legitimate state interests or free exercise of self-determination. It seems clear that nationalism is in great need of critical analysis which goes beyond political appraisals of its different expressions in this or other countries.

MacCormick was intellectually honest to introduce the topic of nationalism in the practical philosophy syllabus, which was and still is largely influenced by liberalism. Thanks to his valuable contribution, [liberal] nationalism is a contemporary issue not only in political philosophy, but also in jurisprudence, and it is also a tenable position in normative philosophy. *Legal Right and Social Democracy* published in the mid-1980s already had a final chapter which showed how some forms of nationalism are compatible with the liberal, democratic and egalitarian principles, in short, the enlightened principles, which he defended in the book, and add something which is crucial to complement individualistic principles: namely, collective identity. *Questioning Sovereignty*, published seventeen years later, further spelt out these ideas in the context of the European Union and shared sovereignty. This is

[1] See my own *La Europa Peter Pan* (Oñati: IVAP, 2005).

precisely the debate: is it possible to remain liberal while affirming the normative importance of the group, the nation?

Radical versions of liberalism, denying the possibility of group rights, deprive national identities of any moral significance for individuals or any cultural context (of choice) through which politics is accessed.[2] On the other hand, liberal and federal versions of nationalism or regionalism[3] conceive identities as democratic processes of participation and deliberation. Individuals are not the only possible subjects of moral and political discourse, and in any case they are not devoid of cultural identity, as abstract, methodological or contractarian individualism would have us believe. Groups are also moral subjects and they are composed of unique, contextual individuals.[4] A discursive, deliberative, approach is necessary to understand collective identity and the pluralistic *demos*, rather than the approach that merely affirms a reified and monist collective, and negates its equally reified internal or external neighbours.

MacCormick's contribution to the debate has been to consider the philosophical credibility of "a kind of social-democratic liberal nationalism" based upon subsidiarity – as proximity to the people and respect for the distinctiveness of collective civic institutions, legal and other traditions, and culture – respect for persons as autonomous, self-determined contextual individuals and voluntary membership – member-shared allegiance to certain civic institutions. For MacCormick, "cultures have value in terms of identity to their possessors" (*Questioning Sovereignty* as fully refereed in fn 3, and hereafter QS: 171) and linked to this principle is the *prima facie* value of the nation, "the political relevance of the shared national consciousness,

---

[2]For a view contrary to the existence of group rights, see Luis Rodríguez Abascal, "El debate sobre los derechos de grupo", in: J.L. Colomer & E. Díaz (eds), *Justicia, estado y derechos* (Madrid: Alianza, 2002), pp. 63–81.

[3]With varying nuances, on Liberal Nationalism, see Y. Tamir, *Liberal Nationalism* (Princeton NJ: Princeton University Press, 1993), Neil MacCormick, *Questioning Sovereignty* (Oxford: Oxford University Press, 1999); W. Kymlicka, "Territorial Boundaries: A Liberal Egalitarian Perspective", in: D. Miller & S. Hashmi (eds), *Boundaries and Justice* (Princeton NJ: Princeton University Press, 2001), Alain Gagnon, "The moral foundations of Asymmetrical federalism: a normative exploration of the case of Quebec and Canada", in: A. Gagnon & J. Tully (eds) *Multinational Democracies* (Cambridge: Cambridge University Press, 2001); W. Norman, *Negotiating Nationalism* (Oxford: Oxford University Press, 2006). Regionalism is not a term normally used in this context, but it would be interesting to associate it with nationalism, communitarianism or multi-culturalism, politics of recognition, and identity politics of politics of difference.

[4]The term is taken from Yael Tamir, note 3 *supra*, and MacCormick's *Questioning Sovereignty*, note 3 *supra*, in which the idea develops in this sense: "To become a full human individual involves things like acquiring a name, learning to speak a language and becoming acculturated into some culture, or into some sub-culture in some idiosyncratic mix with some wider and more inclusive culture or cultures. Schooling and further education, work and the workplace, marriage and family, friendship, engagement in sport or voluntary activity or politics, and all suchlike engagements and relationships with other persons, make us the persons we come to be. Such things account for the continual evolution of character and individuality in our lives as human persons." (p. 180)

however many share it" (*QS*: 172). The formulation of liberal nationalism is based upon the following principle:

> the members of a nation are as such in principle entitled to effective organs of political self-government within the world order of sovereign or post-sovereign states. (*QS*: 173)

And the corollary follows:

> if many humans, as humans are today, include in their subjective sense of individuality and identity the idea of belonging to a certain nation or national culture, then respect for persons as contextual individuals must include respect for that aspect of their individuality. (*QS*: 182)

Clearly, nationalism is not a necessary normative consequence of enlightened principles, only a possible one, and the form it will take in the different countries of the EU, depends on the availability of governance and sovereignty models in our contemporary world, on the institutional expression of collective identity, and on the particular stage of development of European integration. MacCormick was one of the pioneers in this direction (*QS*: 188–192). Radical forms of liberalism, however, deny the compatibility of any version of nationalism with liberal values; in taking these positions, they place themselves in idealist or utopian normative discourse outside any plausible analysis or interpretation of the political forms known to us.

But is nationalism plausible at this level of ideal discourse? If the question is meant normatively, we go back to the claim of liberal non-organic nationalism, and we can, perhaps, discuss the merits of adhering to a term that is most probably *passé* and discredited. If the question is meant descriptively, the answer is clearly affirmative: in spite of its intellectual disrepute, nationalism is actually everywhere, from the US Patriot Act to the Olympic games, to the Greek veto on the name of the Republic of Macedonia, to the Spanish Constitution and its invocation by the Constitutional Court to justify the refusal to allow a consultation on the political will of the Basque People,[5] and, perhaps, also in the Basque Government's intention to proceed with the consultation upon the basis of a weak parliamentary majority of one, or the *Académie Française*'s zealous defence of the French language.[6] One only has to look around at the practice and discourses of most established states and state-related organs and at the claims, practices and discourse of most political parties. At a descriptive-interpretative level of analysis, the question should rather be, is cosmopolitanism or other forms of non-nationalism plausible in a nationalist world?

[5]The law providing for a consultation of the Basque people – on two points, on peace negotiations to bring about a permanent ceasefire and on negotiations between political parties to bring about the recognition and practice of the right of the Basque people to decide on their preferred political status – was passed with a narrow majority by the Basque Parliament as law 9/2008. The consultation was to take place on the 25 October 2008. The Spanish Constitutional Court declared this law (un-) constitutional on the grounds that only the Spanish State has the competence to call for referenda and that the said consultation is really a form of referendum. See the ruling of 11 September 2008, available at: http://www.tribunalconstitucional.es/jurisprudencia/Stc2008/STC2008-05707.html

[6]See its Declaration of 12 June 2008, opposing the constitutional amendment aimed at declaring that the regional languages are part of the French heritage.

On the other hand, if nationalism is taken to imply the classical formal sovereignty of states, then it becomes more of an ideal than a reality, and perhaps not a highly desirable ideal. Full sovereignty of the nation-state, if it ever existed, belongs to the past, and advocating full sovereignty as a normative aspiration seems dated and stale. This is nowhere more challenging than in the European context. In many meaningful ways, the European experiment is an attempt to overcome nation-state nationalism, but the question is, once nationalism is regarded as an obstacle towards integration, what sort of ideology is there to replace it: national interests are simply not going to disappear and their defence is not going to be considered unjustified. Furthermore, nationalism is a pervasive ideology when it comes to identity issues: national identity is seen as challenged both by internal processes of regionalism and self-determination, and by external processes of globalisation and European integration, and this sometimes leads to a re-deployment of state-nationalist strategies, taking new and different forms. Therefore, if nationalism is flatly rejected, it will very probably re-surface into some form of post-nationalism or neo-nationalism.

The classical identification of nation and state will also need serious revisions. Nation encompasses the *demos*, the people, and the state becomes the legal and institutional format of the nation, backed by means of the monopoly of the use of force and the claim to legitimate recourse to coercion. The identification of state and law is so powerful, that even expressions of law outside the state format such as the law of international organisations or the *lex mercatoria* phenomena, are still considered as creatures of the outcome of their recognition by states. In this area, another of MacCormick's key contributions, his theory of law as institutional normative order conceptually independent from the state, allows us to separate state and law, and to disentangle law and coercion. This separation has crucial consequences for the theory of sovereignty and of legal order.

The importance of the state can hardly be overstated: it is a coercive organisation which controls a territory and its people, deploying administration and services, using physical force for the enforcement of individual norms, or keeping credible the possibility of its use in order to guarantee "law and order". The state further claims that this use of force by state organs is legitimate while banning as unlawful and wrong the use of force by other, unauthorised, players. Law is the make-up and the output of the state.

But state law is only one kind, the most visible and central case of law and sovereignty. There are interesting legal orders at the conceptual borders of law, which do not rely on coercion, but on co-ordination and co-operation, instead, although the question remains as to what extent they do not somehow depend on the backup of state coercion in order to ensure compliance. If state law does not exhaust the phenomenology of legal orders, the possibility of legal pluralism is not denied, at least not in theory. Different institutional normative orders or sets of norms that we cannot simply discard as non-legal can be simultaneously applicable in a territory. We are now referring to normative orders within the family-resemblance of law, not to morality or ethics. The co-existence of legal, moral and political norms is not found to be problematical from the point of view of state law, even if clashes between law and morality are the gist of most hard legal cases, and clashes between politics (simple majoritarian will in a constituency) and law (rights and guarantees protecting minorities) are in the very essence of constitutionalism. Yet, the state legal system and its legal field, in both stages of law-creation and law-application, does not consider other normative spheres such as ethics, or political morality as legally-challenging, and it finds devices for accommodating them via legal principles, or for tolerating them via justifications and excuses, in a highly-sophisticated institutionalised setting of practical reasoning which is typically legal: judicial institutions.

But where alternative forms of "law" appear, where groups of people guide and justify their social action upon the basis of norms that are not considered to spring from the acceptable sources of the state legal system,[7] problems of legal challenges and co-ordination are inevitable. The question will then open up to what extent these norms are co-ordinated and brought into one single normative system, like state law under the unifying *aegis* of a shared rule of recognition, most likely by considering them to be "customs", or whether, sociologically, we can observe that all these different practical norms, which both guide and justify behaviour, co-exist in other ways, for example, by ignoring each other, by avoiding clashes, or even by acknowledging each other to some extent. To the extent that they require enforcement by coercion, they will need to come to terms with state law and recognise its supremacy or sovereignty. But if other, softer, alternative means of "enforcement" are developed by the actors following those rules, such as peer pressure, social criticism, market exclusion, diversion of investment, de-localisation of production plants, consumer boycotts, then submission to state law loses weight, and state law will prevail in practice only where points of connection between these norms are brought before a state organ of law application. Legal pluralism can then be denied successfully by state law: when the challenge between competing legal sources is brought before a state organ, there is a final reception or rejection upon the basis of state law; but the question from the sociological and anthropological understandings of pluralism is precisely the normative pluralism before the challenge is redirected to judicial institutions.

There are interesting expressions of "co-ordinated" or quasi-official pluralism both above and below the state level. De-centralised and/or federal systems often recognise internal territorial legal orders of public law, even of criminal law, and sometimes also of private law. In principle, these territorial infra-state legal orders are co-ordinated with the state legal order upon the basis of the division of competences between the state and the infra-state entities, the regions. The rule of recognition that ensures the ultimate unity of the state legal system can be seen as the result of an authoritative decision adopted at a higher or at a larger level, but the interpretations made by the infra-state entities need not go along with this authoritative view. Regions might consider themselves to be autonomous and therefore

[7] Although legal order and legal system can be distinguished in a strict sense (see my "Legal System as Regulative Ideal" (1994) 53 *ARSP*, [*Archiv für Rechts- und Sozial-Philosophie*], pp. 66–80. In this section, I use the terms legal system, legal order and law as equivalent.

sovereign, and they might claim to maintain the right to decide on the ultimate rule of recognition or, at least, to co-opt and co-decide on this rule, either bilaterally with the state, or multilaterally with the other "nation-regions" that make up the state. The question of pluralism in these cases is not so different conceptually from the one that exists between the Member States and the supra-state entity, the EU, which has the ultimate authority to decide as to who decides, also seen as the issue of *Kompetenz-Kompetenz*, and to what extent that authority exercises its prerogatives by imposing constitutional dogma or by engaging in discourse argumentation.

With regard to the EU, legal "pluralism" exists in a rather conceptual way, and the debate turns on the question of whether that unifying rule of recognition – using the language of effectiveness and the uniform application of community law, and setting aside incompatible national rules rather than the language of primacy and hierarchy – has moved to the federal supra-state level or remains with the Member State, within the "national" constitution. Ultimately, there will be a case by case judicial solution in a gradual process in permanent motion, and, over time, it might be the case that we detect the shift towards a European rule of recognition, and, when this shift has finally been accepted by all the higher courts of the Member States and by the larger juristic community, we shall be able to infer the existence of a European *Grundnorm*, or it might be that the different norms (and practices) of recognition of state law and "common" law all claim ultimate authority and only tolerate each other in order to avoid overt constitutional disputes. A legal culture might develop amongst European jurists, leading them to consider such ultimate pluralist situations as not necessarily problematical, but permanently contested sources of legitimacy. The institutional theory of law can be of great help for the development of such open and democratic culture. But if the dominant culture tends to see national constitutions as the only source of authority, then state conceptions will carry the day, and if anything like a European *Grundnorm* is to develop, it will require the transformation of the EU into some sort of federal constitution.

It still remains the case that this semi-official pluralism of legal orders, which become operative through courts and agents, co-habits with other domains of practical, normative reason such as morality and political morality, and "other laws", and these remain autonomous. To the extent that organised groups of people govern their social relations or certain aspects of them according to these normative orders, and deliberately avoid following the "official" law, we can speak about legal pluralism in a stronger sense, not unrelated to cultural pluralism. Law seeks its justification, it lays a *claim to correctness* in being a normative order based upon certain values, and this claim necessarily engages moral agents in deliberative discourse and rational action. Critical reflective compliance, which, incidentally, does not rule out civil disobedience in hard cases, becomes the cosmopolitan moral and political position of citizens in modern democracies, at the local, national, state, or global level. The pretension that only official law is valid and commands compliance is often made by established states, but, to the extent that coercion is the major argument to support this pretension, all the state can hope for is precisely that: prudential obedience or covert compliance, not overt alliance. In that case, state sovereignty retains the formal validity of law and the claim to obedience, but it no longer carries any deeper implications of political morality or of functional governance. But, then, it risks failing to be law: all law raises a claim to validity, to correctness and to rightness; if it only obtains a calculated, prudential obedience, it will need other systems of support, morality, ideology, religion, in order to ensure acceptability. Formal validity might remain uncontested, as is the case in totalitarian systems, but then engaging in the practical reasoning underlying the law becomes a mere question of discipline, very far removed from deliberative democracy and practical rationality.

The latest development of MacCormick's institutional theory of law, *Institutions of Law*, revises the strict separation thesis of legal positivism. No law can conceptually be imagined that does not purport to govern social action in a rightful way. That it actually gets it right and achieves fairness is a matter of judgement, and this cannot be finally settled by the law, but the way to engage the law and its officials into a discussion of its merits is precisely by assuming that it purports to govern righteously and to achieve justice. The strict separation of law and ethics might have been a healthy reaction to the ideological confusion of law and morality which totalitarian regimes have accentuated, but it has led to a monologue of legal validity: the law is the law is the law is the law... In order to evaluate it morally, you need to step outside the legal province, but how can a moral debate on the law be engaged *within* the law?

On the other hand, if it is acknowledged that law makes claims to moral and political correctness, the rationality debate must be engaged: but the question is where, in what forum? If it is state law, there is a high possibility that the forum will be in a supreme court, in a constitutional court or in parliament, and the discussion will be juristic in tone. Issues of jurisdiction, of access and representation, of standing and title will then become prominent, and the definition of the majority and of the people in whose name decisions are made also becomes crucial: But who is the *demos* on whose name final *legal* decisions are made about the moral and political *worth* of the law? Inevitably, we need to tackle the issue of relevant majorities in the relevant constituencies and of the protection of those minorities that do not have a chance to become a constituency of their own.

By constitutional definition, the *demos* is the nation in the nation-state model, but who is the *demos* within pluri-national states? How is the *demos* to be defined in such cases, and who has the final authority to settle its delimitation? In pluralistic contexts, there will probably always be contested *demoi* and a majority might eventually carry the day and define the people. And what happens in supranational contexts, is there a new larger *demos* in the making? And can there simultaneously be more than one *demos* over a given polity? If each polity caries its own *demos*, then, the question becomes one of defining the polity. We are now about to reformulate the question of the *demos* in terms of the question of the *polis*, but is it possible to define the *polis,* even of society at large other than by ultimate reference to the state and its law? Could the law, or the plural constitution, recognise different *demoi* corresponding to different polities or constituent bodies as the Treaty of Lisbon does? Perhaps, this makes it easier to conceive of a plurality of *demoi* co-existing in different co-ordinated and overlapping polities, and perhaps Europe is precisely the laboratory for such ideas: over one concrete territory there are several overlapping polities and jurisdictions of different sizes, co-ordinated upon the basis of several structural principles such as the division of competences, subsidiarity-proportionality, loyalty, institutional autonomy, representation, accountability and participation: regional, national, supranational. Each of these levels of government would have its own *demos*, understood as a pluralistic body of citizens deciding on common issues of crucial interest, and creating their own law.

12.3 Plural Polities and Plural *Demoi* in a Polycentric European Federation

One of the corollaries of this position is, as MacCormick explains, that the EU makes it possible to have not only systems of law and government, but also politics beyond the sovereign state. I take this to be a very moderate, but forceful, response to the "no *demos*" objection, which often tends to be nationalist or nation-state oriented. These will bc a different type of politics with a completely different notion of the *demos* and popular representation, political debates, political culture, accountability, participation, representativeness, media participation and (mis-) representation, a different type of *Öffentlichkeit* or public lifeworld. It is not politics *without* the sovereign state or simply *beyond* it, nor is it exclusive or dismissive of it, instead, it is inclusive of member statehood and of other forms of polity above, beyond and underneath the Member State,[8] and also across it to engage the agents and stakeholders involved in the process of governance that are expressed outside institutional *fora*.

The extent of normative power in the EU today depends on the division of competences between the EU and its Member States, and also on the distribution of competences within each of these Member States. To the extent that sovereignty amounts to legitimate norm-making capacity, it is divided or shared between the supranational or supra-state, the state-national and the infranational or infra-state regions, and, in a constant flux, it is both dynamic and dialectic. This would take us to a concept of shared sovereignty based upon two guiding principles: the distribution of competences and subsidiarity, which encompasses other principles such as efficiency, proportionality, proximity.... Yet, there are surprisingly few political debates revolving around subsidiarity, on the effectiveness of local *versus* global approaches, on economies of scale, on allowing local standards to prevail. These debates would require rather subtle and informed arguments, as well as judgements based upon social-scientific and policy knowledge, whereas dominant political

[8]Whether democracy is possible in any polity, even in the nation-state is a loaded question, which requires clarification of the principles that inspire democracies. Local and regional democracy and democracy at a multi-national federal state level are quite different, too. According to the logics of subsidiarity, the local and regional levels would be closer to the citizens, and, in principle, they would be the "natural" forum for the adoption of decisions, unless greater efficiency and economies of scale be obtained by taking the decisions at a larger level, i.e., the state or the supra-state levels or even the global level. The difficult issue will, then, be *how* those decisions are adopted at a higher level, by which representatives, and under what possibilities of citizen control.

debates tend to simplify and choose cleavage issues that more easily appeal to popular sentiment.

Formal sovereignty, therefore, implies title or competence to decide. Real or material sovereignty is sometimes reduced to this formal legal aspect of competence and capacity, although it would need to involve something more than that: a real opportunity to determine the state of affairs. If formal sovereignty means having the title to make norms, material or factual sovereignty would imply being able to make any decision, unfettered by financial constraints or any limit imposed by the powers that be. The visibility of power and sovereignty is again a different matter, and it takes us back to the issue of state coercion: it is easier to perceive sovereignty behind an armed policeman bringing an accused before a female judge in a local court than behind the executive board of an equities firm moving spectacular investments around the world to countries where wages are low and trade unions weak, although, arguably, the latter exercises much greater power.

Besides having the title to decide and having the means and know-how to carry out decisions, sovereignty also implies having the administrative and bureaucratic means to implement decisions, and here, again, we find different formulae. Even EU competences are exercised or implemented by means of national (state, regional or local) administrations, which means that, even when the decision was adopted at supranational level, it is actually implemented at local level. On top of this, the areas where the Member States retain competence, such as social control – criminal law and justice systems – protection – law and order, police and defence – the creation of infrastructures – roads, major transport and engineering projects – or welfare – social security and other social advantages – and, of course, the raising of taxes to make sure all these "regal" services can be provided, are all exercised with serious consequences on the lives of the citizens by state organs. As a result, state authorities tend to acquire maximum visibility and social presence in contrast with the EU bodies that have made the original norms in cases where they had the title, or simply coordinated and recommended state action. The mass media pay attention to these tasks, which adds to the impression that the state remains the real centre of power. Setting the limits of political debate and liberties by means of the criminal law will give us a wrong impression of the dilution or the transformation of sovereignty and of the polycentrism of power, competences and decision-making. We tend to forget that important spheres of power are deployed at a higher transnational level, often outside the "normal" institutional settings, and that the possibilities for innovation, adaptation and success depend on the local fabric/setting. Yet the local and the global are presented as powerless spheres; the focus of political debate is still thought to be the state, and our models and theories of democracy – parliamentary control, counter-majoritarian technocratic decision-making – remain anchored at that level. However, other non-state versions of the *demos* might very well be in the making. They are subtle and silent, and will involve new forms of governance. The interesting question is whether they can be *democratic* forms of governance.

Can there, then, be different expressions of democracy at the three or four levels – local, regional, state-national, supranational – that we have identified? Can there even be non-territorial democracies? We begin to understand that the *demos* is not always clearly-defined and that the better conception of democracy is one that operates with inclusive procedures[9] of participation in the decisions that shape the way of life or the lifeworld in a community. This is the essence of politics, the discourse of the *polis*. But we can see that the higher the level removed from citizens and their communities is, the less opportunities for participation and the greater the risk of alienation and disconnection between citizens and relevant decision-makers becomes. Other stakeholders with particular interests can reach the decision-makers at higher levels. Where normative decisions on the lifeworld, and the market are adopted, they take the form of legally predefined sources of law, following legally predefined procedures. Decision-makers are to be formally mandated or authorised to make decisions representing their constituencies, but it is often the case that their constituencies are not fully aware of what is being decided and what is at stake in the adopted decisions. The responsibility of the decision-makers and the opposition candidates is, therefore, to be as informed as possible about the implications and repercussions of all proposed legislation and to seek the advice and the opinions of their constituents. Subsidiarity can imply precisely this *awareness* of impact.

Perhaps, there is excessive juridification or legalism in the EU, and politics is dominated by technical, institutionalised law-making and new modes of governance. Perhaps, there is fragmentation from the inside, with each sub-system having its own particular logic and perhaps it is difficult to interpret these processes from a coherent standpoint. The discussion at the EU law- and policy-making levels becomes technical, rather than principled, is subject to pressure from interest groups specialised in each field and from stakeholders that are more influential than relevant, and, accordingly, the feeling of a genuine political discussion is lost, and thus the elements to reintroduce overall coherence are called for in order to bring the whole legal and political process under meaningful action, at least meaningful to those affected. As mentioned above, this seems more plausible the closer the decisions are made to citizens. But the counter-argument usually runs that the important processes are not locally decided, but globally decided, and this seems to justify action at the higher levels, removed from the citizens. For democracy to be at all meaningful, citizens would then need to be properly involved in these processes, including the transnational processes that bring about the effects which we tend to call globalisation: understanding procedures, having the relevant factual information and understanding it, being able to foresee the consequences of their decisions, mandating their representatives with precise terms and being in a position to call their representatives into account, and having a forum to question decision-makers based in other jurisdictions. If these forms of participation required by modern versions of democracy are to be meaningful, it becomes crucial for citizens to detect a sense of direction at all levels of the *polis*: this is the only way to expect them to

---

[9]See S. Besson, *The Morality of Conflict, A Study on Reasonable Disagreement in the Law* (Oxford: Hart Publishing, 2005); and W. Kymlicka, *Liberalism, Community and Culture* (Oxford: Oxford University Press, 1989); *Multicultural Citizenship* (Oxford: Oxford University Press, 1996); and *Multicultural Odysseys: Navigating the New International Politics of Diversity* (Oxford: Oxford University Press, 2007).

partake in the *demos* and have a sense of identity. Macro-economic objectives such as those set out in the Lisbon Agenda, now 2020 Strategy, especially with the sustainable development turn it took in the Gottemborg summit, combating all forms of discrimination or protecting human rights and fighting climate change are all higher level aims which provide the EU with a *telos* and a sense of direction.

It is not certain whether citizens will actually develop a sense of identity upon the basis of such universal ambitions, thereby allowing a European *demos* gradually to emerge and develop, but it seems plausible that, without them, politics at the EU level will remain a domain reserved for initiates, élites, experts and lobbies. But if the media are not there to report what is at stake and whose interests are dominating, and if public opinion, civil society, NGOs and political parties are not interested, then how can the citizens be expected to remain involved and supportive to the extent that the entity can be said to enjoy some form of democratic legitimacy, assuming, that is, that citizen involvement is something that interests not only the key decision-makers, but also all those who believe in democratic governance.[10] The risk of the no-*demos* (i.e., no pan-European *demos*) is, therefore, that the important decisions adopted in a polity go, largely, unchecked by those who are greatly affected by those decisions. The alternative picture of the EU is that a purely technical and bureaucratic intergovernmental forum, left to the diplomacy and policy-negotiation skills and know-how of government officials, trusted to bring about welfare and benefits to their respective *demoi*. The history of European integration shows constitutional episodes or moments, which can be understood from either of these standpoints, and the recent developments from the 2001 Laeken Declaration to the 2008 Irish referendum on the Treaty of Lisbon confirm the difficulties the EU is encountering in coming to terms with its own democratic aspirations. Resistance to the so-called European super-state can sometimes be interpreted as the perceived risks of the decline of the sovereign nation-state, and as agonistic and sentimental attempts to preserve it, or to save whatever is left of it. For some, this is a futile attempt, akin to resisting the incoming tide; for others, it is the only way to make sure that this process will not develop into something truly supranational.

Purely formal sovereignty is thus analysed as an all-or-nothing question, equivalent to state personality in international law. Traditionally, this has been interpreted as the unrestrained prerogative to make laws, and immunity from external interference or pressure in norm-making, but, in the EC, EU and ECHR, this full power and immunity no longer hold, they have become system-relative or competence-bound. The sovereignty of the states has an interesting common projection into the European Community and into the European Union. Formally, the EC was a very special type of international organisation, so special that it developed into its own

[10]On the other hand, when an issue decided at European level gets sufficient public attention, the citizens are keen to have a voice, as the discussions on the services (for example, the Bolkenstein) directive showed.

genus, the EU, an unclassifiable entity: the type of sovereignty that the EU might enjoy comes from its legal personality as an international organisation, and from the powers and competences exercised, in concert, by the sovereign Member States or attributed by them to the Common Institutions.

The resulting scenario is one in which different polities, below and above the state, exhibit formal sovereignty along with traditional nation-state sovereignty. The fact that these new forms of sovereignty can ultimately be traced back to the state, both formally and conceptually, no longer implies that they are state dependent or state forms of sovereignty. Below the state, the development of constitutional regions has actually transformed the very understanding of complex states. Take the example of contemporary Belgium in the EU or of Switzerland, outside the EU: they are inconceivable as anything other than consociational states constituted by their infra-state entities. The formation of the will of the state is a complex result of participation and concert between these regions. Similarly, when talking about the criminal laws of the Member States, one cannot sidestep the fact that states such as the UK have more than one system of criminal law, that there is no national criminal law above that of Scotland, Northern Ireland, and England and Wales, and possibly other special cases for some of the islands, for example, Jersey, the Isle of Man, *etc*. Thus, the formal sovereignty of a state transforms into something more nuanced if we are talking about criminal law in the UK or if we are talking about corporate taxation in Spain, where there are five different quasi-sovereign legislators: the three historic territories of the Basque Autonomous Community, the Foral Community of Navarre, and the common regime of the rest of Spain.

Going beyond the slightly misguided impression that Member States are now powerless, whereas the EU would be almighty, or that infra-state levels of governance such as the regions, not to mention cities, have no role at all to play in the sovereignty game, the analytical maps show more nuanced and complex ways in which classical state-national sovereignty has been transformed in the world context since the creation of the UN and other international organisations, and, in the case of postwar Europe, since the creation of the European Communities and the Council of Europe.

If we take nation-states such as Luxembourg, Estonia, Portugal, Malta, Ireland or Bulgaria, would we say that they have altogether lost or gained in sovereignty as a result of these processes? Clearly, if sovereignty is to be understood as the formal normative capacity to make laws, unrestrained by external influences or commitments, then those states have willingly limited or reduced that capacity by assuming certain international law obligations, but, even theorists of formal sovereignty – except those who hold on to the theory that the Queen in Parliament has no limits – will say that they have done so exercising their external sovereignty as the relevant subjects of international law. A country such as Ireland can stop the entry into force of a treaty (the Treaties of Lisbon) that it has formally signed with 26 other Member States, and the rest accept this as constitutional orthodoxy because the Treaty which they have signed consecrates precisely this model of the necessary ratification by each and everyone of the national *demoi*. Formally speaking, Ireland acquired formidable weight, and a formidable responsibility as well, for although it had signed the Treaty of Lisbon, it did not ratify it on a first referendum and, for a number of months it was blocking the entry into force of the Treaty, which requires ratification in all the Member States: this gave Ireland extraordinary power, Likewise, a small Member State enjoys over-representation in the European Parliament and a quality vote in the Council (the part of the vote not related to its population) as compared to the larger Member States, as the Federal Constitutional Court of Germany has observed in its Lisbon ruling of 30 June 2009.[11]

This extraordinary formal power gained by smaller Member States involved in the current stage of the development of European integration might be a powerful argument in favour of internal enlargement and independence in Europe. For those nation-regions that are currently part of a larger Member State, the suggestion might be to secede from those plurinational states and to set up their own Member State, in order to gain the type of formal sovereignty afforded by member statehood.

It comes as no surprise, that sub-state national parties such as the Scottish National Party, to which Neil MacCormick contributed, should have argued for Member State status within the EU. In these proposals, the vision of the EU tends to be rather static, remaining as it is – a commonwealth – or, alternatively, a confederation. My own approach differs slightly from that of MacCormick's, precisely because it takes the evolution of the EU into account. If something like the United States of Europe develops, the issue of independence in Europe becomes, at the same time, both less tragic and less attractive. For one, the Member States would relinquish part of the formal sovereignty which is ensured by the power of veto, thus making it less attractive to become a federated state and making it more attractive to form part of a larger voting-*bloc*. On the other hand, alliances between smaller federated states will be possible, and one cannot always take it for granted that the larger federated state will defend the interests of one of its nation-regions. But the choice becomes less tragic for those who are against it: secession is currently a traumatic decision because a formally sovereign Member State loses one of its component nations, but, if all these nations agree to federate into a larger state, there would simply be a re-arrangement of the federation, and thus there is no real secession to combat. I argue for a federal Europe to which, even formally, the current Member States would have vested not just specific powers, but formal or external sovereignty as well, maintaining the right to exit and regain formal sovereignty. This is not the way that I would reconstruct the current EU, but, rather, how I would like to see it transforming in the near future, as a European Federation. In this ideal scenario, the current nation-states would become nation-regions and there would be nothing dramatic in the current multinational Member States dividing up and generating new nation-regions, unless they choose to develop their multi-national status and federate, as multi-national regions with other European nation-regions. This is, of course, a claim for the transformation of Europe.

[11] BVerfG, 2BvE 2/08 vom 30.6.2009, Absatz-Nr (1–421).

The development of the EU follows efforts that pull in different directions, some towards greater integration and efficiency, others towards self-respect for the traditions and regional identities of the Member States, thereby seeking the preservation of different centres of decision-making, but still calling for a successful operating Union. If Europe is diverse and polycentric, as I certainly want it to be, it will hardly move forward smoothly without tensions or contradictions. What is essential is that it is not blocked in deciding what to do, thus failing to deliver internally and as a world actor.

Chapter 13
Nationalism, Patriotism and Diversity – Conceptualising the National Dimension in Neil MacCormick's Post-sovereign Constellation

John Erik Fossum

13.1 Introduction

Nationalism is probably the dominant political ideology in today's world, and it is also deeply institutionalised. In all nation states, there is a whole gamut of mechanisms and symbols that serves to remind us constantly that we are living in a national place and in a world of nations; and "this reminding is so familiar, so continual, that it is not consciously registered as reminding".[1] Nationalism has been so widely accepted because the nation state has been understood as the foremost (many see it as the only convincing and historically tested) carrier of popular democracy.

The term "nation" is generally understood to refer to a specific type of community based upon a form of fraternity and solidarity. This form of fraternity and solidarity translates into a sense of community – which is maintained and shaped by patterns of communication and interaction. There is now considerable agreement among analysts, certainly of a liberal bent, that a nation is an invented, or even an imagined, community,[2] i.e., some symbols and aspects of a community's past are highlighted at the expense of others:

> Only the symbolic construction of 'a people' makes the modern state into a nation-state.[3]

The raw material for the construction of national identity is also generally understood to be:

> a historic territory: common myths and historical memories; common, mass public culture; common legal rights and duties for all members; [and] a common economy with territorial mobility for members.[4]

J.E. Fossum (✉)
ARENA, University of Oslo, Oslo, Norway
e-mail: j.e.fossum@arena.uio.no

[1] M. Billig, *Banal Nationalism* (London: SAGE, 1995), p. 8.

[2] B. Anderson, *Imagined Communities* (London: Verso, 1991).

[3] J. Habermas, *The Postnational Constellation: Political Essays* (Cambridge: Polity Press, 2001), p. 64.

[4] A. D. Smith, *National Identity* (London: Penguin, 1991), p. 14; see, also, Neil MacCormick, *Questioning Sovereignty* (Oxford: Oxford University Press, 1999), p. 186.

A.J. Menéndez, J.E. Fossum (eds.), *Law and Democracy in Neil MacCormick's Legal and Political Theory*, Law and Philosophy Library 93,
DOI 10.1007/978-90-481-8942-7_13,

National identity is based upon the conception of a collective national consciousness, whose sources are culturally based, but need not be pre-determined or given, and can be forged. There are different views on how "thick" this sense of community and belonging is, and from where it is derived. A widely accepted distinction is between a civic and an ethnic nation.[5] The former locates the sources foremost in politico-legal institutional traits, the latter in ethno-cultural social traits.

In today's world, there are several important trends which suggest that the role of nationalism is changing. Globalisation, Europeanisation and sub-state regionalisation are three important developments that raise questions regarding the continued link between the state and the nation within a world in which the state's system of sovereign control is weakened.

It is against this backdrop that I will consider an important contribution to the debate, namely, that of Neil MacCormick. The focus of this chapter is on MacCormick's conception of national identity and nationalism in a world in which both the state and state sovereignty are undergoing important changes.[6] MacCormick's position is particularly interesting for at least three reasons.

The first is his effort to address this situation by devising a conception of nationalism that is culturally imbued, but certainly not essentialist. If anything, MacCormick goes to great lengths to point out the excesses of nationalism – historical as well as contemporary. His effort should therefore be understood as a serious critical attempt to consider whether we may be able to rescue nationalism in a changing global context – a context which he finds, on balance, to be more favourable to such a rescue operation. But this rescue operation, he argues, can only be ensured through the manner in which liberal autonomy can be put to the task of transforming nationalism, as set out in the notion of liberal nationalism.[7]

The second is that MacCormick takes the present changes and transformation seriously. He explicitly and self-consciously casts his discussion of nationalism within a post-sovereign frame. MacCormick underlines that the contemporary world

---

[5] J. Hutchinson and A. D. Smith (eds), *Nationalism*, Vol. I (London: Routledge, 2000).

[6] The most comprehensive statement and the one most systematically addressed here is *Questioning Sovereignty* (from here on, this work is referred to as QS), note 4 *supra*. But see, also, MacCormick's writings in: "Beyond the Sovereign State", (1993) 56 *The Modern Law Review*, pp. 1–18; "Liberalism, Nationalism and the Post-Sovereign State", (1996) 44 *Political Studies*, pp. 553–567; "The Rise of Scottish Nationalism", (1974) 44 *The Round Table*, pp. 425-438; "The Health of Nations and the Health of Europe", (2005) 7 *The Cambridge Yearbook of European Legal Studies*, pp. 1-16; "Nation and Nationalism", in: R. Beiner (ed), *Theorizing Nationalism*, (Albany NY: SUNY Press, 1999), pp. 189–204; "Does a Nation need a State?" in: E. Mortimer and R. Fine (eds), *People, Nation and State: The meaning of Ethnicity and Nationalism*, (London: I.B. Tauris, 1999), pp. 125–137; "Independence and Constitutional Change", in: Neil MacCormick, *The Scottish Debate: Essays on Scottish Nationalism*, (Oxford: Oxford University Press, 1970), pp. 52–62; *idem*, *Legal Reasoning and Legal Theory*, (Oxford: Clarendon Press, 1978).

[7] As initially developed by Yael Tamir, *Liberal Nationalism*, (Princeton NJ: Princeton University Press, 1993). See, also, D. Miller, *On Nationality*, (Oxford: Oxford University Press, 1995). Here, I do not distinguish between liberal nationalism and civic nationalism, as there are quite a few affinities between those generally listed under the second wave of nationalism, be they formally labelled as civic or liberal nationalists.

is one in which nationalism is undergoing important changes, mainly because of transformations in the constitutive features of its main organisational carrier, the sovereign state. This applies, in particular, to the European Union as a "post-sovereign entity".[8] It might also be said to apply to the UK as a multi-national state. Both entities represent cases of the de-linking of the nation and the state.[9] This raises the issue, as to whether, and, if so, the extent to which, nationalism can be made compatible with the simultaneous patterns of supra-state integration driven by the European integration process, on the one hand, and state fragmentation driven, for instance, by the case of Scottish nationalism, on the other.

The third reason for the focus on MacCormick's work is, broadly speaking, about theory. This has two facets. On the one hand, MacCormick's conception of nationalism will necessarily draw on his institutional conception of law, since the law plays such a vital role in the liberal reading of nationalism to which MacCormick also subscribes. How nationalism, and – in broader terms – attachment and allegiance, figure in this institutional theory of law is an important topic unto itself. On the other hand, there is the broader question of attachment and allegiance in a changing world. How can political systems attach citizens when the key legal-political institutions that have sustained state sovereignty are undergoing significant changes? Will nationalism be up to the task?

MacCormick does not see the need to abandon nationalism in the light of the changes in the constitutive features of the state (i.e., the post-sovereign constellation). He does nevertheless argue for the need to reconsider nationalism in order to ensure that it can properly accommodate itself to this changed context. Viewed in this light, one critical issue is to clarify MacCormick's position on nationalism. Doing so includes three sets of investigations. The first is to outline his conception of liberal nationalism, including its underlying theory of allegiance formation and sustenance. Given that the law will obviously play a role here, it is necessary to spell out the link to, or the role of, the institutional theory of law. The second is to assess critically whether liberal nationalism is a tamed version of nationalism. The third is to discuss whether the European Union qualifies as a post-sovereign liberal nationalist vanguard, in the sense of properly tamed nationalism.

One central aspect pertaining to MacCormick's position on attachment and allegiance is whether a transformation of revolutionary proportions can be adequately captured within the nationalist framework that he has devised. The issue is not only one of MacCormick's conception of nationalism and whether it is apt for such a changed context, it is also a matter of the underlying assumptions that modern nationalism rests upon. This brings into focus assumptions about the role of the state and its attendant presuppositions of sovereignty – legal and political. Will salvaging nationalism promote the development of the post-sovereign constellation in today's Europe? Or does it require a different perspective on attachment and allegiance? This requires us to focus on the character of the European construct, and whether

---

[8]QS, note 4 *supra*, p. 95 and pp. 137–56.

[9]QS; see, also, MacCormick, "Does a Nation need a State?", note 6 *supra*.

there are modes of allegiance that not only serve as real alternatives to the national and nationalism, but also capture the distinct features of the European Union as a post-sovereign constellation. I will argue that cosmopolitanism is not only suitable to the post-sovereign constellation, but that it is also in line with MacCormick's broader conception of the European legal-political configuration.

13.2 Liberal Nationalism

Liberal nationalism might be construed as a form of "tamed" nationalism.[10] It is a response to the many problems embedded in nationalism, in particular, the numerous tragic excesses which we have witnessed from its ethnic variant. MacCormick is very much aware of these problems, and consequently underlines that a central concern for adherents of nationalism is to subject it properly to the requirement of individual autonomy that lies at the very heart of the liberal project; hence the prefix "liberal".

> Autonomy is indeed a fundamental human good, and thus it is a great social value to uphold societies that facilitate it.[11]

At the same time, MacCormick is highly sceptical of the peculiar understanding of methodological individualism that posits persons as atomised or as a-social individuals,[12] and which informs some of the liberal positions. He, instead, underlines that individuals are socially embedded persons, or "contextual individuals".[13] Liberal nationalism seeks to reconcile nationalism's onus on the socio-cultural context (as expressed in the notion that individuals are socially-embedded persons) with liberalism's onus on rights-based individual autonomy. How this is reconciled is a key to the broader understanding of MacCormick's conception of society, community, and law, in the post-sovereign constellation.

There is, of course, a clear cultural reference to the notion of "contextual individuals", because the context in which individuals are shaped, is conditioned by the particular or distinct community in which they live.

> Culture and institutions are attached to a given place, a country, and are of special significance to those who live there, because they belong to (or in) it as much as it belongs to them. This is a critical part of the context of the contextual individual in many parts of the contemporary world.[14]

---

[10]MacCormick notes that this is a form of tamed nationalism; see QS, p. 167. It might also be added here that MacCormick's main empirical reference, Scottish nationalism, was very different from the context within which Tamir's notion emerged, namely, the Israeli context, which, if anything, would expose a deep ambivalence.

[11]QS, p. 164.

[12]QS, p. 162.

[13]QS, p. 162.

[14]QS, p. 182.

In line with this, MacCormick's notion of liberal nationalism embraces nationalism as an ideology of communal self-determination, and as "a political culture: it colours how we identify ourselves, how we justify policies and political programmes, and how we mobilize support for such programmes".[15] The nationalism that is embedded in liberal nationalism is, therefore, a mode of attachment that elicits support and sustenance from those elements that are constitutive of us as persons. As MacCormick notes,

> humans as moral and practical beings have ties and links of sympathy and fellow-feeling with other individuals. They have like ties in a more diffuse way with larger groups and communities of people. These particular links of sentiment are not just accidental features of phenomenal human beings aside from their rationally intelligible moral character. They are a part of what makes it possible for people to have moral character at all.[16]

An important point is that the liberal's freedom of choice has socio-cultural preconditions. Kymlicka underlines the cultural dimension of this:

> it is only through having access to a societal culture that people have access to a range of meaningful options.[17]

In a sense, then, and seen from this angle, liberal nationalism should be seen as an attempt to reconcile a liberal *ethos* with a communitarian ethos.[18] What this suggests is, therefore, that the tension that is built into liberal nationalism is one that pits autonomy against authenticity – the notion that there are certain ways of living communally that are more appropriate reflections of a person's sense of self, including basic values and worldviews. Whether or how the relation between autonomy and authenticity can be worked out is obviously important, but with the important proviso that, for MacCormick, the social dimension must be properly included in this equation.

MacCormick 's position on how this putative tension within liberal nationalism can be worked out is very interesting, because he situates the notion of liberal nationalism not in the sovereign democratic state, but instead within the post-sovereign constellation. The point of departure is precisely that the sovereign state has not struck a viable balance here. It inculcates an assimilationist and exclusivist mode of nationalism which curtails autonomy understood as communal self-governing. The majority can easily use the state's powers to subject minoritarian nationalisms to

---

[15]W. Norman, *Negotiating Nationalism*, (Oxford: Oxford University Press, 2006), p. xvi.

[16]QS, p. 180.

[17]W. Kymlicka, *Multicultural Citizenship*, (Oxford: Oxford University Press, 1995), p. 83.

[18]As Wayne Norman has noted, "nationalism can be considered to be one of the most successful forms of communitarian politics in the modern world". (Norman note 15 *supra*, p. viii) MacCormick's emphasis on "contextual individuals", then, also has clear resonance with Charles Taylor's notion of the modern identity. See C. Taylor, *Human Agency and Language*, (Cambridge: Cambridge University Press, 1985); *Philosophy and the Human Sciences*, (Cambridge: Cambridge University Press, 1986); and notably *Sources of the Self: The Making of the Modern Identity*, (Cambridge MA: Harvard University Press, 1989).

strong homogenising measures, and effectively deprive a minority nationalism of its right to democratic self-government.

The post-sovereign constellation changes this. It entails a significant reconfiguration of sovereignty, which may either entail a significant change in the internal dimension of sovereignty, or in both its external and internal dimensions. One aspect is that it opens the way for territorial exit of sub-units (which is very difficult under prevailing international law). Another aspect is that the internal relations within the political order are reconfigured. This constellation has democratic potential: it offers new possibilities for dealing with minority national exclusion since state sovereignty is weakened or undermined through the creation of, and/or recognition of, legal orders below, above and beyond the nation-state. Possibly, this is precisely because law is not coterminous with the state. MacCormick understands law as an institutional normative order. Law understood as an institutional normative order may overlap with the state, but the two do not need to cohere fully. Law can exist as a normative order without a supportive state, and a political system can harbour several institutional normative orders.[19] Thus, law as institutional normative order is entirely compatible with legal pluralism, which is the type of legal structure that is most conducive to liberal nationalism and the post-national constellation. This type of legal structure is more conducive to minority nationalisms, because there is no longer a sovereign state that can harness the law in the service of national assimilation. Legal pluralism offers a bulwark or protective device for minority nationalisms, and also operates simultaneously as an effective brake on every majoritarian assimilationist attempt.

MacCormick thus addresses the tension built into liberal nationalism in several related manners. The first is through considering certain aspects of the socio-cultural context in which individuals are located as being autonomy-enhancing. Whether these individuals are able to govern themselves in and through their community is important to their autonomy. Self-government in this sense establishes or protects, through collective means, those features of the socio-cultural context that the individuals collectively understand as important to their individual autonomy.

> If autonomous individuals require the context of some sort of freedom-enabling society, then the collective autonomy of the society itself seems a part of the necessary context.[20]

Democratic self-governing is autonomy-enhancing in that it is a vital component to ensure that the community undertakes those social functions that permit individuals to be fully autonomous in a social sense. This argument, as we shall see, also extends to aspects of culture.

The second is to reconsider the possible answers to the inherent dilemma of democracy, namely, that there is no democratic method – intrinsic to democracy itself – of determining the *who* of democracy, or the democratic *demos* within the

---

[19] QS, p. 25.

[20] QS, p. 164.

post-sovereign constellation which is marked by reconfigured relations between territory and systems of governing.[21]

In order to address this dilemma, what is required is a set of presuppositions of membership (and citizenship) to determine who are accepted as part of the community, and of how, and in what sense, they are part; of identity (people need to identify with the community for this to make up a community in the first place); and of legitimacy, as people must believe that the community's basic norms are just and valid for this to make up a democracy.

The third is that subsidiarity within the post-sovereign constellation opens the conceptual and political space for reconsidering the problem of size in democracy. In principle, subsidiarity can configure the polity in such a manner that those elements of our existence that are constitutive for us as persons can be dealt with in local-regional contexts (communal subsidiarity), without this preventing legally-binding political and economic co-operation at higher levels (rational-legislative and market subsidiarity) that is properly subject to deliberative-democratic norms and procedures.[22] This structure makes it possible to reconcile (minority) nationalisms within an overarching non-state communal framework that does not need to assume the character of a nation.

MacCormick argues that nations have a right to democratic self-government.[23] Every nation has that right, but it does not amount to exclusive territorial control along the lines of the sovereign state. What constitutes a nation is therefore important to establish.

> A nation is constituted by a sense in its members of important (even if internally diverse) cultural community with each other based in a shared past, a 'heritage' of common ways and traditions, including at least some of a family of items such as language, literature, legend and mythology, music, educational usages, legal tradition, and religious tradition.[24]

Autonomy-guaranteeing democratic institutions combine with a sense of communal attachment and identification to render the political system legitimate. But this system differs from the sovereign state, in that the membership conditions – and requirements – are very different. The post-sovereign constellation is configured along the lines of subsidiarity, which entails that citizens have membership in multiple communities, which undertake different, albeit complementary, functions. Thus,

---

[21] This is a matter of vital importance to the contemporary conception of justice. It brings up the issue of the proper frame within which to consider substantive questions of justice. See, for instance, N. Fraser, "Reframing Justice in a Globalizing World", (2005), 36 of the second series *New Left Review*, pp. 69–88.

[22] The notion of comprehensive subsidiarity refers to how representative democracy is supplemented with extensive processes of open and effective deliberation (QS, p. 154).

[23] "(T)he members of a nation are as such in principle entitled to effective organs of political self-government within the world order of sovereign or post-sovereign states." (QS, p. 173).

[24] QS, p. 186.

> (c)hoices between claims of different nations can cease to be choices between rival claims to sovereign statehood over disputed territories and populations. They can become choices about allocation of levels of political authority within a transnational commonwealth embracing many nationalities and cultural traditions or groupings.[25]

Thus, there are new and more inclusive opportunities for democratic self-governing in the contemporary post-sovereign context because of the changes which it ushers in, which promise to reconfigure our established and largely taken-for-granted state-based national societies.

This position should locate MacCormick as one of the very early forerunners of the "second-wave" nationalism theorists.[26] MacCormick shares with "first-wavers" the need to legitimise nationalist enquiry, but, in doing so, he also moves the discussion forward and into the "second wave" by explicitly associating liberal nationalism with the post-sovereign constellation. In this sense, he, arguably, also goes further than the liberal theorists who seek to formulate ways for national minorities to co-exist within the framework of the multi-national federal state.[27]

13.3 Post-sovereign Liberal Nationalism Assessed

The post-sovereign framework is designed to replace domination with justification. One obvious advantage with this framework is that the overarching structure must justify why the community should stay together. The point is that the post-sovereign structure places a much stronger onus on the need for such a justification (perhaps even in an ongoing manner), because there is no recourse to either the form of coercion or to the strong mechanisms of assimilation that the sovereign state has available. Thus, there is a greater scope for reflexivity, which entails that the polity is open to challenge, re-interpretation, and amendment. A reflexive polity is not only open to deliberative challenge, it is also a forum for critical self-examination on who we are, who we should be, who we are thought to be, and who we think we are.

The onus on justification is also intrinsic to subsidiarity, whose three core principles are specifically designed to render the overarching structure reflexive:

---

[25]QS, p. 191.

[26]Neil MacCormick spoke of a liberal version of nationalism as early as 1982, in his *Liberal Right and Social Democracy*, (Oxford: Oxford University Press, 1982). See, also, Joxerramon Bengoetxea's chapter in this volume. For the distinction between "first" and "second-wave" nationalism, see Norman, note 15 *supra*.

[27]Consider notably W. Kymlicka, *Liberalism, Community, and Culture*, (Oxford: Oxford University Press, 1989); *Multicultural Citizenship. A Liberal Theory of Minority Rights*, (Oxford: Clarendon Press, 1995); *Finding our way*, (Oxford: Oxford University Press, 1998); Norman, note 15 *supra*; A.-G. Gagnon and J. Tully (eds), *Multinational Democracies*, (Cambridge: Cambridge University Press, 2001). I say "arguably" because I would also claim that the key reference case for theorists of multinational federalism, namely, Canada, has clear built-in cosmopolitan traits.

> The first is linked to the idea of inviolate and inalienable rights. Not only individuals but also communities have such rights. There are some rights a higher level under no circumstances can revoke, or a lower level give away...
> The second proposition is that a higher level has a duty to support a lower level to the degree that this helps the lower level to fulfil its true potential...
> The third proposition is that 'the principle of subsidiarity governs the burden of proof'... The higher level is obliged, through arguments, to make it clear why a decision should be taken at a higher level.[28]

We might add that MacCormick's notion of comprehensive subsidiarity is intended to inject a deliberative component as a vital supplement to representative democracy into the entire structure.

Having said that the post-sovereign scenario also brings up a number of problems and challenges. One critical issue is to clarify whether the answer to who has a right to self-government will end up enhancing democracy or stymieing it. Finding a proper answer to this question is a major challenge for democratic theory, with some of the most innovative solutions coming from transnationalists such as James Bohman.[29]

Nationalism figures as a central component in triggering the right to minoritarian self-government in the post-sovereign constellation. MacCormick argues that, in today's societies, the main problem rests with the state and state sovereignty, not with the nation and nationalism.[30] There is, as he notes, a close link between nationalism and the right to self-government, and this link has a bearing on the social significance of national identity:

> (c)ontextual individuals may have as one among their most significant contexts some national identity. To that extent, respect for national identities, and commitment in principle to the nationalist principle stated above [the members of a nation are as such and in principle entitled to effective organs of political self-government], are not merely not incompatible with nationalism, but are actually required by it.[31]

Given nationalism's central role, it is important to clarify how it figures here. It is, after all, the ability of citizens to understand themselves as the authors of the laws that they are affected by that is the core condition for democratic self-government, and this is clearly also present in MacCormick's line of reasoning.[32] But, for

---

[28] L.C. Blichner and L. Sangolt, "The Concept of Subsidiarity and the Debate on European Cooperation: Pitfalls and Possibilities", (1994) 7 *Governance*, pp. 284–306, at 289. This also has a clear affinity to MacCormick's conception of subsidiarity; see QS (notably Chapter 9); see, also, his *Institutions of Law*, (Oxford: Oxford University Press, 2007), p. 266.

[29] See J. Bohman, *Democracy across Borders. From Dêmos to Dêmoi*, (Cambridge MA: The MIT Press, 2007).

[30] QS, p. 190.

[31] N. MacCormick, note 7 *supra*, p. 132.

[32] But it should be noted that regional nationalism, in MacCormick's framework, has a kind of federal-democratic role. With regard to the Scottish case, he notes, in his "Independence and Constitutional Change,", note 6 *supra*, p. 53, that: "the centralization of political and economic power round the centre of government, which necessarily characterises modern states, makes it necessary to diversify centres of government. Centralization in its present form will reduce

MacCormick, what triggers this right is the existence of a nation or a national community, regardless of whether it forms a majority or a minority within a larger political entity.

One problem this raises is that, in so far as we assign a right to self-determination to a nation, when and under what conditions can this right be triggered? If all potential nations were to cash in on this claim, we could end up with thousands of nations; thus the principle relies on some element of self-restraint. This has prompted Ronald Beiner to note that "(i)t seems a strange kind of normative principle that relies on its coherence on the willingness of most national groups not to cash in the moral voucher that the principle gives them."[33] We therefore need clear criteria for establishing that this something actually is a nation. This raises the question as to whose claims to this effect are authoritative? One important problem which I see here pertains to the fact that nationalism enjoys such a great legitimacy and prestige in today's world that there is a great propensity, on the part of élites, to want to define a political system as national. In the extension of this, there is what we may term a "reification fallacy": to accept as an already established fact that which one wants to come into existence.[34] This is at the heart of what we may label the ideology of nationalism. The risk for the analyst, the decision-maker, and the public is to be co-opted into type-fixing an entity according to the entity's own self-description, rather than through critical and detached scrutiny. In effect, it renders us vulnerable to the ideology of nationalism, and might prevent us from developing a deeper sense of when a nation is, and *when it is not*. The additional problem is that, in accepting a nationalist claim, one may simply contribute to reify nationalism, and in so doing, also gloss over changes in the modes of allegiance and the sense of community in a more globalised world.

In order to address these issues, it is important to look more closely at the type of nationalism that MacCormick has in mind, and how he understands it to be both produced and sustained. In what sense is MacCormick's liberal nationalism different from mainstream ones? The point is that the appropriate nationalism must somehow provide us with assurances that minority nationalisms will not develop exclusivist propensities, or discriminate against either minorities within, or members of the majority within. It also follows that they cannot prevent the members of a minority

Scotland the worst sort of provincialism and parochialism, unless a real centre of power is established in Scotland." To this effect, it should also be added that Scotland already had its own legal system and a distinctive political culture, related to the specific path the reformation took in the most northern parts of Great Britain.

[33] See R. Beiner (ed), *Theorizing Nationalism*, (New York: SUNY Press, 1999), p. 5.

[34] Jacob Levy has cogently argued that: "'Nation' does not denote a kind of community describable apart from nationalist projects and the claim of national self-determination. Once we have a sociologically persuasive account of where a 'nation' is, we find that one way or another the political mobilization that nationalist theory is supposed to justify is already part of how we have picked the community out. In other words the political program of nationalism is built into the category of nation to begin with; the normative argument is always circular." J. Levy, 'National Minorities Without Nationalism', in: A. Dieckhoff (ed), *The Politics of Belonging: Nationalism, Liberalism, and Pluralism*, (Lanham MD: Lexington Press, 2004), pp. 155–174, at 160.

within, or members who are part of the majority, from relating to other minorities outside, including, presumably, those members who are pursuing alternative nationalist projects.

The liberal dimension of liberal nationalism is supposed to ensure that the community is open to the inclusion of outsiders. Furthermore, the liberal *ethos* posits that there is ready-exit from the community. Subsidiarity is an additional safeguard. But it should be noted that, subsidiarity figures more as a doctrine for social organisation than as an alternative mode of belonging to nationalism, in MacCormick's scheme. Therefore, the question of whether, or in what sense, exit is possible under nationalism still has relevance. In order to address this, we need to look more closely at the mode of attachment that is associated with nationalism, because the *ethos* of nationalism is very much about loyalty. This has bearings on nationalism's civicness, according to Bernhard Yack,[35] who speaks of the myth of the civic nation. This myth is created by the pre-supposition in the civic nation that there is a close connection between political and cultural community. Yack underlines that there is no necessary connection between the two. To show this, he compares the modern situation with the situation of Ancient Greece in order to extrapolate the distinctive feature of modern nationalism. Despite civic nationalism's assertion of civicness, there is a particular form of identity associated with modern nationalism that links loyalty to the nation directly to the sense of personal identity:

> Because it brings political and cultural community together in a way that was foreign to the ancient Greeks, modern nationalism, whether of the civic or the ethnic variety, combines political loyalty with loyalty to oneself.[36]

Thus, in the modern context, to be disloyal to the nation is the same as to betray oneself. This is distinctive of the nationalist *ethos* and locates it in direct conflict with liberal autonomy. From this highly sceptical reading, we find that liberal nationalism is based upon two incompatibles. Is there such an incompatibility in MacCormick's conception of liberal nationalism? There are two issues here which have a direct bearing on MacCormick's theory. The first pertains to the post-sovereign constellation. Is the situation changed in the post-sovereign constellation, in the sense that there is no longer a requirement for the co-existence of cultural and political community? If this is the defining characteristic of the post-sovereign constellation, then the tension to which Yack refers does not exist. The second, and related, issue is whether the post-sovereign constellation is one in which the very notion of nationalism changes, or whether the post-sovereign constellation is one that operates different constraints on nationalism. In other words, does nationalism's onus on loyalty change, or does it remain the same within the post-national constellation? This issue is important in terms of both the durability and the sustainability of the post-sovereign constellation, as well as of the prospects for slipping back to more standard versions of sovereignty.

---

[35] B. Yack, "The Myth of the Civic Nation", (1996) 10 *Critical Review*, pp. 193–211.

[36] Ibid., p. 206.

Is the mode of nationalism that MacCormick depicts one that is clearly and unambiguously different? There are two aspects to this. One is the conception of nationalism; the other is whether communal subsidiarity (where the cultural identities of people are formed and sustained) is sufficiently inclusive. On the latter, the answer has not been spelled out in much detail. On the former, however, he notes that differences in forms of nationalism are matters of degree, and liberal nationalism can also develop ethnic roots (thus communal subsidiarity can also harbour ethnic nationalism). The emphasis on "contextual individuals" and the general manner in which MacCormick depicts nationalism sit rather well with quite mainstream definitions of nationalism.[37] The reliance upon the same basic definition and the onus on different forms as different gradations suggest that it is more a matter of taming nationalism "from the outside" than through liberal nationalism somehow altering the genetic code or ushering in a qualitatively different conception of nationalism *per se*. Central "taming" devices are rights that ensure individual autonomy, together with an emphasis on voluntary membership in the community, the possibility of exiting from the community, and legal pluralism, as such.[38]

This suggests, then, that there may be a built-in tension also in MacCormick's thoughts on nationalism: precisely because he takes both nationalism and liberalism so seriously, he also ends up with a conception of liberal nationalism that harbours a certain tension between a liberal and a communitarian *ethos*.

How significant this tension is requires attention to how liberal nationalism figures in his broader intellectual scheme. This requires attention to the relationship between nationalism and the broader structure that is set up not only to ensure autonomy, but which also conditions the entire manner in which individuals understand themselves as community members and citizens, namely, law. This is also of particular interest because MacCormick has devised a distinct theory of law, namely, the institutional theory of law.

Legal pluralism is understood as a national taming device. Clearly, the post-sovereign constellation operates with weaker mechanisms of power because it is no longer supported by the same levers of power that are found in the sovereign state. This is one of the key elements in taming nationalism: it is no longer possible for any form of nationalism, be it majority or minority, to draw (to the same extent at least) on the mechanisms that have sustained majority forms of nationalism in the sovereign state. But this could also mean that the mechanisms for taming nationalisms would be similarly weakened. This is clearly not MacCormick's

[37]He notes that: "Our sense of identity arises from our experience of belonging within significant communities such as families, schools, workplace communities, religious groups, political associations, sports clubs – and also nations, conceived as cultural communities endowed with political relevance. A nation is constituted by a sense in its members of important (even if internally diverse) cultural community with each other based in a shared past, a 'heritage' of common ways and traditions, including at least some of a family of items such as language, literature, legend and mythology, music, educational usages, legal tradition, and religious tradition." (QS, p. 186)

[38]The two latter points are not only among the designative features of liberal nationalism, they are also positions that the entire body of "second-wave" nationalist theorising has embraced.

view,[39] but it is useful to touch upon it because it sheds light on law's nationally-stabilising role in the post-sovereign constellation, and, in particular, on the question of whether law depends on nationalism for its stability at all. To access this, we need to consider whether nationalism is a necessary complement, or a more contingently-related element, to law in MacCormick's scheme. This is a broad question to which I cannot do full justice here. Consequently, I will confine myself to some brief remarks.

In order to look at this, we should start by considering how nationalism figures in relation to the institutional theory of law. This is relevant because it tells us something about law's underlying socio-cultural foundation, which, in turn, helps us to clarify its relationship to nationalism.[40] Does the sense of belonging to a community, accompanied by loyalty and trust, which nationalism seeks to instil, provide law with a set of necessary or requisite social stabilising devices? This issue matters to MacCormick's theory because it is an *institutional* theory of law. Law programmes social and political institutions, but law is also programmed by more informal social and cultural norms and traditions. Furthermore, it should also be added that many of the institutions that law does, in fact, programme, are institutionalised organisations that develop informal institutional cultures and repertoires of action that may help their sustenance.[41] The gist of this is that the more salient nationalism is in conditioning the law, the weaker will be the law's taming effects on nationalism.

Clearly, the strongest case would be if nationalism were somehow to infuse the "gene code" of law, and to contribute to shape the rationale for the law abidance of the people.[42] This would probably be the case on the far ethnic side of the national scale, but this is also a scenario that MacCormick seeks to guard against. An alternative view is that it is a more complex process that works through the way in which nationalism links in with democracy (with democracy as the means for enlisting the participation of citizens and for instilling in them the notion that they are a self-governing community).

MacCormick's institutional theory of law is not explicitly set up to account for allegiance formation. This is something we need to discern more indirectly through

---

[39]MacCormick could also point to the very resilience of Scotland here, as reflected in its retention of its own legal system, and notably its own common law tradition.

[40]MacCormick, *Institutions of Law*, note 28 *supra*, underlines the central role of what we may label political culture as a central underpinning of law. An important issue, here, is how prominent is the political, as opposed to the cultural, component of such an underpinning element.

[41]See Kymlicka 1998, note 17 *supra*, and Norman note 15 *supra*, Chapter 2, for two comprehensive lists of relevant factors.

[42]In this scenario, if nationalism were to figure as a necessary complement to law, and law is understood as a social institution, we should expect nationalism both to underpin and to give sustenance to a political culture that supports law-abidance. Furthermore, we should expect nationalism to render such an underpinning through a unique or distinct type of – national – support. This would mean that law would be socially embedded; that this social embedding would be vital to law's stability as a socially regulatory mechanism; and that the social embedding would be steeped in a distinct national culture within a distinct national community.

interpretation. The institutional theory of law starts from the notion of normative order, which refers to something that is norm-based and ideal. A normative order is not ideal in a normative-prescriptive sense, understood as "the best of all worlds" sense, but in terms of being norm-based and providing guidelines to direct *praxis*. As such, it is concerned with putting ideals into a practically realisable state.[43] Institutional normative order is normative in the sense that norms are understood to guide conduct; it is also normative in that the relevant norms carry value, in the sense of being valuable. It is institutional in that it forms a system capable of both passing and enforcing judgments. When institutionalised the normative order has a certain self-referential quality,

> there is a way, conclusive within the system, for determining what counts as an authoritative norm of the system, or a definitely established right or duty of some person under the system.[44]

Human beings are inculcated into this order through patterns of nurture, socialisation and education. Law is institutional normative order and is distinct from politics, which is about power and capability. Law, in contrast, being a normative order, is not value-free or ethically neutral, and as such resembles critical morality. But it is, nevertheless, also distinct from critical morality. Law is positive and "jurisdiction-relative", in contrast to morality that may be controversial, but whose moral judgements have universal applicability.

MacCormick's institutional theory of law is thus based upon the notion of humans as norm-oriented actors.[45] It also clearly recognises that law has informal social roots and anchorings. MacCormick notes that the institutionalisation that underpins the constitutional state is one where "the formal rests on informal, customary foundations".[46] Furthermore, he notes that "law [is] indeed a part of culture in its broader sense".[47] But the way in which he depicts humans as norm-oriented does not programme them as reliable *national* carriers. MacCormick also underlines the notion of spontaneous order, which is deeply rooted in universalistic moral principles of justice and fairness. This is to highlight that the law embodies a clear connection between the normative imagination and inclination of human beings, on the one hand, and institutional structures, on the other. One way to approach this is to underline that law has built into it a coherent regulatory ideal, which pertains not

---

[43] There is a clear ambiguity here, however. Norms do prescribe certain courses of action and rule out others, and, in doing so, they promote certain values and world-views and downplay other.

[44] QS, p. 8. He further notes that "the characteristic of an institutional normative order is that competent judgement in it is conclusive within its own order, except to the extent that there is coordinated cross-recognition of different orders". Ibid.

[45] Consider the strong emphasis on habits about rules and of how rule following becomes routinised behaviour because the human mind is in the habit of forming habits, (see MacCormick *Institutions of Law*, note 28 *supra*, Chapter 4.

[46] Ibid., p. 304.

[47] QS, p. 173.

only to systemic coherence, but which, in the modern world, is also infused with the norms of democratic constitutionalism.

This also means that it is where the institutional theory of law operates in a national context that law might be, somehow, nationally imprinted. But since law does not need nationalism for its sustenance, there is nothing, as such, that translates the notion of human beings as norm-oriented beings into vehicles for institutionally encoding nationalism into law. It should be added that MacCormick's notion of law as institutional order underlines law's built-in reflexivity and defeasibility.[48] These are factors that render any system of established truths about national origins, national character, and national distinctness open to deliberative challenge and contestation.

From these comments, it should be clear that, whereas law has socially-integrative functions, they are not dependent on a particular communal doctrine such as nationalism. In this sense, the relationship between law and nationalism is clearly contingent, at the very most. Nationalism *may* increase the socially-integrative functions of law, but then through various mechanisms. One is the manner in which nationalism contributes to define the community by adding criteria regarding who is a member of the national community and who is not, and by programming procedures and institutions to inculcate national allegiance.[49] The legal means for regulating exit and entry and for social inculcation could, however, also be tailored to suit other social doctrines entirely compatible with law as institutional normative order. Thus, the relationship between law and nationalism appears *quite contingent*. From this, we can see that there is not such a great tension within MacCormick's overarching scheme because nationalism figures less prominently here. However, when we look at the more concrete portrayal of nationalism, the tension re-appears. How much of the tension thus remains will, to a great extent, hinge upon the taming effect of the post-sovereign constellation, which requires explicit attention to the European Union as the foremost example of the post-sovereign constellation.

13.4 Some Further Reflections on Nationalism

Before doing so, I will look a bit more closely at what taming nationalism might entail. Can nationalism be properly tamed? Investigating this also serves as a prelude to the discussion of the possible alternatives to nationalism. This brief assessment should be seen, first and foremost, as a methodological attempt to establish which factors we need to bear in mind when thinking about how nationalism – as political doctrine, ideology, and institutional reality – actually shapes our conceptions of

---

[48] MacCormick, *Institutions of Law*, note 28 *supra*. See, also, his *Rhetoric and the Rule of Law*, (Oxford: Oxford University Press, 2005.

[49] Through citizenship provisions, the law programmes the access of immigrants to the polity, and erects high barriers against collective, and, notably, territorial, exit. It also programmes the system of education and socialisation, the main levers for inculcating nationalism.

community and allegiance in the contemporary world. With this in mind, we also obtain a better sense of what "taming nationalism" in the contemporary world really requires.

I will start by looking closer at how Charles Taylor, as a "holistic liberal",[50] conceives of contextual individuals, because Taylor has devised the most advanced conception, including the most developed methodology, for analysing this.[51] Taylor sees human beings as self-interpreting animals.[52] They see and discover themselves through the kinds of values that they endorse. These values are culturally entrenched, and the individual derives his or her self-interpretations from the interaction with the community. The values are often expressed in emotive terms, and emotions are vital to the understanding of human motivations, as well as of human actions.[53] Emotions are also cues to the moral and ethical evaluations that humans make. Such evaluations can be either strong or weak.[54] Humans distinguish themselves from animals in their ability to be morally self-reflective, and their morally-salient self-reflections are expressed through strong evaluations,[55] which denote not wishes, but visions of life and who the person wants to be. Thus, these self-reflections entail a qualitative evaluation of the worth of one's desires.[56] Strong evaluations refer to emotive claims that are morally salient, because they are related to our conceptions of self and who we are, i.e., they are standards of assessment that are embedded in human beings as persons or as a species. In this sense, language is not simply a means of communication, but also a means through which the people within a language community become cognisant of, and are able to sustain, their identity. To Taylor, then, the protection of a cultural language community is important to the protection of identities,[57] which also suggests that cultural protection is an important means to ensure symmetrical relations of esteem among both individuals and groups.

Viewed in this light, what is particularly important is that nationalism has obtained a similar status in modern societies. It is, perhaps, best understood as a kind of umbrella over, and a form of unifying device for, a range of community-defining (and sustaining) features, such as language, religion, and shared tradition, all of which are expressed through strong evaluations. Nationalism thus not only draws upon but also subsumes under it – and gives a unified communal shape to –

---

[50] See S. Mulhall, "Articulating the Horizons of Liberalism: Taylor's Political Philosophy", in: R. Abbey (ed), *Charles Taylor*, (Cambridge: Cambridge University Press, 2004), pp. 105–126.

[51] See, in particular, Taylor, *Sources of the Self: The Making of the Modern Identity*, note 18 *supra*.

[52] See Taylor, *Human Agency and Language*, note 18 *supra*, Chapter 2.

[53] Taylor, *Sources of the Self: The Making of the Modern Identity*, note 18 *supra*.

[54] Ibid.

[55] Ibid.

[56] Ibid., Chapter 1.

[57] C. Taylor, *Reconciling the solitudes: Essays on Canadian federalism and nationalism*, (Montreal & Kingston: McGill-Queen's University Press, 1993), and "The Politics of Recognition", in: C. Taylor and A. Gutmann (eds), *Multiculturalism*, (Princeton NJ: Princeton University Press, 1994), pp. 25–74.

a range of factors that are understood not only as designative of us as persons, but also as emotionally-salient categories (considered in terms of strong evaluations). These can, therefore, be harnessed to serve the political ends of nationalism, which is to ensure not only that the community governs itself, but also that it governs itself in such a manner as to ensure that the national *ethos* properly permeates the community's self-understanding. In such a context, there will always be strong social pressures on individuals and groups to conform.

One re-inforcing element here – and a distinguishing mark of nation-building – has been that it has both shaped and conditioned other modes of allegiance. Precisely through the marriage with the state, nation-builders were able to eliminate competitors, or to subsume them under the national label, or even to relegate them to the private sphere. Nationalism has, therefore, not only become a deeply internalised mode of attachment, in modern societies, it also effectively forms the top of a hierarchy of modes of attachment. It is this element (the historical forging of which has often taken place entirely devoid of democracy) which, in turn, is used to justify claims to democratic self-government. It is in this sense that nationalism's justification for democratic self-governing rests on shaky historical foundations (effected through morally unjustifiable procedures).

Nationalism has a prescriptive communal *ethos*, namely, to create a national community. This not only permeates the different spheres of society (political-administrative system, culture, economy, sports, education, defence, *etc*), it also produces mutually reinforcing effects across all these spheres.[58] This strong internalisation of the national dimension raises the threshold (and cost) of exit. It also makes it clear that all those that enter (and want to stay in) the community go through quite a process of national inculcation.

At the same time, it is less clear precisely how (and how well) nationalism attaches citizens. The affective ties that a shared culture furnishes are understood to provide the effective motivation for actors to sustain the patterns of cultural reproduction and socialisation required for proper social integration. The problem is that some of the arguments that have been mustered in support of this view fail:

> People can affectively identify with each other despite not sharing particular norms or beliefs; the trust indispensable to social integration is not dependent upon shared national culture; national-cultural diversity may raise the costs of, but does not rule out, achieving higher degrees of communicative transparency; and the higher economic costs of national-cultural diversity, even if not fully balanced by diversity's economic benefits, do not render homogeneity an 'objective imperative' for industrial liberal democracies.[59]

The relationship between cultural nationalism and social integration is far more contingent than what is generally held. The same argument also applies to the role of nationalism in supplying social justice. Prominent liberal nationalists,[60] including

---

[58] See Norman, note 15 *supra*.

[59] See Arash Abizadeh, "Does Liberal Democracy Presuppose a Cultural Nation?", (2002) 96 *American Political Science Review,* pp. 495–509, at 507.

[60] Consider, notably, Miller, note 7 *supra*, p. 96.

MacCormick, attach great importance to social rights and social justice. National identity is widely held to supply the type of solidarity and interpersonal trust that are required for sustaining social justice and welfare arrangements. Many studies have found no support for such a relationship, and even a very carefully crafted study on the relationship between national identity and the welfare state in Canada finds this to be a more contingent relationship than what is generally thought, but also that a critical factor is trust in government.[61] These studies point to the need to consider other important factors that attach citizens to the political system. Trust in government could for instance mean that national identity is the product of an underlying constitutional patriotism.

Nationalism's strength no doubt derives at least in part from its very ubiquity, which adds to both its attraction and its taken-for-grantedness. Nationalism is not just sustained by factors internal to each state; this internal process of national inculcation draws sustenance and re-inforcement from the fact that each state (and many regions) is similarly encoded. This is by now a systemic feature of the system of states and exercises a mutually reinforcing effect on all the components (nation-states and aspiring regions) in the structure (the system of states). The system is literally encoded in the conceptual categories and the prescriptive mode of community embedded in nationalism. These are universally shared, and their hallmark is that each state and nation should be the bearer of a distinct national identity. This isomorphic pressure takes a distinct form, which we might label as the "universal programming of national specificity". In other words, nationalism is programmed to highlight certain forms of specificity as being distinctive of the community; these are not natural distinguishing features, but are raised to prominence by those in charge of the nation-building process. A successful nation-building process presents these features as "natural", distinctive and designative of a given community. They appear as institutional facts. In a world of states, national self-government at regional level will always have state-based national self-government as its model.

This raises the question as to whether the development of a post-sovereign vanguard in Europe will sufficiently weaken these conditioning structures, or whether it will, itself, be conditioned by them, instead. If the European Union is the only post-national vanguard, it will continue to face significant isomorphic pressures from the states outside it. Thus, it might be that the system of states needs to turn post-sovereign for this to be effective in taming nationalism.

Liberal nationalism portends to include these contextual factors, but it does not explicate nationalism through the language of strong evaluations and does not spell out how nationalism orchestrates those other ethically salient features it portends to overlay. Thus, in a world made up of national entities, liberal nationalism effectively under communicates the problem of reconciling autonomy and authenticity.

What is important to bear in mind, when it comes to taming nationalism, is nationalism's ability to put a range of ethically-salient features of modern societies

---

[61] R. Johnston, K. Banting, W. Kymlicka and S. Soroka, "National Identity and Support for the Welfare State", (2010) 43 *Canadian Journal of Political Science*, pp. 349–377, at 351.

to its own ends. The liberal nationalist must take proper heed of the deeply institutionalised nature of nationalism: its very taken-for-grantedness, and the liberal nationalist must, in addition, recognise that this also applies to how analysts relate to it. Many analysts and political commentators simply take the nationalist pattern of thought, vocabulary, the assumptions of mode of community and belonging, and the attendant notion of political organisation as their frame of reference, without questioning whether this is a relevant and/or a viable reference-point or not. Nationalism, in this sense, has come to dominate the conceptual categories and modes of seeing society to such an extent that this particular social construction of reality has become increasingly objectified, taken for granted, and, in normative terms, also elevated to the only meaningful way of organising a political community.[62] The result is a "methodological nationalism", which:

> assumes this normative claim [every nation has the right to self-determination within the frame of its cultural distinctness] as a socio-ontological given and simultaneously links it to the most important conflict and organisation orientation of society and politics. These basic tenets have become the main perceptual grid of social science. Indeed, the social-scientific stance is rooted in the concept of nation state. A nation state outlook on society and politics, law and justice and history governs the sociological imagination. To some extent, much of social science is a prisoner of the nation state.[63]

The right to self-government gives further normative credence to this, and gives it a democratic justification. The problem is that the democratic licence is then also understood as a licence to inculcate a certain conception of the good. Even if we think of the community as being open to exit and entry, the *ethos* of nationalism is to seek to bring to fruition the greatest possible degree of congruence between cultural and political community; thus it must instil as far as possible the mode of loyalty that Yack associated with the modern national condition.

The problem facing minority nationalists is to single out those features that can be seen as constitutive of nationalism at regional level and, at the same time, contain the urge to impose this programming also on all the other aspects of the community. If we relate this to MacCormick's communal subsidiarity, there is no clear prioritisation; it is, in principle, open to such re-inforcing effects.

Thus, there are grounds to argue that the only fail-safe way to prevent this from happening is to alter the communal *ethos*. In my view, the best way of doing so is by considering alternatives to nationalism. To illustrate the mind-frame of one alternative, let us consider federalism and its view of fraternity, a value that is central to both nationalists and federalists:

> It is the imagining of fraternity... that gives meaning to the nationalist's idea of the nation and motivates citizens willingly to die for it. The fraternity of nationalism unites a strong

[62] A highly instructive account of how such a process of conceptual retooling took place over time in connection with the development of the modern nation-state is provided by Michael Oakeshott in his "The vocabulary of the modern European state", (1975) 2–3 *Political Studies*, pp. 319–341, and (1975) 4 *Political Studies*, pp. 409–415.

[63] See U. Beck, "Toward a New Critical Theory with a Cosmopolitan Intent", (2003) 10 *Constellations*, pp. 453–468, at 454.

> emotional content with the sentiments of kinship, friendship, and love in the heightened atmosphere of something like religion. Nationalists embrace a primordial idea of fraternity, attach it to the nation, and use it to characterize the type of relation that exists between those who share a culture or a language or a way of life. But the concept of fraternity is more complex than nationalists appear willing to allow. What they fail to notice is that the idea of fraternity looks two ways. It looks to those who share a way of life; it also looks to those who have adopted alternative ways of life. There is no greater fraternity than the brotherhood and sisterhood of all people. Moreover, it may not be possible to confine fraternity in the way that the nationalist program presupposes. If fellowship... is morally compelling in part because it connotes respect and concern for others..., is it not compromised when confined in expression to a particular group of people?[64]

Federalism injects a more complex and inclusive mode of attachment into the notion of fraternity, which permits a more inclusive conception of identity and community than is to be found in nationalism.[65] Federalism, of course, begs the question of the terms under which one enters into such an arrangement, and is premised on some form of formal constitutional contract or federal covenant. But modern federalism, as Elazar has steadily reminded us, has itself been tamed because it has been directed to serve the nation-state, and it has also frequently been mistakenly relegated to a mere organisational device.[66] The post-sovereign constellation presents new scope for federal theorising.[67]

The question, then, is whether the post-sovereign constellation might usher in greater opportunities with regard to forging and sustaining other, more inclusive, modes of attachment, than nationalism. The European Union is the most obvious, but it is far from the only possible candidate to consider in this regard.

13.5 The Case of the European Union

In Europe, states have rescinded sovereignty through acceding to the European Union, and the European Union has become an institutional normative order with a self-referential legal system. The European Union has a democratic vocation, is configured as an institutional normative order, but it does not embed this in state sovereign form. The European Union is the world's foremost manifestation of re-configuring Member State sovereignty along post-sovereign lines within a legal (moderately) pluralist structure. Can this system tame nationalism and deliver the form of liberal nationalism that MacCormick propounds?

---

64 S. V. LaSelva, *The Moral Foundations of Canadian Federalism*, (Montreal & Kingston: McGill-Queen's University Press, 1996), p. 26.

65 D. J. Elazar, *Federalism as Grand Design: Political Philosophers and the Federal Principle*, (Lanham MD: University Press of America, 1987); *Exploring Federalism*, (Tuscaloosa AL: The University of Alabama Press, 1987); LaSelva, note 64 *supra*.

66 Elazar, note 65 *supra*.

67 See Daniel J. Elazar, "From Statism to Federalism: A Paradigmatic Shift", (1996) 17 *International Political Science Review*, pp. 417–429.

MacCormick is carefully optimistic on this point. In his *Questioning Sovereignty*, he depicts the European Union as a Commonwealth based upon a mixed constitution. It is a consensus-based system with a modicum of democratic institutions that ensure a limited measure of self-government coupled with an oligo-bureaucratic structure and a system of indirect legitimation.[68] One key taming-device is the fact that this system is neither set up as a sovereign state, nor does it have the vocation to become one. But the European Union does express a set of common objectives, it is an institutional normative order, it has established direct links to the citizens (through European citizenship provisions), and thus it requires some mode of citizen attachment. The Union's more narrow remit of action, its large size, and the sheer distance to the citizen implies that there is no need for a European nation. These factors suggest that the citizens can feel themselves to be attached to the Union through some form of civic identity akin to a form of constitutional patriotism.

A second taming-device is found in the Union's distinct form of legal pluralism, which is characteristically non-hierarchical (it could be, as Menéndez notes in his chapter, resting on *the plural but equal standpoints thesis*). This system provides the proper legal-institutional framework for subsidiarity to serve as the key organising principle that can help to render this system legitimate. This complex structure would then balance several modes of subsidiarity in order to ensure a common market within a multi-levelled structure of representative-democratic institutions and deliberative arrangements, in such a manner as to keep the tasks of primary concern to the citizens – as close to the citizen as possible. The point about this structure in national terms is three-fold: to prevent an overarching hegemonic nationalism from arising and overpowering those at the lower levels; to permit the development and flourishing of nationalism at the sub-unit or regional level as a more democratic (because it is closer to the citizen) way of incorporating citizens; and to render the entire structure attentive to autonomy through commitment to liberal rights and justificatory procedures at all levels.

This depiction of the European Union raises three questions. One pertains to the prospects of subsidiarity fulfilling this overarching structuring role in today's European Union. MacCormick emphasises that subsidiarity must "go all the way down", notably to the regions. This also pertains to the democratic authorisation of the system, which must encompass all the relevant levels of society. In today's European Union, the general tendency has been for the Member States to appropriate this principle and to place limits on its applicability to the regions.[69] We see this

---

[68]QS, p. 149.

[69]Consider for instance Protocol 2 of the Treaty of Lisbon (on subsidiarity and proportionality), which provides national parliaments with a subsidiarity check on Union legislation. Lisbon Treaty Consolidated, OJ C 115, Volume 51, 8 May 2008. See A. Føllesdal, "Subsidiarity and democratic deliberation", in: E. O. Eriksen and J. E. Fossum (eds), *Democracy in the European Union*, (London: Routledge, 2000), pp. 85–110. Justus Schönlau in the recently published paper, "The Committee of the Regions – The RECON Models from a Subnational Perspective", RECON Working Paper, 2010/10, shows some modest gains for the Committe of Regions in the Treaty of Lisbon but the general picture is still one of subsidiarity privileging the Member State, not the regional, level.

institutionally in the development of the European Council, notably in the central role which it has in the constitution-making process. The most explicit example of this was in the closed and secretive process of forging the Treaty of Lisbon (2007–2009). Thus, empirically speaking, there appears to be little hope for this principle to play an overarching structuring role along the lines that MacCormick depicts (not the least because of the prominent role of Member States).

The second issue pertains to the emphasis on installing a form of constitutional patriotism at European level, which would be conducive to a "civic *demos*" in which the attachment of the people is to a common constitutional order. A viable constitutional patriotism presupposes that:

> those who are subject to a special legal system should have the ultimate say about its contents, hence the residents of such a territory should also possess democratic legislative institutions.[70]

The mode of allegiance that constitutional patriotism refers to is one that draws on *democratic* constitutionalism. The question is whether it is possible to instil a viable constitutional patriotism in a setting that is not wholly democratic. In a setting that is marked by a mixed constitution, the commitment to instil a viable constitutional patriotism is therefore concomitantly a commitment to replace the mixed constitution with a democratic constitution in order to ensure both citizen support and legitimacy.

In the literature, there are also very different versions of constitutional patriotism, which draw variously on some form of cosmopolitanism[71] and on nationalism.[72] In the latter version, Craig Calhoun criticises Habermas' cosmopolitan-inspired stance on a European form of constitutional patriotism for placing too little onus on the need for the constitution to foster bonds of mutual commitment embedded in a common sense of attachment to the constitution. For this attachment to be salient, we would not only need a constitution worthy of its name, but also a set of institutions able to imprint some sense of attachment and an ability to sustain it.

Upon the basis of the above, if a European form of constitutional patriotism is properly installed, this would entail a democratic Union capable of legitimately

---

[70] QS, p. 167.

[71] See J. Habermas, "Struggles for Recognition in the Democratic Constitutional State", in: C. Taylor and A. Gutmann (eds), *Multiculturalism*, (Princeton NJ: Princeton University Press, 1994); *Between Facts and Norms: Contributions to a Discourse Theory of Law and Democracy* (Cambridge, MA: The MIT Press, 1996); *The Inclusion of the Other*, (Cambridge MA: Polity Press, 1998); "Constitutional Democracy: A Paradoxical Union of Contradictionary Principles", (2001) 29 *Political Theory*, pp. 766–781; and *The Postnational Constellation*, (Cambridge MA: The MIT Press, 2001). Patchen Markell, "Making Affect Safe for Democracy? On 'Constitutional Patriotism'", (2000) 28 *Political Theory*, pp. 38–63, detects two different readings of constitutional patriotism in Habermas' works. See, also, J. E. Fossum, "Constitutional patriotism: Canada and the European Union", in: P. Mouritsen and K.E. Jørgensen (eds), *Constituting Communities – Political Solutions to Cultural Difference*, (London: Palgrave, 2008), pp. 138–161.

[72] Craig Calhoun, "Imagining Solidarity: Cosmopolitanism, Constitutional Patriotism, and the Public Sphere", (2002) 14 *Public Culture*, pp. 147–172.

claiming the attachment of its citizens. One question is, therefore, whether this structure might end up being too compelling and attach citizens to itself in such a manner as to privilege the central level. Moreover what would prevent such an entity from claiming that it was a nation, along liberal nationalism lines, and developing institutions to give credence to this claim? After all, the entity (the European Union) would operate in a world of nations, internally and externally, each of which would assert a claim to self-government; thus representing a strong isomorphic pressure on the Union to comply with the prevailing norm (democratic self-government embedded in a nation).

This is not, of course, how MacCormick depicts the European Union, but it does underline that we need to consider other modes of allegiance, which may be viable alternatives to nationalism – insofar as they do not have these effects. This takes us to the third point, namely, the need to ensure that the current EU structure (which falls well short of MacCormick's notion of subsidiarity) retains sufficient devices to render the existing forms of nationalism subservient to liberal principles. In its current shape, and judging on the track-records of both new and old Member States alike (consider, for instance, the recent case of how Slovakia, Italy and France have dealt with the Roma people), we see clear breaches of core liberal principles.

In its present shape, the EU clearly provides inadequate safeguards for taming state-based forms of nationalism, with implications for both the European level and for regional-national self-government. But what are the implications for MacCormick's general framework?

13.6 The Post-sovereign Constellation and the Cosmopolitan Option

The previous discussion has revealed that none of the modes of allegiance discussed thus far sits well with the notion of the post-sovereign constellation, as manifested in the European Union. Liberal nationalism is prone to reify the ideology of nationalism. It might also downplay the identitarian changes that occur when the decline of sovereignty unleashes the politics of identity from the shackles of the nation-state. Federalism may hold promise in terms of depicting the more complex fraternal relations that the sustenance of such an entity requires, but it pre-supposes an explicit agreement or a commitment to submit to the federation. Federalism is also so closely associated with the sovereign state that it is necessary to devise a proper federal road-map for the post-sovereign constellation. This has not yet been done.

Does this fling us into an incessant search for developing new modes of allegiance, or might there be a solution closer to home? To approach this, it is first necessary to re-visit the European Union. The Union is, MacCormick underlines, an autonomous institutional normative order. But, in its present form, it is neither a fully-fledged manifestation, nor an adequate representation of the theory of law as an institutional normative order. It could, of course, be added here that every actual manifestation is, in some sense, at most an approximation to theory. But, for the EU, we need to include the proviso that there must be an adequate and clearly articulated theory that can capture the distinct constitutional character of the EU. MacCormick, as Menéndez shows in his chapter, provides most of the intellectual basis for such a theory, which both of us have developed into a theory of constitutional synthesis (with applicability, perhaps, also beyond the European Union)[73].

My point of departure is that the theory of constitutional synthesis offers a better view on how we can ensure allegiance in a democratic post-sovereign constellation such as the EU. This theory starts from the notion that the European Union is a constitutional union of already constitutionalised states. The European Union is a "synthetic polity" built on the legal-constitutional foundations of the Member States, albeit, in a particular trapping, namely, in the form of the common constitutional law of the Member States. In this structure, they combine their old role as national constitutional systems (each of which has a distinct constitutional identity), with their new role as part of the collective supranational constitution. The process of constitutional synthesis thus represents the development of the distillation of a common constitutional system from a range of diverse legal orders (normative synthesis) within a set of supranational institutions with a strong Member State imprint. The present European Union is the result of a gradual and stepwise creation of a supranational supporting institutional structure, a structure that has been super-imposed on the national institutional structures without aiming at a hierarchical structure or even a clear-cut division of labour when it comes to competences.

This structure deals with the identitarian-democratic problems which we found in MacCormick's scheme, but is nonetheless at the same time, quite compatible with core traits of MacCormick's approach to law and the EU, especially and critically so if it were to inform the re-construction of both European and national constitutional law (in the latter case, *vis-à-vis* regional constitutional orders). There are several reasons for why this is so. First, the process of constitutional synthesis is powered by the notion of a common constitutional law as a powerful regulatory ideal. This propels the integration process. The regulatory ideal is infused with the core norms and principles of democratic constitutionalism, and, as such, reins in legal pluralism and renders it subservient to the basic tenets of democratic constitutionalism. Second, the structure retains the justificatory element of subsidiarity that MacCormick underlined. But it strengthens it through expanding its applicability: it is not only a matter of a vertical structure in which the higher level must justify to the lower level why it should take on added tasks; it is a matter of compelling all constitutional agents to justify, to each other, that they abide by democratic constitutionalism. The process of constitutional synthesis injects a powerful horizontal justificatory dimension, in that only those norms that are true reflections of what is common (and in accordance with democratic constitutionalism) in the common

---

[73]See John Erik Fossum & Agustín José Menéndez, *The Constitution's Gift – A Constitutional Theory for a Democratic European Union* (Lanham, MD: Rowman and Littlefield, 2011). There, we develop and apply the theory with reference to both the European Union and Canada.

constitutional traditions of the Member States will be uploaded to European level (as already indicated, it could also be extended to the regional level in a similar fashion; the national constitution will reflect the common constitutional law of the regions which make up the state). Third, the structure presupposes the forging of a form of constitutional patriotism at European Union level. This is steeped in cosmopolitan principles (because it reflects the universalistic norms and principles embedded in democratic constitutionalism). This structure also has stronger built-in safeguards against undue centralisation and nation-building, for two reasons. One is because it is embedded in a pluralistic institutional structure with significant centrifugal elements (an institutional field). The other is because the institutional structure has a strong built-in Member State presence as an additional safeguard to prevent the central structure from straying from the democratic path. MacCormick is also well aware of this institutional pluralism; the advantage of constitutional synthesis is that it has a clear theory to account for the democratic authorisation of the EU structure, which MacCormick's scheme lacks.

The theory of constitutional synthesis thus addresses several problems with which MacCormick's scheme could not adequately deal. Of direct relevance to the liberal-nationalism in the post-national constellation, two such problems stand out. The first is the question of European democracy. The second is how best to tame and transform nationalism. Constitutional synthesis is ultimately steeped in a form of cosmopolitanism, but, as noted, with a particular twist: a clear anchoring in the basic norms underpinning democratic constitutionalism. Constitutional synthesis thus provides a way of addressing the problem of ensuring individual autonomy, and does so through the manner in which the synthetic constitution embodies basic liberal rights of applicability across all levels of the polity. It does so in a manner that is faithful to a cosmopolitan-oriented form of constitutional patriotism because the entire structure is informed by the regulatory ideal of democratic constitutionalism. Note that this mode need not initially replace, but may, instead, initially co-exist alongside, deeply institutionally-entrenched national identities. It is the process of ongoing constitutional synthesis – legal-constitutional harmonisation and institution-building – that sets the outer limits for the ability of this system to tame the existing forms of nationalism. But, precisely *because* it represents the injection of a cosmopolitan impetus into the system from across levels, it offers a greater assurance of reflexivity. In this sense, it is also entirely open to the system's morphing into new and more inclusive modes of allegiance.

13.7 Conclusion

In this chapter, I have critically assessed Neil MacCormick's highly innovative approach to law, democracy and community in the post-sovereign constellation. MacCormick pinned his hopes on a *liberal* nationalism in an effort to rescue cultural cohesion and social solidarity in a rapidly changing world in which the established normative and institutional templates were increasingly being questioned.

MacCormick was intellectually bold and open-minded. He was concerned with adequately capturing the new. But he combined this intellectual inquisitiveness with due prudence. Precisely because he saw the central role of normative factors in human existence, he not only sought to devise an approach to law that would fully capture this, but his recognition of the normative dimension also informed his efforts to strike a proper balance between change and continuity in the post-sovereign constellation. From this perspective, it is clear that, when faced with uncertainty and rapid change, one should focus on that which needs protecting, lest the changes will eradicate what we cherish. In this connection, it is easy to understand the support for civic national identities that play the role of safe haven and protection from the anomie and havoc which, for instance, a very specific path to globalisation has brought about.[74]

I am very sympathetic to MacCormick's overall approach. I also agree on the need to ensure that what is presently wrought is properly infused with a sense of fraternal community and social solidarity. But I think this can be ensured through focusing on the prospects for a viable form of cosmopolitanism rather than liberal nationalism. The two main reasons for this are because nationalism is saddled with too many negative connotations and conditions which behave in an exclusivist direction, and also because cosmopolitanism is already more deeply ingrained in our contemporary world than we often admit. These are conclusions that MacCormick might have disagreed with, but which he, in his familiar reflexive manner, would engage with seriously, not least because he was a cosmopolitan local, as Neil Walker puts it so well in his chapter.

[74]This is, indeed, the same structural reason that MacCormick famously employed to turn von Hayek's argument on its head and sustain a defence of the welfare state against neo-liberals. See "Spontaneous Order and the Rule of Law: Some Problems", (1989) 2 *Ratio Juris*, pp. 41–54.

Index

A.J. Menéndez, J.E. Fossum (eds.), *Law and Democracy in Neil MacCormick's Legal and Political Theory*, Law and Philosophy Library 93,
DOI 10.1007/978-90-481-8942-7,